D1327796

A PASSION FOR PHYSICS

Geoff discussing bootstrap ideas in his office at the Lawrence Berkeley Laboratory.

A PASSION FOR PHYSICS

Essays in Honor of Geoffrey Chew
Including an Interview with Chew

Edited by
Carleton DeTar
J. Finkelstein
Chung-I Tan

World Scientific

Published by

World Scientific Publishing Co Pte Ltd.
P. O. Box 128, Farrer Road, Singapore 9128.
242, Cherry Street, Philadelphia PA 19106-1906, USA

The publisher is grateful to Jacqueline Capra for the frontispiece and cover photographs and to *The Washington Post* for permission to reprint a photograph of "Just an Atom-Smasher" in p. 10 of this book.

Library of Congress Cataloging-in-Publication Data
Main entry under title:

A Passion for Physics.

    1. Particles (Nuclear physics) — Addresses, essays,
lectures.   2. S-matrix theory — Addresses, essays,
lectures.   3. Bootstrap theory (Nuclear physics) — Addresses,
essays, lectures.   4. Chew, Geoffrey F. — Addresses, essays,
lectures.   5. Physicists — United States — Biography — Addresses,
essays, lectures. I. Chew, Geoffrey F. II. DeTar, Carleton.
III. Finkelstein, J. IV. Tan, Chung-I.
QC793.28.P384   1985   539.7'21   85-2377
ISBN 9971-978-29-6
ISBN 9971-978-24-5 (pbk.)

Printed in Singapore by Kyodo-Shing Loong Printing Industries Pte Ltd.

PREFACE

A sixtieth birthday offers an opportunity to reflect upon the achievements of a lifetime and an occasion to honor a great scientist and teacher at the peak of his career. Geoffrey Chew's firm vision of the unity and self consistency of physical law has inspired a generation of students and colleagues. Many of them gathered in Berkeley on September 29, 1984 for a one-day symposium and banquet (entitled the "Chew Jubilee") marking his sixtieth anniversary (which actually took place June 5, 1984). The first part of this volume collects written versions of the talks delivered at the Chew Jubilee and includes essays by other friends and colleagues. The second part contains the text of an interview with Geoff by Fritjof Capra. The title of this volume is taken from Murph Goldberger's after-dinner talk, also included here.

Carleton DeTar
J. Finkelstein
Chung-I Tan

January, 1985

CONTENTS

A PASSION FOR PHYSICS

PART I

THE ANALYTIC AND UNITARY S MATRIX

William R. Frazer

This talk, on the occasion of the Chew Jubilee, is a collection of observations and reminiscences on the development of the theory of the analytic S matrix. It does not presume to be a history of that development, because to write such a history would impose a burden of completeness and fairness which I am not prepared to assume! I shall select the developments I describe, simply because I was fortunate enough to observe them, and not because I make any claim that they are more important than others I do not describe.

The method I shall use is a diagrammatic method, a sort of "intellectual history" diagram. A typical diagram is shown in Fig. 1.

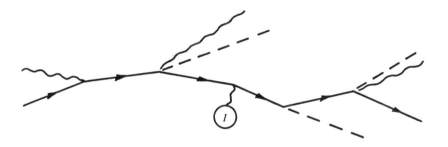

Fig. 1. A typical intellectual history diagram.

The diagram rules are as follows: A solid line represents the Chew world-line (see Fig. 2).

Fig. 2. Chew world-line.

Those of you who, along with Geoff, have played a fundamental role in the development of S-matrix theory, please do not feel slighted at not seeing your world lines — this is not your jubilee!

Another diagram element is shown in Fig. 3:

Fig. 3. Emission of a student or postdoc.

The emission of a student, which occurs so remarkably frequently along the Chew world-line, illustrates the profound analogy between our diagrams and other more familiar diagrams; namely, the emission of a student is quite analogous to bremsstrahlung. Students are, with high probability, emitted in the forward direction, and tend to remain moving along the direction Geoff taught them, even after Geoff himself has turned in another direction!

Another important diagram element, the absorption of a collaborator, is shown in Fig. 4:

Fig. 4. Absorption of collaborator.

Again, the absorption of a collaborator is a frequent phenomenon along the Chew world-line. This interaction is a singularly strong one, with Geoff absorbing the ideas and talents of a succession of eminent collaborators and turning them to his own clearly-defined ends.

I observed with fascination the absorption of Stanley Mandelstam, and benefited immensely from the resulting Chew-Mandelstam collaboration. Geoff had been struggling for some months to derive partial-wave dispersion relations, and had realized that he needed some sort of then-unknown double dispersion relation. I remember him describing to Pauli, who was listening intently and nodding inscrutably, what important things one could accomplish with partial-wave dispersion relations, if only one understood more about the analytic structure of the S matrix in two variables. Thus, when Stanley gave a cryptic ten-minute paper at the Washington meeting of the American Physical Society in 1958, Geoff was uniquely appreciative of its significance. The folk tale has it that Geoff whisked Stanley out of the meeting room and directly onto a plane to Berkeley!

Our diagram rules are completed by the two types shown in Figs. 5 and 6, which I shall discuss later in my talk:

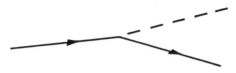

Fig. 5. Radiation of an important new idea.

Fig. 6. Interaction with an external field (Inspiration), with consequent change of direction.

In Fig. 7 I have represented some of the exciting events of the period 1958–61, in which the Chew-Mandelstam collaboration produced so many exciting new results.

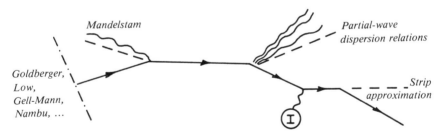

Fig. 7. The 1958–61 period: development of partial-wave dispersion relations.

Let me say a few words about the change in the direction of Geoff's world-line toward the right-hand side of Fig. 7. I was the first of the students emitted during the period shown, and went to the Institute for Advanced Study for a very exciting year in which I had the pleasure of preaching the new gospel to a very attentive and interested audience. I returned to Berkeley the following summer, to find to my shocked surprise that Geoff had made a major change of course in the meantime. He had seen the limitations of our old "nearby singularities" approach and was now intent on understanding the asymptotic behavior of scattering amplitudes. I was still attempting to follow the old course, and was shocked at how completely he had lost interest, and how completely he was convinced that the new direction was the one true pathway to truth! I have continued to marvel at Geoff's ability to adopt a working hypothesis with absolute conviction, and yet preserve the mental agility to change course as necessary — and to adopt the new working hypothesis with the same absolute conviction!

In Fig. 8 I show a little more detail on the 1959–60 "shower" of students and ideas:

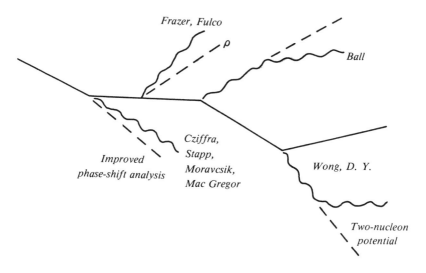

Fig. 8. The 1959–60 shower of students, ideas.[1-4]

Students and ideas are emitted, with students occasionally radiating their own ideas and students, to produce a veritable shower. Fulco and I were so fortunate as to predict a resonance, which bore our names for a time, before we lost out to Sakurai's more euphonious "rho-meson". Geoff advised us every step of the way, but generously decided not to put his name on the paper. In addition to his evident desire to help two young physicists gain recognition, Geoff gave me a unique reason: He said that if he were to put his name on the paper, he would feel a continuing commitment to the problem of nucleon structure — he would be making it "his problem". He thought physicists should feel a commitment to a problem, rather than "skipping around" so much. Much as I admire Geoff's deep commitment, I'm afraid I proceeded to "skip around"!

Some of the developments in Fig. 8 led to quantitative results; or, to use the euphemism of the era which has, I hope, passed out of fashion, "semi-quantitative" results. For example, the proton-proton phase shift analysis which explicitly included pion exchange was used to determine the pion mass, yielding[5] $m_{\pi^0} \approx 125$ MeV, against the actual $m_{\pi^0} = 135$ MeV. The same analysis determined the pion-nucleon coupling constant as $g^2 = 14$, whereas the Chew-Low[6] effective-range analysis of pion-nucleon scattering gave $g^2 = 15$. The analysis by Fulco and myself of electron-nucleon scattering predicted $m_\rho \approx 550$ MeV, *vs* the actual[7] 769 MeV. Coming as they did after decades of failure to formulate a quantitative theory of strong interactions, these results were very exciting.

From the perspective of two decades later, these accomplishments may seem quite modest compared to the present, when QCD provides a systematic theory of strong interactions. It is hard to find anyone who will admit to being a QCD skeptic today, but let me present an imaginary dialog between such a skeptic (*S*) and an orthodox QCD believer (*Q*):

Q: QCD is a major advance, in that it provides a systematic theory of strong interactions. Its perturbation expansion is quantitatively successful.

S: Yes, but that expansion is not valid in the region of the S-matrix results we have discussed.

Q: Non-perturbative QCD, especially lattice gauge theory, promises to make systematic calculations which have never been possible before — such as, hadron masses.

S: But in fact even the modest advances discussed above compare favorably with the accomplishments of lattice QCD to date!

Q: But is the S-matrix approach used in those calculations fundamental, or does it just relate nearby singularities of the S matrix?

S: No, it wasn't a fundamental theory, but *is QCD fundamental*?

In his contribution to the proceedings of this Jubilee, Weinberg discusses the question of what form the fundamental theory of matter might take, when examined on energy scales beyond those available at accelerators. I commend his paper to your attention, because it recounts the vicissitudes of S-matrix and field theory approaches, and because it points out eloquently the need to keep an open mind concerning the form of whatever may turn out to be the really fundamental theory which describes all particles, including gravity. Let me summarize Weinberg's argument briefly.

1. Our current "standard model" will break down before we reach some large mass scale, characteristic of gravity or grand unification. "Perhaps the theory of the new ultra-high energy scale will not be a quantum field theory at all. We don't know." But if the ultimate theory is not a quantum field theory, why do simple, beautiful field theories work so well today? In answer, Weinberg quotes two "folk theorems". He says, "I quote them partly because I think they can probably be

formulated in precise terms and proved, and though I haven't done it, they are true."

2. Folk Theorem I: General quantum field theory, with the most general Lagrangian, is without content, it's just a way of implementing the axioms of S-matrix theory. Examples of quantum field theory used in this way are (i) the effective field theories used to derive soft-pion theorems, and (ii) Sakuraï's vector meson theory of strong interactions.

But if this theorem is true, why do we find that our successful field theories are so simple and beautiful? The answer lies in the second folk theorem:

3. Folk Theorem II (Harmonic Oscillator Theorem): At energies much lower than the natural energy scale of the fundamental theory, an effective field theory can be found, whose Lagrangian is dominated by terms with the fewest fields and/or derivatives. "Where possible, the interactions in this effective field theory will be so simple that they allow the cancellation of infinities to go through as they did in quantum electrodynamics."

I call this a "harmonic oscillator theorem", because it points out that apparent simplicity and beauty can arise through nothing more fundamental than a power series expansion. Could it be that we who marvel at the profound beauty and simplicity of gauge field theories will appear to future generations to be as naive as a freshman who marvels at the simplicity of Hooke's law?

Weinberg concludes, "If our quantum field theories of which we're so proud are just the debris of some really fundamental field theory which describes all of physics including gravity, it may be that the really fundamental theory will have nothing to do with fields; it may not look like a quantum field theory at all. I think we have to leave this as an open possibility and maybe, in fact, that it will be something like an S-matrix theory."

Whatever the form of the fundamental theory which underlies our current efforts, experience tells us that much of what we have done will find a place in that theory. Let me attempt, at the peril of angering the reader by sins of omission and commission, to list some key ideas and concepts which have proved important in the development of S-matrix theory. Directly or indirectly, Geoff's influence has been felt in the development of all of them. Many are candidates for inclusion in a fundamental theory.

— ANALYTICITY: Dispersion relations, Mandelstam representation, partial-wave dispersion relations.
— NEAR-BY SINGULARITIES: Peripheral interactions, strip approximation, multiperipheral model.
— NUCLEAR DEMOCRACY: Bootstrap models.
— UNITARITY: Asymptotic behavior, Froissart bound.
— AXIOMATIC S-MATRIX THEORY.

— REGGE POLES.
— CROSSING: Duality, string models, topological expansion.

Let me conclude by an even lengthier list, the list of Geoff's Ph.D. students. My list (I hope it is complete!) numbers 60 students to date. If this is not unique in theoretical physics, it certainly has not been exceeded often!

Ph.D. Students of Geoffrey F. Chew

Noyes, Pierre[a]	Berkeley	1950
Blair, John[a]	Illinois	1951
Segall, Benjamin	Illinois	1951
Friedman, Marvin H.	Illinois	1952
Schey, Harry	Illinois	1953
Gartenhaus, Solomon	Illinois	1955
Lichtenberg, Don B.	Illinois	1955
Salzman, Freda	Illinois	1956
Franklin, Jerrold	Illinois	1956
Frazer, William R.	Berkeley	1959
Ball, James S.	Berkeley	1960
Cziffra, Peter	Berkeley	1960
Wong, How-Sen	Berkeley	1960
Desai, Bipin R.	Berkeley	1961
Young, James A.	Berkeley	1961
Kim, Yong Duk	Berkeley	1961
Fulco, Jose R.[a]	Buenos Aires	1962
Balazs, Louis A. P.	Berkeley	1962
Singh, Virendra	Berkeley	1962
Thiebaux, Martial L. Jr.	Berkeley	1962
Muzinich, Ivan J.	Berkeley	1963
Sakmar, Ismail A.	Berkeley	1963
Taylor, John R.	Berkeley	1963
Der Sarkissian, Michael[a]	Penn State	1963
Ahmadzadeh, Akbar	Berkeley	1964
Jones, C. Edward	Berkeley	1964
Arndt, Richard Allen	Berkeley	1964
deLany, Vincent M.	Berkeley	1965
Stack, John D.	Berkeley	1965
Chu, Shu-Yuan	Berkeley	1966
Gross, David J.	Berkeley	1966
Schwarz, John H.	Berkeley	1966
Rothe, Heinz J.	Berkeley	1966
Chau, Ling-Lie	Berkeley	1966
Finkelstein, Jerry L.	Berkeley	1967
Markley, Francis L.	Berkeley	1967
Scanio, Joseph J.	Berkeley	1967
Wang, Jiunn-Ming	Berkeley	1967
Arbab, Farzam	Berkeley	1968
Dash, Jan W.	Berkeley	1968
Lee, Huan	Berkeley	1968

Tan, Chung-I	Berkeley	1968
Brower, Richard C.	Berkeley	1969
Misheloff, Michael N.	Berkeley	1970
Ting, Peter Di-Hsian	Berkeley	1970
DeTar, Carleton E.	Berkeley	1970
Sivers, Dennis W.	Berkeley	1970
Tow, Don Mei	Berkeley	1971
Chan, Chun-Fai	Berkeley	1972
Chen, Chih Kwan	Berkeley	1972
Sorensen, Cristian	Berkeley	1972
Ghandour, Ghassan I.	Berkeley	1974
Shankar, R.	Berkeley	1974
Koplik, Joel I.	Berkeley	1974
Millan, Jaime	Berkeley	1977
Lucht, Philip H.	Berkeley	1978
Sursock, Jean-Pierre	Berkeley	1978
Weissmann, George	Berkeley	1978
Levinson, Mark A.	Berkeley	1983
Espinosa-Marty, Raul	Berkeley	1983

[a] *De facto*, but not *de jure* Ph.D. students

References

1. A good general reference for this period is Chew, G. F., *The Analytic S Matrix* (Benjamin, New York, 1966).

2. W. R. Frazer and J. R. Fulco, *Phys. Rev. Lett.* **2**, 365 (1969).

3. P. Cziffra, M. MacGregor, M. Moravcsik, and H. Stapp, *Phys. Rev.* **114**, 880 (1959).

4. D. Y. Wong, *Phys. Rev. Lett.* **2**, 406 (1959); H. P. Noyes and D. Y. Wong, *Phys. Rev. Lett.* **3**, 191 (1959); A. Scotti and D. Y. Wong, *Phys. Rev.* **138**, B145 (1965).

5. P. Signell, *Phys. Rev. Lett.* **5**, 474 (1960).

6. G. F. Chew and F. E. Low, *Phys. Rev.* **101**, 1570 (1956).

7. E. B. Hughes, T. A. Griffy, M. R. Yearian, and R. Hofstadter, *Phys. Rev.* **139**, B458 (1965).

HOW GEOFF GOT STARTED?

James S. Ball

19-YEAR OLD GEORGE WASHINGTON STUDENT EXPOSES U.S. ATOMIC BOMB
PROJECT

Security Agent Interrogating Physics Student Geoff Chew
About Knowledge of Manhattan Project

While not all of the above actually happened something rather close to
this scenario did and may have hastened Geoff's assignment to the Los
Alamos project. The real story, as well as I have been able to reconstruct it,
is as follows:

In 1943, with national price and wage controls in effect, all requests for
salary increases were reviewed by the War Labor Board. One request in
October, 1943 came from a physicist operating a cyclotron. Salary increases
were usually justified by the importance of the worker's contribution to the
war effort. This physicist's work was so far removed from the popular
stereotype of the female riveter in the war plant that his request was treated
as some kind of joke and the review board thought the case very amusing.

A young Washington Post reporter, Jean Craighead, was at that time
assigned to write feature articles about the actions of the board. She didn't
find the physicist's request particularly funny and she remembered that in a
physics class taken several years earlier the professor had said that the next
war would very likely be won by technological superiority. As a result she
decided to write an article to illustrate how this physicist's work might lead
more or less directly to winning the war.

Her first step was reviewing her college physics text, which, as it was
published in 1939–40, contained some information on nuclear fission. I
mention this because in texts published later, this material had been
removed. To make sure that her facts were up to date she needed to consult
someone currently studying physics. This problem was solved when she
discovered that her friend, Ruth Chew had a brother who was a physics
major at George Washington University.

After consulting with 19-year old Geoff Chew, she wrote the following
article which was published in the Washington Post on Sunday, October 31,
1943. While the reaction of the general reader is not known, the discussion
of an atomic bomb fueled by uranium was very exciting reading for the U.S.
security agencies guarding the secrecy of the Manhattan project. They
moved swiftly, confiscating all copies of the article, including removing it

Just an Atom-Smasher
He Can't Get a Raise—Hasn't Accomplished Anything

By JEAN CRAIGHEAD

A young fellow who has been studying much of his life on the matter of blowing up nations with an atom would like to get a wage increase from the War Labor Board.

Preoccupied with discovering the formula for demolishing Berlin with a teaspoonful of dust,

An atom-smasher is just an atom-smasher

before the Berlin boys master this upsetting trick, he nevertheless needs a new pair of shoes and a winter overcoat.

In the laboratory where the young man lives, one seldom has such simple thoughts as the corner grocery and the Nation's wage stabilization policy.

The drift of the conversation usually tends toward bombarding isotopes, the effect of an alpha particle on the electric forces of an atom of uranium, and the explosive annihilation of Berlin.

So that it must have been with some bit of embarrassment that he found himself wondering about time and a half and incentive payments. Nevertheless, the very ordinary thought that he needed a wage increase for razors and cigarettes, outweighed the science of isotopes, and he took time to write to the War Labor Board to ask how it might be done in his case.

Why Not Another Job?

The letter stumped the WLB, and they looked through their directives and executive orders to see what could be done in the way of a pay adjustment for an atom smasher.

Teey suggested the Little Steel Formula, but the young man's natural inclinations run to bigger things, and 15 per cent of the amount he was receiving would hardly be enough to buy one new shirt for Wednesday evening forums, much less the latest textbook on extra-nuclear electrons.

The board then suggested that he be reclassified and given a raise on the basis of another job. But an atom smasher is an atom smasher, and after studying seven years to understand the trade, one would hardly want to make a shift.

On the other hand, the board stated, one can always obtain a merit increase.

In labor circles a merit increase means many things, but to a person occupied with the spontaneous desintegration of Axis cities and the Nazi war machine by bombarding an atom, a merit increase means only one thing: Finding the formula that will unlock uranium and with a dull roar of separating particles, buckle and rupture Berlin and Tokyo into fire and dust.

Don't Expect It Very Soon

Chances are slim that either side will have the formula before the next war, and that is a little long to wait for a merit increase.

Now this young man is no fictional character; he is very much alive, and very much kicking. But, because of the secret nature of his work, his name cannot be published.

In regards to the work he is doing, let me suggest that you keep on buying war bonds and turning out rifles. Although the dramatic effect of an atomic explosion in the Ruhr Valley is overwhelming, artillery is still a good thing in the absence of a formula.

Even the inspiration of a wage increase won't advance the research out of proportion, and we

Sketches by Jean Craighead.
A stadium around Germany, so we can see the show

can make use of the Flying Fortresses for some time to come.

When the young man with labor problems and his fellow genii do discover how to use the energy in an atom, it would be nice if they would throw up a stadium around Germany and invite the United Nations to the explosion of the Nazi war machine.

It would be a great spectacle—guns and war plants would spin apart under the violence of the impact, and erupt skyward in a fanfare of colors and electronic reactions.

Jean Craighead's article as it appeared in the Sunday, October 31, 1943 edition of the Washington Post.

from the Washington Post's archives. Miss Craighead was questioned intensively and forced to reveal that she had consulted with Geoffrey Chew. After a long session of interrogation of both Geoff and Miss Craighead, it became clear that this was not a case of a leak in security but simply an intuitive guess which happened to be uncomfortably close to the truth.

While no security records of this incident have been found, the following seems consistent with the security practices of that time: (1) Geoff knew too much to be allowed to be on his own; (2) he had done nothing wrong so he couldn't be legally locked up, therefore send him to Los Alamos where, to the first approximation, everyone was locked up and certainly where he could be watched. In any case, within 4 months of the publication of this article, Geoff had joined the scientific staff at Los Alamos.

Miss Craighead married in January 1944 and has since become a successful author under her married name of Jean George. As for Geoff Chew ....

INTERACTIONS WITH GEOFF CHEW

Owen Chamberlain

Geoff Chew and I were both at Los Alamos during the last half of World War II, though we had little contact most of that time. I came to notice Geoff as we were returning to graduate school after the interruption of the war.

We had all learned that Enrico Fermi and a number of the world's best physicists were going to the University of Chicago and that Sam Allison had a good number of University of Chicago fellowships to hand out. I applied for one of these fellowships but was turned down. I remember pounding Allison's desk at Los Alamos and saying I hoped to demonstrate that I deserved a fellowship and that my being refused was a mistake in judgment. (I was not one to pound desks, but on this occasion I felt very strongly.)

A month or so later Sam Allison called me back to his office. This time he reported that Geoff Chew had received a National Research Council fellowship, and that freed up a University fellowship which was awarded to me.

Well, that was only the beginning of Geoff's beneficial influence on me.

When I arrived at Chicago, about March of 1946, I found one room of Eckart Hall in which there were the desks of Frank Yang (C. N. Yang), Murph Goldberger and Geoff Chew. Frank Yang sometimes helped us with problems, but for the most part I think he was going his own way, rather than interacting with the others. I felt I was befriended by Murph. Frequently I joined with Geoff and Murph to make a sort of working trio. Our object was to solve any interesting problem in sight. That was the real fun of physics! Murph seemed to know the most math, Geoff to provide the ideas, and I served to remind us of a method that had worked on a problem the previous week.

One of the high points in our graduate education was Clarence Zener's course: The Fundamentals of Solid State Physics. In the front row of seats there were, sitting side-by-side, Murph, Geoff, and I. I don't think we had any agreement among ourselves, but we worked out a pattern of behavior that we delighted in. Whenever Prof. Zener would say it can be proved that such-and-such is true, one of us would put up his hand and say: "Oh, Prof. Zener, how do you show that?" Well, this would take the lecture completely off the material he had planned on. It would take Zener into areas in which he was not fully prepared. But we found out a lot about how Zener thought about things.

We were afraid of Zener, I think. When we went to his office to complain that the problems were too hard we always went in groups of six or seven students.

One day we complained that a problem as given didn't contain enough information to make a solution possible. He said, "Of course they don't have enough information. Do you think that when you have a problem in the laboratory, it comes with a list of the assumptions you must make in order to solve it? Make the necessary assumption!"

I thought that, apart from Enrico Fermi's private night course, the Zener course was the best course I ever had. When it was repeated the following year it was generally agreed that it fell flat by comparison. I think it lacked that extra stimulus that Geoff and Murph and I provided.

Those were great days in all our lives. We had had our education interrupted by war work, but we came back to the classroom with a more mature attitude, with a better idea of just what we wanted to learn, as well as a real determination to learn it. Several days a week we ate lunch with Enrico Fermi. If we had had a question Fermi couldn't answer we could always have taken it to Edward Teller or Gregor Wenzel or Maria Mayer.

In the academic year 47–48 I watched Murph and Geoff working together on various thesis topics. It was generally recognized that they were both ready to be awarded the degree, but still the right thesis topics had to be found. Several times it happened that they would turn out a nice piece of work that looked like good material, and, just as they were finishing up, there would appear in the *Physical Review* someone else's paper that covered pretty much the same ground. Then they would have to start all over again. In the end Geoff submitted a very respectable paper on proton-deuteron scattering, but Murph had to settle for a Monte Carlo calculation of a proton making successive collisions inside a carbon nucleus, which did not display the full capability of the man.

The proton-deuteron scattering became a steady topic for Geoff. He made successive improvements in his theory, then I think he made one improvement that was not an improvement. Then he made more real improvements. He invented the approximation known as the impulse approximation. Some said it should have been called the Chew approximation. It was the theoretical basis for a number of experiments I took part in at the 184-inch cyclotron.

During the earliest years in Berkeley, Geoff was the star at the annual Physics Department Picnic, for he dominated the baseball game between the faculty and students. (Anyone with a PhD played with the faculty.)

Geoff could hit the ball the full length of the Meadows picnic area. I remember remarking to Geoff on how well he had hit the baseball. He answered that that was not a really squarely hit ball. That a well-hit ball would go a lot farther than that. In fact, I believe at one time Geoff had to make a choice between being a professional physicist and being a professional baseball player. It's a good thing for physics that he decided as he did. It was also a good thing for Geoff, for in later years it became clear that Geoff's back would never have stood the strain of professional baseball.

Then there came the year of the Oath. It took Geoff away from Berkeley to the University of Illinois. I think it was at that time that Geoff took on the chairmanship of the FAS (Federation of Atomic Scientists) committee on passports. This was in the period when many scientists were being denied passports if the Government felt that the U.S. would be better off if the scientist in question did not go abroad. Geoff very ably collected the information about who were being denied passports and made the information known to the public and to the Congress. His committee was an important element in the focus that caused the government to change its ways. We are now much better off.

Now it is well known that Emilio Segre is a great teacher. One of the things that I learned from him was that it was a good idea to stop in and see Fermi once in a while. He stopped in Chicago to see Fermi almost every time he went to the East Coast. I followed suit, stopping to see Fermi whenever I went East. But I did him one better. Not only did I spend a day in Chicago, but I spent the next day in Urbana seeing Geoff. These contacts were particularly valuable while Geoff was concentrating on the p-d scattering, for they directly affected our experimental program.

Later, when Geoff did return to Berkeley he became the work-horse of the theoreticians on whom everybody relied. There were several times that Geoff gave lecture series aimed at helping us experimentalists to understand current theory. I remember one series about the analyticity of the S matrix and another on Regge-pole theory.

Throughout his career he has been ready and able to explain in simple terms recent developments in theory.

I once asked Geoff how he decided which experimentalists were reliable and which unreliable in reporting their results. Geoff answered that he didn't judge experimentalists on the basis of their reliability, but on the interest of the problem they were working on. I think his answer is most appropriate and I think this attitude has served him well over the years.

And, over the years, we have all benefited from Geoff. He has at every turn been both a help and a stimulus. I am pleased to have this opportunity to express my pleasure in having him as a colleague.

Thank you.

MY YEARS WITH PROFESSOR CHEW

Georgella Perry

My acquaintance with Professor Geoffrey Chew began shortly after December 5, 1949 when I started working in the Theoretical Group for Professor Robert Serber at the Radiation Laboratory of the University of California. Professor Chew was mainly on the campus, but it didn't take me long to notice that good-looking campus fellow. Regretfully, he left the University of California and went to the University of Illinois for the fall semester of 1950.

At the time I started, Oppenheimer had left the Lab and the Group had been settled in Building 50. The PhD's and some of the graduate students were located on the first floor, facing the parking lot, and the remaining graduate students were located in one large room on the second floor. The girls from Personnel were afraid to venture in that graduate room to obtain time cards. The Personnel Office was across the hall and the Director's Office was just two doors down the hall. I have a feeling that it was Personnel and the Director's Office that decided that the Group needed a secretary and not the theorists. I started as a part-time secretary and part-time computer operator using the old Friedan and Marchant calculators. After a few days of signing forms for me to get a desk, typewriter, and telephone, Professor Serber said that if he had known that it was going to be that much trouble, he wouldn't have had a secretary.

This closeness to the Director's Office brought the Group under the scrutiny of Professor Ernest Lawrence. I distinctly got the impression that Professor Lawrence did not like to drive up and see the fellows just sitting there thinking. It really upset everyone in the Director's Office if they saw some members of the Group pitching pennies for relaxation for a few minutes. When Professor Lawrence would be going down the hall, he would drop by and talk to them. Quite often he left them with the remark that if they hadn't made their "mark" by the time they were 29 years old, they wouldn't make it.

As you know 1949, 1950, and 1951 were very turbulent times at the University of California. The Loyalty Oath issue had created an emotionally charged atmosphere. Although it was a very exciting time, it was also very sad. Theorists were leaving! The reasons for this exodus were as numerous as the number of people leaving; for some it was time to move on, for others it was the Loyalty Oath and the prevailing atmosphere. However, it had a snowball effect and by the end of the spring term of 1951 Professors Serber, Gian Carlo Wick, Kenneth Watson, Jack Steinberger, Hal (Harold) Lewis, Chew, and W. (Pief) Panofsky, an experimentalist, (those are all that I can recall) had left the Lab. Their graduate students (Pierre Noyes, Ernest Henley, Sidney Fernbach, Richard Christian, Keith Brueckner and others) made an extra effort to finish. The beginning of the summer of 1951 found the Group ravaged and weak, without a leader for a short time, but the fever had run its course.

There was a gap of about seven years during which time I had no contact with Professor Chew. Meantime the Group was being rebuilt under the leadership of David Judd. When the climate at the campus and at the Lab changed, Chew accepted an offer to come back to the University as a full Professor and to the Lab. He returned in 1957 and very shortly built up a wonderful group of graduate students who were very stimulating. Some of these first students that I can recall at this time were James Ball, William Frazer, Jose Fulco, How-sen Wong, Yong Duk Kim from Korea, Bipin Desai, Peter Cziffra, James Young, and Virendra Singh. Fabio Ferrari and Modesto Pusterla from Italy and Udgaonkar from India were also with him. His students have just kept on coming from all around the world.

It is with pleasure that I remember Chew, Ferrari and Pusterla being at the surprise housewarming that the Group gave me in December 1958.

In 1964 *Life* magazine wanted to write a feature article about Chew and he gave his consent for one of their reporters to come and live with him and his wife, Ruth, and their two children, Berk and Bev, in order to obtain background material and understand his work. The reporter trailed him around for several days, attending seminars and talking with people. When the reporter decided he would talk with one of the girls in the office, he asked if she understood what she was typing. He was told, "No." It was explained that she knew how to do the work but that she didn't know what it meant. The reporter was aghast that none of us knew what most of the reports we typed meant; maybe we had a vague idea but we were not physicists. When we told Professor Chew about it, he waited a few minutes and laughingly remarked, "I sometimes wonder if we physicists know what we mean." Very shortly afterwards the reporter took off to cover the wedding of Senator Goldwater's daughter in Phoenix. Sorry, Professor Chew, that you didn't get an article in *Life* magazine.

You did not work around Professor Chew very long before you realized that his main interests were his work and his graduate students, even though he was a good baseball player and loved music. If the telephone fell apart in his hand, he had no intention of wasting his time fixing it; "call the repairman.'' He was completely absorbed in his work and in his students. His students inspired and stimulated him and I believe it was reciprocated. When one of his students submitted a paper to him ready for publication without previous consultation, he was surprised, but admired the student and was impressed by him.

Since returning to Berkeley in 1957, Professor Chew has had numerous tragedies and has come through them using the method he applies to his work and to his administrative duties. It seems to me that he has an unusual ability to look at a situation, decide what needs to be done, or what he wants to do, and then proceed with his life and work. He is not without feeling, but he doesn't wear his feelings on his shoulder ready to be knocked off. He can see when he makes a mistake but he doesn't let it weigh on his mind. He doesn't take on other people's problems. He lets them have their say, but assumes that they will solve the problem. He'll give assistance if they want it and need it. He was not one to ''press my buttons'' and get me upset. (I could get upset all by myself.)

In 1967, Professor Chew became Group Leader of the Theoretical Group. He accepted this job knowing that it would take time away from his physics, his students, and his family. As I saw it, he felt that he had some obligation to the Group. I remember a time when he demonstrated to the Director's Office that he would stand up for what he believed. The office space of the members of the Group was being taken just when our summer ''bulge'' of personnel was starting to take place. He objected and when nothing was done about it, he moved out of his office, giving it to visitors, and went to a small office on another floor. The Director's Office took note of this and at least quit shoving as much. As I see it he realizes that he has 24 hours in a day and he sets his priorities as to how much time he wants to spend on an article or on a memorandum. I have known him to admit that something wasn't as good as it could be, but that was all the time he wanted to devote to it.

I am glad that I, the girl from Arkansas, stayed on with the Theoretical Group and enjoyed the privilege of working with Professor Chew until my retirement in 1979. He was a wonderful boss, and I have always envied him and been astonished and fascinated to see how efficient and productive he could be.

If my impression of Professor Chew is wrong, all I can say is that he is the best actor I have seen or known — even to his dark, Ronald Reagan-like hair.

COMPLETE SETS OF WAVE-PACKETS

Francis E. Low

Watching Geoff Chew over many years — more than 32 years now — has been a remarkable experience. His work has had an extraordinary unity, almost as if he had always worked on the same problem. Throughout, he has incorporated many new ideas and many generations of students into his goal of understanding the strong interactions. Geoff has always had an uncanny ability to recognize the usefulness of new developments, and to exploit them enthusiastically. One thinks of Goldberger's dispersion relations, of Mandelstam, of Veneziano, of Stapp, and many more, too numerous to count. I shared some of these experiences with him — first in Illinois, and later on several occasions in Berkeley. I learned much of what I know from Geoff, and treasure our time together.

I want to tell you today about a problem that has one of its origins in some work with Geoff. In Urbana I shared an office with Arnold Nordsieck. One year Geoff and Arn and I spent a number of Saturday mornings studying von Neumann's famous paper[1] on the ergodic theorem in quantum mechanics. (When we got to the end, we realized of course that the ergodic time was $\sim e^{S/k} \sim e^{10^{23}}$, and therefore not of immediate physical interest.) In the course of his work, von Neumann considers classical wave-packets of the form

$$\phi_{n,m}(x) = \left[\frac{\alpha}{\pi a^2}\right]^{1/4} \exp\left\{-\alpha \frac{(x-an)^2}{2a^2} + 2\pi im \frac{x}{a}\right\},$$

which he claims form a complete set. In fact they do, but not in a very useful way; that is the subject of this talk.

1.   Instead of the special functions $\phi_{n,m}$ we consider general functions $\psi_{n,m}$ such that

$$\psi_{n,m}(x) = f(x-n) e^{2\pi imx},$$

where we have introduced dimensionless variables. Note that the Fourier transform of $\psi_{n,m}$ is

$$\tilde{\psi}_{n,m}(p) = \tilde{f}(p - 2\pi m)\,e^{-ipn}\ ,$$

where $\tilde{f}$ is the Fourier transform of f. Thus the mean position and momenta of the functions $\psi_{n,m}$ (which we assume normalized but not necessarily orthogonal) occupy lattice points through space and momentum space given by

$$\bar{x}_{n,m} = n + \int_{-\infty}^{\infty} x\,|f(x)|^2\,\mathrm{d}x\ ,$$

and

$$\bar{p}_{n,m} = 2\pi m + \int_{-\infty}^{\infty} |\tilde{f}(p)|^2\,\mathrm{d}p\ .$$

In order to represent a classical wave-packet, $f(x)$ should go to zero rapidly for large $|x|$, as should $\tilde{f}(p)$ for large $|p|$. The requirement of completeness turns out to make this property relatively useless, and that of orthonormality makes it impossible.

Consider as a first example the obviously complete orthonormal set

$$\psi_{n,m}(x) = h(x - n)\,e^{2\pi i m x}\ ,$$

where

$$h(x) = 1,\ -\tfrac{1}{2} \leqslant x \leqslant \tfrac{1}{2} \quad \text{and} \quad h(x) = 0 \quad \text{otherwise}\ .$$

We see that $h(x)$ has very desirable properties in x; however the discontinuity of $h(x)$ at $x = \pm 1/2$ produces a very slow fall-off in p:

$$\tilde{h}(p - 2\pi m) = \sqrt{\frac{2}{\pi}}\ \frac{\sin(p/2 - \pi m)}{p - 2\pi m}\ ,$$

so that although $\bar{p} = 2\pi m$, $\bar{p}^2$ is linearly divergent.

One might hope to cure this disease by smoothing the function at its boundaries, and adding appropriate wiggles to ensure orthogonality. This cannot be done in a way which permits desirable behavior at large values of both x and p without destroying the orthogonality. Even then, completeness problems remain, as we now show.

2. Consider the improper function

$$\chi(k, q; x) = \sum_p e^{-ikp} \, \delta\left(x - \frac{q}{2\pi} + p\right),$$

with $0 \le k, q \le 2\pi$. Here p runs over all integers between $\pm\infty$.

We shall show that if $f(x)$ and $\tilde{f}(p)$ fall off sufficiently rapidly there exists a value of the pair $(k, q) = (k_0, q_0)$ such that $X(k_0, q_0; x)$ is orthogonal to every $\psi_{n,m}$. This does not in itself show a lack of completeness of the set for ordinary functions, but it does cause serious problems, as we shall see.

The inner product $(\chi, \psi_{n,m})$ is easily calculated. It is

$$(\chi, \psi_{n,m}) = \int \sum_p e^{+ikp} \, \delta\left(x - \frac{q}{2\pi} + p\right) f(x - n) \, e^{2\pi imx} \, dx$$

$$= e^{-i(kn - qm)} \, g(k, q) \, ,$$

with

$$g(k, q) = \sum_p e^{ikp} \, f\left(\frac{q}{2\pi} - p\right) .$$

If f goes to zero sufficiently rapidly for large values of its argument, g will be periodic in k, and periodic except for the phase factor e^{ik} in q:

$$g(2\pi, q) = g(0, q) \, ,$$

and

$$g(k, 2\pi) = \sum e^{ikn} \, f(1 - n)$$

$$= e^{ik} \sum e^{ikn'} \, f(0 - n')$$

$$= e^{ik} \, g(k, 0) .$$

If in addition f is continuous, g will be continuous.

These three conditions are sufficient to prove that g has a zero in the range $0 \le k \le 2\pi$, $0 \le q \le 2\pi$. The following elegant proof is due to Professor Frank Morgan.

Since g is continuous and $g(2\pi, q) = g(0, q)$, the values of g form a closed curve in the complex plane as k goes from 0 to 2π.

Let $\Phi(k, q)$ be the (continuous) phase of g. Then by the first periodicity property of g,

$$\Phi(2\pi, q) = 2\pi n(q) + \Phi(0, q) ,$$

where $n(q)$ is the number of times the closed curve circles the origin.

As q varies from 0 to 2π, the second periodicity property of g tells us that $n(2\pi) = n(0)+1$, so that the curve must have crossed the origin — that is, the function g has a zero.

The zero of g affects the completeness properties of the $\psi_{n,m}$. Let us expand the well-behaved function $F(x)$ in terms of the $\psi_{n,m}$'s:

$$F(x) = \sum a_{n,m} \, \psi_{n,m}(x) .$$

The coefficients $a_{n,m}$ are given by the formula

$$a_{n,m} = \int \frac{dk \, dq}{(2\pi)^2} e^{i(kn-qm)} \frac{F(k,q)}{g(k,q)} ,$$

where

$$F(k, q) = \sum_p e^{ipk} \, F\left(\frac{q}{2\pi} - p\right) .$$

The integral determining $a_{n,m}$ above is defined if the zero of g is linear and essentially complex in the neighbourhood of the zero. That is

$$\left(\frac{\partial g}{\partial k}\right)^* \left(\frac{\partial g}{\partial q}\right)\Bigg|_0 \neq 0 \quad \text{and not real. With that assumption the high } n \text{ and}$$

m behavior of $a_{n,m}$ is given by

$$a_{n,m} \rightarrow e^{i(k_0 n - q_0 m)} \frac{F(k_0, q_0)}{2\pi} \cdot \frac{\epsilon\left(\text{Im}\, \dfrac{\partial g}{\partial k}\Big|_0 \dfrac{\partial g^*}{\partial q}\Big|_0\right)}{\dfrac{\partial g}{\partial q}\Big|_0 n + \dfrac{\partial g}{\partial k}\Big|_0 m} ,$$

(where ϵ is the usual sign function) so that even for $F(x)$ and $f(x)$ very narrowly confined in x and p, and indeed close to each other, large values of n and m are needed for the completeness sum. Note that the functions $\psi_{n,m}$ are not orthogonal. In fact, the assumption of orthogonality would preclude the narrow definition of x and p in $f(x)$, as we will see in the next section.

3.   We consider next the constraint that orthonormality of the $\psi_{n,m}$'s imposes on the function $f(x)$. It is easy to see that the equation

$$\int_{-\infty}^{\infty} \psi_{n',m'}^{*}(x)\, \psi_{n,m}(x)\, dx \;=\; \delta_{n'n}\, \delta_{m'n} \;\;,$$

is equivalent to the condition

$$|g(k,q)| = 1 \;\;,$$

where $g(k,q)$ is the function defined in (2.9). The theorem proved in the last section then tells us, since g cannot have a zero, that g cannot satisfy the periodicity conditions *and* be continuous. It turns out that violating the conditions makes $\overline{x^2}$ and/or $\overline{p^2}$ diverge linearly.

Provided the periodicity conditions are satisfied, we find for $\overline{x^2}$ and $\overline{p^2}$

$$\overline{x^2} = \frac{1}{3} + \frac{1}{8\pi^3 i} \int dq\; q\; dk \left[g \frac{\partial g^*}{\partial k} - \frac{\partial g}{\partial k} g^* \right]$$

$$+ \int \frac{dk\, dq}{(2\pi)^2} \left| \frac{\partial g}{\partial k} \right|^2 \;\;,$$

and

$$\overline{p^2} = \int dk\, dq \left| \frac{\partial g}{\partial q} \right|^2 \;\;.$$

Since g must be discontinuous, the above expressions will still have convergence problems. I believe the "best" one can do is to choose

$$g = \frac{\lambda(k,q)}{|\lambda|} \;\;,$$

with

$$\lambda = \sum e^{ikn}\, u\!\left(\frac{q}{2\pi} - n \right) \;\;,$$

and u a completely well behaved function. It then turns out that both $\overline{x^2}$ and $\overline{p^2}$ are logarithmically divergent. The relevant formulas follow easily:

Let $\lambda = a + ib$ in the neighborhood of the zero (k_0, q_0), and, after shifting variables, let

$$a = \alpha_1 k + \alpha_2 q \;\;,$$

and

$$b = \beta_1 k + \beta_2 q \;\;.$$

Then the logarithmically divergent parts of $\overline{x^2}$ and $\overline{p^2}$ are given by

$$\overline{x^2} = \frac{1}{8\pi} \frac{\alpha_1^2 + \beta_1^2}{(\alpha_1\beta_2 - \alpha_2\beta_1)^2} \int \frac{dq}{|q|} \quad ,$$

$$\overline{p^2} = \frac{\pi}{2} \frac{\alpha_2^2 + \beta_2^2}{(\alpha_1\beta_2 - \alpha_2\beta_1)^2} \int \frac{dk}{|k|} \quad .$$

Reference

1.   J. von Neumann, Z. *Phys.* **57**, 30 (1929).

SALESMAN OF IDEAS

John Polkinghorne

We used to call Geoff Chew "the handsomest man in high energy physics." I know of at least one senior secretary in a British physics department who kept a photograph of him near her desk. That frank and open face, with just a hint of his one-eighth Burmese ancestry, and his tall commanding figure, made him one of the few theorists in the pin-up class. Allied to this was considerable personal charm and an ingenuous manner. Geoff was definitely a man from whom one would be happy to buy a used car.

Indeed it was as a salesman that Geoff exerted some of his most important influence on high energy physics, peddling, of course, not automobiles but ideas. They could be his own or they could be those of others, for Geoff was remarkably quick to get onto the scent of a new discovery and generous in propagating other men's theories. I remember a "Rochester" Conference at CERN in the late fifties at which Geoff expounded with characteristic vigour and conviction the recent work of the then young and comparatively unknown Stanley Mandelstam. Stanley had just written a paper in which he introduced his conjectured two-variable representation of the scattering amplitude, incorporating analyticity and crossing properties. At the time the paper was not easy reading but Geoff rightly persuaded us all of its importance and the need to get to grips with it. There was a saying at the time that "there is no God but Mandelstam and Chew is his prophet." They were a striking pair together — the long and the short of it, one talkative, the other quiet. The combination was powerful indeed.

There was a sequence of "Rochester" Conferences at which Geoff fulfilled this salesman role. His talks were always eagerly awaited, both because of their inspirational and encouraging tone which helped to sustain one's possibly flagging spirits, and also because of his ability to put his finger on whatever was most promising in the year's crop of ideas. Prompted by Mandelstam, Geoff was among the first to appreciate and attempt to exploit Regge's ideas on high energy behaviour. He also recognized the significance of the bound on high energy behaviour obtained from very general principles by Marcel Froissart. For a while the message was that one should "saturate Froissart", a name, I remember, which Geoff pronounced at the time in a manner more American than Gallic.

But of all the ideas that Geoff presented to the physics community, none was sold with greater fervour than that of the S matrix and the bootstrap. It was a grand notion. When a few years ago I wrote a little book, *The Particle Play*, about the development of high energy physics I was rebuked by some reviewers for having included a chapter on these ideas, now so out of fashion. I remain unrepentant. Bootstrappery was a significant episode in the subject and the concept is one that deserves intellectual appreciation, whatever its eventual fate as a physical principle may prove to be. Its attraction lies in its audacity. The exchange of particles, according to our understanding, creates forces. May not these forces then prove sufficient in turn to create the particles exchanged? In this way the equation of the world would become a gigantic self-consistency condition expressing the possibility that everything is made out of everything else. The universe would, in an act of breathtaking legerdemain, have lifted itself into being by its own bootstraps. It is difficult to think of a more grandiose or exciting proposition.

One of the consequences of bootstrappery would be the abolition of the idea of elementary particles. If everything is made of everything then the supposition of special basic constituents becomes redundant. Geoff coined a slogan for selling this: "nuclear democracy". He proclaimed this anti-elitist physics with enthusiasm. (Oddly enough, in Regge theory he permitted himself a more hiererchical terminology, calling leading trajectories the "Queen" and the "King" and gallantly placing the Queen above the King. This idiosyncratic terminology never caught on.)

All good sales campaigns depend for their success upon timing. In this respect things were perfect. The S-matrix idea cashed in on the disillusionment then current with quantum field theory, so successful perturbatively in dealing with the comparatively weak electromagnetic interactions but apparently powerless to tackle the non-perturbative problem of the strong interactions. Bootstrappery seemed particularly appealing at a time when so-called "elementary" objects were proliferating, as experimentalists discovered resonance after resonance and before the quark model brought recognized order to the chaos of high energy physics.

Geoff proclaimed these ideas with a fervour that went beyond that of the salesman and approximated to that of the impassioned evangelist. There seemed to be a moral edge to the endeavour. It was not so much that it was expedient to be on the mass-shell of the S matrix as that it would have been sinful to be anywhere else.

The intensity of this conviction is summed up for me by the recollection of a small conference at La Jolla in the sixties. It was made clear to us that it was time to decide what our positions were. Speaking with directness and simplicity Geoff said something to the effect that we should all abandon the fruitless pursuit of out-moded field theory and supply our efforts to the elucidation of the S matrix. He had run up his colours and nailed them to the mast. One thought of Martin Luther, "Here I stand, I can do no other." Arthur Wightman, sitting in the front row, turned a bright red but behaved with characteristic courtesy at this labelling of his life's work as vanity.

Geoff's unflagging commitment to the S matrix maintained the momentum of a massive Berkeley programme toiling with ideas of bootstrappery through successive versions of the strip approximation. A great deal of valuable hadronic physics was learnt in the process but in the end it collapsed under the weight of its own complexity. After all, if everything is made of everything that is going to be a rather involved notion to express and manipulate. Moreover it became plain that the times were not after all favourable to egalitarian ideas of nuclear democracy. It became clearer and clearer that quarks were cast for an elitist elementary role.

Intellectual history is full of ups and downs and the years since those heroic times have also seen an astonishing reflowering of quantum field theory. Like Mark Twain, the report of its demise has proved exaggerated.

Theoretical physicists of my generation owe a great debt of gratitude to Geoff Chew. He was our inspirer and encourager, guiding and leading us by his enthusiasm and example through an era of great activity in the subject. He spoke always with integrity and intensity, so that you readily bought his ideas. We also owe him a great debt of affection, for he was and is one of the nicest men you could wish to meet.

THIRTY YEARS OF ONE-PARTICLE EXCHANGE

Michael J. Moravcsik

In selecting a topic for my contribution to this volume I found one-particle exchange a particularly suitable one, for several reasons. To start with a general one, one-particle exchange, in one of its many forms of reincarnation, has been the leading dynamical idea in particle physics for almost 50 years now. It is hardly an exaggeration to say that in as much as we have been able to make quantitative predictions for the dynamics of elementary particle reactions (as distinct from dealing with the spectroscopy of particle states) this was almost always done on the basis of one-particle exchange. This state of affairs continues today, and there is no foreseeable change on the horizon, though of course, as Max Born said, it is difficult to predict, especially ahead of time. Thus in discussing some aspects of one-particle exchange, we touch upon some of the central elements of particle physics.

The second reason why this topic is appropriate for the occasion is that my earliest interaction with Geoff Chew was in connection with one-particle exchange. It was in the late 1950's and early 1960's, at the Berkeley Radiation Laboratory, when S-matrix theory, with Geoff as perhaps its most magnetic high priest, rode high. The semiphenomenological black art of polology was practiced then with great enthusiasm and also with some instances of beautiful and stunning success. Geoff's particular approach[1] was the extrapolation of experimental data to the pole (outside the physical region) where other, non-pole or remote-pole contributions would be negligible, and where therefore the existence of the pole and the size of its coupling constant could be ascertained. I was somewhat attuned to this way of looking at things through some previous work of mine on pion photoproduction[2] in which the analysis of the angular distribution and hence of the multipole expansion could be dramatically improved by separating out the so-called meson-current term (which, in terms of the later S-matrix language, was nothing but a pole term). Indeed, I became an avid contributor[3] to the use of the Chew extrapolation procedure, particularly in nucleon-nucleon elastic scattering.

It is for that particular reaction that a new and perhaps more powerful variant of the utilization of one-particle exchange poles was invented, undoubtedly also stimulated by Geoff Chew's interest in and devotion to one-particle exchange processes. This new phenomenological method, which came to be called the modified phase shift analysis,[4] used the one-pion exchange process to describe the angular momentum states in nucleon-nucleon scattering matrices beyond a certain upper limit (all the way to infinitely high angular momentum values), thus considerably improving the economy and power of the phase shift analysis of nucleon-nucleon scattering. The method had a self-consistency check built into it since the coupling constant of the one-pion exchange contribution could be used as an adjustable parameter in the modified phase shift analysis and the coincidence of its optimal value with the already well-known pion-nucleon coupling constant therefore confirmed the correctness of the method. Indeed, with this modified method the analysis of the two-nucleon interaction up to a few hundred MeV's became a very active program in many institutions around the world for years to come, and in fact this is still an ongoing concern of researchers, now extending up to and even beyond a GeV.

This semiphenomenological work also served as support for further developments involving one-particle exchange, namely for the creation of the one-particle exchange models[5] of nucleon-nucleon interaction. With the experimental establishment of the existence of various heavy mesons the door was opened to constructing a more elaborate one-particle-exchange mechanism for the two-nucleon interaction in which one of each of a half dozen or so mesons participated in the interaction. This work might also be called semiphenomenological by the strictest reckoning, since the meson masses were taken from the experimental determinations, and not calculated from theory, and because not all mesons needed in the model were well established experimentally. Yet the model was highly economical and was also well-defined, since all one-particle-exchange contributions could be precisely calculated. The remaining parameters with any room for adjustment were the coupling constants and in some cases the widths, forming a total list of about ten. With these ten parameters several thousand quite accurate pieces of data on nucleon-nucleon elastic scattering, involving a variety of polarization quantities, and encompassing a broad range of energies up to several hundred MeV's, could be explained with a statistical significance of a chi-square very close to 1 per degree of freedom. Up to this day, the above model represents the high point of strong interaction theory, quantitatively far superior to anything we had before or since. We know that such a model cannot be exactly correct, and the addition of approximate semiphenomenological calculations of the uncorrelated two-pion exchange contributions[6] in fact managed to further improve the agreement with experimental data. Yet, for the first and so far only time in the history of strong interaction physics, we managed to create a quantitatively significant first approximation to the dynamics of a strong interaction process.

All this is now history. So let me now turn to a third reason why I found one-particle-exchange a very appropriate topic for this occasion, and turn to the present. It concerns a new angle in our exploration of strong interaction dynamics and in particular in our probing the extent to which one-particle mechanisms dominate that dynamics.

In recent years the study of polarization phenomena in atomic, nuclear, and elementary particle reactions has undergone a huge expansion. There are reasons for this both experimentally and theoretically. As to the former, the technology of high-current accelerators, of polarized beams, of polarized targets, and of polarization detectors has evolved rapidly, so that experiments are feasible today that were technically impossible a decade or two ago. On the theoretical side, the realization grows that in most situations the unpolarized differential cross section represents such a weak test of our understanding of particle dynamics that the door remains open for various questionable theories to fit such cross sections with the help of a few loose parameters. Indeed, on several occasions during the last 2-3 decades, theoretical constructs scored apparent partial successes with differential cross sections only to be disproven when polarization data became available, even if the latter were only of relatively low accuracy. Using only unpolarized differential cross sections for experimental information is akin to trying to guess the shape of a complicated three-dimensional object on the basis of snapshots taken always from the same distance and same direction. These show, at best, a two-dimensional projection of the three-dimensional shape, thus leaving much ambiguity. In fact, the case of the differential cross section is even worse, since it provides only one dimension of an entity that exists in a complex multidimensional space.

In taking advantage of the richness of the polarization phenomena, the first task is to construct a phenomenological description of them which is as general, as flexible, and as economical as possible. The aim is to relate the polarization quantities to the bilinear combination of reaction amplitudes, since these latter amplitudes contain all the information on the reaction that can be obtained. The objective, therefore, is to evolve a formalism for the amplitudes and the observables in which the matrix relating observables and amplitude products is as close to diagonal as possible. Complete diagonality can be shown to be prevented by certain Hermiticity requirements, but there is a class of formalisms[7] (called the optimal formalisms) in which the matrix in question is zero everywhere except for small submatrices along the main diagonal. These submatrices, for a general four-particle reaction containing particles with arbitrary spins, are always only 1-by-1, 2-by-2, 4-by-4, and 8-by-8, but never larger.

The optimal formalisms form a whole infinite class because although the form of the matrices used in them to describe spins and observables is determined and the rows and columns are labeled by the spin-projections along quantization axes, the *orientation* of these quantization axes (a different one, if so wished, for each participating particle) remains arbitrary. If in addition to Lorentz invariance further symmetries are also imposed on the reaction, the originally multiply infinite set of optimal formalisms becomes somewhat more limited. For example, for a reaction which conserves parity, the only possible optimal frames are those in which the orientations of the quantization axes are either normal to the reaction plane or are in the plane. Time reversal invariance and identical particle constraints produce correlations among the orientations of the quantization axes of the various particles in the reaction. Thus, for elastic proton-proton scattering which is constrained by all three of the above mentioned symmetries, the optimal formalisms are limited[8] to the transversity frame (in which all four quantization axes are normal), and a singly infinite set of planar frames in which the four quantization axes are all in the reaction plane and are correlated with each other. A special case of the planar optimal frame is the helicity frame.

The utilization of such formalisms for the spin structure of reactions presupposes the existence of an at least substantial and preferably very extensive variety of polarization data. It is not necessary that such data cover an energy range and/or an angular range. On the contrary, data at a single energy and angle suffice. What is important, however, is that we have measurements for many different types of polarization quantities, that is, simple polarizations, asymmetries, spin correlations, spin transfer coefficients, etc.

It is perhaps not an accident that in creating such a data base, the elastic nucleon-nucleon scattering reaction took the lead again. Perhaps the most extensive and ambitious such experimental program was undertaken at the ZGS accelerator at Argonne.[9] Over a span of several years, over ten different polarization quantities were measured, particularly at 6 GeV/c, but, to a lesser extent, also at higher energies. Very extensive programs were also undertaken at other accelerators, at somewhat lower energies. The ZGS program raced against time, working furiously in the shadow of the scheduled permanent shut-down of the accelerator, to release funds for the operation of new accelerators at higher energies but without facilities to pursue such polarization studies. Less extensive sets of polarization data were also produced for pion photoproduction and for meson-nucleon scattering. In addition, extensive sets of polarization data were being accumulated at much lower energies for nuclear reactions involving very light nuclei.

The analysis of such polarization data can have various different objectives. One can test the validity of various conservation laws through very sensitive null-experiments, using polarization quantities which exactly vanish if the symmetry holds rigorously. One can determine the reaction amplitudes phenomenologically from the measured set of polarization quantities. One can do the same from a partial set of such measurements,

hoping to be able to acquire information on a partial set of amplitude parameters. One can compare amplitudes with those predicted by various theoretical models. One can, from the phenomenologically determined amplitudes, search for dynamical clues in cases when theory for the dynamics
does not exist. Such an analysis also helps in planning future polarization
experiments, since the analysis can show which future experiments provide
genuinely new information, not duplicating the amplitude combinations
already measured previously in seemingly quite different types of polarization experiments.

Of these various possible uses of polarization analyses, I want to discuss,
in our present context, only one, namely that one which leads us back to our
overall topic of one-particle-exchange. I will give a qualitative account of
this application, and will give some quantitative and mathematical details of
it in the Appendix for those whose professional work lies fairly close to
particle physics.

One might ask whether there is a particular type of "amplitude signature" for one-particle-exchange mechanisms. In other words, for a given
reaction a one-particle-exchange mechanism predicts the reaction amplitudes, and the question then is whether these amplitudes show a particular
pattern characteristic for such mechanisms.[10]

In exploring this, one first needs to specify what one means by one-
particle-exchange mechanism. We focused on two particular properties.
One was factorization, that is, the property that the one-particle-exchange
contribution can be written as a product of two parts, each describing one
of the two vertices. The other property was that the object being exchanged
by the two vertices has to have a definite angular momentum and parity.
These are very general and "minimal" requirements for identifying one-
particle-exchange mechanisms, and they are quite independent of the particular form of the vertices and of other technical details.

Following the consequences of these two conditions in the structure of
the reaction amplitudes is not overly arduous and has in fact been carried
out. It was found that, indeed, one-particle-exchange mechanisms exhibit a
characteristic amplitude signature. It was also found that the signatures dis-
tinguish between exchanges of particles with two different types of parities
("natural" or "unnatural"), but that the signature is independent of the
masses of the particles being exchanged, or, in many cases, of the value of
the spin of the exchanged particle. Furthermore, the signature is present
even when we have a superposition of several simultaneous one-particle-
exchange mechanisms of the same type of parity. These latter properties
make such polarization tests of one-particle-exchange mechanisms broadly
applicable and of wide scope.

The test can be used both for direct-channel resonances and for the usual
t-channel exchange processes. In the former, the signature is most con-
veniently expressed in the helicity frame. In the t-channel case, however, the

most convenient formalism to use is one of the optimal planar formalisms, rotated from the helicity frame by a "magic" angle, the formula for which can be easily given. In such a "magic" frame the constraints imposed on the amplitudes by the one-particle-exchange nature of the dynamics are particularly simple: They involve simple equality between pairs of reaction amplitudes, or equality in magnitude with opposite signs.

The tests were then applied to the proton-proton elastic scattering data mentioned earlier, since those data yielded a definite determination of the reaction amplitudes. The test showed[11] that, as one expected, at the lower energies of 570 MeV and 800 MeV there is no dominance of one-particle-exchange mechanisms of a given type of parity, in accordance with the one-boson-exchange models in which one-particle-exchanges of both types of parity play significant roles. To our surprise, however, the test indicated that at 6 GeV/c, one-particle-exchange mechanisms with natural parities, play a dominant role. It would be an exaggeration to claim that this role is exclusive, since the differences in *magnitude* of the two amplitudes required to be equal by one-particle-exchange are slightly more often different from zero outside the experimental errors than they should be for an exclusive dominance, and in the differences between the two amplitudes in terms of phases there is also room for a 15-20° difference within the experimental errors. Yet the effect is very pronounced, and now awaits theoretical explanation. Interestingly, the effect shows up in the entire momentum transfer range in which data are plentifully available, that is, up to $t = -1.0$.

Thus the search for imprints of one-particle-exchanges continues by constantly changing methods and in an ever broadening range of kinematic parameters. Although Geoff Chew's present interests have branched out from such exchanges into more abstract features of particle physics, his impact in this area remains and is gratefully and pleasurably acknowledged by those of us who continue to contribute to this apparently pivotal aspect of elementary particle physics.

Appendix

Proton-proton elastic scattering (with the assumption of Lorentz invariance, parity conservation, time reversal invariance, and identical particle constraints) has five complex reaction amplitudes at each energy and angle. We will denote these five amplitudes as follows:

$$a = \langle ++|++ \rangle \qquad b = \langle ++|+- \rangle \qquad c = \langle ++|-- \rangle$$

$$d = \langle +-|+- \rangle \qquad e = \langle +-|-+ \rangle , \qquad (1)$$

where the four signs in the brackets represent the spin projections of the four protons in the following order: first final state particle, first initial state particle, second final state particle, second initial state particle.

The quantization direction of the spins of the four protons is yet unspecified, except that the constraints of the symmetries additional to Lorentz invariance are different for the transversity amplitudes from what they are for the planar amplitudes, and so the above amplitudes were derived using the constraints for the planar amplitudes. But within the infinite class of planar amplitudes, we can still choose any one by specifying the particular spin quantization direction in the reaction plane. So we can have the usual helicity amplitudes (subscript h) or sets of amplitudes rotated for each particle by angle β with respect to the helicity frame (subscript β).

The test of the one-particle-exchange (OPE) mechanisms mentioned in the text is simple in terms of the "magic" planar frame, which is a particular a_β, ..., e_β with β given by

$$\cos \beta_m = \left[1 + \frac{4m^2}{s} \cot^2 \frac{\theta}{2} \right]^{-\frac{1}{2}} , \qquad (2)$$

where θ is the c.m. scattering angle, s is the c.m. energy squared, and m is the proton mass.

These amplitudes will be denoted by a subscript m.

The OPE test then can be formulated in the following exceedingly simple form

$$a_m = \pm c_m , \qquad (3)$$

where the upper and lower signs hold if the OPE or OPE's involve particles with natural and unnatural parities, respectively.

The results of this test as applied to p-p elastic scattering[9] at 6 GeV/c are shown in Figs. 1 and 2. Ambiguities in the amplitude analysis permit four sets of discrete solutions. The values for the difference in magnitude and phase of a_m and c_m are shown for each set. The normalization of the amplitudes is such that the sum of the absolute value squares of the five amplitudes is unity, which means that, on the average, the magnitude of each amplitude is about 0.45. The four discrete solutions exist because at the time when the analysis was made the number of observables measured and the uncertainties associated with the data points were sufficient only to eliminate all *continuum* of ambiguities, but still leaving several *discrete* solutions resulting from the bilinear nature of the relationship between amplitudes and observables. Such discrete ambiguities can be eliminated through the measurement of a few additional observables, the number of which will depend on the specific circumstances.

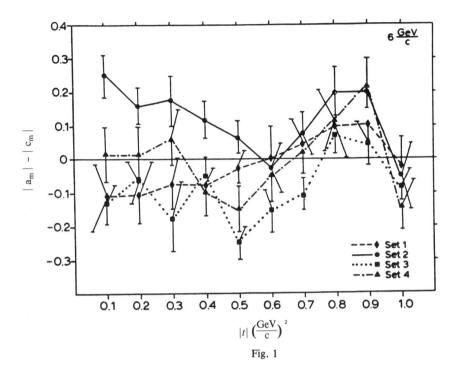

Fig. 1

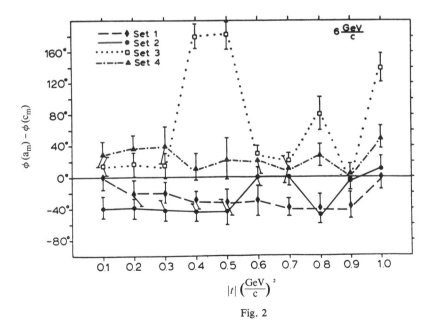

Fig. 2

References

1. G.F. Chew, *Phys. Rev.* **112**, 1380 (1958).

2. M.J. Moravcsik, *Phys. Rev.* **104**, 1451 (1956).

3. P. Cziffra and M.J. Moravcsik, *Phys. Rev.* **116**, 226 (1959).

4. M.J. Moravcsik, *Nucleon-nucleon Scattering and the One-Pion Exchange,* UCRL-5317-T (August 1958); P. Cziffra, M.H. MacGregor, M.J. Moravcsik, and H.P. Stapp, *Phys. Rev.* **114**, 880 (1959).

5. For a summary of the various one-particle-exchange models up to about 1972, see M.J. Moravcsik, *Rep. Prog. Phys.* **35**, 587 (1972).

6. The early history of these modified one-particle-exchange models is discussed in Sec. 4.2 of the review article referred to in Ref. 5.

7. G.R. Goldstein and M.J. Moravcsik, *Ann. Phys.* (N.Y.) **98**, 128 (1976).

8. G.R. Goldstein and M.J. Moravcsik, *Ann. Phys.* (N.Y.) **142**, 219 (1982).

9. A. Yokosawa, *Phys. Rep.* **64**, 50 (1980); I.P. Auer *et al., Measurements of Triple- and Double-Spin Parameters in Elastic p-p Scattering at 6 GeV/c,* ANL-HEP-PR-84- (submitted for publication).

10. G.R. Goldstein and M.J. Moravcsik, *Phys. Rev.* **D30**, 55 (1984).

11. G.R. Goldstein and M.J. Moravcsik, *Phys. Lett.* **152B**, 265 (1985).

IS THERE A $\Delta\Delta\pi$ PROBLEM?

Duane A. Dicus and
Vigdor L. Teplitz

We first reminisce about Chew's dedication to the goal of strong interaction dynamics and his attention to all aspects of the problem and then present him with potential grist for his mill. Specifically we point out that deduction of $g_{\Delta\Delta\pi}$ from P33 πN inelasticity appears to give a value significantly less than almost all theoretical calculations and review efforts to date to resolve this apparent discrepancy.

1. Introduction

One of us (VLT) spent the years 1962–64 at the Lawrence Berkeley Laboratory as a research associate where he was fortunate enough to collaborate with Chew on the Reggeized bootstrap; it was for him and his wife a most productive,[1] educational and agreeable period.

Chew had, VLT recalls, infinite patience with research associates, and everyone else. He always had time to hear a new idea or a new result, to check a calculation or to suggest a new approach. In part this patience reflected his warm personality. In part, however, it reflected his goals. Chew wanted a dynamical understanding of strong interactions. He wanted to know of anything that could conceivably help that goal. He tended then, as no doubt now, to work one approach at a time, but always to be searching for new techniques, new facts from experiment, and new ideas from other areas of physics or mathematics. Leonard Rodberg,[2] who was a research associate at Berkeley in the late 50's says that he sat beside Chew at a session of contributed papers at a Washington Physical Society meeting when a young physicist named Mandelstam gave a ten-minute talk on an iterative procedure involving several variables. Rodberg says he turned to Chew and told him that nothing that complicated could be useful. Chew never heard, he was on his feet moving toward Mandelstam.

The search for new inputs to the strong interaction problem went on continuously. In addition to a parade of visitors, Chew saw just about all the preprints and casually, but not by chance, asked at lunch or coffee about the details of any that he didn't have time to digest thoroughly but thought could contain something useful. For a major initiative, there would be an internal seminar or a series of seminars to master it. There was a sense of being in "strong interaction central"; all information on strong interactions was either generated there or flowed there to be absorbed. Also information from other areas was to be sifted for potential applicability. Therefore Chew asked irrelevant questions: at an experimental solid state colloquium he would ask about some item incidental to the experiment, but with a hint of a twist that made him wonder whether there was a possible application of the idea to strong interactions. It was probably always clear to members of the theory group that he had asked the question because of such a possibility but the connection for any particular question was often very hard to fathom — especially for the speaker.

In such an atmosphere it was easy to be productive. Chew always had lots of ideas for problems in strong interaction dynamics that needed solving, ideas for calculations to solve them with, time to help make certain the calculations were done correctly, and interest in integrating the results into the continually growing understanding of strong interactions.

It is in this spirit of bringing our result to "strong interaction central" to see how it fits in, or whether, conceivably, it is just plain wrong, that we sketch below our work on $g_{\Delta\Delta\pi}$. Our result is, in brief

$$\frac{g^2_{\Delta\Delta\pi}}{4\pi} \text{ (experimental)} \leq \left(\frac{1}{3} \text{ to } \frac{1}{2} \right) \frac{g^2_{\Delta\Delta\pi}}{4\pi} \text{ (theory) .} \tag{1}$$

We arrive at this result as follows:

2. $g_{\Delta\Delta\pi}$ — Experimental

We considered[3] the reaction

$$\pi(Q) + N(p_i) \rightarrow \pi(q_2) + \pi(q_1) + N(p_f) . \tag{2}$$

We assumed that the dominant contribution to (2) comes from the isobar model[4] diagram of Fig. 1 together with its crossed diagrams. The contri-

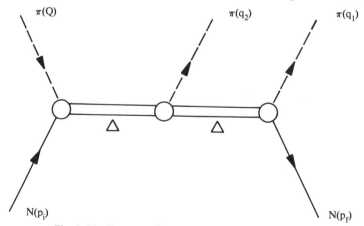

Fig. 1. The Feynman diagram for PP33($\pi\Delta$) production.

butions from these diagrams to φ_{33}^{inel} is of the form

$$\sigma_{33}^{inel} = g_{\Delta\Delta\pi}^2 g_{\Delta N\pi}^4 \kappa . \tag{3}$$

In Ref. 3 we calculated the proportionality constant κ for both pseudo-scalar and pseudovector $\Delta\Delta\pi$ coupling using the spin 3/2 Rarita-Schwinger field, taking into account the work of Johnson and Sudarshan[5], Nath, Etemadi, and Kimel[6], and Hagen[7] on freedom and constraints of spin 3/2 fields and using the dressed isobar model propagator of Woloshyn, Moniz, and Aaron.[8] For the pseudoscalar case, the matrix element for Fig. 1 is given by (for the case $\pi^- p \to \Delta^\circ \to \pi^- \Delta^+ \to \pi^- \pi^+ n$)

$$M = g_{\Delta^+\pi^-\Delta^\circ} \, g_{\pi^+n\Delta^+} \, g_{\pi^-p\Delta^\circ} \, q_1^\alpha \, Q^\mu \, \bar{u}(p_f) \, (g_{\alpha\beta} - \gamma_\alpha\gamma_\beta)$$

$$\times \; S^{\beta\rho}(p_f + q_1)\gamma_5(g_{\rho\nu} - \gamma_\rho\gamma_\nu)S^{\nu\sigma}(p_i + Q)$$

$$\times \; (g_{\sigma\mu} - \gamma_\sigma\gamma_\mu)u(p_i) , \tag{4}$$

where $S^{\alpha\beta}(p)$ is given by

$$S^{\alpha\beta}(p) = (\not{p} + m_\Delta)\left[-g^{\alpha\beta} + \frac{1}{3}\gamma^\alpha\gamma^\beta + \frac{1}{3m_\Delta}(\gamma^\alpha p^\beta - \gamma^\beta p^\alpha)\right.$$

$$\left. + \frac{2}{3m_\Delta}p^\alpha p^\beta\right]\left[p^2 - (m_\Delta - \frac{i}{2}\Gamma_\Delta)^2\right]^{-1} . \tag{5}$$

There are a large number of terms involved in squaring the 800 terms of (4) and summing over spins. We calculated the contributions to σ_{33}^{inel} using SCHOONSHIP, thereby obtaining the coefficient κ in (3).

To compare with experimental data we used: (i) our analysis of 4140 $\pi^- p \to \pi^+\pi^- n$ bubble chamber events at total center of mass energies between 1330 and 1380 MeV[3]; and (ii) the Berkeley Carnegie-Mellon elastic πN phase shift analysis.[9] Comparing the cross section from our analysis at 1340, 1360, and 1375 MeV for the PP33 $(\pi\Delta)$ wave with (3) alone (using the results from (4) and (5)) gave the values of $g^2/4\pi$ of Table 1. In these calculations the most sensitive parameter is the value chosen for the mass of the Δ. In our view the appropriate value is the real part of the Δ pole position, (1211 MeV), rather than the resonance position (1236 MeV). In the table, as discussed in Ref. 3, the "EPP values" of $g^2/4\pi$ are obtained by searching the PP33 $(\pi\Delta)$ wave under the assumption that its phase is related to the elastic phase through a two-channel K matrix in the approximation that the inelastic to inelastic K-matrix element is small. For the "SPP

Table 1. The $\Delta\Delta\pi$ coupling constant as determined for various combinations of the Δ mass, pseudoscalar (P) versus axial vector (A) interaction, and isobar-analysis solutions. W is the total center of mass energy.

W(MeV)	M_Δ(MeV)	Coupling	$g^2/4\pi$ (SPP)	$g^2/4\pi$ (EPP)
1340	1211	P	$19.7 \begin{array}{l} +11.6 \\ -\ 9.0 \end{array}$	$0.1 \begin{array}{l} +5.2 \\ -0.1 \end{array}$
1360	1211	P	$35.7 \begin{array}{l} +10.9 \\ -\ 9.5 \end{array}$	$13.0 \begin{array}{l} +6.9 \\ -5.4 \end{array}$
1375	1211	P	$17.9 \begin{array}{l} +8.0 \\ -6.5 \end{array}$	$2.3 \begin{array}{l} +3.1 \\ -1.8 \end{array}$
1340	1236	P	$35.7 \begin{array}{l} +21.1 \\ -16.2 \end{array}$	$0.3 \begin{array}{l} +9.4 \\ -0.3 \end{array}$
1360	1236	P	$64.1 \begin{array}{l} +19.6 \\ -17.0 \end{array}$	$23.4 \begin{array}{l} +12.4 \\ -\ 9.8 \end{array}$
1375	1236	P	$32.3 \begin{array}{l} +14.4 \\ -11.8 \end{array}$	$4.1 \begin{array}{l} +5.6 \\ -3.2 \end{array}$
1340	1211	A	$23.4 \begin{array}{l} +13.8 \\ -10.6 \end{array}$	$0.2 \begin{array}{l} +6.2 \\ -0.2 \end{array}$
1360	1211	A	$39.6 \begin{array}{l} +12.1 \\ -10.5 \end{array}$	$14.5 \begin{array}{l} +7.6 \\ -6.0 \end{array}$
1375	1211	A	$19.1 \begin{array}{l} +8.5 \\ -7.0 \end{array}$	$2.4 \begin{array}{l} +3.3 \\ -1.9 \end{array}$
1340	1236	A	$44.4 \begin{array}{l} +26.2 \\ -20.1 \end{array}$	$0.3 \begin{array}{l} +11.7 \\ -\ 0.3 \end{array}$
1360	1236	A	$74.6 \begin{array}{l} +22.8 \\ -19.8 \end{array}$	$27.2 \begin{array}{l} +14.4 \\ -11.4 \end{array}$
1375	1236	A	$36.0 \begin{array}{l} +16.1 \\ -13.1 \end{array}$	$4.6 \begin{array}{l} +6.2 \\ -3.6 \end{array}$

values" of $g^2/4\pi$, the phase of the P33 ($\pi\triangle$) wave is searched as a free para-meter. Because of the small magnitude of the PP33 ($\pi\triangle$) amplitude and the reasonable nature of the EPP assumption, we believe the EPP solutions are more reliable. One sees from the table that each of these considerations weighs one toward the smaller values of $g^2/4\pi$. After judicious considera-tion of Table 1, we quote a value for $g^2/4\pi$ of

$$\frac{g^2_{\triangle\triangle\pi}(\text{VTNB})}{4\pi} = 40 \pm 20 \ . \tag{6}$$

This $g_{\triangle\triangle\pi}$, those in Table 1, and those below have had a CG coefficient removed and therefore should be multiplied by the appropriate CG coeffi-cient to find the coupling for a particular charge state; for example,

$$g_{\triangle^0 \pi^- \triangle^+} = \langle \tfrac{3}{2}, \tfrac{1}{2}; 1, -1 | \tfrac{3}{2}, -\tfrac{1}{2} \rangle g_{\triangle\triangle\pi} \ .$$

It should be noted that the main features of the analysis of Ref. 3 were reproduced in a new, largely independent analysis of $\pi N \rightarrow \pi\pi N$ over the larger energy range 1320 — 1950 MeV.[10] The latter analysis began at 1440 where a large data set exists and eliminated waves with decreasing energy. A specific search on the small PP33 ($\pi\triangle$) was not conducted, but the results for the large waves — PP11 ($\pi\triangle$), PS11 (εN), DS13 ($\pi\triangle$), and DS33 ($\pi\triangle$) — were in approximate agreement in both magnitude and phase.

The Berkeley-Carnegie-Mellon elastic phase shift analysis gives even more stringent limits on $g_{\triangle\triangle\pi}$; attributing the entire πN P33 inelasticity to $\pi\triangle$ production allowed us to deduce

$$\frac{g^2_{\triangle\triangle\pi}(\text{BCM})}{4\pi} = 2^{+25}_{-2} \ . \tag{7}$$

3. $g_{\triangle\triangle\pi}$ — Theoretical

We know of one theoretical calculation that yields a $g_{\triangle\triangle\pi}$ in agreement with the experimental value above. R. C. Brunett and R. W. Childers[11] obtained, from a two-channel N/D calculation,

$$\frac{g^2_{\triangle\triangle\pi}(\text{N/D})}{4\pi} \simeq 27 \ . \tag{8}$$

They consider their calculation "ambiguous", however, because they find a second, unphysical bound state below the $\pi\triangle$ threshold.

All other theoretical values for $g_{\triangle\triangle\pi}$ that we know of are significantly larger. Some examples are: (i) SU(6) gives[12]

$$\frac{g^2_{\Delta\Delta\pi}(SU_6)}{4\pi} \cong 130. \tag{9}$$

(ii) U(12) gives about the same result as SU(6).[13] (iii) Using the Goldberger-Treiman relation,[14] with the axial vector coupling constant evaluated in the MIT bag model,[15] gives[3]

$$\frac{g^2_{\Delta\Delta\pi}(Bag)}{4\pi} = 102 \text{ or } 133. \tag{10}$$

Similar results are obtained by Kiehlmann and Schmidt from superconvergence relations, by S. Oneda *et al.* by deriving the axial vector coupling of the Δ from considering asymptotic level realizations of SU(2) symmetry in the chiral SU(2) $\times$ SU(2) algebra, and by Duck and Umland in a "cloudy" bag model.[16] (iv) Sum rules that follow from evaluating the matrix element of the commutator of the pion field with the electromagnetic current between Δ and N states give a higher value[17]

$$\frac{g^2_{\Delta\Delta\pi}(\gamma p \to \pi\Delta)}{4\pi} \cong 250. \tag{11}$$

(v) An earlier calculation[18] along the lines of (iv) gives a value closer to those of (i) — (iii). (vi) Similarly, finite energy sum rules also give a higher value[19] close to that of (11). (vii) The quark model gives a value slightly larger than (9).[20] (viii) Kuriyan and Sudarshan[21] use the technique of non-invariance groups; for the strong coupling groups SU(4), SL(4,R), or T(9) $\times$ (SU^I(2) $\times$ SU^J(2)) they predict a value of 80. (ix) The topological theory of elementary-hadron coupling constants finds[22] $g_{\Delta\Delta\pi}$ to have the value predicted by SU(6)$_W$. It encompasses all the predictions of Mandelstam's Veneziano representation-based relativistic quark model which itself reproduced SU(6) predictions for baryon and meson particle spectra, masses, and coupling constants.[23]

4.   Discussion

With the exception of Brunett and Childers[11] all theorists whose work is known to us get higher values for $g_{\Delta\Delta\pi}$ than we find from the data (Sec. 2 above). For a while we thought that the discrepancy might be eliminated by taking into account the off mass shell dependence of the $\Delta\Delta\pi$ form factor. We investigated this possibility in some detail.[24] Single-channel form factors make the disagreement worse; they tend to be *rising* toward higher mass (effective) poles and hence predict *larger* cross sections than uncorrected coupling constants. Coupled channel calculations are complicated; one needs to continue in both Δ energies. In Ref. 24 we give arguments that the off-shell F33($\pi\Delta$) channel can be ignored and address the resulting 2×2 P33(πN)-P33($\pi\Delta$) problem, using the N/D parameterization of Ball, Garg, and Shaw.[25] We find in each case considered in Table 1 two solutions — one smaller than that of Table 1 and one on the order of 1000. Neither, of course, resolves the discrepancy between experiment and theory.

What then are the possible explanations for the apparent discrepancy? We list a few below:

(1) There is some error in principle or in execution in the calculation of Ref. 3 of the coefficient κ in Eq. (3) above. A larger $g_{\Delta\Delta\pi}$ would both remove the discrepancy and would discriminate among the models of Sec. 3.

(2) Low energy P33 inelasticity is in fact much larger than found in the data analyses cited in Refs. 3 and 9.

(3) The contribution of the diagram of Fig. 1 (plus that with the π's interchanged) is cancelled in the P33 state by some other contribution.

(4) Our form factor calculations are too naive. Perhaps more elaborate (coupled channel) ones could correct $g_{\Delta\Delta\pi}$ to agree with theory.

(5) The models listed in Sec. 3 are all inadequate for the calculation of $g_{\Delta\Delta\pi}$ — an idea guaranteed to be unpopular.

Whatever explanation is in fact the case, it is important to resolve the present disagreement between theory and experiment. It is our firm expectation that Chew, the participants in the September 29 Jubilee for him, and the readers of this volume will focus on this problem. The Δ plays too important a role in strong interaction dynamics to allow discrepancies in $g_{\Delta\Delta\pi}$ to remain unanswered; we are confident "strong interaction central" will not allow such an unnecessary lacuna.

Acknowledgements

We are grateful to our collaborators of Refs. 3, 10, and 24, R. Aaron, R. A. Arndt, J. B. Cammarata, Y. N. Goradia, R. H. Hackman, R. S. Longacre, and D. M. Manley for their help. We also thank C. E. Jones for a useful discussion. This work was supported in part by the U.S. Department of Energy and by the National Science Foundation.

References

1. See for example G. F. Chew and V. L. Teplitz, *Phys. Rev.* **137**, B139 (1965); P. Tarjanne and V. L. Teplitz, *Phys. Rev. Lett.* **11**, 340 (1963); D. C. Teplitz and V. L. Teplitz, *Phys. Rev.* **137**, B142 (1965); R. C. Hwa and V. L. Teplitz, *Homology and Feynman Integrals* (W. A. Benjamin Co., New York, 1966).

2. Private communication, 1962.

3. R. A. Arndt, *et al., Phys. Rev.* **D20,** 651 (1979).

4. R. M. Sternheimer and S. J. Lindenbaum, *Phys. Rev.* **109,** 1723 (1958); and *ibid.* **123,** 331 (1961). For an early application to $\pi N \to \pi\Delta$, see S. Mandelstam *et al., Ann. Phys.* (N.Y.) **18,** 198 (1962).

5. K. Johnson and E. C. G. Sudarshan, *Ann. Phys.* (N.Y.) **13,** 126 (1961).

6. L. M. Nath, B. Etemadi, and J. D. Kimel, *Phys. Rev.* **D3,** 2153 (1971).

7. C. R. Hagen, *Phys. Rev.* **D4,** 2204 (1971).

8. R. M. Woloshyn, E. J. Moniz, and R. Aaron, *Phys. Rev.* **C13,** 286 (1976).

9. R. Kelly and R. Cutkosky, *Phys. Rev.* **D20,** 2782 (1979); R. Cutkosky *et al., Phys. Rev.* **D20,** 2804 (1979); R. Cutkosky *et al., Phys. Rev.* **D20,** 2839 (1979);

10. D. M. Manley, R. A. Arndt, Y. Goradia, and V. L. Teplitz, *Phys. Rev.* **D30,** 904 (1984).

11. R. C. Brunett and R. W. Childers, *Nuovo Cimento* **48,** 890 (1967).

12. F. Gursey, A. Pais, and L. A. Radicati, *Phys. Rev. Lett.* **13,** 299 (1964).

13. B. Sakita and K. C. Wali, *Phys. Rev.* **139,** B1355 (1965).

14. M. L. Goldberger and S. B. Treiman, *Phys. Rev.* **110,** 1178 (1958).

15. T. DeGrand, R. L. Jaffe, K. Johnson, and J. Kiskis, *Phys. Rev.* **D12,** 2060 (1975). Also see E. Golowich, *ibid.* **12,** 2108 (1975); R. H. Hackman, N. G. Deshpande, D. A. Dicus, and V. L. Teplitz, *ibid.* **18,** 2537 (1978).

16. H.-D. Kiehlmann and W. Schmidt, University of Karlsruhe reports, 1978 (unpublished); M. Slaughter, S. Oneda, and T. Tanuma, *Phys. Rev.* **D26,** 1191 (1982); I. M. Duck and E. A. Umland, Rice Univ. preprint. See also H. F. Jones and M. D. Scadron, *Nuovo Cimento* **48A,** 545 (1967) and *ibid.* **52A,** 62 (1967).

17. M. Chaichian and N. F. Nelipa, University of Helsinki preprint HU-TFT-80-36 (unpublished).

18. L. V. Laperashvili and V. Kh. Shoikhet, *Sov. J. Nucl. Phys.* **6,** 772 (1968).

19. D. G. Sutherland, *Nuovo Cimento* **48,** 188 (1967); see also C. D. Froggatt and N. H. Parsons, *J. Phys.* **G3,** 159 (1977); we are grateful to Dr. Sutherland for helpful correspondence.

20. R. P. Feynman, M. Kislinger, and F. Ravndal, *Phys. Rev.* **D3,** 2706 (1971).

21. J. Kuriyan and E. C. G. Sudarshan, *Phys. Lett.* **21,** 106 (1966); *Phys. Rev.* **162,** 1650 (1967).

22. G. F. Chew, J. Finkelstein, and M. Levinson, *Phys. Rev. Lett.* **47,** 767 (1981).

23. S. Mandelstam, *Phys. Rev.* **184,** 1625 (1969) and *ibid.* **D1,** 1745 (1970).

24. R. A. Arndt, J. B. Cammarata, D. A. Dicus, and V. L. Teplitz, *Off Mass Shell Effects and the* $\Delta\Delta\pi$ *Coupling Constant,* (unpublished), Univ. of Texas preprint 03992-471.

25. J. S. Ball, R. C. Garg, and G. L. Shaw, *Phys. Rev.* **177**, 2258 (1969).

MY EXPERIENCES WITH THE S-MATRIX PROGRAM

Steven Frautschi

Arriving at Berkeley as a postdoctoral fellow in September 1959, I was placed in an office with Stanley Mandelstam (as well as, at various times, Adam Bincer, Dan Zwanziger, Marcel Froissart, and the late Jerzy Sawicki), and exposed to the visionary leadership of Geoff Chew. In addition to ordinary seminars, etc., Chew was regularly available at lunchtime and in weekly meetings with his large circle of students and postdocs. It was an inspiring environment for learning the new physics and discussing it from all points of view, philosophical as well as technical.

After learning how to handle the new techniques in an S-matrix treatment of low energy πN scattering with my college classmate Dirk Walecka,[1] I had an idea for handling high energy scattering which led to the "strip approximation" and working directly with Chew.[2,3] We also wrote a paper[4] giving a general definition of the relativistic "potential" for elastic scattering.

It was the dynamics of the strip approximation that made the need for some kind of "boundary condition" controlling high energy behavior clear to me. Mandelstam played a crucial role in pointing both Chew and myself towards Regge poles as providing the needed boundary condition. We soon came to realize that the Regge pole[5-8] was far more interesting than the strip approximation, and was indeed the simple, general concept that captured the essence of our subject.

Apart from the theoretical consistency of dynamical models such as the strip approximation, the fact that 30 GeV accelerators at Brookhaven and CERN were about to start operation, with early emphasis on exclusive small-angle two-body reactions such as NN $\rightarrow$ NN and πN $\rightarrow$ πN, helped focus our attention on Regge poles as the dominant terms in high energy scattering amplitudes.

A central idea in the Regge pole papers was the "principle of equivalence" — the suggestion that all hadrons are dynamically formed composites lying on Regge trajectories. With regard to this principle, the Chew-Low model, with its attractive potential in both the 1-1 and 3-3 states, had played a crucial role in making the nucleon look dynamically equivalent to the $\triangle$(3-3) resonance. The difficulties of treating the $J = 3/2 \triangle$ particle as an elementary field (e.g., its interactions couldn't be made renormalizable) were well known, and were reinforced for S-matrix theorists by the discovery of the Froissart bound. Regge poles gave us an experimentally testable way out of the $J = 3/2 \triangle$ problem, [by looking at the energy dependence of backward $\pi^- p \rightarrow \pi^- p$] and an exciting chance to see if the nucleon similarly lay on a Regge trajectory. And if the nucleon, the best-known and most fundamental-appearing hadron lay on a Regge trajectory, why shouldn't all hadrons?

Another important factor leading us to extend the hypothesis that hadrons lie on Regge trajectories to *all* hadrons was certainly Gell-Mann's enormous enthusiasm. I had my first serious encounter with Gell-Mann in the summer of 1961. He visited the Lawrence Laboratory at a time when Chew happened to be away, so the firehose of Gell-Mann's inquiries was turned on the grad students and postdocs. Shaken after an afternoon of heavy interrogation, several of them asked me to be present the next day to take some of the heat. The first question Gell-Mann asked me concerned the relation between the $J^p = 1/2^+, 5/2^+, ...$ sequence of nucleon states and the $J^p = 3/2^-, 7/2^-, ...$ sequence. As luck would have it, I had been thinking about that very issue the previous week. I had realized that "exchange potentials" would split the trajectories associated with these two sequences, as experiment appeared to require, and had worked out how to express this fact technically. Consequently I was able to answer Gell-Mann's questions — no doubt a minor episode in the history of S-matrix theory, but a major impetus to my eventual employment by Caltech!

While Regge poles thrust the strip approximation and Mandelstam representation off center stage, the calculational possibilities they afforded did provide us with some significant insights into Regge poles:

(i)   Chew and I, in Ref. 3, considered the buildup of powers of logarithms $(c(t) \log s)^n$ in iterated exchanges, and showed that the logarithms *might* sum to a Regge trajectory (although we couldn't really prove it). This subject was later developed to great heights of technical expertise in studies of leading logs in perturbation theory by Gell-Mann *et al.*, Hung Cheng *et al.*, and others.

(ii)   In a less happy vein, I found indications of what were later called "Regge cuts" [an extremely oblique allusion to this can be found on the last page of Ref. 7]. After a period when Chew hoped these would cancel out, we eventually had to accept that Regge cuts existed and, indeed, represented the physics of multiple scattering. But our inability to calculate such complicated objects accurately, and the need for messy phenomenological parametrizations of them, became a major limitation of the Regge pole program.

After the initial preprints applying Regge poles appeared, the reception accorded Regge poles by the physics community went through a "boom and bust" cycle. While partly a bandwagon effect of mass psychology, this cycle also reflected experimental developments. In addition to placing all known hadrons on Regge trajectories, we had tentatively associated the diffraction peak with exchange of a "vacuum" or "Pomeranchuk" trajectory. Experiments on the new 30 GeV accelerators started with the diffraction peak, since it gave the highest counting rate for each incoming beam, and only later measured the charge exchange and backward peaks where particle exchange is not obscured by Pomeranchuk exchange. Initial enthusiasm when the PP diffraction peak "shrank" as predicted turned to bemusement when the πN diffraction peak didn't shrink and the pp peak even anti-shrank. Finally, later experiments on πN charge exchange and other nondiffractive reactions exhibited beautiful Regge behavior, and it was recognized that the elastic diffraction peaks stand apart as a special case, not necessarily associated with particle exchange.

It always helps if something turns out simple, and we were certainly fortunate with linear trajectories. As far as I'm aware, Chew and I originally drew straight-line trajectories purely for simplicity. In the early days of Regge poles, speakers who had calculated the trajectories for some nonrelativistic potentials could always get a good laugh by contrasting our straight lines with their non-linear, crooked, cusp-ridden results. But later the hadronic trajectories determined by the particle spectrum and high energy amplitudes turned out to be remarkably straight. Eventually this became an ingredient in dual models and string theory.

After leaving Berkeley, my work in S-matrix theory went off in several directions:

1.   Inelastic processes at high energies.
2.   Symmetry breaking in S-matrix theory.[9] After my move to Caltech, I was naturally made aware of the empirical rules for octet dominance in flavor SU(3) symmetry breaking. Roger Dashen and I attempted to explain the data by considering the response of hadrons to electromagnetic and weak (and strong SU(3) breaking) perturbations in S-matrix language. These studies did very well when based on the Chew-Low model, but foundered in a welter of slowly converging terms when they tried to go beyond Chew-Low.
3.   Spin factors in Regge pole couplings.
4.   The statistical bootstrap.[10-12] The statistical bootstrap studies used statistical assumptions in an attempt to shortcut the complexities introduced by the rapid growth in number of coupled channels at high energies. A count of the growth in number of states was achieved which is in striking agreement with the results of dual and string models.

In retrospect, I would list some of the weak and strong points of the S-matrix program as follows. A major weak point was the relative lack of predictive power. The theory tended to relate things rather than predict them. S-matrix calculations had trouble dealing with the proliferation of amplitudes entering into unitarity relations, with the complex cut structure in inelastic amplitudes, with the complexities of Regge cuts in the *J*-plane. Consequently the dynamics closed only in principle, not in practice; the dynamical calculations were woefully inadequate compared to the soaring aspirations of the program. Also the inability to deal effectively with massless particles limited the S-matrix program to strong interactions.

But the attractive features and accomplishments of S-matrix theory were substantial. It worked with finite observables. It was nonperturbative. With the general principles available to it, it succeeded in making physically significant statements on strong interactions at a time when the fundamental degrees of freedom (the quarks), the fundamental interaction (presumably QCD), and essentially the entire body of data that now validates the fundamental interaction was unknown. It provided a program for comprehending strong interactions — a program never disproved, though eventually superceded by the greater predictive power of the quark model and the broader unification (extending to weak and electromagnetic interactions) of the gauge theories. It provided lasting insights into the Regge family relations among particles of different spin, and the relation between the hadron spectrum and high energy scattering at small momentum transfers.

Looking over my publication list, I find more than 50 papers on the S-matrix program, the latest among them dated 1978 — seventeen years after leaving Berkeley! Exposure to Geoff Chew and his program truly shaped my career, and provided the opportunity of a lifetime to contribute to physics.

References

1. *Pion-Nucleon Scattering in the Mandelstam Representation* (with J. D. Walecka), *Phys. Rev.* **120**, 1486 (1960).

2. *Unified Approach to High- and Low-Energy Strong Interactions on the Basis of the Mandelstam Representation* (with G. F. Chew), *Phys. Rev. Lett.* **5**, 580 (1960).

3. *Dynamical Theory for Strong Interactions at Low Momentum Transfers but Arbitrary Energies* (with G. F. Chew), *Phys. Rev.* **123**, 1478 (1961).

4. *Potential Scattering as Opposed to Scattering Associated with Independent Particles in the S-Matrix Theory of Strong Interactions* (with G. F. Chew) *Phys. Rev.* **124**, 264 (1961).

5. *Principle of Equivalence for all Strongly-Interacting Particles Within the S-Matrix Framework* (with G. F. Chew), *Phys. Rev. Lett.* **7**, 394 (1961).

6. *Regge Trajectories and the Principle of Maximum Strength for Strong Inter-actions* (with G. F. Chew), *Phys. Rev. Lett.* **8,** 41 (1962).

7. *Regge Poles in $\pi - \pi$ Scattering* (with G. F. Chew and S. Mandelstam), *Phys. Rev.* **126,** 1202 (1962).

8. *Experimental Consequences of the Hypothesis of Regge Poles* (with M. Gell-Mann and F. Zachariasen), *Phys. Rev.* **126,** 2204 (1962).

9. *Bootstrap Theory of Octet Enhancement* (with R. Dashen), *Phys. Rev. Lett.* **13,** 497 (1964).

10. *Statistical Bootstrap Model of Hadrons, Phys. Rev.* **D3,** 2821 (1971).

11. *Determination of Asymptotic Parameters in the Statistical Bootstrap Model* (with C. J. Hamer), *Phys. Rev.* **D4,** 2125 (1971).

12. *Ericson Fluctuations and the Bohr Model in Hadron Physics, Nuovo Cimento* **12A,** 133 (1972).

THE S-MATRIX THEORY OF NUCLEAR FORCES

R. Vinh Mau

The use of the S-matrix theory for deriving the nucleon-nucleon interaction is reviewed. Fits to recent NN data are described. Applications to nuclear structure properties and nucleon-nucleus reactions are also discussed, and the results compared with data.

1. Introduction

Many of us certainly remember the great excitement aroused by the S-matrix theory in the early 60's. We also remember the prominent role played by Professor Chew in the development of this theory, and it seems to me appropriate at the celebration of Professor Chew's Jubilee to recall some of the successes of the S-matrix theory. Nowadays, there is a tendency to regard as obsolete the concepts, such as analyticity, unitarity and crossing symmetry attached to this theory. I hope that this talk will provide some support in their favor.

I chose, for this purpose, the illustrative example of the theory of nuclear forces. I believe this example to be relevant because

(i)   nuclear forces are central to physics

(ii) the field of nuclear forces is the one where theory can be severely tested by experiment.

We will see that several thousand nucleon-nucleon scattering data, most of them of very high accuracy, have been accumulated during the last decade. This vast wealth of data provides a very difficult test which, if it is passed successfully, would warrant to any theoretical model the correctness of its physical content.

2. General properties of the Nucleon-Nucleon Interaction

We now believe that nucleons and, more generally, hadrons, are made up of subhadronic constituents (quarks, gluons, etc.). One is, therefore, entitled to demand that the whole theory of nuclear forces should be derived from the degrees of freedom of those fundamental constituents. The problem in its full generality is however very difficult to carry out with accuracy, and present attempts in this direction[1] lead to still inconclusive results. On the other hand, simple arguments based on the confinement of quarks and gluons can provide us some guidance for the approximations to be adopted[2]: Consider a system of two nucleons. When they are far apart, i.e., for inter-nucleon distances r larger than some value of r_0, they can only exchange colorless objects, namely *mesons*, since quarks and gluons must be confined. In the process of these exchanges, the nucleons can also find themselves, during part of the time, in excited states, namely *isobars*. On the contrary, when the overlap of the nucleons is significant, *i.e.,* for small separation distances $(r < r_0)$, the various subhadronic constituents can interact with each other and contribute to the nuclear interaction energy. The dividing line between the two phases depends of course on the size of the confinement domain. A realistic estimate for the value of r_0 gives 0.5 fm $< r_0 < 1$ fm.

From the previous simple arguments, a reasonable approach[2] to the problem of nuclear forces can be based on the breaking of the interaction into two parts:

(i)   the long range (LR) and medium range (MR) part $(r > r_0)$, where the *meson* and *isobar* degrees of freedom are expected to provide a good approximation. In this part, consideration of quark degrees of freedom is probably unnecessary, uneconomical, and in any case does not yield reliable results at the present stage.

(ii)   the short range (SR) part $(r > r_0)$, where the subhadronic (quarks, gluons, etc.) degrees of freedom can play, in principle, a significant role. However, their contribution can be made meaningful only through a proper account of the quark and gluon dynamics. This latter point is still unresolved.

Following the above line of reasoning, the LR part of the NN interaction is given by the exchange of one pion (OPE), since the pion is the lightest meson. The one-pion-exchange potential (OPEP) is well established and every theoretical NN potential contains it. The next lightest system that can be exchanged between the nucleons is the two-pion system. Consequently, the two-pion-exchange (TPE) must be considered in the MR part. The

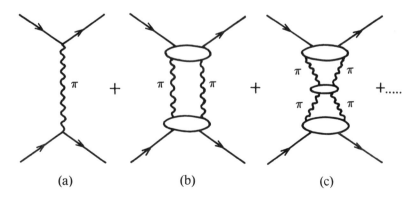

Fig. 1

exchanged pions in the TPE can be uncorrelated (Fig. 1b) or strongly correlated (Fig. 1c), since the $\pi\pi$ interaction is known to be very strong. Multipion exchanges give rise to shorter and shorter range contributions.

The S-matrix theory provides a natural framework for the calculation of these particle exchange contributions to the NN interaction. Only very general properties of the S matrix, such as unitarity conditions crossing relations and dispersion relations[3] are needed.

3.   The Paris NN potential[4]

This potential is representative of the philosophy described above. This means:

(i)   The LR + MR parts ($r \gtrsim 0.8$ fm) are given by the OPE, the TPE and the ω-meson exchange, as part of the three pion exchange. The TPE is calculated carefully via dispersion relations and unitarity from the πN amplitudes and the dominant S and P waves of the $\pi\pi$ interaction. The inputs of the calculation are, thus, the πN phase shift $\delta_\ell^{\pi N}$ and the $\pi\pi$ phase shifts $\delta_0^{\pi\pi}$ and $\delta_1^{\pi\pi}$. The values of $\delta_\ell^{\pi N}$ are taken from phase shift analyses, and $\delta_0^{\pi\pi}$ and $\delta_1^{\pi\pi}$ directly from experiments. In doing so, one includes automatically all the πN *isobars* and the $\pi\pi$ *resonances* in the S wave (the ω-meson) and in the P wave (the ρ-meson) as well as the πN and $\pi\pi$ non-resonant backgrounds. In this way the uncorrelated and correlated two-pion exchange is completely *fixed*. The coupling constant of the ω to the nucleons can be varied, although its value can, in principle, be derived from SU(6). The interested reader can find the details of these rather complicated calculations in Ref. 4.

(ii)   As mentioned above, the presently available theoretical results on the SR forces are still uncertain. On the other hand, there exists a rich body of experimental data. For $T_{\text{Lab}} \lesssim 350$ MeV, several thousand data points have been accumulated.[5] For these reasons, we provisionally take a phenomenological viewpoint for the description of the SR part ($r \lesssim 0.8$ fm). An immediate question to the whole project arises: is this description of the actual LR + MR forces realistic? This question can be answered by comparing the high partial wave phase shifts (F, G, H waves) with the empirical ones. This comparison was done in Ref. 6 and the agreement with experiment is satisfactory. An even better way to check the validity of the LR + MR forces of the Paris potential is to compare the predictions with data for observables that are sensitive to these forces. This is the case for very low energy analyzing powers or polarizations, since at very low energies the S wave is accurately known from the effective range formula, and the P and higher waves are only sensitive to the LR + MR forces. High precision analyzing power and polarization measurements, both in pp and np scattering, have been performed recently.[7] A comparison with these data of the predictions

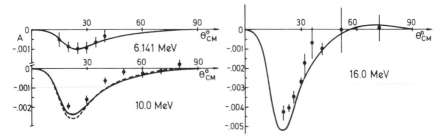

Fig. 2a. The analyzing power in pp scattering. The solid lines refer to the Paris-potential predictions. The dashed lines to phase shift analysis.[8] Experimental data are from Ref. 7.

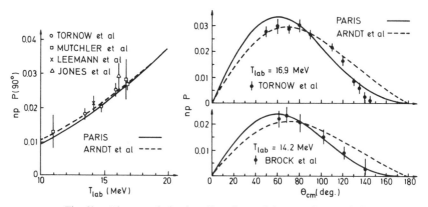

Fig. 2b. The np polarization. Experimental data are from Ref. 7.

obtained with the LR + MR part of the Paris potential is shown in Fig. 2.

Concerning the SR part, it was proposed[9] as a first step, to describe the core with a very simple phenomenological model: namely, the LR + MR (π + π + ω) exchange potential is cut off rather sharply at an internucleon distance $r \sim 0.8$ fm and the SR ($r > 0.8$ fm) is described simply by a constant soft core. This introduces a *minimum* number (five) of adjustable parameters corresponding to the five components (central, spin-spin, tensor, spin-orbit, and quadratic spin-orbit) of the potential for each isospin state. On the other hand, it was found that the central component of the theoretical LR + MR potential has a weak but significant energy dependence and this energy dependence is, in a very good approximation, linear. One then expects also an energy dependence in the SR part. Indeed, fitting the data required an energy dependent core for the central potential, the energy dependence being again linear. This introduces one additional parameter, the slope of the energy dependence. The proposed SR part is then determined by fitting all the known phase shifts ($J \lesssim 6$) up to 330 MeV and the deuteron parameters. Although the number of free parameters is small (six in total for each isospin state) the quality of the fit is very good.[9] The χ^2/data are as good as the ones given by the best phenomenological potentials, which contain many more free parameters:

$$\chi^2/\text{data} = \begin{cases} 2.5 \text{ for pp scattering} \\ \\ 3.7 \text{ for np scattering} \end{cases} \text{with the Paris potential}$$

χ^2/data = 2.4 for pp + np scattering with the Reid soft core potential.

Examples of the fit are shown in Table 1 and Fig. 3.

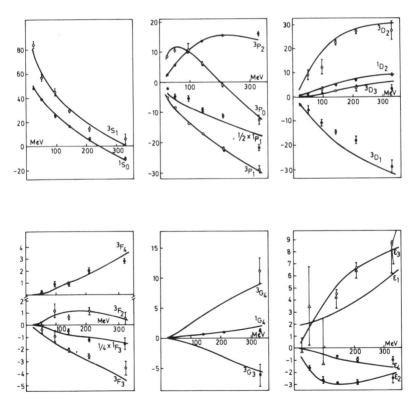

Fig. 3.   Comparison of the phase shifts calculated from the Paris potential with the experimental results of Ref. 8.

Table 1. The deuteron and effective range parameters. Experimental results are given in brackets.

E_D	Q_D	$P_D\%$	μ_D
-2.2246	.290	6.75	.8392
$(-2.2246 \pm .001)$	$(.2875 \pm .002)$		$(.8574 \pm .000006)$

a_{np}	r_{np}	a_{pp}	r_{pp}
5.4179	1.753	-7.817	2.747
$(5.413 \pm .005)$	$(1.748 \pm .005)$	$(-7.823 \pm .01)$	$(2.794 \pm .015)$

The previous model was purposely chosen in its simplest form to demonstrate that, once the LR + MR forces are accurately determined, the (SR) forces can be described by a model with few parameters that does not affect the LR + MR part. This simple model, in which a definite separation between the theoretical and phenomenological parts is made, is designed to provide a clear physical insight into the problem. However, the explicit expression of the resulting potential is not very convenient for practical use in many-body calculations.

In a subsequent paper,[10] an analytical expression for the *complete* potential was developed in terms of a parametrization as a discrete sum of Yukawa terms. This has the advantage of being simple in both configuration and momentum spaces. This parametrization is convenient enough to facilitate its use in many-body calculations. Also, several improvements over the previous version[9] have been incorporated. Another part of the 3π exchange represented by the A_1-meson is included. The determination of the core parameters is now performed by fitting not only the phase shifts but

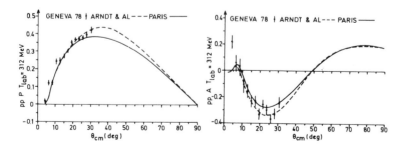

Fig. 4.   pp polarization and the Wolfenstein parameter A.

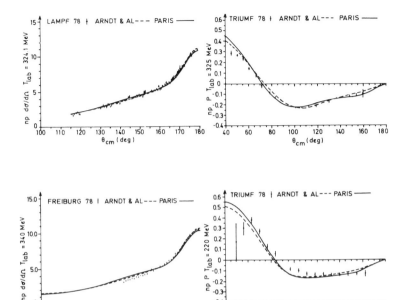

Fig. 5. np differential cross section and polarization.

also the scattering data themselves. The fit was carried out via a two-step procedure. First, the best fit to the phase shifts was searched for, and then the results were further tuned by fitting the data themselves. Use was made of the world set of data consisting of 913 data points for pp scattering ($3 \leqslant T_{\text{Lab}} \leqslant 330$ MeV) and 2239 data points for np scattering ($13 \leqslant T_{\text{Lab}} \leqslant 350$ MeV). This set includes recent measurements on cross sections, polarization, Wolfenstein parameters and spin correlations. Some examples of the fit are displayed in Figs. 4 and 5.

The fit yields a total χ^2/data shown in Table 2. In this table, these values are compared, for reference with those of the most recent phase shift analysis.[8] The total χ^2/data for the same set of data was also calculated in Ref. 11 for the Reid soft core potential. The values are also shown in Table 2.

Table 2.

	χ^2/data for pp scattering	χ^2/data for np scattering
Paris	1.99	2.17
P.S.A.[8]	1.33	1.80
R.S.C.	4.76	9.99

To date, we do not know of any theoretical or even purely phenomenological NN potential that has achieved such a degree of accuracy in fitting the *data*.

In the literature, one still finds NN potential builders who are satisfied with a good comparison of their results with the empirical phase-shifts. We would like to emphasize that, for an accurate quantitative test of models (theoretical or phenomenological), it is more decisive to compare theoretical predictions with experimental data directly rather than through phase shifts. This point is illustrated with the example of the Reid soft core and the Paris potentials. For the fit to phase shifts, the χ^2/data obtained by both of them are very similar, as seen above. On the contrary, when the fit to the data itself is considered, the results are drastically different, as can be seen in Table 2. A phase shift representation is useful and gives a good idea of the overall properties of the NN interaction. It is, however, not constraining enough to put a severe test on the models.

Of course, in the derivation of the Paris potential, the procedure of using theory for the description of the LR + MR part and phenomenology for the SR part is only meaningful if the theoretical inputs are not washed out by the phenomenological part in the final results. Care was taken in this respect. In Fig. 6 the theoretical ($\pi + 2\pi + \omega + A_1$) exchange potential is

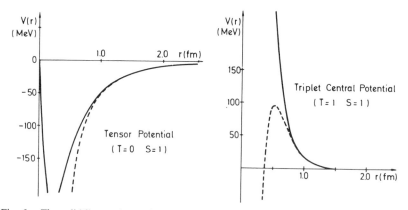

Fig. 6.   The solid lines refer to the complete potential, the dashed lines to the theoretical ($\pi + 2\pi + \omega + A_1$) potential.

compared with the full Paris potential for two examples, the triplet central potential, $T = 1$, and the tensor potential, $T = 0$. Deviations of the long and medium part from the full potential occur only at distances $r > 1$ fm. This provides an *a posteriori* justification to the philosophy adopted from the beginning in the construction of the Paris potential.

This also suggests that, in the framework of the S-matrix theory, we have achieved a reasonable and quantitative understanding of the low energy NN interaction for distances larger than 0.8–1 fm, and that any ultimate theory of strong interactions should recover the same results in that region.

3. Applications to complex nuclei

a) The Trinucleon System (^3H, ^3He)

Those systems are, of course, the first ones to be studied for a test of the previous two-body forces. In this case, given the two-body forces, the problem can be solved exactly with the help of large computers. The observables of interest are the binding energies E_B and the form factors.

In Table 3, are listed the values of the ^3H binding energy yielded by different potentials, the phenomenological ones like the Reid soft core (R.S.C.) and the V14 potentials, as well as the Paris potential. In comparison with the experimental value, all potentials underbind by 1 to 1.5 MeV.

Table 3.

Potential	E_{KIN}(MeV)	E_{POT}(MeV)	E_B(MeV)	References
			−7.1	J.J. Benayoun *et al., Phys. Rev.* **C23**, 1854 (1981)
R.S.C.			−7.022	J.L. Friar *et al., Phys. Rev.* **C25**, 1616 (1982)
	49.925	−57.157	−7.232	C. Hadjuk and P.U. Sauer *Nucl. Phys.* **A369**, 321 (1981)
PARIS	43.034	−50.418	−7.384	*ibid.*
VI4	46.5	−53.5	−7	J. Carlson *et al., Nucl. Phys.* **A401**, 59 (1983)
EXPERIMENT			−8.48	

The ^3He form factor is, in general, correctly described for low momentum transfers, but all models disagree with experiment for $q^2 > 10$ fm^{-2}.

b) Nuclear Matter

Because of the lack of time, I will skip the applications to finite nuclei and consider the extreme case of infinite nuclear matter. The quantities of interest here are the binding energy per particle E/A and the Fermi momentum k_F at the saturation point. Although infinite nuclear matter is theoretically a simpler system than finite nuclei, the methods of calculating the saturation parameters require various approximations. In the Brueckner theory, the lowest order leads to the Brueckner-Hartree-Fock (BHF) approximation. Different choices of the single particle spectrum can be made. The conventional choice has the disadvantage of presenting a gap at $k = k_F$. This difficulty is circumvented by the so-called continuous choice of the single particle spectrum[12] or by a model-space approach[13] which leads also to a continuous single particle spectrum at $k = k_F$. This method is denoted (MBHF) in Table 4. In this table, are shown the saturation parameters calculated with different potentials using different methods.

Table 4.

Potential		E/A (MeV)	k_F (fm^{-1})	Method	Reference
R.S.C.		-9.8	1.36	BHF	Z.Y. Ma, T.T.S. Kuo, *Phys.*
		-13.3	1.4	MBHF	*Lett.* **127B**, 137 (1983)
M.R.S.C.		-10.5	1.4	BHF	B.D. Day, *Phys. Rev. Lett.* **47**, 226 (1981)
OBEP	HM1	-11.8	1.48	BHF	K. Holinde and R. Machleidt, *Nucl. Phys.* **A247**, 425 (1975)
	HM2	-23.5	1.77	BHF	*Nucl. Phys.* **A256**, 479 (1976)
PARIS		-11.22	1.51		M. Lacombe *et al.*, *Phys. Rev.* **C21**, 861 (1980)
		-11.2	1.5	BHF	B.D. Day, *Phys. Rev. Lett.* **47**, 226 (1981)
		-11.5	1.5		Z.Y. Ma, T.T.S. Kuo, *Int. Conf. on Nuclear Physics*, Florence, (I) Sept. 83
		-15.5	1.6	MBHF	*ibid.*
		-16.1	1.62	BHF	A. Lejeune, M. Martzolff, P. Grangé, Preprint (1983)
				with continuous choice of S.P.S.	
		-21[a]	1.6	same	M.A. Matin, M. Dey, *Phys. Rev.* **C27**, 2356 (1983)
V14		-20	1.7–1.8	Variational FHNC	J. Carlson *et al.*, *Nucl. Phys.* **A401**, 59 (1983)
Empirical value		-16	1.33		

[a] In their paper, Lejeune *et al.*, indicate an error of about 5 MeV in the results of this reference.

The table shows that the results obtained with the same method are now consistent with each other. The improved BHF method (MBHF or BHF with a continuous choice of the single particle spectrum) gives, for the Reid soft core potential, too low an energy: $E/A = -13.3$ MeV at about the correct value $k_F = 1.4$ fm^{-1}, and, for the Paris potential, a correct value of the energy: $E/A = -16$ MeV but at too large a value $k_F = 1.6$ fm^{-1}.

c) *The NN interaction in Nucleon-Nucleus Reactions*

Once the free NN interaction is known, one can try to construct a two-nucleon effective interaction in the presence of nuclear medium. Much progress has been achieved during the last few years in the theoretical attempts to construct such effective interactions from the free NN interactions.[14] From these effective interactions, calculation of cross sections and polarizations in elastic and inelastic nucleon-nucleus reactions can then be performed. This was done by various groups and comparison made with accurate measurements on (p, p') and ($\vec{p}$, p') reactions in the energy region $100 < E_p < 400$ MeV. This provides a test of the free NN interaction inputs and also of methods used to derive the effective interactions. Complete references to these works can be found in Ref. 14. In Figs. 7–10 are shown only some examples: $^{12}C(p, p')^{12}C$, $^{16}O(p, p')^{16}O$ and $^{28}Si(p, p')^{28}Si$ for $80 < E_p < 200$ MeV.

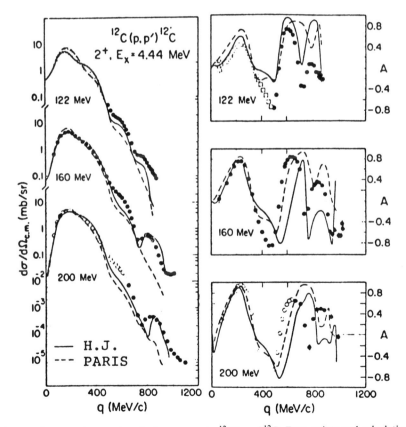

Fig. 7. Cross sections and analyzing powers in $^{12}C(p, p')^{12}C$. Data points and calculations are from Ref. 15.

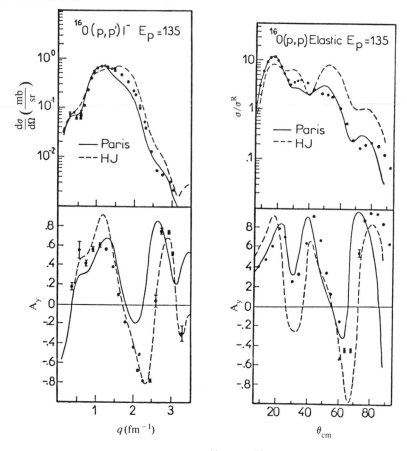

Fig.8.   Cross sections and analyzing powers in $^{16}O(p, p')^{16}O$. Data points and calculations are from Ref. 16.

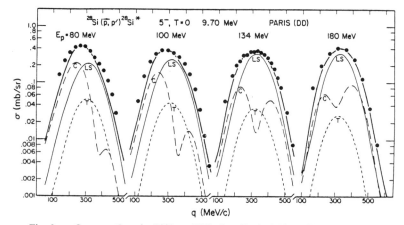

Fig. 9a.   Cross sections in $^{28}Si(p, p')^{28}Si$, 5^-, $T=0$, 9.70 MeV. Data points and calculations using the Paris (DD) potential are from Ref. 17.

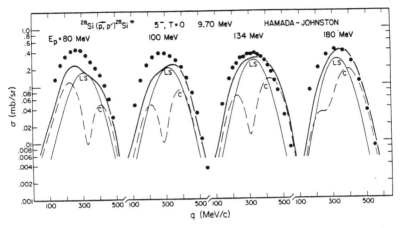

Fig. 9b. Cross sections in ^{28}Si(p, p')^{28}Si, 5$^-$, $T=0$, 9.70 MeV. Data points and calculations using the Hamada-Johnston are from Ref. 17.

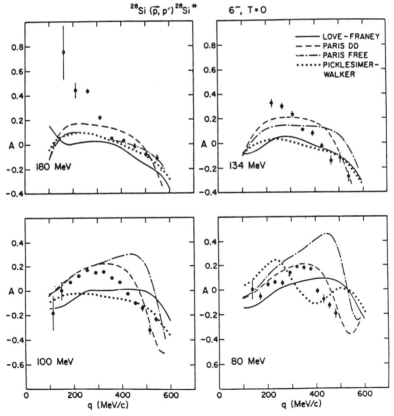

Fig. 10. Analyzing power in ^{28}Si(p, p')^{28}Si,* 6$^-$, $T=0$, 11.58 MeV. Data points and calculations are from Ref. 17.

In general, the different interactions (calculations have been performed mostly with the Hamada-Johnston and the Paris potentials) can manage to reproduce the cross sections. The behaviour of polarizations, however, varies with the NN potential inputs.

In conclusion of this section one can say that in various applications to complex nuclei the results obtained with the Paris potential compare well with experiment. This achievement is far from being trivial. To quote only one example, the nucleon-nucleus differential cross sections span several orders of magnitude. Here also, the data are of a very high precision.

Conclusions

It is fair to say that the long-standing problem of the interaction between two nucleons at low energy still resists any fundamental theory of strong interactions like QCD. On the other hand, as shown in this talk, a *quantitative* understanding has been reached in terms of hadronic (mesonic and isobaric) degrees of freedom, at least for the outer part of the interaction. The crucial role played by the S-matrix theory here is to be emphasized. It provides a unique framework for carrying out with accuracy fairly complicated calculations.

Recently, it has been conjectured[18] that, at low energies (and for large number of colors), QCD can be approximated by effective Lagrangians where quark and gluon degrees of freedom are averaged out. These effective Lagrangians are constructed from meson fields, and baryons emerge as solitons. The Skyrme model[19] is of this type. The NN interaction has been derived from the Skyrme model.[20] It is remarkable that some connection can be made between the results obtained and those from the S-matrix theory.

Acknowledgements

This work was supported in part by the Director, Office of Energy Research, Division of High Energy and Nuclear Physics of the U.S. Department of Energy under Contract DE-AC03-76SF60098.

I would like to thank N.K. Glendenning and the Nuclear Theory Group of the Lawrence Berkeley Laboratory for the kind hospitality extended to me during part of the summer of 1984.

References

1. D. A. Liberman, *Phys. Rev.* **D16,** 1542 (1977); C. DeTar, *Phys. Rev.* **D17,** 323 (1978); M. Oka and K. Yazaki, *Phys. Lett.* **90B,** 41 (1980), *Prog. Theor. Phys.* **66,** 556 and 572 (1981); C. S. Warke and R. Shanker, *Phys. Rev.* **C21,** 2643 (1980); H. Toki, *Z. Phys.* **A294,** 173 (1980); M. Harvey, *Nucl. Phys.* **A352,** 302 and 326 (1981); A. Faessler *et al., Phys. Lett.* **112B,** 201 (1982).

2. R. Vinh Mau, Proceedings of the Symposium "From Collective States to Quarks in Nuclei", eds. H. Arenhovel and A. M. Sarius. Bologna, 1981 (Lectures Notes in Physics, Springer-Verlag).

3. D. Amati, E. Leader, B. Vitale, *Phys. Rev.* **130,** 750 (1963); W. N. Cottingham and R. Vinh Mau, *Phys. Rev.* **130,** 735 (1963); G. E. Brown and J. W. Durso, *Phys. Lett.* **B35,** 115 (1971); M. Chemtob, J. W. Durso, D. O. Riska, *Nucl. Phys.* **B38,** 141 (1972); R. Vinh Mau *et al., Phys. Lett.* **44B,** 1 (1973); W. N. Cottingham *et al., Phys. Rev.* **D8,** 800 (1973); G. Bohannon and P. Signell, *Phys. Rev.* **D10,** 815 (1974); G. B. Epstein and B. H. J. McKellar, *Phys. Rev.* **D10,** 1005 (1974).

4. R. Vinh Mau, *Mesons in Nuclei,* eds. M. Rho and D. Wilkinson (North-Holland, Amsterdam, 1979), p. 179, see also *Proceedings of the VII International Conference on Few Body Problems in Nuclear and Particle Physics,* eds. A. N. Mitra, I. Slaus, V. S. Bashin and V. K. Gupta (North-Holland, Amsterdam, 1976) p. 472.

5. J. Bystricky and F. Lehar, *Physics Data* 11 (Karlsruhe, 1978) 1.

6. R. Vinh Mau *et al., Phys. Lett.* **44B,** 1 (1973).

7. G. Bittner *et al., Phys. Rev. Lett.* **43,** 330 (1979); J. D. Hutton *et al., Phys. Rev. Lett.* **35,** 429 (1975); P. A. Lovoi *et al., IVth Int. Symp. on Polarization Phenomena,* Zurich, 1975, p. 450; W. Tornow *et al., Nucl. Phys.* **A340,** 34 (1980).

8. R. A. Arndt, private communication.

9. M. Lacombe *et al., Phys. Rev.* **D12,** 1495 (1975).

10. M. Lacombe *et al., Phys. Rev.* **C21,** 861 (1980).

11. M. Lacombe *et al., Phys. Rev.* **C23,** 2405 (1981).

12. J. Jeukenne, A. Lejeune and C. Mahaux, *Nucl. Phys.* **A245,** 411 (1975).

13. Z. Y. Ma and T. T. S. Kuo, *Phys. Lett.* **127B,** 137 (1983).

14. See the recent reviews by C. Mahaux and by H. von Geramb in *1982 IUCF Workshop on the Interaction between Medium Energy Nucleons in Nuclei,* AIP Proceedings No. 97, ed. H. O. Meyer (1983).

15. M. Hugi, W. Bauhoff and H. O. Meyer, *Phys. Rev.* **C28,** 1 (1983).

16. J. Kelly *et al., Phys. Rev. Lett.* **45,** 2012 (1980).

17. C. Olmer *et al.,* private communication.

18. See for example, E. Witten, *Proceedings of the Workshop on Solitons in Nuclear and Elementary Particle Physics,* eds. A Chodos, E. Hadjimichael and C. Tze (World Scientific, Singapore 1984), p. 306.

19. T. H. R. Skyrme, *Proc. Roy. Soc.* **A260,** 127 (1961).

20. A Jackson, A. D. Jackson and V. Pasquier, *Nucl. Phys.* **A438,** 567 (1985); R. Vinh Mau, M. Lacombe, B. Loiseau, W. N. Cottingham, and P. Lisboa, *Phys. Lett.* **150B,** 259 (1985).

QUARK LOOPS AND OPEN CHANNELS IN HADRON MASS-SPECTRUM DYNAMICS

Louis A. P. Balázs

Chew's S-matrix theory program has, from the beginning, attempted to exploit to the fullest constraints arising from certain general principles governing open hadronic-channel amplitudes. Its most extreme expression is the bootstrap theory, where these are assumed to be sufficient to determine the complete hadronic spectrum. On the other hand, in a "confined" theory like QCD, "closed" channels like $q\bar{q}$ also contribute. In fact, these are often assumed to dominate. Since there is accumulating evidence to the contrary we have embarked on a program in which the closed-channel-only spectrum is taken as the input but in which non-pertubative methods are then used to build up the contributions of the open hadronic channels. Unlike earlier attempts to "unitarize" the quark model, our approach does not exclude the possibility of formally switching off all the closed channels, thereby allowing the data itself to eventually decide how important the latter should be. Our preliminary results are so far very promising.

Most of Chew's work has been concerned with the role of "open" hadronic channels, such as $\pi\pi$, $\pi\omega$,...N$\overline{\text{N}}$,... in generating the hadron spectrum. Indeed, in the bootstrap limit, it was assumed that such channels may be sufficient to self-consistently generate this spectrum. When quarks are used, they are taken to be purely mathematical entities.

In recent years the more popular view has been that "closed" $q\bar{q}$, qqq,... physical channels, with nonperturbative gluon-exchange forces, dominate in generating the hadron spectrum (see Fig. 1). This is the point of view adopted in lattice calculations and in bag models, for example, where the gluonic exchanges are assumed to form stable narrow (rotating) flux tubes or "strings", which become spherical for ground states.

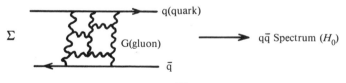

Fig. 1

In a fundamental quark-gluon theory like QCD there is, of course, no *a priori* reason to believe that open hadronic channels are unimportant. In such a theory they arise from $q\bar{q}$ creation (and annihilation), which leads to the fragmentation (and re-formation) of the flux tube (see Fig. 2). It is sometimes argued that such $q\bar{q}$ effects can be neglected on the basis of a $1/N_{color}$ expansion. However, the controlling parameter in any realistic $1/N_{color}$ expansion turns out to be, not $1/N_{color}$ itself, but, rather N_{flavor}/N_{color}, which is effectively of order unity in the real world, suggest-

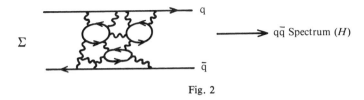

Σ $\longrightarrow$ $q\bar{q}$ Spectrum (H)

Fig. 2

ing that, even in QCD, open hadronic channels might be at least as important as closed ones.

Phenomenologically, of course, interquark flux tubes are known to fission quite readily in jet-formation experiments, typical hadronic couplings are known to be quite large experimentally and the inclusion of hadronic channels is known to lead to important mass shifts in explicit hadron mass calculations.[1] All of these are a consequence of $q\bar{q}$ creation, which also turns out to be quite important in recent explicit field-theory-model estimates.

The dynamical effect of $q\bar{q}$-creation seems to be particularly important at the moderately long-range interquark confinement-region distances which are so important in any hadron mass-spectrum calculation. This is perhaps seen most vividly in deep-inelastic lepton-hadron scattering, where "sea" quarks, which arise from $q\bar{q}$-creation, give a major contribution for smaller momentum fractions (or Feynman x-values) within hadrons — precisely the x-region which corresponds to smaller energies, and hence larger distances, within the hadron rest frame. It is also seen in the usual difficulties that calculations which ignore $q\bar{q}$-creation have with chiral symmetry, and in accounting for the smallness of the pion mass. A standard way of overcoming such difficulties has recently been to assume a "chiral bag" or "cloudy-bag" model,[2] in which a cloud of mesons is explicitly added to a core of valence quarks — a picture which also helps to explain the many real successes of meson-exchange forces in nuclear physics. But such a cloud of mesons is clearly reconcilable with a theory like QCD only if we assume that the "hadronization" arising from $q\bar{q}$-creation is a non-negligible part of confinement dynamics.

We have therefore embarked on a program in which such "hadronization" is assumed to play an important role from the beginning. As in the $1/N_{color}$ expansion or in the more recent hadronic Skyrme and static strong-coupling models, a natural starting point would be graphs of the type shown in Fig. 3, which have the hadronic spectrum (H_0) of Fig. 1 and could in principle be calculated by using lattice methods (from fundamental QCD parameters) or some variant of the bag model (from more phenomenological parameters). But we would then use non-pertubative S-matrix methods to build up the higher-order quark-loop graphs of Fig. 4. In such an approach we would normally also, as a first approximation, take the latter graphs to be planar in the quark lines, although non-planar corrections can eventually

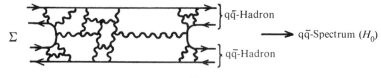

Fig. 3

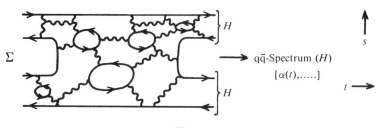

Fig. 4

be calculated with the help of an appropriate topological expansion.[3,4] In such an expansion it is also possible to argue that diquark breakup and formation are suppressed so that, in lowest order, the quark lines of Figs. 3 and 4 should be generalized to represent intact anti-diquarks ($\bar{q}\bar{q}$) as well as quarks q.

In a "perturbative" version of the above scheme, the graphs of Fig. 4 would be approximated by the hadron-line Feynman graphs of Fig. 5, where H_0 represents the zeroth-order spectrum of Figs. 1 and 3. An improved version of this would replace Fig. 5 by Fig. 6 with $W = H_0$, where the hadrons H are required to be self-consistent with the "output" hadrons H generated by the sum of Fig. 6 and therefore include quark loops. In the Törnqvist variant of this scheme, the vertical $W = H_0$ lines of Fig. 6 would be replaced by horizontal H_0 lines in the usual sense of (Regge-resonance) duality.

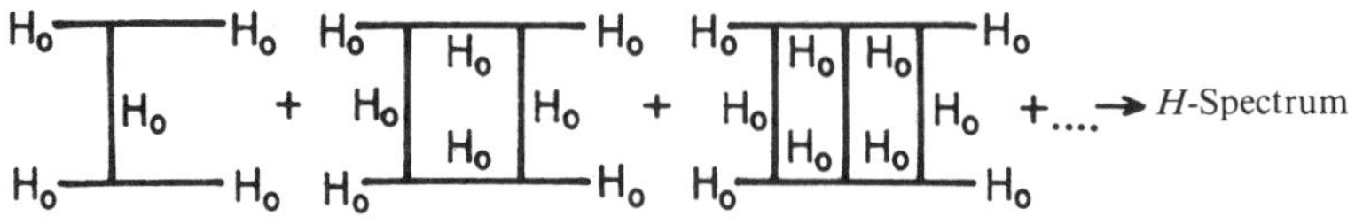

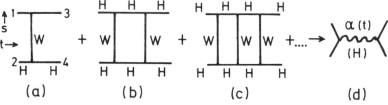

Fig. 5

Fig. 6

The schemes of the preceding paragraph are the principal ones which have been used in the past for estimating unitarity (open-channel) corrections to the quark-model spectrum (H_0). They do, however, neglect quark-loop effects in the vertical-line exchanges H_0 and W of Figs. 5 and 6, which, as we have seen, are known to be important at long-range distances, which can be shown to correspond to small values of the Mandelstam variable s. We have therefore adopted a further improvement which does take this into account, and in which the exchanges W of Fig. 6 are given by Fig. 7, where all the (corrected) hadrons H, including the low-s ($< s_0$) vertical-line H exchanges which give rise to the long-range forces, are required to be self-consistent with the output hadrons H generated by the sum of Fig. 6 (and therefore include quark loops). Unlike the cruder schemes of the preceding paragraph, the present approach permits the possibility of formally switching off the closed channels without ending up necessarily with a zero amplitude, thereby allowing the data itself to ultimately decide how important such channels should be.

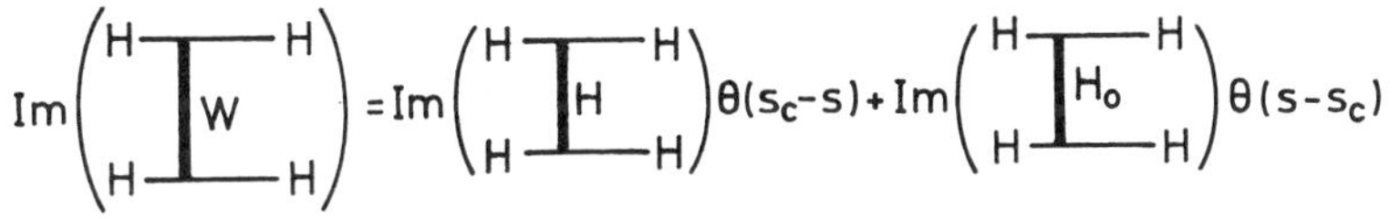

$$\mathrm{Im}\left(\begin{matrix}H & \!\!\!\!\!\!\! H \\ & W & \\ H & \!\!\!\!\!\!\! H\end{matrix}\right) = \mathrm{Im}\left(\begin{matrix}H & \!\!\!\!\!\!\! H \\ & H & \\ H & \!\!\!\!\!\!\! H\end{matrix}\right)\theta(s_c-s) + \mathrm{Im}\left(\begin{matrix}H & \!\!\!\!\!\!\! H \\ & H_0 & \\ H & \!\!\!\!\!\!\! H\end{matrix}\right)\theta(s-s_c)$$

Fig. 7

One way of dealing with the sum of Fig. 6 is to formally associate a coupling parameter ϕ with each of the vertical W-lines of Fig. 6 and to approximate the resulting Mellin-transformed expansion in ϕ by its $[1,N]$ Padé approximant. As a first step, we have also dropped the $s > s_c$ high-s (short-range) "tail" contribution of Fig. 7 and made a peak approximation for hadronic loop contributions like Fig. 6(b). If we then use finite-energy sum-rule duality to relate the lowest (particle and background) contribution [a] of Fig. 6(a) to the leading "output" Regge trajectory $\alpha(t)$ of Fig. 6(d), and impose uniqueness on the latter, we obtain the simple "generic" formula[5,6]

$$\alpha(t) = \max[S_1 + S_2, S_3 + S_4] - \frac{1}{2} + 2\hat{\alpha}'\left[m_a^2 + \frac{1}{2}\left(t - \sum_{i=1}^{4} m_i^2\right)\right]$$

(1)

for light-quark hadrons; here the S_i and m_i are the spins and masses of the external hadrons $i = 1,2,3,4$ in Fig. 6, and m_a is the effective mass of [a]. An approximately linear-t trajectory therefore arises quite naturally in our approach, despite the presence of strong open hadronic channels.

In applying Eq. (1) we require that allowed couplings vanish only if they are required to do so by consistency with other processes and constraints. We also require secondary contributions to [a] (backgrounds or other states), whose net effect would be to shift the effective (average) value of m_a away from the mass m_{aL} of the lowest contributing single-particle state, to be as small as possible. In other words, we simultaneously minimize $|m_a^2 - m_{aL}^2|$ in Eq. (1) for all the dominant processes, with m_{aL} as low as possible. This procedure has enabled us to successfully determine (partly in collaboration with B. Nicolescu) the masses of all the light-quark ground-state $q\bar{q}$, qqq and $qq\bar{q}\bar{q}$ states,[7] except the Ω^-, and the Regge trajectories on which they lie; the only input parameters were m_{K*} and m_ρ, one of which merely serves to fix the overall energy scale of our mass-spectrum. Specifically, we obtained

$$\alpha_{\hat{\rho}} - \alpha_{\hat{\pi}} = \frac{1}{2} = \alpha_\Delta - \alpha_N = \alpha_{M_2^4} - \alpha_{M_1^4} = \alpha_{M_1^4} - \alpha_{M_0^4} \ ,$$

$$\alpha_{\hat{\rho}} - \alpha_\Delta = \frac{1}{4} \ , \qquad \alpha_\rho - \alpha_{M_2^4} = 1 \ ,$$

where each $\alpha = \alpha(t)$ is linear in t, $\alpha_{\hat{\rho}}(0) = 1/2$, and $\hat{\rho} = (\rho,\omega)$, $\hat{\pi} = (\pi,\eta_{ud})$ are the (degenerate) planar ground-state $q\bar{q}$-mesons and M_0^4, M_1^4, M_2^4 the $J^P = 0^+$, 1^+, 2^+ ground-state $qq\bar{q}\bar{q}$ states. In addition, if H, H_s, H_{ss},... are hadrons with 0, 1, 2,... s-(quarks + antiquarks), we find, in all cases, that $\alpha'_H = \alpha'_{H_s} = \alpha'_{H_{ss}} = \alpha'_{\hat{\rho}}$ and

$$m_{H_s}^2 - m_H^2 = m_{H_{ss}}^2 - m_{H_s} = \ldots = \Delta_H \ ,$$

with $4\Delta_{q\bar{q}} = 2\Delta_{qqq} = \Delta_{qq\bar{q}\bar{q}}$. These results are in good agreement with experiment, and in contrast to many other calculations, give a small pion mass quite naturally.

Our results also lead to interesting predictions for $qq\bar{q}\bar{q}$ states. Since the decay of these particles into $q\bar{q}$ mesons can only proceed via highly suppressed graphs involving diquark breakup and reformation, they are narrow if they occur below the relevant $(qqq) - (\bar{q}\bar{q}\bar{q})$ threshold to which they couple.[4] For example, we predict a narrow sub-$\Lambda\bar{\Lambda}$-threshold 2.19 GeV $J^P = 2^+$ state containing two strange and two nonstrange quarks which would be a natural candidate for the recently-observed narrow $\xi(2.22)$ state. Another candidate might be our predicted narrow sub-$\Xi\bar{\Xi}$ 2.32 GeV $J^P = 0^+$ $ss\bar{s}\bar{s}$ state, if the ξ should turn out to be a scalar. Our predictions were first made before the discovery of the $\xi(2.22)$ state.

Our derivation of Eq. (1) depended on a semilocal duality between [a] and the Regge exchange of Fig. 6(d). This may be reasonable if $\alpha(t)$ is a light-quark system, since the s-channel resonance spacing is then comparable to $\alpha_{output}'^{-1}$. If $\alpha(t)$ is a heavy-quark system, however, this spacing $\ll \alpha_{output}'^{-1}$, so that we would probably need more than one resonance in any sensible finite-energy sum rule implementing our duality. For this reason we are forced to consider a more explicit and complicated set of equations based on Fig. 6. This is in any case necessary if we are to obtain any results on couplings, even if $\alpha(t)$ is a light-quark system; a partial step in this direction has recently been made by Matute-Carvajal[8] for such systems, who obtained a set of couplings in good agreement with experiment. It is also necessary if we are to include the $s > s_c$ "tail" of Fig. 7, whose effect we have begun to investigate recently.

As an additional preliminary step towards the above programs we have been studying simple models based on a rotating "flux tube" joining two valence quarks q and $\bar{q}$. As a result of "sea"-quark $q\bar{q}$-creation, however, such a tube is no longer stable but must condense into a string of hadronic "beads" (of total mass M) which stick together for a time τ and then break up.[6] Of course τ must be long enough for at least a metastable string picture to be meaningful, since hadronic ground states and their orbital excitations are in fact fairly narrow and therefore relatively long-lived. In this case we might then expect the "tension" (or rest-frame energy distribution) along such a string to continue to be independent of the flavors of the valence quarks or hadrons 1,2 at the ends. We have found that for a broad class of models of this type we have the approximately separable structure

$$f(M - m_1 - m_2) = h(m_1) + h(m_2) , \tag{2}$$

where $f(m)$ and $h(m)$ are flavor-independent functions of m, with $f(m)$ monotonic and non-constant at the same time.[9]

If we now apply Eq. (2) to a variety of flavor-configurations and require self-consistency we are able to derive simple mass formulas of the type

$$m_\phi = 2m_{K^*} - m_\rho , \qquad m_\psi = 2m_{D^*} - m_\rho ,$$

$$m_\Upsilon = 2m_{B^*} - m_\rho , \text{ etc.} \tag{3}$$

Each of the Eqs. (3) continues to hold, moreover, if each particle is replaced simultaneously by any given excitation of itself or of the corresponding pseudoscalar with the same flavor content.

Suppose we next use the fact that, if one of the valence quarks is $q_v = $ (u,d) or s, the low-($M - m_1 - m_2$) dynamics of any $\bar{Q}_v q_v$ system with $Q_v = c$ is essentially the same as that of the corresponding system with $Q_v = b$, since in both cases we have basically the same light-quark cloud around an almost-static heavy-quark center; this gives

$$m_{D^{*r}} - m_{D^*} = m_{B^{*r}} - m_{B^*} , \text{ etc.} , \tag{4}$$

where D^{*r} is any given excitation of D^* or D, etc. If Eq. (4) is combined with the results of the preceding paragraph, we obtain

$$m_{\psi^r} - m_\psi = m_{\Upsilon^r} - m_\Upsilon \ .$$

(5)

This latter relation only involves heavy valence-quark systems, which can always be described in terms of an effective non-relativistic potential $V(r)$ between the valence quarks. Since ψ^r and Υ^r can be *any* given excitations of ψ (or η_c) and Υ (or η_b) in Eq. (5), this potential must then be of the Quigg-Rosner form

$$V(r) = V_0 \ln(r/r_0) \ ,$$

with flavour-independent V_0, at least if we assume that m_b and m_c are arbitrary and can take on a continuum of possible values. Many similar results can also be obtained for baryons by treating them as quark-diquark systems.[9]

This work was supported in part by the U.S. Department of Energy.

References

1. See e.g. N. A. Törnqvist, *Ann. Phys.* (N.Y.) **123**, 1 (1979); *Nucl. Phys.* **B203**, 268 (1982).

2. See e.g. G. E. Brown and M. Rho, *Phys. Today,* p. 24 (Feb. 1983).

3. G. F. Chew and C. Rosenzweig, *Phys. Reports* **41**, 263 (1978); L. Montanent, G. C. Rossi and G. Veneziano, *Phys. Reports* **63**, 149 (1980).

4. G. F. Chew and V. Poenaru, *Z. Phys.* **C11**, 59 (1981); H. P. Stapp, *Phys. Rev.* **D27**, 2445, 2478 (1983).

5. L. A. P. Balázs, *Phys. Rev.* **D26**, 1671 (1982).

6. L. A. P. Balázs, *Phys. Lett.* **120B**, 426 (1983).

7. L. A. P. Balázs, and B. Nicolescu, *Phys. Rev.* **D28**, 2818 (1983).

8. E. A. Matute-Carvajal, *Calculations of the Leading Meson Regge Trajectory and Meson Couplings in a Planar Bootstrap Model,* Purdue Univ. Ph.D. thesis (May 1983), unpublished.

9. L. A. P. Balázs, *Simple Dynamical Hadron Mass-Spectrum Calculations Incorporating Hadronic Channels Arising From $q\bar{q}$-Creation,* Purdue University preprint PURD-TH-84-16 (August 1984), unpublished.

WHAT ARE THE QUARK AND GLUON POLES?

Carleton DeTar

1. Introduction

Perhaps no issue has divided orthodox bootstrap proponents from field theorists more than the treatment of quarks and gluons in hadronic physics. There is little doubt that the language that treats quarks and gluons on the same footing as electrons and photons has been enormously successful in explaining a wide range of short distance phenomena, such as deep inelastic electron and neutrino scattering from hadrons and hadron production at large transverse momentum. These successes are attributed to asymptotic freedom, which allows the perturbation series to converge rapidly at distances and time intervals much smaller than the confinement scale (about 1 fm). Going beyond perturbation theory, recent advances in numerical methods, i.e. the numerical simulation of quantum chromodynamics (QCD) on a space-time lattice, promise to give a good accounting of the hadron spectrum and, perhaps, even give an accounting for hadronic structure, although the full scale treatment of interactions seems remote at present. Thus QCD appears to be a remarkable field theory that embraces both short and long distance phenomena. Now as Geoff has taught us, poles of the S matrix correspond to particles that can occur in asymptotic states. In quantum chromodynamics quarks and gluons are evidently confined, so they do not occur in asymptotic states — instead the color singlet hadrons occur. Therefore, quarks and gluons are not associated with poles in the S matrix. This property is one reason bootstrap proponents have been unwilling to place quarks and gluons on the same footing as electrons and photons. Nonetheless quarks and gluons are useful at least for treating short distance phenomena in perturbation theory. From the standpoint of perturbation theory quarks and gluons are associated with poles in energy and momentum in propagators or correlation functions. These propagators represent the result of a potentially physical measurement over a finite range in space and time. For example, the quark propagator from the space-time point x to the point y represents the probability amplitude for observing a quark at y, having created a quark at x. This process may be studied in perturbation theory as long as the distance between x and y in both space and time is very short compared with the confinement scale. Of course to find the correct pole positions in energy and momentum, it is necessary to carry out a Fourier transform that requires knowledge of the propagator at large distances. Indeed, it is precisely the large distance behavior that determines the pole positions. Thus the quark and gluon poles in the perturbative propagators are unobservable and approximate. To study the large distance behavior goes outside the range of applicability of perturbation theory. To the extent the "fully dressed" or non-perturbative quark or gluon propagator has a meaning, it is expected that its momentum space poles correspond to asymptotic states, i.e. color singlet hadrons!

It is perhaps not surprising that the true poles in the quark and gluon propagators must correspond to color singlet states, but it is an amusing exercise to see how this result comes about in QCD. That is the subject of this contribution in honor of Geoffrey Chew on the occasion of his sixtieth birthday. A more detailed exposition with references to other work can be found in Ref. 1.

2.   Axial Gauge Propagators for the Electron

The first problem we must face is to define the propagators. Because they are gauge-dependent, one must refer to a specific gauge when defining them. The gauge choice is not merely a minor inconvenience; indeed it can even affect the position of the pole, as we shall see. Let us see "temporal axial gauge". This gauge is preferred over Coulomb gauge in QCD. For pedagogical simplicity, consider first the propagator for the electron in quantum electrodynamics (QED).

The electron propagator is constructed from the correlation product

$$S(y, x) = \langle 0 | \psi(y) \psi^\dagger(x) | 0 \rangle , \tag{1}$$

where $\psi(x)$ is the Heisenberg-Dirac electron field and $| 0 \rangle$ is the normalized vacuum state in QED. Suppose $y_0 > x_0$. The correlation product then gives the amplitude for finding an electron at y, having created it at x. Now the temporal axial gauge has the property that the fourth component of the vector potential vanishes ($A_0 = 0$) and Gauss' law is satisfied as an operator condition on the states, i.e.

$$(\nabla \cdot \mathbf{E} - \rho) | \text{phys} \rangle = 0 , \tag{2}$$

defines the "physical" states. Here $\mathbf{E}$ is the electric field and

$$\rho = -e : \psi^\dagger \psi : , \tag{3}$$

is the charge density. Because of gauge invariance, once Gauss' law is satisfied by a state, the state remains in the physical Hilbert space as time evolves. Usually the vacuum state $|0\rangle$ is physical. It is important to notice that as a consequence the one-electron state $\psi^\dagger(x)|0\rangle$ is not physical, i.e. does not satisfy (2). However, it does satisfy the condition

$$[\nabla \cdot \mathbf{E}(\mathbf{z}) - \rho(\mathbf{z}) + e\delta^3(\mathbf{z} - \mathbf{x})]\,\psi^\dagger(x)|0\rangle = 0 \ . \qquad (4)$$

That is to say, it satisfies a modified version of Gauss' law — as though a fixed charge of strength $+e$ were placed at x where the electron is created. This fixed charge alters the propagation of the electron from x to y. The states intermediate between x and y must occur in a modified Hilbert space that satisfies the modified version of Gauss' law. The eigenstates of the Hamiltonian on the modified Hilbert space in the one-electron sector are similar to the bound states and scattering states of the hydrogen atom, except that the proton has been replaced by a fixed, spinless, point source. These are not the states usually associated with the free electron.

Why does this peculiar result occur in temporal axial gauge? The reason is that in this gauge, unlike the more familiar Coulomb gauge, the creation of an electron is not automatically accompanied by the creation of an electric field. If no field is created and no field exists to begin with, then Gauss' law requires that the total charge that is created be neutral. The result, then is a fixed positive charge at the point of creation and a moving negative charge.

If we want to study free electron propagation, then it is important to keep the fixed charges out of the way. One solution is to put them in the initial state so that the intermediate state satisfies Gauss' law in the form (2). The physical state is then

$$\psi^\dagger(x)\,|0,\mathbf{x}\rangle \ , \qquad (5)$$

where the state $|0,\mathbf{x}\rangle$ is the vacuum state in the unphysical zero-electron sector with a fixed charge of $-e$ located at $\mathbf{x}$. Notice that the fixed charge now has the same strength and sign as the electron.

To complete the definition of the electron propagator three more technical details need to be mentioned. First, these fixed charges are point-like and so have infinite self energy. Thus as usual, a suitable regularization procedure must be followed so that finite physical quantities can be obtained. Second, even though we have arranged for the intermediate states to be free of fixed charges, the final state must have one at $\mathbf{y}$, since

$$[\nabla \cdot \mathbf{E}(z) - \rho(z) - e\delta^3(\mathbf{z} - \mathbf{y})]\,\psi(y)\,\psi^\dagger(x)|0,\mathbf{x}\rangle = 0 \ . \qquad (6)$$

It is more tidy to define propagators on the same vacuum so we must

arrange somehow to get the fixed charge from **y** back to **x**. The operator
that does the trick is

$$C(\mathbf{x}, u_0; \mathbf{y}, u_0) = \exp\left(ie \int_R A_\mu \, dx^\mu\right),$$ (7)

where the line integral follows a path $R(\mathbf{x}, u_0; \mathbf{y}, u_0)$ connecting **x** and **y** at a
fixed time $t = u_0$. The operator C creates an infinitesimal line of electric flux
running from **x** to **y**, thereby causing a displacement of the fixed charge.
Third, to be sure that the intermediate state is not the physical vacuum (it
should be a one-electron state) we explicitly project out any vacuum contribution. This operation is irrelevant in QED but needed in QCD. The revised
correlation product with physical intermediate state is

$$S(x, y) = \frac{\langle 0, \mathbf{x} | C(\mathbf{x}, u_0; \mathbf{y}, u_0) \, \psi(y) \, (1 - |0\rangle\langle 0|) \, \psi^\dagger(x) | 0, \mathbf{x} \rangle}{\langle 0, \mathbf{x} | 0, \mathbf{x} \rangle},$$

(8)

where $u_0 > y_0 > x_0$.

Is there a deeper significance to the operator C? Its presence is associated with the gauge fixing process. In classical field theory the gauge is not
completely fixed by the condition $A_0 = 0$. A gauge transformation

$$A_\mu(x, t) \rightarrow A_\mu(x, t) + \partial_\mu \lambda(x, t),$$ (9)

is still permitted if λ is independent of time. Therefore it is possible to
arrange, by further gauge transformations, so that

$$A_1(\mathbf{x}, u_0) = 0,$$ (10)

at a fixed time u_0. Let us suppose $u_0 >> y_0 > x_0$. Even then, further gauge
transformations (9) are permitted if λ is independent of x_1 and t. Therefore
one can arrange that

$$A_2(u_1, x_2, x_3, u_0) = 0,$$ (11)

for a fixed u_1 and u_0. Finally it can be arranged that

$$A_3(u_1, u_2, x_3, u_0) = 0,$$ (12)

leaving only a residual global gauge freedom. It is not hard to show that
every pair of space-time points x and y can be connected by a unique path
$R(x, y)$ parameterized by $x_\mu(s)$ for $s \in [0, 1]$ such that

$$x_\mu(0) = y, \qquad x_\mu(1) = x,$$

$$A_\mu[x_\mu(s)] \frac{dx_\mu(s)}{ds} = 0, \tag{13}$$

i.e. the vector potential tangent to the path vanishes. Such a completely fixed gauge[2] has been called "superaxial gauge".

To impose the residual gauge condition on the quantum expectation value, one may use a projection operator $Q(t = u_0)$ that acts at a fixed time and projects onto the subspace of the Hilbert space satisfying (10–12). Because of the residual gauge freedom this projection operator can be inserted in the numerator and denominator of (8) without changing the ratio. But as long as the path R in the definition of C satisfies (9) the operator C is irrelevant, since

$$CQ = Q, \tag{14}$$

and the correlation product assumes a somewhat more familiar form

$$S(x,y) = \frac{\langle 0, x | Q \psi(y) (1 - |0\rangle\langle 0|) \psi^\dagger(x) | 0, x \rangle}{\langle 0, x | Q | 0, x \rangle}. \tag{15}$$

The difference in appearance between (15) and (1) is entirely attributable to the details of gauge fixing and boundary conditions.

Now that we have painstakingly constructed the axial gauge correlation function, let us see where the low lying poles in frequency occur. To find them we take y_0-x_0 to infinity along a ray in the complex time plane such that $\text{Im}(y_0 - x_0) \to -\infty$. As long as u_0 is taken to infinity first along this ray, the intermediate states of lowest energy survive. The leading term has the behavior

$$S(x,y) \sim \exp[-i(m - m_1)(y_0 - x_0)] \quad \text{as } \text{Im}(y_0 - x_0) \to -\infty, \tag{16}$$

up to possible powers in y_0-x_0. The mass m is the physical mass of the electron and the mass m_1 is the vacuum energy in the Hilbert space with one fixed charge. The result suggests a singularity in frequency in the retarded propagator at $\omega = m - m_1$, which becomes a pole when the Fourier transform to zero momentum is carried out.

The result for the electron propagator in axial gauge is not as elegant as the result in Coulomb gauge, since it involves the divergent energy and momentum shift m_1. However, Coulomb gauge is beset with ambiguities in

QCD,[3] but axial gauge is not. The results for QED can be readily transferred to QCD and compared.

3. Axial Gauge Propagators for Quarks and Gluons

We proceed to QCD first by listing the changes in the formalism. Gauss' law now reads

$$(D_b^a \cdot E^b - \rho^a)\,|\,\text{phys}\,\rangle = 0 \;, \tag{17}$$

where a,b are color octet indices and the covariant derivative is, as usual

$$D_{\mu b}^a = \partial_\mu \delta_b^a - g f_{bc}^a A_\mu^c \;. \tag{18}$$

The charge density is

$$\rho^a = g : \psi_\beta^\dagger \lambda_\beta^{a\alpha} \psi_\alpha : \;, \tag{19}$$

g is the color coupling constant, f_{bc}^a is the structure constant for SU(3), λ_β^{α} the SU(3) generator matrix in Gell-Mann's notation and α and β are color triplet indices. The quark operator $\psi^\dagger$ in temporal gauge creates a quark and adds a fixed antiquark source or removes a fixed quark source. The state $|0,x,\alpha\rangle$ with a fixed quark source at x is a multiplet in the triplet representation of SU(3) and satisfies

$$\left\{ [D_b^a \cdot E^b(z) - \rho^a(z)]\,\delta_\beta^\alpha - \lambda_\beta^{a\alpha} \right\} |0,x,\alpha\rangle = 0 \;. \tag{20}$$

The QCD operator C is a matrix in SU(3):

$$C(x,u_0;y,u_0) = P \exp\left(ig \int_R A_\mu^a \lambda^a \, dx^\mu \right) \;, \tag{21}$$

where P denotes path-ordering in the exponential. The correlation product analogous to (8) is

$$S(x,y) = \frac{\langle 0,x,\beta\,|\,C_{\beta\gamma}(x,u_0;y,u_0)\,\psi_\gamma(y)(1 - |0\rangle\langle 0|)\,\psi_\alpha^\dagger(x)\,|0,x,\alpha\rangle}{\langle 0,x,\alpha\,|\,0,x,\alpha\rangle} \;. \tag{22}$$

Where are the poles if QCD confines color singlets? The intermediate states are physical states with no fixed sources. Therefore the lowest lying state is the lowest mass physical color singlet that "contains" the quark in question, i.e. in the valence quark language, the quark appears in at least one of the components of the hadronic wave function. Let the mass of this hadron be m. The initial state is the vacuum state in the sector containing a fixed triplet source. This state must also be a color singlet state, if QCD is confining. Let its energy be m_1. Of course to be a color singlet, it must contain at least one dynamical antiquark or two quarks that are bound to the fixed source. These additional quarks attach themselves to the dynamical quark when it is created at x and form the intermediate hadron that carries the quark from x to y. The asymptotic behavior is still (16), but the masses now refer to color singlet states. Therefore, the pole in frequency in the retarded propagator is expected to be at $\omega = m - m_1$.

The same procedure can be applied to gluons. The only change is that the fixed sources are now color octets instead of triplets.

At distances and time intervals $y_0 - x_0$ much smaller than 1 fm, confinement effects are unimportant. The fellow travelling quarks and gluons are now at a respectable distance and presumably play no dynamical role. In this case it is expected that the usual temporal gauge perturbative form of the propagator is obtained with boundary conditions appropriate to having fixed sources in the initial and final states.

4. Discussion

Because of the gauge dependence of the quark and gluon propagators, they have no preferred definitions. However, it should be plausible from the preceding discussion that regardless of how the propagators are defined, as long as they involve local operators, the long distance and large time behavior is controlled by physical and/or unphysical color singlet states, even though the short distance behavior may be found approximately in perturbation theory. In this way we see that QCD shuns the poles of the quarks and gluons and produces only poles corresponding to color singlets.

Acknowledgement

I am, of course, indebted to my collaborators, James King, Sai Ping Li, and Larry McLerran, for their participation in the development of the ideas presented here. This work is supported in part by the National Science Foundation under grant NSF 8405648.

I want to thank especially the model teacher and advisor who, even when he had seven or eight research students somehow always managed to find time for each one, and who set a stellar example for conducting theoretical research as a broad ranging inquiry into even the most fundamental questions (e.g., why only four space-time dimensions, why quantum mechanics, etc.) in accordance with rigorous standards of consistency, still paying close attention to experimental developments.

Thanks, Geoff.

References

1. C. DeTar, J. E. King, L. McLerran, *Nucl. Phys.* **B249,** 644 (1985); C. DeTar, J. E. King, S. P. Li and L. McLerran, *Nucl. Phys.* **B249,** 621 (1985).

2. S. P. Li, Ph.D. thesis, University of Washington, Seattle, 1983 (unpublished).

3. V. N. Gribov, *Nucl. Phys.* **B139,** 1 (1978).

THE POMERON STORY*

A. Capella, Uday Sukhatme, Chung-I Tan and J. Tran Thanh Van

1. Introduction

In their seminal paper[1] of 1961, Chew and Frautschi asserted: "All hadrons are composite; they lie on Regge trajectories." A successful description of the energy dependence of many hadronic processes has subsequently been developed in terms of exchanging Regge poles. In the same spirit, in order to account for the near constancy of hadron total cross sections, it was necessary for them to postulate the existence of a Regge trajectory with vacuum quantum numbers and a zero-energy intercept near $J = 1$, even though no physical particles were known to lie on the trajectory. This Regge singularity, which was also proposed independently by Gribov,[2] is known as the Pomeron, in honor of I. Ia. Pomeranchuk who first addressed the general question of the possible equality of total cross sections for particle-particle and particle-antiparticle interactions at high energies.

Strong interaction phenomena can be loosely grouped into three seemingly distinct categories: (a) Low-energy particle spectra, (b) High-energy particle production, and (c) Diffraction and diffraction dissociation. Searching for regularities within each category has been a primary concern of hadron physicists. Two decades of intense efforts have taught us that the observed regularities can be characterized respectively by the following assumptions: (A) Hadrons lie on linear Regge trajectories obeying a Harari-Rosner rule; (B) The multiparticle production predominantly consists of pions emerging with limited transverse momenta and having approximate short-range rapidity correlations (SRC); and, (C) There is a Pomeron trajectory with a zero-energy intercept $\alpha_p(0) \sim 1$ and a slope $\alpha'_p \sim 0.3$ GeV^{-2}. A well-posed challenge to hadron theorists has been to provide theoretical links among these properties, without having to wait futilely for

*This work was supported in part through funds provided by the U.S. Dept. of Energy under Contract No. DE-AC202-76 ER03130. A013–Task A and Grant No. 40169.

the ultimate dynamical theory of hadrons. In this paper, we discuss some of the efforts made towards this goal. In particular, we present evidence supporting topological schemes where the Pomeron corresponds to a cylinder topology.

2. Skepticism about the Pomeron

(i)   Experimentally, the order of magnitude of hadron total cross sections corresponds roughly to the geometric "radius" of the particles. In a Regge framework, the scale for total cross sections is controlled by the Pomeron residue functions. Without a detailed dynamical calculational scheme, it is unclear how geometrical considerations can enter.

(ii)   An immediate consequence of the Regge hypothesis is the shrinkage of a forward peak in the differential cross section. Denoting the elastic peak width by B^{-1}, we have asymptotically $B = \text{constant} + 2\,\alpha'_p \ln s$. However this behavior was masked by lower trajectories as well as by other low energy effects in early experiments at lab energies below 100 GeV.

(iii)   Unitarity requires the presence of branch points in the complex-J plane. Granting the presence of a Pomeron trajectory with $\alpha_p(0) \sim 1$, the singularity structure at $J = 1$ necessarily becomes complicated. Can a pole dominance prescription remain meaningful?

(iv)   With ordinary vector-tensor trajectories having intercepts near $J = 1/2$, what is the dynamical origin of $\alpha_p(0) \sim 1$? Why is it that vector-tensor and other lower lying trajectories all have slopes $\alpha' \sim 1$ GeV^{-2} whereas the Pomeron trajectory is much shallower? Indeed, why were there no particles on the Pomeron trajectories?

(v)   It has become clear since the early seventies that total cross sections, instead of converging towards constants, increase slowly with energy.

Although the uncertainty (ii) has since been alleviated by experiments at higher energies, skepticism about the existence of a Pomeron trajectory remains. At the minimum, (v) forces one to entertain the notion of a "bare Pomeron" with an intercept greater than 1. To restore unitarity, a non-perturbative sum of multi-Pomeron exchanges must then be performed, and one finds Gribov Reggeon-field-theory. Although this is conceptually acceptable, does the notion of a single Pomeron pole still remain meaningful at current available lab energies?

3. Topological Expansion

One of the more remarkable features of flavor symmetry is that mesons come in nonets, whose decays obey the Okubo-Zweig-Iizuka (OZI) rule.

Together with Regge behavior, this can serve as a test for the viability of any approximate description of the strong interactions.

The topological expansion (TE) based on the large N_c (number of colors) limit[3] has been advanced as a promising calculational scheme for non-perturbative studies of QCD, where one hopes, in the leading order, quarks and antiquarks are permanently bound to form zero-width mesons. The dual TE, which is based on a large N expansion with N_c, N_f (number of flavors) large, and N_c/N_f fixed,[4,5] has also been advocated as a unified approach to the study of soft hadronic phenomena. Common to both expansions is the requirement that the planar component, i.e., the leading component of the expansion, must provide a good approximation to the observed low-energy particle properties. One advantage of a dual TE approach is the admission of resonance widths at the planar level. Since internal quark loops are not suppressed, it leads to a unitarized OZI-rule already at the leading order of the expansion. Furthermore, the presence of internal quark loops allows a simultaneous description of elastic scattering and particle production. Therefore, it is much more appropriate for making direct contact with high-energy reactions where soft hadronic productions predominate.

Comprehensive reviews of TE can be found in Refs. 6 and 7. Here we only mention certain key features of the low order dual TE. The leading order, in a QCD language, includes all planar graphs with an external quark loop to which particle lines are attached. These graphs contain planar internal quark loops, and they satisfy a planar form of unitarity. The spectrum contains Reggeons which are ideally mixed and obey an OZI-rule exactly. Since the trajectories are exchange degenerate, there is no room for a Pomeron at this level. Furthermore, since the J-plane contains only poles, it follows from a Mueller analysis that one has short-range correlations for particle production.

The next order involves the cylindrical topology, planar diagrams with two quark-loop boundaries. For instance, for an elastic process $a + b \rightarrow a + b$, type-a particles are attached to one boundary and the b's to the other. A general positivity argument then shows that, in the forward limit, a J-plane singularity higher than the Reggeons now appears in the vacuum channel, e.g., even signature, $I = 0$, etc., which we identify as the bare Pomeron. Again, because of the absence of cuts, particle production satisfies SRC in rapidity.

These mechanisms for generating Reggeons and the Pomeron have their exact analogs in the string model. More directly, under certain plausible approximations, it has been shown[8] by H. Lee and also by G. Veneziano that, with the Reggeon intercept 1/2 as the input, a Pomeron with an intercept 1 is automatically generated at the cylinder level. Therefore, within a TE approach, an answer to the point (iv) raised earlier can be provided.

4.   Evidence for Cylinder Topology and the Dual Parton Model

We have just seen that in a topological description of the strong inter-actions, a unified treatment of both the low-energy particle spectra and the presence of a Pomeron can be achieved. The systematics of the higher order contributions indeed leads to a Gribov Reggeon Calculus. However, analyses during the seventies have revealed that the essential features of high energy production processes can be understood in terms of a multiperi-pheral cluster production picture. Past experience assures us that this production mechanism automatically leads to the desired qualitative features such as limited transverse momenta, SRC in rapidity, a slow increase of multiplicity, limiting fragmentation and a rapidity plateau. These are precisely the expected features provided that the dual TE is dominated only by the planar and the cylinder terms. This in turn suggests that higher order terms, corresponding to Pomeron cuts, can be treated per-turbatively, so that a nonperturbative analysis like Gribov field theory is perhaps unnecessary at current machine energies.

It has been noted by Veneziano[4] that a unitarity cut of the planar com-ponent corresponds to a "one-chain" event, with particles having limited transverse momenta and obeying Feynman scaling. Similarly, a unitarity cut of the cylinder component yields a "two-chain" configuration. It is this unique topological feature which we have been able to identify from high energy data. This is accomplished by organizing and interpreting multipar-ticle data in terms of an explicit phenomenological model for soft hadronic production, the *Dual Parton Model*,[9] which we will briefly review next.

A convenient way to achieve a topological description of a scattering process is to make explicit use of the color degree of freedom. One envisages that a collision corresponds to a two-step process. The interaction first gives rise to a color separation for each initial particle. Fragmentation next takes place through the formation of chains of secondaries between the colored fragments of the projectile and the target. The contribution from each allowed configuration can be identified with a term in the dual TE.

For definiteness, consider the dual parton model diagram for pp scatter-ing shown in Fig. 1. The interaction can separate the valence quarks of each incident proton into two systems of color 3 and $\bar{3}$, corresponding to a quark and a diquark respectively. The fragmentation occurs in the form of two quark-diquark chains, i.e., each chain consists of a quark fragmentation region and a diquark fragmentation region. These two chains correspond exactly to multiparticle intermediate states obtained by making a unitarity cut of the cylindrical Pomeron.

To be quantitative, it is necessary to specify the probability that the inter-action separates the protons into two quarks with momentum fractions x_1 and x_2 and two diquarks with the remaining momentum fractions $(1 - x_1)$ and $(1 - x_2)$. Here, for simplicity, the probability $\rho(x_1, x_2)$ is taken to be pro-

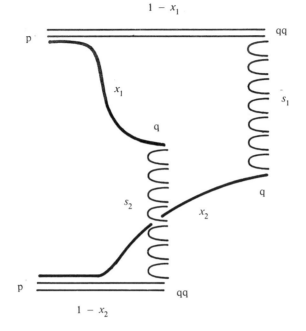

Fig. 1. Two chain Pomeron contribution to pp scattering.

portional to the valence quark structure functions in a proton, $\rho\,(x_1, x_2) = cV(x_1)V(x_2)$, where ρ is normalized to 1. Since the structure functions are peaked near $x=0$, $V(x) \sim x^{-1/2}$, it results in two "held back" quarks near $x_1=0$ and $x_2=0$ respectively, with typically, an average value around 0.05. This held-back effect is indeed general and it can be detected experimentally.

The total energy in the overall pp CM frame, $s^{1/2}$, is shared between the two chains labelled 1 and 2 in Fig. 1, $s_1 \sim sx_2(1-x_1)$, $s_2 \sim sx_1(1-x_2)$, where $s_1^{1/2}$ ($s_2^{1/2}$) is the energy of chain 1(2) in its own CM frame. The rapidity shifts necessary to go from the overall pp CM frame to the respective CM of chain-1 and chain-2 are $\Delta_1 \sim (1/2)\ln\,[(1-x_1)/x_2]$ and $\Delta_2 \sim (1/2)\ln[x_1/(1-x_2)]$. The single particle inclusive cross section for pp $\to h + X$ is then given by the superposition (see Fig. 2)

$$\frac{d}{dy}N(s,y)^{pp \to h} = \int_0^1 dx_1\,dx_2\,\rho(x_1,x_2)\left\{\frac{d}{dy}N(y-\Delta_1,s_1)\Big|_1\right.$$

$$\left. + \frac{d}{dy}N(y-\Delta_2,s_2)\Big|_2\right\}\ ,$$

where $dN/dy|_{1,2}$ are the contributions from chains 1 and 2, and are known from quark and diquark fragmentation functions extracted from planar processes, e.g., for phenomenological purposes, they can be taken from hard processes. More detailed discussions and justifications for the model can be found in Ref. 10.

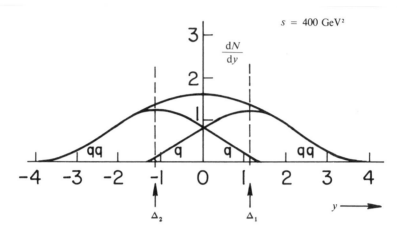

Fig. 2.   Diagram illustrating how the contributions from two quark-diquark chains add up to give the total inclusive cross section in pp scattering. As the total energy increases, the chains overlap more, and the rapidity plateau rises.

Having identified the two-chain Pomeron as the dominant diagram, one must also include corrections coming from multiple Pomeron exchanges. However, these additional contributions always involve chains terminating on sea quarks or antiquarks, which have structure functions proportional to $1/x$. Therefore, these chains span a smaller rapidity range than those involving valence quarks or diquarks. Since there is a physical minimum threshold requirement in each chain, one finds that up until the highest ISR energies ($s^{1/2} < 63$ GeV), the two-chain contribution dominates. However, at higher energies, (as for example at the CERN p̄p collider), there is sufficient energy available to share between four (and more) chains, and multiple Pomeron exchanges give a noticeable contribution.

The formalism outlined above has proved to be remarkably successful in quantitatively describing many diverse facets of multiparticle production: *Inclusive single particle rapidity distributions, rising rapidity plateaus, charged particle multiplicity moments and approximate KNO scaling, charge distributions in rapidity, the held-back effect, forward-backward correlations, heavy flavor production, two-particle inclusive distributions, hadron-nucleus and nucleus-nucleus interactions.* For example, rising rapidity plateaus occur naturally for our model. For $s^{1/2} < 63$ GeV (highest ISR energy) the increasing overlap between the two chains produces a rise in the central plateau height. At higher energies, additional multi-chain contributions appear in the central regions, thus producing a continuous increase of dN/dy. This prediction was made in 1981 and was subsequently observed at the CERN-SPS collider. A comprehensive list of references for studies mentioned above can be found in Ref. 11. We believe that the overwhelming phenomenological successes of the model suggest that the general ideas underlying the dual TE must be correct.

5. Concluding Remarks

QCD is generally believed to be, if not the correct theory, at least the most promising theory for the strong interactions. However, until a practical analytic nonperturbative technique for treating QCD is developed, it is difficult to confront the theory with soft hadronic phenomenon. Since multiparticle production at low transverse momentum constitutes the bulk of the cross section in a hadron-hadron collision, either one accepts the view that soft hadronic phenomena are basically not worth paying attention to, or one must adopt a more phenomenological approach.

We have seen that, by adopting a topological viewpoint, the Pomeron concept fits in nicely with the description of the rest of soft hadronic phenomena. However, since our approach is basically phenomenological, some skepticism will always remain. Instead of having a unified treatment for soft processes, why doesn't one simply adopt a geometric approach for hadron cross sections? To this we point out that ''diffraction as the shadow of inelastic production'' has been a long held physical picture for the occurrence of a forward diffraction peak. Therefore, a consistent description of elastic scattering requires a simultaneous accounting of inelastic production. Indeed, in our unified approach, the structure of inelastic processes and that of the Pomeron are tightly intertwined.

Since no geometric concept has been introduced, being able to account for the observed diffraction peaks quantitatively becomes a non-trivial constraint for the topological approach. An attempt[12] to provide an understanding for both the diffraction widths and the magnitude of hadron total cross sections from the dual TE viewpoint has been made with ''semi-quantitative'' success. One finds that the smallness of the pion-to-nucleon mass ratio allows a natural mechanism for the pion mass scale to enter in determining the nucleon-Pomeron residue function. Our analysis is rather crude and further refinement and extension are clearly needed. Nevertheless, the result is quite encouraging.

What can one say about the rising total cross sections? We have concluded earlier that this necessitates having a bare Pomeron with an effective intercept greater than 1. In view of the nearly constant pp total cross section below the ISR energies, how can this come about? The answer lies in the notion of trajectory ''renormalization'' due to the dynamically delayed threshold for heavy "flavor" production (in this particular case, the production of nucleon-antinucleon pairs[13]). Indeed, the bulk of the rise in the pp total cross section over the ISR energies is nondiffractive, and it coincides with the magnitude of the sudden increase in the $N\overline{N}$ production cross section over the same energy range. This mechanism has subsequently been dubbed as "flavoring of the Pomeron".

Ultimately, in order to respect the unitarity bound, a nonperturbative use of Gribov field theory is needed, leading to a log-type increase with energy. Alas, at superhigh energies, the Pomeron is not a simple pole! This new chapter of the Pomeron story will undoubtedly be told by its own aficionados elsewhere.

Lastly, where are the particles associated with the Pomeron trajectory? Are they glueballs? Baryonium? In fact, can our phenomenology possibly suggest a new avenue of attack for the fundamental theory?

We began our story by first setting a rather modest goal: Instead of searching for fundamental answers, we merely want to make an attempt to relate three seemingly unconnected features of the strong interactions. ((A), (B), and (C) listed in the Introduction.) It is comforting to have recognized that these features can be treated in a unified fashion when a topological approach is adopted. It is particularly gratifying to have constructed a phenomenological model based on the topological approach so that the cylinder nature of the Pomeron can be identified from high energy data. Much remains to be understood. However, we have no doubt that future development for the strong interactions, theoretical as well as experimental, will further embellish the Pomeron. More than twenty years after it was first proposed, we hope many will join us in the continuing effort to elucidate the mystery of the elusive Pomeron.

Acknowledgements

We wish first to thank our friends and past collaborators who have helped to shape our understandings of soft hadronic processes. Special thanks should go to H.-M. Chan, M. Goldberger, A. Krzywicki, F. Low, G. Veneziano, and many others who have taught us much about the Pomeron. We have also benefited greatly from discussions with participants of the hadronic sessions of *Rencontre de Moriond* where the Pomeron has always been a hotly debated topic since the early seventies. But, foremost, we owe much of our impetus for the Pomeron study to Geoff who has been the leading light for more than a generation of hadron physicists. Lastly, one of us (CIT) would like to express his deep gratitude to Geoff for his guidance. He has the fondest memory of his graduate student days at Berkeley and, in particular, those evening "secret seminars". With ideas freely exchanged and scrutinized, these were weekly gatherings which Geoff's students always looked forward to. He remembers Geoff's telling them about his experience working with Fermi. (To demonstrate his adoptation of the American way of life, Prof. Fermi asked his students to call him by his first name; apparently not all did.) He also vaguely remembers Geoff mentioning about their performing "numerical experiments" using dice, (presumably as a random-number generator.) One wonders how physics would have evolved had current super-computers been available then. During another session, Geoff asked the question "Why is the proton stable? Can one understand this fact from basic S-matrix principles?" More than a decade later in a provocative talk on his recent effort in unifying the strong and the electroweak interactions given at the 1984 hadronic session of *Rencontre de Moriond,* Geoff described how his topological theory would predict absolute proton stability. It appears that the question he asked one evening in the late sixties has, consciously or subconsciously, always stayed with him.

Happy Sixtieth Birthday, Geoff!

References

1. G. F. Chew and S. C. Frautschi, *Phys. Rev. Lett.* **7**, 394 (1961).

2. V. N. Gribov, *Sov. Phys. — JETP* **14**, 478, 1395 (1961).

3. G. t Hooft, *Nucl. Phys.* **B72**, 461 (1974).

4. G. Veneziano, *Nucl. Phys.* **B74**, 365 (1974), and **B117**, 519 (1976).

5. H. M. Chan, J. E. Paton, and S. T. Tsou, *Nucl. Phys.* **B86**, 479, and **B92**, 13 (1975).

6. G. F. Chew and C. Rosenzweig, *Phys. Reports* **41C**, 263 (1978).

7. G. Veneziano, in *Proceedings of XIIth Rencontre de Moriond,* edited by J. Tran Thanh Van (Editions Frontiéres, Paris, 1977); E. Witten, *Nucl. Phys.* **B160**, 57 (1979).

8. H. Lee, *Phys. Rev. Lett.* **30**, 719 (1973); G. Veneziano, *Phys. Lett.* **43B**, 413 (1973).

9. A. Capella, U. Sukhatme, C-I Tan, and J. Tran T V., *Phys. Lett.* **B81**, 68 (1979).

10. A. Capella, U. Sukhatme, and J. Tran T. V., *Zeit. Phys.* **C3**, 329 (1980).

11. A. Capella, U. Sukhatme, C-I Tan, and J. Tran T. V., *Heavy Flavor Production in Dual Parton Model,* Brown preprint HET-547 (1985).

12. U. Sukhatme, C-I Tan, and J. Tran T. V., *Zeit. Phys.* **C1** 229 (1979).

13. T. Gaisser and C-I Tan, *Phys. Rev.* **D8**, 3881 (1973); and C-I Tan, in *Proceedings of IXth Rencontre de Moriond,* edited by J. Tran Thanh Van (Éditions Frontiéres, Paris, 1974).

A CRUCIAL PROBE OF THE CONFINEMENT MECHANISM IN QCD; LINEARLY RISING REGGE TRAJECTORIES

Carl Rosenzweig

Linearly rising Regge trajectories provide direct insight into the nature of the QCD vacuum and the mechanism of quark confinement. They provide us with the experimental and theoretical challenge and opportunity to study in detail quark, antiquark interactions at large distances. I review the history of Regge trajectories and explain why their properties are crucially reflective of the dynamics of confinement.

Geoffrey Chew has had a remarkable and profound influence on physics and several generations of physicists. In this essay I would like to examine one of Geoff's major contributions to particle physics — Chew-Frautschi plots and the idea of linearly rising Regge trajectories.[1] The idea was born more than twenty years ago and has reached its maturity nurtured by modern ideas of gauge theories. We now understand that linearly rising Regge trajectories offer crucial insight into one of the most difficult and profound problems in modern field theory-quark confinement. My motivation in this essay is to introduce the newest generation of particle physicists to the great significance of Geoff's idea for QCD. It is offered in this Jubilee volume to Geoff with gratitude and affection.

Upon plotting the angular momentum of hadrons *versus* their (mass)^2, a pattern, remarkable for its simplicity and accuracy, emerges. In Fig. 1, I exhibit this Chew-Frautschi plot for the highest spin natural parity mesons. The spin and (mass)^2 are related via the linear function

$$J = \alpha' m^2 + \alpha_0 \ ,$$

with $\alpha' = 0.87 \, \text{GeV}^{-2}$ and $\alpha_0 = 0.49$. About ten years ago, Geoff and I had occasion to check such a plot with the data then available. I fondly remember his amazement at how accurate the straight line fit was. If Geoff, or the reader have not yet seen the recent data contained in Fig. 1, I am sure they will have a new sense of amazement. Such an impressive regularity calls for explanation. It is warmly satisfying that the explanation probes deeply into fundamental, non-perturbative properties of gauge theories.

1. What is a Regge Trajectory?

There are many ways to enumerate energy levels of bound states for non-relativistic potentials. For a given energy (k^2) there are numerous possible

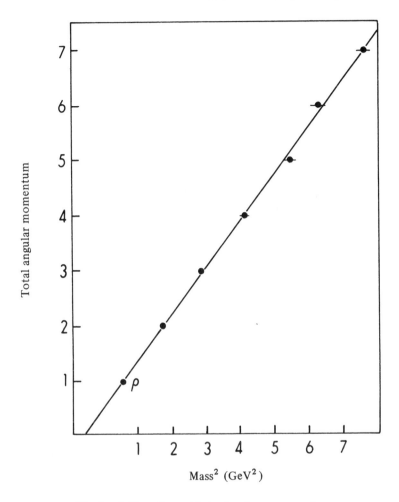

Fig. 1.   A Chew-Frautschi plot for the ρ-meson trajectory.

angular momentum states. In Fig. 2 are displayed all possible angular momentum states, for a given energy, in the case of three radial potentials.[2] The states have been related by drawing a line through all those having the same number of nodes in the radial wavefunction. A "trajectory" is traced out in (ℓ, k^2) space.

In the radial Schrodinger equation, we can treat both k^2 and ℓ as variables. Bound states can be uncovered by searching for the poles in the partial wave amplitudes $f_\ell(k^2)$. If ℓ is also a variable we can consider a generalized function $f(\ell, k^2)$. At a fixed k^2 this may have a pole at some non-integer value of $\ell = \alpha(k^2)$, a Regge pole. As we vary k^2, ℓ may approach an integer value and we would find a familar bound state. The k^2 dependence of this generalized angular momentum leads to the curves plotted in Fig. 2.

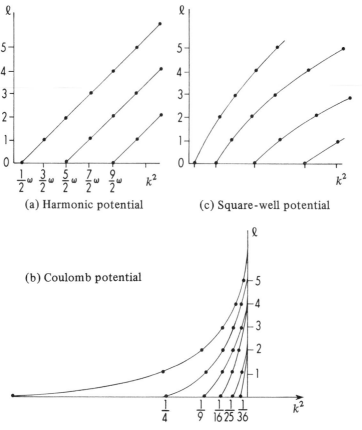

Fig. 2.   Bound states of various angular momentum for a given energy for three radial, non-relativistic potentials.

By studying the properties of solutions to the general Schrodinger equation as functions of both ℓ and k^2 we reproduce the trajectories introduced on other grounds above.

A remarkable, if seemingly sterile, property of Regge poles is that they determine the asymptotic behavior of the full scattering amplitude $f(k^2, \cos\theta)$ as $\cos\theta \rightarrow \infty$: $f(k^2, \cos\theta) \approx (\cos\theta)^{\alpha(k^2)}$. (This is demonstrated by studying the scattering amplitude in the complex ℓ-plane by means of a Sommerfeld-Watson transformation.) The unphysical limit of large $\cos\theta$ becomes fecund when we extend our horizons to relativistic domains. A relativistic scattering amplitude describes more than one reaction. For example the amplitude for $\pi N \rightarrow \pi N$ can be analytically continued via crossing symmetry to describe $\pi\pi \rightarrow N\bar{N}$. What was a momentum transfer (proportional to $\cos\theta$) for one reaction becomes the energy s for the crossed reaction. A Regge pole expansion for $\pi\pi \rightarrow N\bar{N}$ $(\cos\theta)^{\alpha(t)}$ with $\alpha(t)$ a Regge pole for $\pi\pi$, becomes, via crossing, the asymptotically dominant contribution to $\pi N \to \pi N$ at large s: $F(s,t) \approx s^{\alpha(t)}$.

We can now explore and exploit Regge trajectories $\alpha(k^2)$ over a wide range of k^2. For k^2 positive we look for bound states or resonances. When $k^2 < 0$ we look at crossed reactions with k^2 a momentum transfer. The study of Regge poles was a major concern of particle physicists in the 60's.[3]

2. How Can a Regge Trajectory Rise Linearly?

In potential scattering an infinitely rising Regge trajectory is possible only for infinitely high potentials (Figs. 2a and 2b). The Yukawa potential, at one time considered most relevant for particle physics, has a trajectory which (Fig. 3) turns over. Several years of effort in the mid-60's established

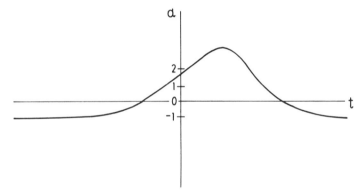

Fig. 3.   Typical Regge trajectory behavior for a Yukawa potential.

the difficulty of achieving, in standard dynamical schemes, a particle spectrum consisting of infinitely rising (linear) trajectories. Simultaneous with this theoretical activity experimentalists were accumulating evidence that just such behavior was Nature's choice. The simple elegance of this regularity was finally matched by the elegantly simple string theory which emerged from dual resonance models. Consider two massless quarks at the end of a spinning string. Let the string tension (energy density) be k. The massless quarks must be moving at the speed of light $v = 1$. A string rotating with angular frequency ω will have a length of $1/\omega$. Each segment will have $v = \omega\ell$. The total energy of the string will be

$$E = 2 \int_0^{1/\omega} \frac{k\,d l}{\sqrt{1 - v^2}} = \frac{k\pi}{\omega}.$$

The total angular momentum is

$$J = 2 \int_0^{1/\omega} \frac{kvldl}{\sqrt{1-v^2}} = \frac{k\pi}{2\omega^2} \ ,$$

or $J = \alpha'E^2$ with $\alpha' = \frac{1}{2\pi k}$. Finite quark masses m will change the argument in a controllable way. Linearity will now emerge only when $E >> m$ and $J >> \alpha'm^2$.

3. What do Strings have to do with QCD?

Confinement is, of its essence, a highly non-perturbative effect. It is best approached, not by starting from the fundamental QCD Lagrangian, but from a more physical picture. In this way we can break the shackles of perturbative prejudice and gain insight into essential features of the confinement mechanism. An especially evocative and productive approach views the QCD vacuum as a medium whose complex properties can be modelled and explored. Only under extreme conditions (e.g., high temperature, density or chromoelectric field) will it be transformed into the simple perturbative vacuum. This is similar to the approach of solid state physicists. They do not start their solutions from Schrodinger's equation, but rather begin with crystals, phonons, energy bands, etc. Under extreme conditions (e.g., temperatures high enough to vaporize the solid) Schrodinger's equation may again be convenient.

Mandelstam and t'Hooft[4] suggested that the QCD vacuum is a chromomagnetic superconductor. Quark confinement (or the impossibility of physical states which are not color singlets) would be the analog of the Meissner effect. The exclusion of magnetic fields from a physical (electric) superconductor is analogous to the vacuum's inability to tolerate chromoelectric fields. (For recent attempts to justify this picture see Ref. 5 and the references therein.) To simplify the discussion I will refer to magnetic monopole confinement in an electric superconductor. The reader can make the transformation to quark confinement in QCD by replacing monopoles by quarks, electric superconducting material by chromomagnetic vacuum and then ignoring some potentially interesting effects coming from the full non-Abelian nature of SU(3). Nevertheless, my example of a U(1) superconductor will, I am confident, provide most of the physics of the dynamics of quark confinement.

When a monopole and an antimonopole ($m\bar{m}$) find themselves in a superconductor they fall victim to two competing influences. The superconductor, because of the Meissner effect, wants to expel all magnetic fields. The fields, however, must stay because they are tied to the monopoles. The conflict is resolved by the formation of a restricted region of normal (non-superconducting) material including the monopole-antimonopole pair. The magnetic field is restricted to this normal region. A static snapshot of the system will reveal an axial symmetry about the $m\bar{m}$ axis. If the $m\bar{m}$ separation is larger than any other scales characteristic of the medium, the normal region will be a tube connecting the $m\bar{m}$. This is the monopole amputated remnant of the celebrated (and infinite) Abrikosov vortex. Its existence is the physical distillation of the very general topological arguments which lead to vortices. As such, monopole-sealed flux tubes are a general and intrinsic feature of a superconducting medium. The flux tube is the physical realization of the mathematical string. It immediately implies a linear potential between monopoles at large $m\bar{m}$ separation and asymptotically linearly rising Regge trajectories. Conversely the observation of these regularities provides evidence for the superconducting nature of the medium in which quarks are embedded — physical vacuum.

We can now appreciate why QCD-inspired bag models, which seem so different from strings, reproduce string model results.[6] Bag models emerge as a special limit of a superconductor (Nair and I[7] argue that bag models exist most naturally in type I superconductors, while strings prefer type II). I have just shown, however, that any superconducting model of confinement must produce a string limit for sufficiently large monopole separation. A major distinction between bags and strings will be the limits for which asymptotic string behavior emerges.

4. Linearly Rising Regge Trajectories as a Crucial Probe of the Confinement Mechanism

In a world of quarks, rising Regge trajectories intrinsically reflect quark confinement. A high spin $q\bar{q}$ meson must, by centrifugal effects, have widely separated quark constituents. High spin mesons are thus probes of the large distance, hence non-perturbative QCD quark interactions. The spin-7 meson on the ρ trajectory, the M(2750), is the longest, experimentally established, $q\bar{q}$ system. The basic string model relation $E = \ell/2\pi\alpha'$ implies a flux tube length of about 3 fm. By contrast quarkonium potentials are known out to a distance of only 1 fm and are not very sensitive to the confining force.[8] Every higher spin meson discovered extends our knowledge of the long distance, non-perturbative QCD force. This claim is basically model independent. The study of high spin states on Regge trajectories is, as far as I know, the only experimental means of answering the extremely important question of whether the interquark force increases, decreases, or remains the same as quarks are pulled further apart. The challenge to experimentalists is clear.

The challenge facing theorists is to understand better the data at hand by understanding the approach to asymptotic linearity. If, as seems true (cf. Fig. 1), linearity commences with the lowest lying states, we must explain such precocity. In the spirit of the analogy with superconductivity a flux tube can be characterized by three scales: (1) the linear energy density $1/2\pi\alpha'$; (2) the London penetration depth (this tells us how far into the superconductor the forbidden fields can actually penetrate; (3) the Ginzburg-Landau coherence length (this gives the radius of the non-superconducting core of the flux tube). These parameters provide vital structural information about flux tubes and details of QCD vacuum structure. They can be determined if we understood better how linearity sets in. Ultimately of course, all three numbers will be predictively related to each other and to Λ_{QCD}.

At the moment the only deviation from linearity which seems well understood is that caused by finite quark masses at the ends of the strings.[9] Reasonable quark masses can account for the observed differences between the ρ, K* and ϕ trajectories and imply a universal slope parameter between 0.87 GeV^{-2} and 0.97 GeV^{-2}.

Mesons decay. Strings break. The decay of high spin mesons, especially into two other high spin mesons, offers an excellent laboratory to explore the dynamics of string breaking.[10] Fascinating information about the details of QCD flux tubes can emerge from such explorations.

The continued, detailed study of Regge trajectories and their high spin members by theorists and experimentalists offers us our best opportunity for a quantitative study of the mechanism of quark confinement.

I wish to close first, by examining history and displaying the original Chew-Frautschi plot as it appeared in their *Physical Review Letters* article. I am amazed and impressed with what fragile material intuition allows

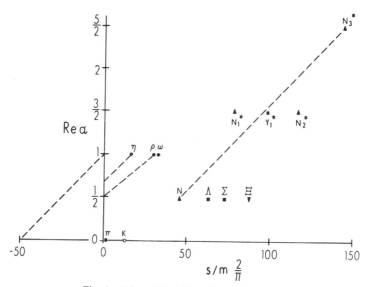

Fig. 4.   The original Chew-Frautschi plot.

genius to unveil Nature's secrets. Second, I present the result of Professor C. G. Callan's prophetic vision.[11] The linear Regge trajectory is familiar, the scale is unknown. The Chew-Frautschi plot may yet be a guide for many, many future generations of physicists.

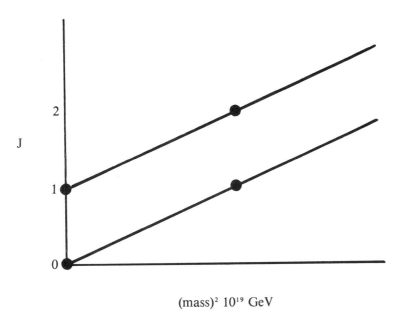

$(\text{mass})^2\ 10^{19}\ \text{GeV}$

Fig. 5.   A projection into the future, by C. G. Callan.

Acknowledgements

I wish to thank F. Lizzi and V. P. Nair, my collaborators on Refs. 5, 7, 9 wherein further elaborations of these ideas are found. It is with great pleasure that I thank G. F. Chew for all the physics I have learned from him and for all that he has taught me about physics as a profession, a craft, and a calling.

References

1 . G. F. Chew and S. C. Frautschi, *Phys. Rev. Lett.* **8,** 41 (1962).

2. R. Omnes and M. Froissart, *Mandelstam Theory and Regge Poles,* (W. A. Benjamin, New York, 1963). This book provides an excellent and painless introduction to the subject matter of its title.

3. P. D. B. Collins and E. J. Squires, *Regge Poles in Particle Physics,* (Springer-Verlag, Berlin, 1968). One of the few "modern" books with a discussion,

albeit brief, of Regge poles is D. H. Perkins, *Introduction to High Energy Physics* (Addison Wesley, Reading, Mass, 1982).

4. G. t'Hooft, *Physica Scripta* **25**, 133 (1982); S. Mandelstam, *Phys. Reports* **23C**, 245 (1976).

5. V. P. Nair and C. Rosenzweig, *The QCD Vacuum as a Chromomagnetic Superconductor; Microscopic Physics,* to appear in *Phys. Rev.* D.

6. K. Johnson and C. B. Thorn, *Phys. Rev.* **D13,** 1934 (1976).

7. V. P. Nair and C. Rosenzweig, *Bags vs. Strings: Hadrons in Type I and Type II Superconducting Vacua,* to appear in *Nucl. Phys.* B.

8. C. Quigg, H. B. Thacker and J. L. Rosner, *Phys. Rev.* **D21,** 234 (1980).

9. A. Chodos and C. Thorn, *Nucl. Phys.* **B72,** 509 (1974); K. Johnson and C. Nohl, *Phys. Rev.* **D19,** 291 (1979); F. Lizzi and C. Rosenzweig, *Linearly Rising Regge Trajectories and Bag and String Models for Hadrons,* Syracuse University preprint 295.

10. C. Rosenzweig, work in progress.

11. C. G. Callan, *Theoretical Summary,* International Conference on Particle Physics, Leipzig, Princeton Univ. preprint 1984.

COMPOSITE VECTOR MESONS AND STRING MODELS

Stanley Mandelstam

1. Introduction

The theme underlying my talk today is the general question of gauge mesons in extended supergravities. We should like to know, of course, whether such theories can produce the gauge mesons corresponding to a group at least as large as SU(3) $\times$ SU(2) $\times$ U(1). An exciting conjecture in this direction was made a few years ago by Cremmer and Julia,[1] who suggested that there might be composite SU(8) gauge mesons in a supergravity model known as the $N = 8$ model. Until we have a consistent, renormalizable theory of supergravity we cannot really obtain any indication of the truth or falseness of the Cremmer-Julia conjecture. One form of the Neveu-Schwarz string model has been shown by Green and Schwarz[2] to be a theory of supergravity; it is finite at the one-loop level and probably in any order of perturbation theory. Our discussion will be within the framework of this model.

Before I go further, let me emphasize one thing that will be well-known to the older members of the audience; the string model originated as a model for the S matrix, and it may well not have been discovered if S-matrix theory had not been vigorously pursued at the time. It is therefore intimately related to the work of Geoff Chew. Of course this does not imply that he necessarily supports later developments of the model.

To return to our question; we know that string models contain many multiplets of *massive* vector mesons. We therefore have to ask the question *whether massive vector mesons can possibly lose their mass due to interactions.* Arguments have been given on both sides of this question; I shall mention the argument due independently to Forster, Ninomiya and Nielsen and to Shenker (FNNS), which in my opinion is convincing and which shows that this *can* occur under certain circumstances. At the same time I should like to clear up one point, namely, the question of any rigid symmetry the system may possess. Our conclusions will be that the FNNS mechanism will create a gauge symmetry *in addition to* the rigid symmetry;

it cannot turn a rigid symmetry into a gauge symmetry. The FNNS mechanism does *not* therefore violate the Weinberg-Witten[4] theorem. As an example, if some modified form of QCD had an extra parameter, we could imagine changing that parameter until the ρ became a massless gauge meson. In fact, the process of massive vector mesons becoming massless is precisely the reverse of the Higgs effect.

Our conclusion will thus be that it is plausible that the superstring model may have composite massless vector mesons. Whether or not it does can only be decided by doing non-perturbative dynamical calculations. We shall end by making one or two speculations on the gauge group which may be expected, and possible connections with the Cremmer-Julia conjecture.

2.   Gauge Mesons in Supergravities

One might obtain gauge mesons in supergravity theories by one of three methods.

(i)   The supergravity multiplet may interact with a matter field containing gauge mesons. This method gives us an infinite range of possibilities; always on the assumption that a consistent dynamical theory can be found. We should like to get massless vector mesons out of supergravity theories rather than put them in, and we shall not consider this possibility further.

(ii)   The massless vector mesons occurring in the minimal supergravity multiplet may be gauged. It is possible at least to write down supergravity Lagrangians where the vector mesons are gauged. Unfortunately the $N = 8$ model is the largest model without particles of spin $\frac{5}{2}$ or greater and, at present, it is not known how to construct a theory of massless particles with such spins. The 28 vector mesons in the $N = 8$ multiplet correspond to the gauge group SO(8), and SO(8) does not contain SU(3) × SU(2) × U(1) as a subgroup.

(iii)   The vector mesons may be composite. We shall be interested in this possibility.

I shall now review very briefly the conjecture of Cremmer and Julia. The line of reasoning to be used when discussing massive and massless vector mesons will be rather different from that to be presented in this section. Nevertheless, I believe that they both concern the same problem, and the two approaches do lead to similar conclusions with regard to the relation between local and global symmetries.

I shall begin by discussing, not the complete SU(8) symmetry, but an SO(7) sub-group which is easier to understand qualitatively. The quickest way of obtaining the $N = 8$ model in four dimensions is by dimensional reduction of the simplest, $N = 1$ model in 11 dimensions, i.e., by compactifying seven of the dimensions to a point. Before dimensional reduction, let us consider a certain sub-group of general co-ordinate transformations, namely, the rigid rotations or deformations

$$\delta x^i = a^{ij} x^j \,, \tag{1}$$

in the extra seven dimensions. If we restrict ourselves to the transformations where $|a^{ij}| = 1$, we have an SL(7) group of transformations. The SO(7) subgroup is realized linearly; the particles occur in SO(7) multiplets. The remaining symmetries in the SL(7) group are realized non-linearly. Though one does not usually think of Goldstone bosons in connection with space-time symmetries (we have not yet carried out the dimensional reduction), it nevertheless can be, and has been, argued that the gravitons are the Goldstone bosons associated with the extra symmetries in the SL(7) group[a]. The question is really one of semantics.

The SL(7) global symmetry survives the dimensional reduction; the remaining coordinate invariances associated with the seven compactified dimensions do not. The symmetry now appears as an internal symmetry. As before, an SO(7) subgroup is realized linearly. The twenty gravitons with both polarizations in the seven compactified dimension have become scalars. They are, by everybody's definition, the Goldstone bosons associated with the broken symmetries.

Though the local Einstein coordinate invariances do not survive the dimensional reduction, there is another group of local transformation which does, namely the vielbein transformations. Since supergravity theories contain fermions, the only way of formulating them in such a way as to exhibit the invariance under coordinate transformations is to employ vielbeins. The vielbeins associated with the seven compactified dimensions give rise to a local SO(7) symmetry which is completely independent of the Einstein coordinate invariance. The symmetry survives the dimensional reduction as a symmetry local in the four space-time dimension. The internal symmetries of the dimensionally reduced model are thus

SL(7) global (SO(7) realized linearly) × SO(7) local.

We may note that SO(7) is the maximal compact subgroup of SL(7). It should be emphasized that the global subgroup of SL(7) and local SO(7)'s are two different symmetries. The existence of isomorphic local and global symmetries is common to many models.

Cremmer and Julia showed by detailed calculation that, in fact, the

---

[a]Of course, one need not restrict oneself to the seven dimensions subsequently to be compactified, and one can apply similar arguments in four dimensions. We have restricted ourselves to the symmetries relevant to our present problem.

model contained larger, hidden symmetries. The full group of internal symmetries is

$$E_{7(7)} \text{ global (SU(8) realized linearly)} \times SU(8) \text{ local.}$$

The group E_7 is one of the five exceptional Lie groups of Killing and Cartan; the second sub-script (7) indicates the particular non-compact form. As before, SU(8) is the maximal compact sub-group of $E_{7(7)}$, and the two SU(8)'s are different symmetries. The SU(8) local symmetry is certainly large enough to contain SU(3) $\times$ SU(2) $\times$ U(1) as a subgroup; it is perhaps embarrassingly large. I know of no easy way of showing that these larger symmetry groups occur but, in order to understand the main features of the symmetries, we may restrict ourselves to the SL(7) $\times$ SO(7) sub-groups. In particular, the whole local SU(8) group may be regarded as a "vielbein" symmetry.

The existence of the global $E_{7(7)}$ symmetry in the model is of course unambiguous; there is never any ambiguity regarding a global symmetry. The SU(8) local symmetry — in which we are mainly interested — is much more questionable. There are no elementary gauge mesons associated with this symmetry; if such mesons exist they must be composite. Gauge symmetries can *always* be added to, or removed from, a theory by changing the variables. One may remove the vielbein variables from a gravitational spinor theory at the cost of losing manifest co-ordinate invariance. Similarly, in the dimensionally reduced $N = 8$ models, we may remove the gauge variables and obtain a Lagrangian without a local SU(8) symmetry and with an $E_{7(7)}$ symmetry which is not manifest. Can we infer that the variables which render the $E_{7(7)}$ symmetry manifest are the "right" variables, and that the SU(8) local symmetry is therefore physical and may lead to real composite massless vector gauge particles?

There exists a two-dimensional model, the CP^{N-1} model, with all these features. The model possesses a global symmetry; if one chooses variables to make this symmetry manifest, the Lagrangian possesses an extra local U(1) symmetry without elementary gauge mesons. The model can be solved in the large-N limit, and is found to possess all the features of a confined gauge theory. In this case, then, the gauge symmetry is a real, physical symmetry. The Lagrangian with the gauge variable is renormalizable and, when a Lagrangian can be made renormalizable by an appropriate choice of variables, it is plausible to assume that these are the "right" variables. The nonrenormalizability of the $N = 8$ model makes it very difficult if not impossible to examine the Cremmer-Julia conjecture further. We feel that the superstring model, being (probably) perturbatively renormalizable, offers much greater possibilities.

One might ask whether the Cremmer-Julia local symmetry is present in the superstring Lagrangian. Unfortunately, the question of local symmetries in the string Lagrangian is not well understood at present, even when gauge mesons do exist (Yang-Mills symmetries in the open-string model or gravitational symmetries in the closed-string model). However, there is another, more dynamical method of examining the problem. The local gauge invariance in theories without elementary gauge particles, is due to a current-current term in the Lagrangian. Such a term gives rise to an attractive force in the vector-meson channel; this force in turn produces the massless vector meson in the CP^{N-1} model. We might therefore study directly the dynamics in the appropriate channels of the string model. Indeed, it is known that such channels possess towers of massive vector mesons. We have not examined the sign of the forces in detail; however, due to the general feature of repulsion of energy levels, it might be expected that the mass of the lightest vector meson would be lowered. This brings us to the general question of whether massive vector mesons can be made massless by the interactions. After examining this question, we shall make one or two remarks about the possible gauge symmetries which may be expected.

3.   Composite Gauge Vector Mesons and the Inverse Higgs Effect

It is sometimes argued that composite massless gauge vector mesons cannot be generated in a theory without a pre-existing gauge symmetry. A massless gauge vector meson has to interact with a conserved current, and it might appear that such a current does not exist unless there is a gauge symmetry. Nevertheless, we shall outline an argument, due independently to Forster, Nielsen and Ninomiya and to Shenker,[3] which shows that massless gauge symmetries can be generated dynamically. A suitable conserved current may be hidden in the system, even though it is not exhibited explicitly in the Lagrangian.

FNNS consider a lattice model where the Lagrangian has a large term which possesses a certain gauge symmetry and a small term which violates it. They show that, if the gauge-violating term is sufficiently small, the gauge symmetry will be restored by the interactions. This model is perfectly general, since any theory can be formulated as a lattice theory, with a very complicated Lagrangian, by performing the functional integral over the inter-lattice variables. The massive vector meson which gives rise to the approximate gauge symmetry need not even be elementary. In the FNNS lattice model, a gauge symmetry *will* be created if the gauge-violating term is sufficiently small. In a continuum theory, we cannot be sure that a small gauge-violating term will remain small when the theory is reformulated as a lattice theory, and hence we can only say that a gauge symmetry *may* be created; the question is one of dynamics.

Let us consider, then, a lattice action

$$S = S_1 + S_2 \, , \tag{2}$$

where S_1 has a certain gauge invariance. The partition function will be

$$Z = \int \mathscr{D}(A)\, e^S \ . \tag{3}$$

FNNS introduce extra variables Ω, one at each lattice point, which have the mathematical form of the adjoint representation of the gauge group under consideration. The partition function is thus (to within a constant).

$$Z = \int \mathscr{D}(A)\, \mathscr{D}(\Omega)\, e^S \ . \tag{4}$$

Since S does not depend on the Ω's, it is trivially invariant under gauge transformations of the new variables; such a gauge invariance clearly has no physical significance. We define new variables $\tilde{A}$ by applying the gauge transformation Ω to the old variables. The partition function may be expressed in terms of these variables:

$$Z = \int \mathscr{D}(\tilde{A})\, \mathscr{D}(\Omega) \exp\left\{ \tilde{S}_1(\tilde{A}) + \tilde{S}_2(\tilde{A}, \Omega) \right\} \ . \tag{5}$$

Since we have merely redefined our variables, the action in (5) is still gauge invariant, now under simultaneous gauge transformations of the $\tilde{A}$'s and Ω's.

Let us perform the functional integral over the Ω's. We thus obtain a new partition function:

$$Z = \int \mathscr{D}(\tilde{A}) \exp\left\{ \tilde{S}'(\tilde{A}) \right\} \ , \tag{6}$$

where S' is in general very complicated. The functional integration cannot remove the gauge invariance, so we appear to have obtained a gauge invariant Lagrangian without extra Ω variables. Since we have made no assumption about the gauge-violating term in the original Lagrangian, there must be a catch somewhere! In fact, before we can deduce physical results from (6), we must know whether or not the action is quasi-local. A term in S will have the general form

$$\int dx_1\, dx_2 \ldots f(x_1, x_2, \ldots)\, A(x_1)\, A(x_2) \ldots \ . \tag{7}$$

If f decreases sufficiently fast as the distance between the x's increases, we can conclude that the gauge invariance is physical. If, however, the action contains long-range correlations — which will be long-range correlations in space and time coordinates — we can draw no such conclusion.

FNNS now consider the model represented by the partition function (5) as a dynamical system in the Ω's with the $\tilde{A}$'s frozen. The term S_2, as a function of the Ω's, resembles a ferromagnetic system, so that long-range correlations would only be expected if the term were sufficiently large. Thus *if the interaction term is sufficiently small, the system will have no long-range correlations and there will be a dynamically generated gauge symmetry.*

We next consider the case where the Lagrangian has a symmetry which is exact as a global symmetry but approximate as a local symmetry — for instance, a model with a multiplet of light vector mesons. Since a gauge symmetry can be dynamically generated in the absence of any rigid symmetry, we might suspect that a dynamically generated gauge symmetry would appear *in addition* to the pre-existing rigid symmetry. We shall show that this is indeed what happens.

Let us examine the partition function (5) for models of this type. We first notice that the field Ω may be regarded as a physical scalar field. The particle counting is right; if we imagine changing the parameters of the theory past the point where the gauge symmetry is just created, the number of physical polarization degrees of freedom will change from three to two. The number of particles cannot change; a scalar meson must be disgorged. The field Ω corresponds to that scalar meson. There is a kinetic term involving the field Ω in the Lagrangian; if $R_{\lambda\mu}$ is a lattice-link variable, the transformed R will be:

$$\widetilde{R}_{\lambda\mu} = \Omega^{\dagger}_{\lambda\alpha}(x)R_{\alpha\beta}\,\Omega_{\beta\mu}(x + \delta x) , \qquad (8)$$

and in the continuum limit, (8) will contain a term $\phi_{\alpha\lambda}(\partial\phi_{\alpha\mu}/\partial x)\delta x$.

The original Lagrangian possessed a rigid symmetry involving the variables λ and μ; the new gauge symmetry involves α and β. By examining (8) we see that the final theory possesses *two* symmetries; a rigid symmetry involving λ and μ and a gauge symmetry involving α and β. This is the result we were attempting to prove.

We observe that the model under consideration is the inverse of the Higgs model where we start with a scalar field $\phi_{\lambda\alpha}$ possessing a rigid symmetry involving the subscript λ and a gauge symmetry involving the subscript α. In one case the original Lagrangian has a gauge symmetry which is broken by the interactions, in the other a gauge symmetry is created by the interactions. In either case a rigid symmetry is never turned into a gauge symmetry or *vice versa*; the rigid symmetries are always independent of the gauge symmetries.

The existence of separate rigid and gauge symmetries removes any conflict between the dynamical generation of gauge particles and the Weinberg-Witten theorem.[4] Arguments to the contrary always assumed that a rigid symmetry is turned into a gauge symmetry.

Once we understand that the dynamical generation of a gauge symmetry is the inverse of the usual Higgs effect, we may investigate the circumstances under which we would expect a particular multiplet of gauge mesons — SO(3), for instance — to be generated dynamically. We might begin with a theory with a global SO(3) invariance and and SO(3) multiplet of massive vector mesons. The interactions might then make the mesons massless; the resulting system would have a global SO(3) and a local SO(3) symmetry. On the other hand, we might have a system without any exact global symmetry, but with three vector mesons of approximately the same mass. As we changed the parameters of the theory, we might convert one of the mesons into a U(1) gauge meson. The system would then contain positively and negatively charged mesons of equal mass; it might happen that the other two vector mesons formed such a doublet. If we then changed the parameters further, the doublet of vector mesons might lose its mass. We would then have a system with an SO(3) triplet of massless vector mesons.

We hope that the foregoing reasoning sheds some light on the question why many models possess isomorphic but independent global and local symmetries. Examples of such models are the Higgs model with a scalar multiplet $\phi_{\alpha\lambda}$, the Higgs model with a spinor multiplet (Weinberg-Salam without the U(1)), and the Cremmer-Julia model. The vielbein variables of the latter model very much resemble the Ω's of the FNNS model. We also observe that the global symmetry may not be exact; an approximate massive vector multiplet may become massless due to the interaction; it would then be an exact gauge multiplet. Finally, we would like to remark that a so-called gauge symmetry does not appear to be a symmetry in the sense that its presence or absence can be inferred by a simple examination of the Lagrangian, regardless of the strength of the coupling. If the coupling is strong, the existence of a gauge symmetry is a matter of dynamics.

4. Gauge Mesons and String Models

We have seen that it is plausible that some of the massive vector mesons in string models may become massless and thereby generate a gauge symmetry dynamically. In the absence of non-perturbative calculations we can only make rough speculative guesses regarding the gauge group.

The superstring model is ten-dimensional; if it is to represent nature, six of the dimensions would have to become compactified to a region whose dimensions are of the order of the Planck length. The shape of the compactified region is totally unknown at present; if we assume a region of maximum symmetry, namely a sphere, we obtain an SO(6) symmetry, which will be an internal symmetry from the point of view of four-dimensional space-time. Thus, if a multiplet of vector mesons in the adjoint representation were to lose its mass, we would have an SO(6) gauge symmetry. If there were neighboring multiplets of similar mass in suitable representations, they might combine to give a larger gauge symmetry, just as the U(1) singlet and doublet combined to give an SO(3) gauge symmetry in the example of the previous section.

There have been hints of higher symmetries associated in some way with string models. Mathematicians have investigated such symmetries in connection with Kac-Moody Lie algebras. The physical interpretation, if any, of these symmetries is not well understood at present; however, they have a resemblance with the global Cremmer-Julia symmetries which we feel is unlikely to be coincidental. Julia himself has emphasized this point. The mathematical models discretize the momentum spectrum to lie on the root lattice of a Lie algebra; discretizing momentum space is of course equivalent to compactifying position space. It may be, therefore, that, by compactifying in a suitable way, we obtain a symmetry resembling the global Cremmer-Julia symmetry or a subgroup thereof. If a vector meson in the adjoint representation were to become massless, we would have a local Cremmer-Julia symmetry. Of course, we are not allowed to compactify a gravitational theory by hand; the compactification must occur spontaneously. Nevertheless an exact symmetry with a suitably chosen compactification would correspond to an approximate symmetry with more general compactifications. We have seen that an approximate global symmetry can lead to a corresponding exact dynamically generated gauge symmetry under suitable circumstances. In this way, we may possibly envisage the generation of a gauge symmetry of the Cremmer-Julia type in string models.

References

1. E. Cremmer and B. Julia, *Nucl. Phys.* **B159,** 141 (1979).

2. M. B. Green and J. H. Schwarz, *Phys. Reports* **89,** 224 (1982). This article contains further references.

3. D. Forster, H. B. Nielsen and M. Ninomiya, *Phys. Lett.* **94B,** 135 (1980); S. Shenker, unpublished.

4. S. Weinberg and E. Witten, *Phys. Lett.* **96B,** 59 (1980).

FROM THE BOOTSTRAP TO SUPERSTRINGS*

John H. Schwarz

The historical roots of superstring theory in the hadronic bootstrap and Regge-pole theory are recalled. Recent developments in superstring theory are then summarized.

1. The Origins of Superstring Theory

During my graduate student years in Berkeley (1962–66) I had the privilege of being a student of Geoff Chew. I felt that I was at the intellectual center of the universe. Berkeley was the place to be for high-energy physics, and hadronic physics was the main focus. New resonances were being discovered with alarming frequency in Luis Alvarez' bubble chamber. Geoff, Stanley Mandelstam, and others were developing the theoretical framework that should make order out of the chaos.

Among the important ideas developed in Berkeley in the 1960's were the hadronic bootstrap (Chew and Frautschi) and the Regge-pole description of hadronic amplitudes (Chew, Mandelstam and many others). Chew emphasized the importance of concentrating on physically observable S-matrix elements and dispensing with extraneous baggage (i.e., quantum fields for hadrons). Analyticity in angular-momentum variables was stressed as an important ingredient for understanding the hadronic S-matrix, Regge poles being the principle observable consequence.

Shortly after I left Berkeley for Princeton, the study of Regge poles and the bootstrap led to the discovery of duality and "finite-energy sum rules".[1] These ideas culminated in Veneziano's 1968 discovery[2] of a specific mathematical function that embodies these ideas. Superstring theory in its modern form looks so different from all this, that even I find it hard to believe that these were the origins that led to its development.

Shortly after Veneziano's discovery of a "dual" four-particle amplitude, N-particle generalizations that factorize consistently on a well-defined spectrum of states were found.[3] It was shown that the states could be regarded as modes of a relativistic one-dimensional system (string), and the interactions interpreted in terms of breakings and joinings of the string.

*Work supported in part by the U.S. Department of Energy under contract DEAC 03-81-ER 40050.

This string theory turned out to have some serious problems, however. It has tachyons in both the open-string and closed-string sectors, it contains no fermions, it has divergent loop amplitudes, and it requires that space-time have 26 dimensions.

In 1970–71, I was working with André Neveu on various ideas that could make a string theory free from the shortcomings of the 26-dimensional one. In early 1971, we discovered an alternative bosonic scheme, which we called the"dual pion model".[4] It eliminated the tachyon of the Veneziano model, but introduced a new one that we tried to identify as the pion. About a month later, we showed[5] that this bosonic theory could be consistently extended to include interactions with a spectrum of fermions that Pierre Ramond had proposed a couple of months earlier.[6] Ramond had shown that a generalized Dirac equation admitted a set of gauge invariances with generators $\{F_n, L_n\}$ satisfying an infinite graded algebra of the form

$$\left\{F_m, F_n\right\} = L_{m+n} + (c_1 m^2 + c_2)\delta_{m,-n} , \tag{1a}$$

$$[F_m, L_n] = \left(\frac{m}{2} - n\right)F_{m+n} , \tag{1b}$$

$$[L_m, L_n] = (m - n)L_{m+n} + (c_3 m^3 + c_4 m)\delta_{m,-n} . \tag{1c}$$

The subalgebra in Eq. (1c) had appeared earlier in the 26-dimensional model and is known as the Virasoro algebra. Neveu and I found a very similar graded algebra in the dual-pion model with a set of operators $\{G_r\}$ replacing the F's. The index r takes values that are one-half of an odd integer, whereas the indices m and n in Eq. (1) take integral values.

It was discovered by Gervais and Sakita[7] that the dual pion model could be described by a two-dimensional action principle with global supersymmetry. Later it was found that the infinite graded algebras are a manifestation of *local symmetry* of an improved two-dimensional action.[8] In 1972, it was discovered[9] that the critical dimension for the dual pion model is 10, and that the spectrum is ghost-free for that choice.

The spectrum of the dual pion model contains two sectors: An even "G-parity" sector with masses given by $2\alpha'M^2 = 0,2,4,...$ and an odd G-parity sector with masses given by $2\alpha'M^2 = -1,1,3,...$ This G-parity is a multiplicatively conserved quantum number in the bosonic amplitudes. We were intrigued by the fact that the $\pi\pi \to \pi\pi$ and $\pi\pi \to \pi\omega$ amplitudes turned out to have exactly the analytic form that was suggested earlier by others, and took the viewpoint that radiative corrections or a small modification of the theory could shift the pions and other particles to their correct mass value. It was obvious that a truncation to the even-G sector gives a model free from tachyons (and ghosts). This was not emphasized because of our determination to use the model as a theory of hadrons.

The next few years were a period of decline for the popularity of string theory. QCD emerged as the correct description of hadrons. The qualitative successes of the string approach could be understood as due to the fact that in QCD quarks are joined by tubes of color flux, which under certain circumstances can be long and narrow.

In 1974–75, I worked with Joel Scherk at Caltech. We were struck by the fact that the string theories had never yielded to our numerous attempts to shift the masses to other values. In particular, the "ρ-meson" state in the open-string sector was inevitably massless, and the "Pomeron trajectory" in the closed-string sector inevitably had intercept 2, implying the existence of a massless spin-two state. At some point it occurred to us (I don't remember whether it was Joel or I who said it first) that maybe the massless spin-two state is a graviton. This innocent remark had profound consequences. It meant that we were no longer discussing a theory of hadrons. It means that the natural length scale for strings is 10^{-33} cm (the Planck length) rather than 10^{-13} cm. It means that there is no longer any reason to keep the odd-G parity sector with its tachyonic "pion" in the theory. Most important, it means we have a candidate for a quantum theory of gravity! Once we realized we were talking about gravity our attitude toward the extra dimensions also changed. We realized it would be perfectly reasonable to take them seriously as real and physical (as demanded by the theory), with a Kaluza-Klein interpretation. We wrote a number of papers on these matters,[10] but then got involved in the development of supersymmetric point-particle theories.

In 1976, Gliozzi, Scherk, and Olive observed[11] that the number of states at each mass level in the even G-parity sector of the dual pion model was the same as in the fermion sector, provided a suitable Majorana-Weyl condition was imposed on the fermion states. This was compelling circumstantial evidence that the theory, truncated in this way, would be supersymmetrical in the ten-dimensional sense. In particular, the massless closed-string states would consist of a supergravity multiplet. That being the case, it was obvious that the theory could not be consistent without the truncation. The massless open-string states were found to correspond to the $D = 10$ super Yang-Mills theory. (That theory was discovered independently by Brink and me.[12]) By early 1978, I was forcefully advocating that supersymmetric string theory could give a complete theory of all interactions.[13]

In August 1979, during a month at CERN, I started discussing supersymmetric string theory with Michael Green. We didn't make much progress that month, but when we got together the next summer in Aspen, we had our first breakthrough.[14] Specifically, we succeeded in developing a new formalism in which the space-time supersymmetry could be proved and understood. In this formalism the old odd-G states never appear. Since then we have had a very exciting and rewarding collaboration at Caltech, Aspen, and Queen Mary College.

Only after we had already learned a great deal about superstrings (my Physic Reports article[15] had already appeared), did the most important discoveries occur: the discovery of a covariant two-dimensional action principle with ten-dimensional supersymmetry,[16] the formulation of the second-quantized superstring field theory,[17] and the study of anomaly cancellations.[18] I will briefly review these developments in the remainder of this paper.

2. Recent Developments in Superstring Theory

Green and I first formulated superstring theory directly in a light-cone-gauge formalism without deriving it from a covariant starting point. It was unclear for some time whether such a starting point need even exist, but in autumn 1983 we found it.[16] The coordinates of superstrings can be described by space-time coordinates $x^\mu(\sigma,\tau)$ and anticommuting Grassmann coordinates $\vartheta^A(\sigma,\tau)(A=1,2)$. σ and τ parametrize the two-dimensional world-sheet of the string, and x^μ and ϑ^A describe its embedding in super-space. ϑ^1 and ϑ^2 are Majorana-Weyl spinors (16 real components each), which may have either the same or opposite handedness. In the most interesting cases (type I and IIB), they have the same handedness, giving a chiral theory. The dynamics of free superstrings is then given by the two-dimensional action

$$S = \int d\sigma \, d\tau \, (L_1 + L_2) \, , \tag{2}$$

$$L_1 = -\frac{1}{2\pi} \sqrt{-g} \, g^{\alpha\beta} \, \Pi_\alpha \cdot \Pi_\beta \, , \tag{3}$$

$$\Pi_\alpha^\mu = \partial_\alpha x^\mu - i \, \bar{\vartheta}^A \, \gamma^\mu \, \partial_\alpha \vartheta^A \, , \tag{4}$$

$$L_2 = \frac{1}{\pi} \epsilon^{\alpha\beta} \, [-i \, \partial_\alpha x^\mu \, (\bar{\vartheta}^1 \, \gamma_\mu \, \partial_\beta \vartheta^1 - \bar{\vartheta}^2 \, \gamma_\mu \, \partial_\beta \vartheta^2)$$
$$+ \, \bar{\vartheta}^1 \, \gamma^\mu \, \partial_\alpha \vartheta^1 \, \bar{\vartheta}^2 \, \gamma_\mu \, \partial_\beta \vartheta^2] \, . \tag{5}$$

The indices α and β are two-dimensional vector indices, whereas the index μ is a ten-dimensional vector index. $g^{\alpha\beta}$ is an auxiliary two-dimensional metric introduced to ensure manifest local-reparametrization invariance.

In addition to local-reparametrization invariance, this action has global

$N = 2$ super-Poincaré invariance. The infinitesimal transformations are

$$\delta \vartheta^A = \tfrac{1}{4} l_{\mu\nu} \gamma^{\mu\nu} \vartheta^A + \epsilon^A , \tag{6a}$$

$$\delta x^\mu = l^\mu_\nu x^\nu + a^\mu + i \bar{\epsilon}^A \gamma^\mu \vartheta^A , \tag{6b}$$

$$\delta g^{\alpha\beta} = 0 . \tag{6c}$$

It also has local supersymmetry under

$$\delta \vartheta^A = 2 i \gamma \cdot \Pi_\alpha \kappa^{A\alpha} , \tag{7a}$$

$$\delta x^\mu = i \bar{\vartheta}^A \gamma^\mu \delta \vartheta^A , \tag{7b}$$

$$\delta(\sqrt{-g}\, g^{\alpha\beta}) = - 16 \sqrt{-g}\, (P^{\beta\gamma}_- \bar{\kappa}^{1\alpha} \partial_\gamma \vartheta^1 + P^{\beta\gamma}_+ \bar{\kappa}^{2\alpha} \partial_\gamma \vartheta^2) , \tag{7c}$$

where

$$P^{\alpha\beta}_\pm = \tfrac{1}{2}(g^{\alpha\beta} \pm \epsilon^{\alpha\beta}/\sqrt{-g}) . \tag{8}$$

The parameters $\kappa^{A\alpha}$ are Majorana-Weyl spinors (in the ten-dimensional sense) and self-dual vectors (in the two-dimensional sense):

$$\kappa^{1\alpha} = P^{\alpha\beta}_- \kappa^1_\beta \quad \text{and} \quad \kappa^{2\alpha} = P^{\alpha\beta}_+ \kappa^2_\beta . \tag{9}$$

The local symmetries allow one to choose a light-cone gauge in which $x^+ \propto \tau$ and $\gamma^+ \vartheta^A = 0$. In this gauge the remaining x and ϑ coordinates satisfy trivial free-field equations.

Using the transverse coordinates $x^I(\sigma)$ and half the remaining $\vartheta(\sigma)$'s in the light-cone gauge, one can introduce functional superfields $\Phi_{ab}[x^I(\sigma), \vartheta(\sigma), x^+, p^+]$ and $\Psi[x^I(\sigma), \vartheta(\sigma), x^+, p^+]$ to describe the annihilation or creation (depending on the sign of p^+) of open and closed superstrings, respectively. In the case of an SO(N) Yang-Mills group, for example, one has

$$\Phi_{ab}[z(\sigma)] = - \Phi_{ba}[z(\pi - \sigma)] , \tag{10}$$

generalizing the usual rule of antisymmetry. This can be interpreted as though quark-like indices a and b are associated with the ends of the string. The symbol $z(\sigma)$ refers to all x's and ϑ's. Eq. (10) implies that the even mass levels are described by antisymmetric matrices (adjoint representation) and the odd levels by symmetric ones.

The interacting quantum field theory of superstrings is described by the action[17]

$$S = \int [\partial_+\Psi\partial_-\Psi + \text{tr}(\partial_+\Phi\partial_-\Phi)] D^{16}z \, dx^+ \, dx^- - \int H \, dx^+ \,,$$

(11)

where H is the Hamiltonian that gives the x^+ evolution. The integral includes functional integrations over all the $x(\sigma)$ and $\vartheta(\sigma)$ coordinates, which can be given precise meaning by using mode expansions. The Hamiltonian H consists of a kinetic piece plus seven interaction terms.[17,19] In the case of the type IIB theory, which only involves oriented closed strings, just one of these seven terms occurs.

The interaction terms in H fall into two categories — Yang-Mills type and gravitational type, and are depicted in Figs. 1 and 2, respectively. The two Yang-Mills type interactions shown in Fig. 1 involve a breaking or joining of ends. The same local interaction occurs in each case, as is obviously required if the theory is to have a causal interpretation. Mathematically, they involve δ-functionals describing the overlap of the initial and final string configurations, as well as a (functional) derivative at the interaction point, characteristic of a Yang-Mills cubic coupling. The gravity

Fig. 1. The two Yang-Mills-type interactions.

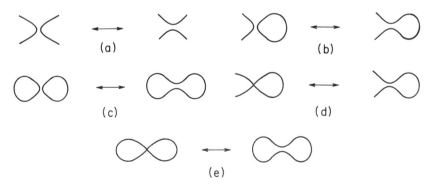

Fig. 2. The five gravity-type interactions.

interaction, depicted in Fig. 2 occurs in five different contexts, but the local interaction is the same in each case. This interaction involves an exchange of string segments, and is topologically distinct from the breaking/joining one. It involves two derivatives at the interaction point, as is characteristic of a gravitational coupling. It should be emphasized that even though the strings are extended in space, the interactions are local. The existence of the gravitational one is a logical consequence of the Yang-Mills ones. Indeed, one finds that $g^2 \sim \kappa T$, where T is the string tension.

It is remarkable that these are all the interactions. This means that the theory is polynomial, even though it contains gravity. All the higher-order contact terms that appear in the expansion of the Einstein-Hilbert action are replaced by exchanges of massive string modes. This is analogous to massive boson exchanges replacing the four-fermion contact terms in weak-interaction theory. As in that case, one obtains improved behavior of quantum corrections in the bargain.

Chiral theories can have anomalous divergences of gauge currents. In fact, when the dimension of spacetime is 2 mod 4 not only the Yang-Mills currents but even the energy-momentum tensor is subject to potential anomalies. A year ago Alvarez-Gaumé and Witten showed[20] that a remarkable cancellation occurs in the case of the IIB supergravity theory, which corresponds to the massless sector of type IIB superstrings. This cancellation makes it appear almost certain that the IIB superstring theory is itself anomaly-free, although an explicit verification still needs to be carried out.

In August 1984, Green and I calculated the Yang-Mills gauge anomaly due to hexagon diagrams of type I superstrings.[18] Much to our surprise, we found that planar and nonorientable loops each give a contribution, but that they cancel in the special case of SO(32). By studying the effective action describing the low-energy expansion of the theory, we were able to clarify the mechanisms that were responsible for the cancellations, and to show that the gravitational and mixed anomalies also cancel. At the level of the effective field theory, we also found (after being told that E_8 has no independent fourth- or sixth-order Casimir invariants) that $E_8 \times E_8$ is another possible gauge group. However, it is not yet known whether a corresponding superstring theory exists.

The SO(32) superstring theory contains all the essential ingredients one would expect of a complete fundamental theory. Although more checks still need to be carried out, the evidence so far suggests that it is anomaly-free[18] and finite[19] in perturbation theory. Not only are the group and the representations unique, but there are no arbitrary dimensionless parameters. Since it is a chiral theory containing elementary gauge fields, there are good prospects that a spontaneous compactification to four dimensions yielding a realistic chiral theory can be found. If an $E_8 \times E_8$ superstring theory exists, the same remarks should apply to it. In fact, that choice might be even more appealing. These recent developments are attracting a lot of interest, and therefore the prospects for more rapid progress are bright. All in all I feel my Berkeley education has served me well, and I feel a special debt of gratitude to Geoff Chew.

References

1. R. Dolan, D. Horn and C. Schmid, *Phys. Rev.* **166,** 1768 (1968).

2. G. Veneziano, *Nuovo Cim.* **57A,** 190 (1968).

3. For reviews see *Dual Theory,* ed. M. Jacob (North-Holland, Amsterdam, 1974); J. Scherk, *Rev. Mod. Phys.* **47,** 123 (1975).

4. A. Neveu and J. H. Schwarz, *Nucl. Phys.* **B31,** 86 (1971).

5. A. Neveu and J. H. Schwarz, *Phys. Rev.* **D4,** 1109 (1971).

6. P. Ramond, *Phys. Rev.* **D3,** 2415 (1971).

7. J.-L. Gervais and B. Sakita, *Nucl. Phys.* **B34,** 477 (1971).

8. L. Brink, P. DiVecchia, and P. Howe, *Phys. Lett.* **65B,** 471 (1976); S. Deser and B. Zumino, *Phys. Lett.* **65B,** 369 (1976).

9. P. Goddard and C. B. Thorn, *Phys. Lett.* **40B,** 235 (1972); J. H. Schwarz, *Nucl. Phys.* **B46,** 61 (1972); R. C. Brower and K. A. Friedman, *Phys. Rev.* **D7,** 535 (1973).

10. J. Scherk and J. H. Schwarz, *Nucl. Phys.* **B81,** 118 (1974); *Phys. Lett.* **52B,** 347 (1974); **57B,** 463 (1975); *Dual Model Approach to a Renormalizable Theory of Gravitation,* Caltech Preprint CALT-68-488, submitted to the 1975 Gravitation Essay Contest of the Gravity Research Foundation.

11. F. Gliozzi, J. Scherk, and D. I. Olive, *Phys. Lett.* **65B,** 282 (1976); *Nucl. Phys.* **B122,** 253 (1977).

12. L. Brink, J. H. Schwarz, and J. Scherk, *Nucl. Phys.* **B121,** 77 (1977).

13. J. H. Schwarz, in *Proc. Orbis Scientiae* 197B, *New Frontiers in High-Energy Physics,* (Plenum Press, NY, 1978).

14. M. B. Green and J. H. Schwarz, *Nucl. Phys.* **B181,** 502 (1981).

15. J. H. Schwarz, *Phys. Reports* **89,** 223 (1982).

16. M. B. Green and J. H. Schwarz, *Phys. Lett.* **136B,** 367 (1984).

17. M. B. Green and J. H. Schwarz, *Nucl. Phys.* **B243,** 475 (1984).

18. M. B. Green and J. H. Schwarz, *Phys. Lett.* **149B,** 117 (1984).

19. M. B. Green and J. H. Schwarz, *Phys. Lett.* **151B,** 21 (1985).

20. L. Alvarez-Gaumé and E. Witten, *Nucl. Phys.* **B234,** 269 (1983).

THE ULTIMATE STRUCTURE OF MATTER

Steven Weinberg

This talk was not given at the celebration of Geoff Chew's birthday, which I was unfortunately unable to attend, but three years earlier, at the celebration of the 50th anniversary of the founding of the Lawrence Berkeley Laboratory. However, my connection with the "Rad Lab" from beginning to end was largely shaped by my connection with Geoff Chew, its leading theorist. During the time I was at Berkeley, from 1959 to 1966, Geoff led a movement that for some years dominated the theory of strong interactions, a movement away from quantum field theory and toward the so-called S-matrix approach. Almost inevitably, therefore, my talk at the Rad Lab's anniversary celebration centered on how I viewed the position of S-matrix theory in the history and the future of theoretical physics. I had rather hoped that Geoff would be pleased that I thought the time might be approaching for a swing back to S-matrix theory, but I later learned that he himself has been moving toward field theory. Nevertheless, it seemed to me that this talk might still make an appropriate contribution to Geoff's *festschrift*, that he will enjoy for old time's sake.

The article presented here is essentially the same as the talk given at Berkeley in October 1981, with only the lightest editing to put it into readable English. I have even left in one scientific mistake; in 1981 I expected that the first intermediate vector boson to be discovered would be the Z^0, because its decay provides a clearer signature, while in fact the available energy in the CERN experiment was so close to the Z^0 threshold that it was the $W^\pm$ that was first discovered.

*   *   *

I want to make it clear from the outset that the rather grandiose title of this talk, *The Ultimate Structure of Matter* was not chosen by me. It was chosen by the organizing committee. However, I did leave it, although I had a chance to change it. This was partly because that way I could blame it on the organizing committee. Also in fact it is precisely what I'm going to talk about. To be a little bit more specific, I want to talk about an old question in physics: What are the fundamental entities of which we regard our universe as being composed — particles or fields?

I don't mean this in the sense of how we should look at our existing theories. It really isn't terribly important, given a theory, whether you describe it in words having to do with particles or words having to do with fields. The important thing is whether it works. The question I'm asking is in what direction we will have to look in the future for more satisfactory theories of matter. In other words, my question is not philosophic but strategic. It is a question that quantum physicists have had to struggle with a great deal and it's appropriate to talk about it here at Berkeley, because many contributions to our enlightenment on this issue have come from here. I'm going to describe something of the history of this old question and then tell you where I think it stands now in today's physics.

In its modern form, the question of a universe of particles or a universe of fields is roughly about as old as the "Rad Lab". In the first decades of the 20th century the question didn't arise, or at least not in its modern form. Physicists then lived comfortably with a kind of dualism. There were undoubted particles like the electron of J. J. Thomson, and the atomic nucleus, discovered by Rutherford. And then there were fields. There was the electromagnetic field, and the gravitational field. True, it was worked out during the period from Einstein in 1905 to Dirac in 1927 that light has a particle nature, that electromagnetic waves can in some sense be thought of as consisting of particles, called (by the Berkeley chemist, G. N. Lewis) photons. Also, there was an effort early in the century by Abraham and Poincaré and others to understand the electron as a bundle of energy of the electromagnetic field. But no one at that time, I believe, dreamed of turning it around and thinking that such material particles as the electron or the proton might have anything to do with an electron field or a proton field. And this was not changed, despite what is sometimes said, by the advent of the quantum mechanics of the 1920's. In that quantum mechanics, as it developed in 1925–26, the description of nature was changed from a description in terms of the trajectories of particles (where a particle is at any one moment and how fast it's going) and fields (what are the values of the electric and magnetic fields at each position in space at any one moment) to a description in terms of wave functions, probability amplitudes, quantities that give you the probability of finding a certain configuration. But these probability amplitudes were still regarded as depending on the positions of particles and the values of fields. The position of every electron in the universe and the values of the electric and magnetic fields at every point in space were taken as the arguments, the independent variables, the things on which the wave function depended.

Dirac attempted in 1928 to formulate a relativistic quantum mechanics; he attempted to take this theory of particles and fields, this dualistic theory, and make it consistent with the principles of special relativity. Dirac's approach was strikingly successful as applied to electrons and electric and magnetic fields, but with the benefit of hindsight we can now say that it could not be extended to the rest of physics, and in particular not to the weak and strong nuclear forces. The fact that it was not generally successful has often been lost sight of because the mathematical machinery invented by Dirac for this purpose has become part of the standard stock in trade of all theorists that followed him. But in fact Dirac's effort to make a relativistic quantum mechanics of particles and fields was not the way of future physics.

Then in 1929, for the first time, there appeared a unified view of the constituents of the universe. I refer to the work of Heisenberg and Pauli in a pair of articles written in 1929, one of them published in 1930. In these articles, Heisenberg and Pauli constructed what we have come to call quantum field theory. The name tells exactly what it is. In this theory, the fundamental constituents of matter are taken to be fields. There is an electromagnetic field: that's no surprise. There's also an electron field; there is a proton field; there is a field for every fundamental particle. The particles emerge when quantum mechanics is applied to these fields, but the particles themselves are mere epiphenomena, just bundles of energy of the field. The energy of the fields are concentrated in little knots and the knots go zipping around and that's what we call particles. But the underlying reality is the field.

The quantum field theory of Heisenberg and Pauli led to a clearer view of what is meant by an elementary particle. An elementary particle is a bundle of energy of one of the fundamental fields that inhabit the universe. Everyone thought the electron, for instance, was an elementary particle, so they assumed that the fundamental field theory would have to involve something called the electron field. Likewise the photon was regarded as a fundamental particle, so the fundamental field theory would be regarded as also containing an electromagnetic field, of which the photon was the quantum or bundle of energy. Other particles, like, say, the nucleus of the iron atom or this blackboard eraser, were regarded as composites. And the fact that they were composites was given a precise meaning in the sense that the basic field equations, which govern the system of fields that makes up the universe, do not contain a field for the iron nucleus or a field for this eraser. These bodies are composed of more elementary particles whose fields do appear in the fundamental equations.

Quantum field theory scored an immediate triumph in 1933 when Fermi used it to develop a theory of the kind of radioactivity known as beta decay, which is the prototype of a whole class of elementary particle interactions which have become to be known as the weak interactions. Beta decay is a process in which a nucleus changes from one element to another element, emitting in the process a negative or a positive electron and a neutrino or an anti-neutrino. This was a process that involved the creation of new particles that could not have existed inside the nucleus. And it was a process that could not possibly be understood within the framework of the old particle quantum mechanics, either in its original form or in the relativistic version of Dirac.

I don't know why Fermi's achievement did not by itself convince physicists of the need for a quantum field theory. Perhaps part of the reason, or perhaps the whole reason, for a hesitancy about quantum field theory after its initial development by Heisenberg and Pauli, was the fact that it immediately ran into a terrible mathematical trouble. In the first few months after the second Heisenberg-Pauli paper was written in 1929, quantum field theory was found to be plagued by a terrible inconsistency, that also afflicted the dualistic particle-field theory of Dirac. One of the first to encounter this problem was a young professor of physics, then new on the faculty at Berkeley, J. Robert Oppenheimer.

Oppenheimer set out to calculate the contribution to the energy of atomic states from the interaction of the atomic electrons with the quantum field of the photon. And Oppenheimer found, to his surprise and chagrin, that the answer was infinite. It wasn't just that the whole zero-point of energy was being shifted by an infinite amount, which wouldn't be observable. Even the energy difference between two atomic energy levels, the quantity which is directly measured when you observe the frequency of light given off by an atom, came out to be infinite in Oppenheimer's calculation.

It was regarded as a disaster. Waller, in Sweden, discovered much the same thing (though he was considering free electrons rather than electrons in atoms), and he told the result to Pauli, and Pauli did not believe it, because it seemed to mean the end for the quantum field theory that he and Heisenberg had just developed. Then other infinites were discovered. Theoretical physicists would set out to calculate some perfectly sensible thing like the energy difference between two states of a hydrogen atom, and the answer they would get would be a perfectly nice number, and then they would carry the calculation to the next order of approximation, and in the next order of approximation they would get an infinite answer. The infinite answer takes the form of an infinite sum over all the ways that momentum and energy can flow between the electron and the radiation field. Other infinites were found in other physical processes. (In fact, more infinites were found than were actually there; there were errors made in some of these calculations which did much to confuse the issue.) There soon developed a general feeling of pessimism about the whole future of the field view of nature.

Many physicists retreated to a position that while the field concept might work as an approximation, there was something basically wrong with it, and if you carried your experiments to, say, one order of magnitude in energy higher than the energies which were then accessible in the kind of accelerator that Lawrence was working with here, that then you would find that the field concept just did not work. (That's always a very common sentiment among physicists, that if you carry experiments to one higher order of magnitude in energy than the energies that are now accessible, that then you'll find that existing ideas don't work. And it's sometimes true.) In particular, Oppenheimer was very much impressed by the fact that in the cosmic ray experiments which were being done at that time, there were discrepancies between the existing theory of electrons and photons and what was observed for cosmic ray showers. At the time no one realized that this was due to the production of particles called mesons, of whose existence physicists were then unaware. Oppenheimer interpreted the cosmic ray data as indicating a breakdown of quantum field theory itself.

Because of the problem of the infinities, there began a return to a view of nature as particles rather than fields. It started with John Wheeler in 1937 and then Heisenberg in 1944. Heisenberg took the point of view, following an ancient and honorable tradition in physics, that the laws of physics should not only make predictions solely about observables, but should not in the formulation of the laws refer to anything but observables. That is, every ingredient in physical law must be something that can be directly observed; physics has no business talking about things that are in principle outside the range of experiment. This satisfied a deep urge in physicists. This philosophic doctrine, which I believe is sometimes called logical positivism, is a recurrent theme in the physics of our century. It was, for instance, very useful to Einstein in his work on relativity. I think physicists often have a feeling that when their theories don't work it's because they've been naughty and introduced unobservable quantities, and if they would only purify themselves and return to things that are observable, then everything would work out.

For Wheeler, and then Heisenberg after him, the observables were the probabilities, or to be more technical, the probability amplitudes, for various collisions among particles. These give the probability for instance, that if you start with two particles coming toward each other at such and such an energy and angle, then you'll end up, say, with three particles going out at such and such energies and angles. All of these probability amplitudes were united by Wheeler and Heisenberg into a quantity called the S matrix, S for *Streung* or scattering. This matrix, an infinite array of complex numbers, would give you all the probabilities for all conceivable collision processes among particles. And the idea was that these were the only things in physics that were ever going to be observed. You would never ever look into a collision and see the local field theoretic processes that had been described by Heisenberg and Pauli so you shouldn't think about them, you should just think about the S matrix and make a theory in which all the laws were formulated in terms of the S matrix.

The issue was now squarely joined. On one side was a field theory of nature in which the underlying reality is a world of quantum fields and in which particles were merely bundles of the energy of the fields. In this view, the laws have to be formulated in terms of the equations that govern the fields — equations like Maxwell's equations, that govern the electromagnetic field. In opposition to this was a particle or S matrix theory, in which the underlying reality is a world of various kinds of particles, and in which when the field idea is useful at all (as everyone knows it is useful in dealing with electromagnetism), the fields are to be regarded as just some kind of collective state of huge numbers of particles, of the sort called a coherent state, but these fields are merely a convenient mathematical abstraction for describing large numbers of particles. In this view, the laws of nature have to be formulated not in terms of field equations but in terms of axioms that describe the S matrix, the array of all the probabilities for all different collision processes.

From the mid 1930's onwards, the mood of physics was going to swing back and forth several times, from S-matrix theory back to quantum field theory, then back again to S-matrix theory, then back again to quantum field theory. I want here to raise the question whether the time is approaching when we will have another swing, back to something like S-matrix theory.

Before I go into this history of these swings of opinion and my comments about where we're headed now, I think I must admit that I have been guilty of a historical oversimplification. Although we may now look back and see a clear opposition between a particle or S matrix view and a quantum field theory, nothing in life is ever that clear. It certainly wasn't that clear in the 1930's or 1940's. One of the great confusions in this story is that for certain problems (though by no means for all problems), Dirac's relativistic quantum mechanics, the dualistic quantum mechanics of particles and fields, of electrons and the electromagnetic field, were equivalent to the quantum field theory of Heisenberg and Pauli. Physicists often referred to them as if they were interchangeable. Weisskopf recently has written in some reminiscences that the paper that he and Pauli wrote in 1934 was designed specifically to demonstrate the need for a thorough-going field theory. (The issue hinged on the nature of anti-matter.) Dirac's view was that in addition to the electrons that we see normally, there is an infinite number of electrons with energies lower than the zero-energy of empty space, the so-called negative energy electrons. Every once in a while there's a hole in the sea of negative energy electrons and that hole we see in the laboratory as an electron but of opposite charge (because a hole in the sea of negatively charged electrons would appear as a positively charged particle). This "anti-electron" or positron was discovered in 1932. Pauli and Weisskopf showed that this view of the nature of antiparticles which was built into Dirac's relativistic quantum mechanics was inadequate; they did this by showing that other sorts of particles also had antiparticles, particles that could not possibly form a sea of negative energy particles. These are the particles that physicists call bosons. They cannot form a stable sea of negative energy particles; if every negative energy state is occupied it becomes even easier for bosons to fall into these states. We now understand that Pauli and Weisskopf were right, and that in fact every non-neutral particle has an antiparticle, and these antiparticles are in no sense to be thought of as holes in a sea of negative energy particles. Among the non-neutral bosons are the $W^\pm$ particles which are exchanged in nuclear beta decay. The fact that every particle has an antiparticle became settled in most people's minds when the antiproton was discovered here in Berkeley in the 1950's. However even now the hole theory still appears in textbooks. I suppose it's an example of physicists not taking the trouble to rewrite their history.

Now back to the main line of my talk. I want to talk now of the swings of opinion between quantum field theory and S-matrix theory. The first revival of quantum field theory came in the late 1940's through the work of a number of people: Feynman, Schwinger, Tomonaga, Dyson, and others. It was found that the infinities that had been discovered by Oppenheimer and Waller and others in the 1930's were in fact due to a simple misinterpretation of the theory. (That is, to what we can now say with the benefit of hindsight was a simple misinterpretation. Nothing is simple when it actually happens.) The misinterpretation was the identification of the quantities e and m which appear in the field equations with the electric charge and mass of the electron as they're actually measured in the laboratory. It became clear that when we measure, say, the mass of the electron in the laboratory, we're not measuring the quantity m which appears in the field equations, but in fact we're measuring the mass m plus the effects of a huge number of so-called radiative processes, in which the electron emits and then re-absorbs photons many times. And all these processes are always going on all the time. You cannot ever measure the mass of the electron apart from these radiative processes. The Department of Energy may turn off accelerators but it can't turn off these processes. As a result, no one has ever seen a bare electron, an electron without its cloud of photons. And once you realize that the quantities appearing in your equations are not the ones that are measured and you reinterpret your equations to express them in terms of the measured quantities, all the infinities simply cancel. I'm making it sound really quite simple, although none of it was easy to see.

Quantum field theory now worked magnificiently. A few years ago, just to give an example, I looked up the numbers for the comparison of theory and experiment for what's called the magnetic moment of the electron. (That's just its strength as a magnet, in natural atomic units.) The experimental value was 1.0011596541 and the theoretical value is 1.00115965234. The discrepancy is in the tenth decimal place and is easily accounted for by both experimental and calculational uncertainties.

There is an interesting historical point here which I suspect not too many people know because probably not many people have read Oppenheimer's 1930 paper. (Incidentally, that paper appeared in a journal which had not, until then, been the scene of many important publications in fundamental theoretical physics, the *Physical Review*.) One of the triumphs of the revival of quantum field theory in the late 1940's was Bethe's calculation of what's called the Lamb shift, which is just the splitting in energy (due to emission and absorption of photons) of two otherwise equal energy levels of the hydrogen atom. He calculated it and it agreed with the experimental value that had just been determined by Willis Lamb. If you look back at Oppenheimer's paper you will find that he had everything there needed for the calculation of the Lamb shift. All he needed to do was to give the crank one more quarter turn and he would have had Bethe's formula for the Lamb shift, and could have calculated the numerical value. Really, all Oppenheimer had to do was put in the numbers and throw away the infinite effects of intermediate states involving relativistic electrons, and he would have gotten the right answer, or at any rate the answer to as good an approximation as Bethe's. He didn't do it because he didn't have confidence in quantum field theory. What happened in the late 1940's was precisely a restoration of confidence in quantum field theory.

But that confidence didn't last very long. More problems were found and there was another revival of S-matrix theory in the late 1950's and early 1960's. One of the problems was that although these infinities beautifully cancelled in the theory of electricity and magnetism and electrons, which is known as quantum electrodynamics, the infinities would not cancel in that way in the theory that Fermi had developed to describe the radioactive process of beta decay. (The generic name for the force that produces these processes, as I said before, is the weak interaction, because it has an intrinsically weak strength, which makes processes like beta decay go very slowly.) For the weak interactions (of which many more examples were known at that time) this lovely trick of cancelling infinities just didn't work. That was, of course, an old story but it was hoped that the new idea of absorbing the infinities into a redefinition or, in other words, a renormalization of the electron's mass and charge, would also work when you applied the idea to the weak as well as the electromagnetic interactions. But it just didn't work.

The second problem was the apparent hopelessness of calculations involving strong nuclear forces. (These are the forces that hold the nucleus of the atom together. It's the strength of these forces that makes the nucleus so much smaller than the atom and that gives rise to such enormous energies when you disrupt the nucleus, typically a million times larger than the energies that are released when you disrupt an atom in an ordinary chemical reaction.) In quantum electrodynamics one has a lovely situation in which the next to lowest order approximation to any calculated quantity is about $1/137$ of the lowest order quantity (in rough magnitude). The next to next to lowest order is another factor of 137 smaller, so if you want values to a certain accuracy you just take a certain number of terms in your perturbation expansion and you get pretty good results. In the strong interactions, the quantity which in quantum electrodynamics is 1/137, the number that defines how strong the force is, is more like 1, and so the first term is of order 1, the second term is of order 1-squared, the third term is of order 1-cubed, and you just don't make any money that way.

Finally, during this period from the late 50's to the early 60's, there was a profusion of new particles being discovered, very largely here at Berkeley at the Bevatron and very largely through the capabilities opened up by the bubble chamber. These particles seemed every bit as elementary as the proton and the neutron which are the constituents of the nuclei of ordinary atoms. In fact some of them even form families with the proton and neutron. And others look just as good. And there were so many of them. Physicists even got to the point where they had to carry around a booklet, which is published now here at Berkeley, listing all the particles. It was clear that anything you need a telephone directory for can't be elementary. Remember, this idea of elementarity was tied to the idea of a field theory. That is, the elementary particles were those that were associated with the fundamental fields described by the field equations that were seen as the basic laws of nature, but it didn't look like there were any particles that were any more elementary than any others.

Here at Berkeley, building on earlier work of Chew, Gell-Mann, Goldberger, Low, Nambu, and others on dispersion relations, Chew and Mandelstam and Stapp and their co-workers set about reviving S-matrix theories, but now with a much more specific and mathematically powerful set of axioms than in Heisenberg's time. I hope the nonphysicists in the audience will forgive me, but I'll just name these by the code words, the buzz words that become common among physicists: unitarity, analyticity, Lorentz invariance and clustering. (I won't tell you what any one of them is.) These were the basic properties which it was argued, a theory would have to have to be physically sensible at all. And the hope was that if you demanded these properties, they would provide so many equations relating different elements of the S matrix that the whole theory would become uniquely defined and you could actually solve the equations and come up with numbers for physical quantities. And on top of this you would have the happy feeling in the back of your mind that you were doing what a scientist should do: You were dealing at every point with physical observables, and you were not getting involved with the mythical quantities, the quantum fields, that Heisenberg and Pauli had used in 1929.

Now the S-matrix theory as developed by Chew and his co-workers did not in fact prove in any sense a failure. It did not lead to results on which we now turn our backs. It was however, to a certain extent, bypassed by the main stream of the history of physics in the following years. This first revival of S-matrix theory was in the 1950's and the early 1960's. But it was followed by a second revival of quantum field theory (the first one was in the 1940's), extending from the late 1960's to the present.

The reasons for the second revival of quantum field theory as I said had nothing to do with any failure of S-matrix theory, but with successes in other directions. First of all, theories of the weak interactions and of the strong interactions were developed during this period which were just as good from the point of view of infinities as the older theory of quantum electrodynamics. When I say they were just as good, I mean again that if you were just careful to properly identify the physical quantities that you're talking about, then all the infinities would cancel. Theories were developed for both the weak and strong interactions in which that was true. In fact, it was not just accidentally true; these theories were built on an analogy with the theory of electromagnetism. In the case of the weak interactions it was more than an analogy; there was actually a unification with electromagnetism, so that increasingly, physicists no longer refer to weak and electromagnetic interactions, but just call them the electroweak interactions. The theory of strong interactions was also constructed in close analogy with quantum electrodynamics; it is called quantum chromodynamics. In fact if you look at a page of equations, until you're told exactly how many values the varying parameters take and what the indices mean, etc., the equations look the same. There are reasons why it took so long to develop these theories, having to do with gauge symmetries and broken symmetries and things like that that I will not have time to go into here.

Another reason for the second revival of quantum field theory was the fact that it was found that the strong interactions, although very strong at distances typical of the size of the particles in the nucleus, get progressively weaker as we go to very, very short distances or, equivalently, to very, very high energies. This means that it is now possible to use our theory of the strong interactions to do actual calculations in the same way that we use quantum electrodynamics to calculate what happens inside an atom. The calculations tell us what happens to elementary particles at very high energy, much higher than is typically found in the nuclei of atoms. And the successes of these calculations in comparison with experiments are sufficient to convince us (or will be in a short time) that this theory is correct. I can't claim that this theory of strong interactions is entirely verified experimentally but there's not much question that it's correct.

Oddly though, the old questions of how to calculate the nuclear forces that hold the nucleus of the atom together, or the kind of thing that was worried about at Berkeley when I was here in the late 50's, like what is the cross section for scattering a pion on a nucleon at 700 MeV, cannot be answered today any more than they could have been 20 years ago. This is an evolution that I think often happens in physics. You don't solve all the problems that concern one generation of physicists; instead, the next generation finds that there are more urgent problems. The important thing in the end is not to solve every problem, but to solve enough problems so that you know you have the right theory. And that is what we're in the process of doing with the theory of the strong forces.

The third thing that happened during the second revival of quantum field theory was the realization that there are particles that seem pretty elementary after all. There's the good old electron, and it comes with a family of siblings, the muon, the tauon, and so on, and related particles called neutrinos. No one has ever found any structure inside them, and there aren't an enormous number of them, just the electron, mu, tau and their corresponding neutrinos. In addition, in place of the proton and the neutron and other particles that were being discovered in Berkeley in the 1950's and early 60's, we now have a much smaller set of strongly interacting fundamental particles called quarks. The proton and the neutron and all those other particles discovered here at Berkeley seem to be composites, made up of quarks. In addition, we have one other class of elementary particles, containing the photon, the good old quantum of light, and its siblings, particles called gluons and other particles too heavy to have been produced yet, called W and Z particles. (The Z particle is due to be discovered in Geneva pretty soon now.) All these particles are regarded as elementary, in the sense that they are manifestations of the quantum fields that appear in the underlying field equations, and they are what they are because of these field equations.

In 1975 I gave a talk about all this at Harvard, and although I don't now remember much of what I said, I remember the title I used for the talk, and it gives a pretty good idea of what I think had been happening in the preceding decade. The title was *The Renaissance of Quantum Field Theory*.

That might seem the end of the story. These have been exciting times. Quantum field theory is riding very high and one might be forgiven for a certain amount of complacency with it. But perhaps we will see another swing away from quantum field theory. Perhaps that swing will be back in the direction of something like S-matrix theory, back to a view of particles as fundamental. There are several reasons that I can point to for this. (By the way, in case you didn't notice, I'm now finished with the historical part of my talk, and up to 1981.) One of the reasons is the continued failure to make a mathematically satisfactory quantum field theory of gravity. The problem again is these damned infinities that Oppenheimer and Waller discovered in 1930. There's no quantum theory of gravity which is free of these infinities and we don't have any good idea of how to make one. From all indications the existing quantum field theory, at least of gravity, and perhaps quantum field theory in general, needs some kind of modification at any energy at or below the very high energy of 10^{19} proton masses. (That's a one with 19 zeros.) Something new has to happen in physics because our existing theories simply break down at these energies.

Another hint of a new energy scale in physics comes from the fact that I've mentioned before, that the strong interaction strength decreases as you go to high energies. If the strength of the strong interactions decreases as you go to high energy, then perhaps it's merely the accident that we are doing experiments at relatively low energy that makes the strong interactions look so much stronger than the other interactions. Perhaps the strong and electroweak interactions really all have the same strength at a fundamental level. The decrease in the strength of the strong interactions is only logarithmic with energy, so the energy at which the strong and electroweak forces become comparable has to be enormously high; in a very wide variety of theories, it is found that that energy is about 10^{15} proton masses. So here again we're led to contemplate enormously high scales of energy.

These hints suggest that there is a fundamental scale of energies in physics far beyond anything that is accessible or will ever be accessible to our accelerators, until someone finds some way of putting a macroscopic amount of energy, like the energy in an automobile tank full of gasoline, on one elementary particle. Perhaps the theory of this new ultra-high energy scale in physics will not be a quantum field theory at all. We don't know. We can't do experiments at these energies.

But if it's not going to be a quantum field theory, the question naturally arises, what are these beautiful theories that we've delighted so much in developing? If the underlying truth is not a quantum field theory, then how come the quantum field theories that we have developed, quantum electrodynamics and then the generalization of quantum electrodynamics to include the weak interactions, and the theory known as quantum chromodynamics that describes the strong interactions, why do these beautiful field theories work so well? What are they if they're not fundamental?

The answer may perhaps be provided by two theorems. These are what I believe Wightman calls "folk theorems", that is, things that have never been proved but are well known to be true. I think these theorems can probably be formulated in precise terms, and proved, though I haven't done it.

The first folk theorem is that if we write down the most general quantum field theory (for the physicists here I'll say the most general Lagrangian) including all possible terms in the theory that satisfy the appropriate symmetries, and if we calculate processes to any given order of perturbation theory, that is to any order of approximation, then what we get, provided we are talking about the most general possible quantum field theory and not some specific theory, is simply the most general possible S-matrix element which to that degree of approximation satisfies the S-matrix axioms of Chew, Mandelstam, Stapp *et al*. Another, briefer, way of saying this is that field theory is in itself without content. Quantum field theory, divorced from specific theories, but just the general idea of quantum field theory, is just a convenient way of implementing the axioms of S-matrix theory.

In fact quantum field theory has been used in precisely this way ever since 1967 in studying the interactions of low energy π-mesons, particles which no one today regards as elementary and yet which are described by a quantum field theory which is widely used to calculate their various reactions. The reason that this field theory works is precisely because all that quantum field theory does for you is to reproduce the most general S matrix consistent with the symmetries that you're assuming and consistent with the axioms of S-matrix theory.

But if that's all quantum field theory is, if quantum field theory is just a clever mathematical trick for implementing the axioms of S-matrix theory, then why are the detailed working theories that we've developed, quantum electrodynamics and quantum chromodynamics and quantum electroweak dynamics and so on, why are these theories so beautifully simple? You expect to find simplicity in physics if you deal with physics at a fundamental level. If you're dealing with something that's just a lot of mathematical trickery, then why should it look so simple? Why, for example, are the field equations of quantum electrodynamics, or Maxwell's equations for that matter, so simple?

The answer to that question may be found in a second folk theorem. The second folk theorem says that theories with a natural energy scale (and I'm thinking here of energies like 10^{19} proton masses or 10^{15} proton masses or whatever), if studied at much lower energies than the natural energy scale, will always be found to be described to a good approximation by an effective field theory which is as simple as possible. (In technical language, the effective Lagrangian is dominated by terms with the fewest fields and/or derivatives.) Where possible, the interactions in this effective field theory will be so simple that they allow the cancellation of infinities to go through as they did in quantum electrodynamics. I suggest that this is why quantum electrodynamics and quantum chromodynamics and quantum electroweak-dynamics are as simple as they are. Where this is not possible, where the symmetries simply don't allow interactions that are that simple, then the physics will be dominated by interactions which do not allow the cancellation of infinities, and which are also very weak, being suppressed by powers of the natural mass scale, whether it's 10^{15} or 10^{19} proton masses or whatever.

We see at least one example of such very weak forces in the world we study today: gravitation. The fact that gravitation seems outside the scope of quantum field theory is from this point of view just due to the fact that the symmetries that it has to satisfy are too stringent to allow field equations which are simple enough for this cancellation of infinities to occur.

Another possible class of extremely weak interactions which has been much discussed lately and which we may discover in the laboratory are the interactions which could lead to the decay of the proton or to the mass of the neutrino. Elaborate experiments are underway now looking for these things, and they may be found.

If our quantum field theories of which we're so proud are just the debris of some really fundamental theory which describes all of physics including gravity, it may be that the really fundamental theory will have nothing to do with fields; it may not look like a quantum field theory at all. I think we have to leave it as an open possibility that maybe, in fact, it will be something like an S-matrix theory.

ON THE UNIQUENESS OF PHYSICAL THEORIES*

David J. Gross

It is a pleasure and an honor to participate in the celebration of the sixtieth birthday of Geoff Chew. Over the years many people have expressed surprise upon hearing that I was a student of Chew. To paraphrase their comments: "Funny — you don't look Chewish". I suppose this has something to do with my role in the development of QCD, a quantum field theory of the strong interactions. I shall take advantage of this special occasion to address the astonishment of all of these people, to acknowledge my debt for the education that I received from Geoff and to explain how my personal journey to QCD was a continuous one.

Although this road has led me in a direction different from that of Chew, the goal was common — the search for a unique theory of hadronic structure, a goal I was inspired to pursue as a student of Chew at Berkeley. The uniqueness of physical theories is the central motif in Chew's approach to physics. It is therefore appropriate to address this issue from the perspective of the modern gauge theory of elementary particles and in light of current attempts to construct unified theories.

1. The Road from N/D to QCD

Let us start in Berkeley in the middle of the 1960's. High energy physics was in a period of rapid change, on both an experimental and theoretical level, and Berkeley was in the middle of much of the action. I was one of a large group of Chew's students. This was a very enjoyable experience. In large part, this was due to Geoff's generous and supportive attitude towards his students. No matter how many students he had he would always find time for each, sharing with us his ideas and insights and treating us as full partners in a common effort.

Most of all it was an exciting time. Geoff transmitted to us his unique passion for physics. We were not merely doing phenomenology of the

*Supported in part by NSF Grant No. PHY80-19754.

strong interactions, but were embarked on a great adventure to find a unique theory of hadrons. There is nothing as important to convey to students as this sense of adventure. Formulas and theorems can be learned from books; attitudes and goals one acquires by personal example. Geoff inspired us to think big, to attempt to achieve ambitious goals and in particular to search for uniqueness in physical theories.

On a more practical level one of the most important things I learned in Berkeley, in large part by observing Geoff, was the correct attitude towards experimental physics. Not just the obvious dictum that one must follow closely and critically experimental developments, but rather that elusive, intuitive sense of which experiments are truly important and must be reckoned with, and which are not and may be ignored. Some of this rubbed off on me at Berkeley and was to serve me well.

From Berkeley I went to Harvard. This was the heyday of current algebra. Like many others I was very impressed with the predictive success of the assumed structure of current commutators. Clearly the properties of these observable hadronic currents placed strong restrictions on hadronic dynamics. By this time most of the easy stuff had been done, and the implications of global current algebra were well understood as consequences of broken chiral symmetry. I therefore studied the less understood properties of the algebra of local currents. These were more model dependent — but that was fine, they thus contained dynamical information which went beyond global symmetry. Furthermore, as it was soon realized, they could be tested in deep inelastic lepton-hadron scattering experiments.

In 1967, Callan and I proposed a sum rule to test the then popular Sugawara model, a dynamical model of local currents. Bjorken noted that this sum rule, as well as dimensional arguments, implies the scaling of deep inelastic electron-proton scattering cross sections. This was shortly confirmed by the new experiments at SLAC. In 1968, Callan and I noted that by measuring σ_L/σ_T one could determine whether the constituents of the hadron had spin zero ($\sigma_T = 0$) or spin 1/2 ($\sigma_L = 0$). The experiments indicated spin 1/2. These experiments had a profound impact on me. They showed that the proton behaved, over short times, as if it were made up of pointlike objects with spin 1/2 and (as later neutrino-proton scattering indicated) baryon number 1/3. From then on I was convinced of the reality of quarks, not just as mathematical objects useful as mnemonic devices for summarizing hadronic symmetries, but as physical pointlike constituents of the nucleon. But how could that be? Surely strong interactions must exist between the quarks which would smear out their pointlike behavior. It soon became clear that in a field theoretic context only free field theory could produce exact scaling. Once interactions were included, scaling and the sum rules went down the tube. Yet the experiments indicated otherwise. This paradox and the search for an explanation of scaling was to preoccupy me for the following four years.

My trust in experiment and my distrust of field theory served me well. In 1970, I met S. Polyakov at the Kiev conference, an uninvited but already impressive participant. We had long discussions about deep inelastic scattering. Polyakov knew a lot about the renormalization group and explained to me that in field theory one expects anomalous dimensions. I retorted that the experiments show otherwise. He responded that this contradicts field theory. We departed, he convinced that experiments at higher energies would change, I that the theory would change.

By the end of 1972 I had learned enough field theory, in particular renormalization group methods from Ken Wilson, to tackle the problem head on. I decided to prove that field theory could not explain the experimental fact of scaling and thus that field theory was not appropriate to describe the strong interactions. The plan of attack was twofold: first to show that ultraviolet stability, later called asymptotic freedom, was necessary to explain scaling and second to prove that no field theory was asymptotically free. In the spring of 1973 Callan and I had completed a proof of the first argument and Coleman and I were close to a proof of the second. There was one hole in the arguments, non-Abelian gauge theories, which for technical reasons were hard to treat. With Frank Wilczek, who had started his graduate work with me that year, we tried to close that hole. The discovery that non-Abelian gauge theories were asymptotically free (made at the same time by Politzer who, working under Coleman, was trying to generalize the Coleman-Weinberg mechanism to Yang-Mills theories) came to me as a total surprise. Wilczek and I quickly realized that color gauge theories of quarks could easily explain the deep-inelastic scattering (albeit with logarithmic modifications of scaling — a bonus since that provided an experimental test of the theory) and that the infrared growth of the coupling (infrared slavery) might provide a mechanism for quark confinement. Rather than killing field theory I was led to a rather unique field theory of the strong interactions. QCD might be wrong, though few would argue that today, but since 1973 it has never had a serious competition.

2.   Arbitrary Parameters

One of the features of QCD that has always appealed to me is its uniqueness. I refer not to the fact that it seems to be uniquely singled out by experiment but rather to the fact that it contains essentially no adjustable dimensionless parameters.

Arbitrary, adjustable parameters in a fundamental theory are embarrassing. The search for uniqueness is often motivated by a desire to explain and fix such arbitrary parameters. Many of us strongly believe that eventually all such parameters will be calculable. Einstein expressed this view eloquently in his autobiographical notes: "I would like to state a principle, which cannot be based upon anything more than a faith in the simplicity,

i.e. intelligibility, of nature; that is to say, nature is so constituted that it is possible logically to lay down such strongly determined laws that within these laws only rationally, completely determined constants occur (not constants, therefore, whose numerical value could be changed without destroying the theory).''

This is a marvelous statement of the ultimate goal of fundamental theoretical physics — the motivating force behind the bootstrap and unified field theory alike. It is a rather arrogant goal and a recent one in the history of physics. This is understandable — until one begins to understand the "how" of things one is in no position to ask for the "why".

The first reference I have found where the issue of the number of fundamental constants of nature is seriously addressed is a book of Eddington, published in 1934. Eddington made a list of the seven *primitive* constants of nature. This was a remarkably good list, considering subsequent developments. It consisted of the following: Planck's constant h, the velocity of light c, Newton's gravitational constant G, the electron charge e, the electron mass m, the proton mass M and the cosmological constant Λ.

Of these seven fundamental constants of nature three are, of course, arbitrary; they simply provide units of length, time and mass. It is customary to pick h, c and G to provide natural units, in which length, time and mass are measured in units of the Planck length $\sqrt{hG/c^3}$, time $\sqrt{hG/c^5}$ and mass $\sqrt{hc/G}$. That leaves four dimensionless ratios, pure numbers, whose precise values are amenable to rational understanding. These four numbers can be thought of as representing four categories of physical parameters. They are:

1.   The fine structure constant, $\alpha = e^2/hc \sim 1/137$. In this category we would also include the values of other gauge couplings, such as α_{strong}. The values of these couplings are typically of order $1-10^{-3}$.

2.   The ratios of the electron and proton masses, $m_e/M \sim 1/2000$. In this category we would, today, include the multitude of mass ratios that particle theories attempt to explain: the ratios of hadronic, quark, lepton and weak boson masses. These ratios range from 1 to 10^{-9}.

3.   The ratio of the proton mass to the Planck mass, $M\sqrt{G/hc} \sim 10^{-19}$. Our ignorance of the origin of this exceedingly small parameter is referred to nowadays as the "hierarchy problem". In this category we also have the ratios of mass scale of gravity and/or unified gauge theories to that of the weak or strong interactions. These ratios are all believed to be of order $10^{-15}-10^{-19}$.

4.   The ratio of the cosmological constant to the Planck energy density, $\Lambda (G/hc)^2 < 10^{-120}$.

The incredibly small bound on this ratio suggests that $\Lambda = 0$, although we do not understand why this must be so.

Thus Eddington's list is quite up-to-date. It includes four of the primary goals in the contemporary search for uniqueness. In the two first categories much progress has been made; the last two are still clouded in mystery. That is not to say that we can predict the precise value of gauge couplings, quark and lepton masses, or even calculate hadronic mass ratios precisely, but we have understood many of the principles that will determine these. In the case of the hierarchy constant, and especially the cosmological constant, we are far from constructing a mechanism that would uniquely determine them.

3. Progress Towards Uniqueness

The fundamental constant that has attracted most attention has been α. Who has not dreamt of calculating $\alpha^{-1} = 137.03604...$? In fact Eddington and many others have tried, with no success. Today we realize that these attempts were premature, that QED is not a complete or internally consistent theory and that the effective α at the unification scale, where its value is of order $1/10$, will most likely be determined by a solution to the hierarchy problem.

However QCD provides us with a gauge theory of the strong interactions which is internally consistent and realistic, in which the strong α_s and hadronic mass ratios are completely determined and calculable. It is instructive to examine how this occurs and to draw some lessons from this, albeit partial, solution to the problem of uniqueness.

Before considering QCD let us first examine a toy "model of the world". Consider the following non-relativistic Hamiltonian, that describes a world consisting of charged particles of equal mass and charges $\pm e$.

$$H = \sum_i \frac{\mathbf{p}_i^2}{2m} + \sum_{i \neq j} \frac{\pm e^2}{|\mathbf{x}_i - \mathbf{x}_j|} .$$

Although there appear to be two free parameters in H this "theory" actually has no adjustable parameters. That is because all physical observables will be expressible in terms of the dimensionful parameters e, m and h: the numerical values of these is therefore a matter of convention. Another way of seeing why the theory contains no adjustable coupling is to note that under a change of scale: $x \to \lambda x$, $t \to \lambda^2 t$, $h \to h$, $m \to m$, we have

$$H(\mathbf{p}/\lambda; \lambda \mathbf{x}; e^2/\lambda) = \frac{1}{\lambda^2} H(\mathbf{p}, \mathbf{x}; e^2) .$$

Therefore a change of the value of the coupling e^2 is equivalent to a change in the scale of length, time and energy.

However this theory does not quite satisfy Einstein's criterion, since there is no reason why the potential must have the form $V = e^2/x$. It could just as well be of the form $V = e^2/x + g/x^2 + fx + \dots$ Therefore the "theory" has an infinite number of free dimensionless parameters: g, f/e^2,... which we have arbitrarily set to zero. What principle could eliminate the non-uniqueness of this theory? One possibility is to demand extra symmetry of the theory. Thus if we demand scale invariance (namely that under a change of scale the potential energy scales like the kinetic energy) then $V(x)$ must equal g/x^2, and ef,... will vanish as a consequence of the symmetry.

Imposing scale invariance leaves us with a theory with three parameters, h, m and g. However the coupling is now dimensionless. Consequently g is a free parameter. Under a change of scale we now have

$$H\left(\frac{\mathbf{p}}{\lambda}, \lambda\mathbf{x}, g\right) = \frac{1}{\lambda^2}H(\mathbf{p}, \mathbf{x}; g) \ ,$$

so that g is unchanged. Thus although we have achieved our goal of explaining why the theory has only three parameters we are left with an arbitrary adjustable dimensionless coupling constant g. Furthermore, this "theory" has a fatal disease. Due to the absence of a length scale in the theory, all energies must be continuous and there can be no discrete states. Such a theory is highly unphysical.

The formulation of QCD, the quantum gauge theory of the strong interactions, also involves three parameters, h, c and g. This is a consequence of a variety of symmetries. The Lagrangian is

$$\mathcal{L} = \frac{1}{4}\operatorname{Tr} F_{\mu\nu} F^{\mu\nu} + \sum_i \bar{\psi}_i (i\not{\partial} + g\not{A}) \psi_i \ .$$

The symmetries that eliminate all but these parameters are the following. Gauge symmetry requires that the gluon-gluon coupling, g_{GGG}, equal the quark-gluon coupling g_{Gqq}. Chiral invariance precludes a quark mass term. Finally the requirement of renormalizability, together with chiral invariance, leads to scale invariance which limits the parameters to three.

A distinction must be made between the status of local color gauge symmetry and global chiral invariance. If we alter the equality of g_{GGG} and g_{Gqq}, breaking gauge invariance, we totally change (if not destroy) the structure of the theory; however the addition of a small quark mass, which breaks chiral invariance, has but a small effect on the theory. This would not please Einstein. In the real world the vanishing of (bare) quark and lepton masses is a consequence of local chiral invariance which cannot be disturbed without totally destroying the full $(SU(3) \times SU(2) \times U(1))$ theory. For the moment, however, we shall ignore the electroweak gauge interactions.

So far QCD is similar to the previous scale invariant toy model, and would appear to suffer from the same difficulties. Although containing only three parameters (h, c, g), one combination is dimensionless and adjustable, $\alpha_s = \frac{g^2}{hc}$ and scale invariance should imply continuous energies. How does QCD avoid this conundrum?

QCD avoids the pitfalls of scale invariant theories with a finite number of degrees of freedom due to the phenomenon of renormalization. The QCD vacuum behaves as a physical medium containing virtual charged particles (gluons and quarks). The polarization of this vacuum produces a distance-dependent coupling. In QCD, the effects of the gluons dominate. They behave as permanent magnetic dipoles, producing a paramagnetic medium with a permeability $\mu > 1$. In a relativistic theory, this yields a dielectric constant $\epsilon = \frac{1}{\mu} < 1$, as if the vacuum anti-screens color charge. Thus the gauge charge g depends on the distance r from the source, decreasing as $1/\ell n(\frac{1}{r})$ for small r and, presumably, increasing without bound for large r. This behavior is responsible for the characteristic dynamical features of QCD; asymptotic freedom, which leads to free pointlike behavior at short distances and infrared slavery, which leads to color confinement at large distances.

Of concern to us here is the fact that renormalization provides a dynamical mechanism for the breaking of scale invariance, without destroying the symmetries of the theory that restrict the number of parameters to three. Consequently g depends on the distance scale. The precise dependence is quite complicated. It is described by the renormalization group which determines how g varies as the scale of lengths is varied. This breaking of scale invariance means that g can be traded off for a choice of a unit of length — dimensional transmutation. For example a unit of length can be chosen to be the distance at which the effective g is equal to one, and this length can be replaced by a more physical choice, say the Compton wave length of the proton. We are therefore in the same situation as in the first toy model considered above — the theory contains three *dimensionful* parameters; h, c and say, m_p = mass of the lowest bound state with quark number equal to 3. All physical observables can be, in principle, calculated in terms of these. All dimensionless parameters can be determined and there are no arbitrary, adjustable parameters.

4.   Lessons and Future Directions

Great progress towards uniqueness has also been achieved in the modern theories of the weak and electromagnetic interactions. As a consequence of unified gauge symmetry the number of independent couplings is greatly reduced; as a consequence of chiral gauge symmetries arbitrary fermionic mass parameters are eliminated. Here too, a crucial ingredient of these theories is the existence of dynamical mechanisms that lead to symmetry breaking but which does not decrease the predictive power of the theory by introducing new arbitrary parameters. Indeed our present frustration with the many (~ 20) arbitrary parameters in the standard model $SU(3) \times SU(2) \times U(1)$ is due to our incomplete understanding of the mechanism of dynamical chiral gauge symmetry breaking.

It is fair to say that we have gone a long way towards determining the parameters of first two entries in Eddington's list (symbolized by α and m_e/m_p). Little progress has been achieved, however, in determining the second pair of constants. This is not surprising since these appear to require an unprecedented extrapolation of present knowledge to distances of 10^{-29}–10^{-33} cm, wherein lie the secrets of gauge theory unification and quantum gravity. What lessons can be extracted from the success of the past decades that could serve as a guide in the ongoing search for uniqueness?

The primary lesson is that the elimination of superfluous constants is a consequence of the discovery of new *symmetries* of nature. However it is not sufficient to simply dream up new symmetries. One must also explain why these symmetries are not apparent. This often requires both the discovery of *new hidden degrees of freedom* and *a mechanism for dynamical symmetry breaking*. Thus the establishment of color gauge symmetry required the discovery of the carriers of color charge (quarks and gluons) as well as the elucidation of the dynamical mechanism of confinement by which these remain hidden. The establishment of the electroweak gauge symmetry required discovery of the dynamical mechanism of spontaneous gauge symmetry breaking that produces the apparent differences in the structure of the weak and electromagnetic interactions. Future progress towards uniqueness will require both new symmetries and new dynamics.

It is no surprise therefore that much of exploratory particle theory is devoted to a search for new symmetries. Some of this effort is based on straightforward extrapolations of established symmetries and dynamics, as in the search for unified gauge theories (SU(5), SO(10), etc.), or in the development of a predictive theory of dynamical chiral gauge symmetry breaking (technicolor, preons, etc.). Ultimately more promising, however, are the suggestions for radically new symmetries and degrees of freedom.

First there is supersymmetry, a radical and beautiful extension of space-time symmetry to include fermionic charges, which has the potential to drastically reduce the number of free parameters. Most of all it offers an explanation for the existence of fermionic matter, quarks and leptons, as compelling as the argument that the existence of gauge mesons follows from gauge symmetry. Supersymmetry will undoubtedly play an important role in a future unified theory. At this point, however, we have not developed an understanding of the dynamics of supersymmetry breaking which is adequate to allow for a direct confrontation with experiment.

An even greater enlargement of symmetry, and of hidden degrees of freedom, is envisaged in the current efforts to revive the ideas of Kaluza and Klein, wherein space itself contains new, hidden, dimensions. These new degrees of freedom are hidden due to the spontaneous compactification of the new spatial dimensions, which partially breaks many of the space-time symmetries of the large manifold. The unbroken isometries of the hidden, compact, dimensions can yield a gravitational explanation of the emergence of gauge symmetries (and, in supergravity theories, fermionic matter). A combination of supersymmetry and Kaluza-Klein has the potential to yield truly unique theories, and could shed light on the hierarchy and cosmological constant problems. The most radical of these attempts to construct unified theories are based on the quantum theory of strings. Here we are contemplating an enormous increase in both degrees of freedom (the basic dynamical entity is not a pointlike object but rather a one-dimensional extended object) and in symmetry. One of the most exciting features of these string theories, which have the possibility of containing all of known low energy physics, is their large degree of uniqueness. If a unified string theory turns out to be correct, it could not only allow us to calculate all of Eddington's fundamental constants but could even determine the number of spatial dimensions.

Finally, recent developments have taught us that gauge symmetries lead to strong global constraints that are not deducible from local considerations. Theories which are apparently symmetric may contain anomalies when one considers the global structure of configuration space. Consistency requires the absence or cancellation of such anomalies and leads to strong constraints on the freedom to adjust parameters. Indeed it appears that as we contemplate even greater extensions of local gauge symmetry, consistency requirements lead to even stronger constraints, thus bolstering our hopes of ultimate uniqueness.

It is unlikely, however, that the ultimate goal will ever be achieved. The more we understand, the more questions we learn to ask. So while we might eventually calculate all of the arbitrary parameters that can now be enumerated, success will most likely produce a new set of questions and parameters whose relevance is not yet appreciated. This is just as well, since the most exciting and enjoyable element of the search for uniqueness is the search itself.

RENORMALONS AND PHENOMENOLOGY IN QCD*

Al H. Mueller

The use of the Borel representation as a means of adding non-perturbative corrections to perturbative calculations is discussed. Non-perturbative corrections to the electromagnetic current correlation function are analyzed. The position and strength of the leading renormalon singularities is determined and a precise definition of $< F_{\mu\nu}^2 >$ is given for QCD.

Before starting the technical part of my talk let me begin by saying that it is a pleasure and an honor to speak to an audience gathered in celebration of Geoff Chew's birthday and to acknowledge his important influence on my own career in theoretical physics. I was not a student of Geoff's, but I did learn physics in a milieu which reflected his philosophy. His *S-Matrix Theory of Strong Interactions* had recently been published which, along with papers of his and his collaborators, served as a vehicle for bringing many of us into the exciting developments of strong interaction physics. Geoff had convinced the physics community that the Lagrangian field theories of that day, using pions and nucleons as fundamental fields, were too *ad hoc* to be sensible approaches to strong interaction physics. His own approach of eliminating interacting fields altogether was philosophically exciting and led to an important understanding of resonances and of high energy scattering. As neophytes becoming involved in this wonderful adventure we learned to set high standards for ourselves and to make great demands on any fundamental theory of nature. For teaching us, for inspiring us and for setting an example of what a theoretical physicist should be, we thank you.

QCD is widely believed to be the correct theory of the strong interactions. As presently treated, QCD predictions are generally classified as perturbative (short distance) or non-perturbative (long distance).

At very high energies perhaps all energy and angular dependences are governed by perturbative QCD. Even such quantities as the total and elastic cross sections may be determined by perturbative calculations as inelastic events become dominated by semi-hard interactions.[1] However, more than a little modesty may be in order when one reflects on the fact that precise tests of perturbative QCD are virtually non-existent. Perturbative calculations always give a correct semi-quantitative description but are somewhat erratic when agreement between theory and experiment at the 15–25% level is required. A good example of the difficulties in obtaining precise quanti-

*This work is supported in part by the Department of Energy.

tative predictions is given by attempts to determine α from 3-jet data of PETRA and PEP. Uncertainties in procedures used in fragmenting quarks and gluons into hadrons lead to 50% uncertainties in α-values.[2]

Non-perturbative QCD is very exciting at the moment. The lattice formulation of the theory very likely gives a complete prescription for calculation. In addition, there has been a very successful phenomenology coming out of quark and bag models. On the other hand, lattice calculations are extremely difficult and the precision attainable is still quite uncertain.

In this talk I would like to discuss a procedure for separating perturbative and non-perturbative effects which may be useful in an intermediate energy region where non-perturbative corrections are competitive with perturbative terms. I shall consider only the current correlation function

$$\Pi_{\mu\nu}(q) = (\delta_{\mu\nu} Q^2 - q_\mu q_\nu) \Pi(Q) , \tag{1}$$

in Euclidean space. The discontinuity of Π, when continued into the Minkowski regime, is proportional to $\sigma_{e^+e^- \to \text{hadrons}}$. Let me also take an approximation where all fundamental quark masses, the current quark masses, are set to zero.

The natural means[3] to attempt a separation between perturbative and non-perturbative terms is through a Borel representation

$$\Pi(\alpha(Q)) = \int_0^\infty db \, e^{-b/\alpha(Q)} \, \tilde{\Pi}(b) , \tag{2}$$

where our notation is such that

$$\alpha(Q) = \frac{\alpha}{1 - \beta_2 \, \alpha \ln(Q/\mu)} , \tag{3}$$

in leading approximation. At the end of this talk I shall come back to the problem of the convergence of the b-integral at $b = \infty$,[4] but for the moment let us ignore this difficulty. The perturbatively defined $\tilde{\Pi}(b)$ has known singularities as shown in Fig. 1.

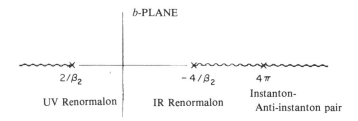

Fig. 1.

There are singularities on the negative real axis of the b-plane, ultraviolet renormalons,[4-6] which come about from high momentum regions of integration in Feynman diagrams. They are not of crucial interest since the Borel integral goes over the positive real axis and so does not encounter these singularities. On the positive real axis there are two types of singularities. Firstly, there are singularities at $b = 4\pi, 8\pi,...$ corresponding to instanton-anti-instanton pairs which show up in perturbation theory through divergences due to large numbers of graphs. However, for QCD, these singularities are far to the right of another type of singularity, the infrared renormalon,[3,4,6] which comes about from regions of soft momenta in Feynman graphs. Such singularities make the perturbatively defined $\Pi(\alpha)$ ambiguous.

In a moment I shall discuss the full Π, including non-perturbative contributions, but first let me indicate a very simple way to find the position and nature of the renormalons. In leading orders the running coupling has the form

$$\alpha(K/\mu, \alpha) = \frac{\alpha}{1 - \beta_2 \, \alpha \ln(K/\mu) + \ln \ln(K/\mu)} \; . \tag{4}$$

The Borel transformed running coupling

$$\tilde{\alpha}(K/\mu, b) = \frac{1}{2\pi i} \int_{a-i\infty}^{a+i\infty} \mathrm{d} \; 1/\alpha \; e^{b/\alpha} \; \alpha(K/\mu, \alpha) \; , \tag{5}$$

is given by[3,7,8]

$$\tilde{\alpha}(K/\mu, b) \sim (K/\mu)^{b\beta_2} \, (\ln \mu/K)^{b\beta_3/\beta_2} \; . \tag{6}$$

Remarkably, for $K/\mu \to 0$ and $b > 0$ or for $K/\mu \to \infty$ and $b < 0$, one can show, using the renormalization group equation, that the K/μ dependence given by (6) remains correct when higher order corrections are included, say in an $\overline{\text{MS}}$ renormalization scheme. When the running coupling given by (6) is inserted into the lowest order radiative corrections to $\Pi(Q)$ the renormalon singularities indicated in Fig. 1 result. Higher order radiative corrections modify the coefficient of the resulting branch point in b but not the position or nature of the singularity.

Infrared renormalons are thus always on the positive real axis. They make perturbative calculations ambiguous at the level of power corrections in Q. Let me simply define $\Pi_{PT}(\alpha)$ by means of a principal value prescription in the b-plane. This is a natural, but certainly not unique, extension of perturbation theory.

Now let us return to consider the exact $\Pi(Q/\mu, \alpha)$. The essential idea[7] is to separate low and high frequency components of the gluon field, A_μ, since it is precisely the low frequency components of A_μ which are not given properly by perturbation theory. The contributions to Π may be separated according to

$$\Pi(Q/\mu, \alpha) = \bar{\Pi}(Q/\mu, \Delta/\mu, \alpha) + \sum_{r=2}^{\infty} \int_\Delta d^4 k_1 \ldots d^4 k_r$$

$$\cdot \mathscr{S}_{\alpha_1 \ldots \alpha_r}(k_1, \ldots k_r) \bar{G}_{\alpha_1 \ldots \alpha_r}(k_1, \ldots k_r, \Delta, q) ,$$

(7)

as illustrated in Fig. 2. Shaded regions in Fig. 2 indicate that only hard gluons are included, $K > \Delta$, while open regions indicate that all gluon frequencies are to be taken. The integrations explicitly given in Eq. (7) have $K_i < \Delta$. $\mathscr{S}$ and $\bar{G}$ may be disconnected. Π does not involve low frequency

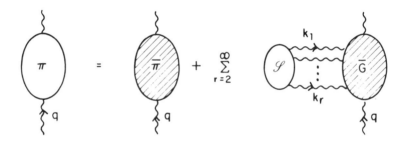

Fig. 2.

gluons and should not have infrared renormalons which are contained in $\mathscr{S}$. We may write an equation identical to Eq. (7), but for the perturbatively defined Π_{PT}. After subtracting the two equations we obtain

$$\Pi = \Pi_{PT} + [\mathscr{S} - \mathscr{S}_{PT}] \bar{G} ,$$

(8)

where integrations are suppressed for notational convenience. Since $\bar{G}$ does not involve low-frequency gluons perturbative factorization should apply. A careful examination of the factorization leads to

$$\Pi(\alpha(Q)) = \Pi_{PT}(\alpha(Q)) + f^2 \exp\left[\int_{\alpha(Q)}^{\alpha_0} d\alpha' \frac{4 + \gamma(\alpha')}{\beta(\alpha')}\right]$$

$$\cdot C(\alpha(Q)) + O(1/Q^6) ,$$

(9)

where

$$\langle F^2 \rangle = \lim_{x \to 0} \frac{1}{z(x^2)} \left\{ \langle T F_{\mu\nu}(x) F_{\mu\nu}(0) \rangle \right.$$

$$\left. - \langle T F_{\mu\nu}(x) F_{\mu\nu}(0) \rangle_{PT} \right\} , \quad (10)$$

and

$$\langle F^2 \rangle = f^2 \mu^4 \exp\left[\int_\alpha^{\alpha_0} d\alpha' \frac{\gamma(\alpha') + 4}{\beta(\alpha')} \right] , \quad (11)$$

as follows from the renormalization group. I believe that the $\langle F^2 \rangle$ given by Eq. (10) is well-defined, but dependent on the prescription used to give meaning to perturbative quantities, in our case a principal value in the Borel plane. The key to Eq. (10) is that the quartic divergence in x cancels as $x \to 0$ leaving only the logarithmic divergences which are then removed by $z(x^2)$ which may be taken from perturbation theory.

The second term on the right-hand side of Eq. (9) is non-analytic in the Borel-plane containing a factor θ $(b + 4/\beta_2)$. Up to the $1/Q^6$ level this is the term we define to be non-perturbative. Only one unknown parameter is involved.

Equations (9)–(11) are in agreement both with the procedure used by the ITEP group[9] and with the results of David[10] who first pointed out the necessity of carefully defining what is meant by perturbation theory before attempting to define non-perturbative condensates such as $\langle F^2 \rangle$.

Let us come back to a point which is potentially troublesome. I have been advocating the use of a Borel representation to separate perturbative and non-perturbative contributions. In particular simply knowing the position of the leading infrared renormalon should immediately tell one what the power decrease of non-perturbative corrections are compared to the leading perturbative terms. However, as discussed by 't Hooft,[4] the Borel representation given by Eq. (2) cannot converge at $b = \infty$. This is easily seen in the following way. As one continues Q from the Euclidean region to the Minkowski region there appear thresholds. Because $\Pi = \Pi(\alpha(Q))$ thresholds in Q must correspond to singularities of Π as a function of α. (One may choose a renormalization prescription, say $\overline{MS}$, such that $\alpha(Q)$ has no threshold singularities.) Thus, every threshold must correspond to a singularity of $\Pi(Q)$ which can be generated by the representation (2) only through exponential growths of $\Pi(b)$ corresponding to each threshold.

Do these exponential growths vitiate our hope that the Borel representation be useful at large Q? I think these divergences at $b = \infty$ probably cause no trouble for high energy applications. Consider Eq. (7). The knowledge of thresholds is completely contained in $\mathscr{S}$ since the high frequency parts of the theory should be given by perturbation theory. Now when one obtains (9) from (8) all knowledge of thresholds is lost as far as the Q-dependence is concerned. Thus, at the level of approximation that we are concerned with there are no threshold singularities in Q. One might worry that in continuing from the Euclidean to the Minkowski region this loss of thresholds will cause incorrect conclusions to be drawn in the Minkowski regime. That is, can one interchange the limit of large Q with the continuation from Euclidean to Minkowski momenta? I believe this interchange is all right because very high thresholds have extremely weak singularities. (It is very difficult to convert all the energy of a quark-antiquark pair into composite particles at rest, the configuration which gives the strength of the threshold singularity.)

At the moment the formalism discussed here could be directly applied to the total cross section for $e^+ + e^- \rightarrow$ hadrons. However, the non-perturbative terms turn out to be very small. Though satisfying in that perturbative QCD and experiment agree very well for this process, it does not allow a testing of our general scheme of adding non-perturbative corrections to perturbative calculations. More work remains in order to determine the nature and position of infrared renormalons for general Minkowski processes.

References

1. L. V. Gribov, E. M. Levin and M. G. Ryskin, *Phys. Reports* **100**, 1 (1983).

2. For a review see S. L. Wu, *Phys. Reports* **107**, 59 (1984).

3. G. Parisi, *Nucl. Phys.* **B150**, 163 (1979).

4. G. 't Hooft in *The Whys of Subnuclear Physics, Erice 1977*, ed. A. Zichichi (Plenum Press, New York, 1977).

5. B. Lautrup, *Phys. Lett.* **69B**, 109 (1977).

6. G. Parisi, *Phys. Lett.* **76B**, 65 (1978).

7. A. Mueller, Columbia Preprint CU-TP-289.

8. Y. Frishman and A. R. White, *Nucl. Phys.* **B158**, 221 (1974).

9. M. A. Shifman, A. I. Vainshtein and V. I. Zakharov, *Nucl. Phys.* **B147**, 385, 448, 519 (1979).

10. F. David, *Nucl. Phys.* **B234**, 237 (1984).

STOCHASTIC VARIABLES IN FOUR-DIMENSIONAL GAUGE THEORIES

G. Veneziano

In this contribution to Geoff Chew's Jubilee volume I will present some work done recently in collaboration with V. de Alfaro, S. Fubini and G. Furlan[1] in which certain four-dimensional gauge theories are shown to possess local "stochastic" variables. Solving these quantum field theories reduces to the classical problem of expressing the original field variables in terms of the stochastic ones and then using the fact that the latter, by definition of stochastic, interact through a trivial S matrix.

I like to entertain the idea that such a reformulation of a field theory does go in the direction long advocated by Geoff in his approach to particle physics.

1. Historical Background

A few years ago H. Nicolai[2] on the one hand and G. Parisi and N. Sourlas[3] on the other have pointed out a very amusing connection between two apparently distinct properties of a certain class of quantum theories.

In the work of Nicolai it is argued that, in supersymmetric theories,[4] the functional integral over the fermionic degrees of freedom (the so-called fermion determinant) cancels against the Jacobian of a (generally non-local) transformation from the original bosonic degrees of freedom to a new set of bosonic variables (Nicolai variables). In terms of the latter the action takes a simple Gaussian form.

Conversely, Parisi and Sourlas have shown that any Gaussian field theory hides some sort of supersymmetry although not always in the form of a *bona fide* (i.e. unitary and renormalizable) field theory.

The elegant results of these two groups have remained somewhat academic since the method could only be applied with success to the cases of one time (quantum mechanics) or one space one time dimensions.[3,5] In the case of physical interest (four-dimensional field theory) either the Nicolai transformation turned out to be non-local or, in the Parisi-Sourlas approach, the equivalent supersymmetric theory was unacceptable (e.g. non-unitary).

2.   Nicolai Map in Four Dimensions

For still mysterious reasons the generalization of the Nicolai-Parisi-Sourlas procedure to four dimensions seems to necessitate a gauge symmetry. This is, of course, welcome since Nature itself appears to have selected this kind of theory.

Quantization of non-Abelian gauge theories is by now well understood. Gauge invariant observables O are given by a functional integral of the form:

$$\langle O \rangle = \int d\,[A]\, \exp(-I(A))\, O(A) \bigg/ \int d\,[A]\, \exp(-I(A)) \,,$$

where $I(A)$ is the gauge invariant Yang-Mills action:

$$I(A) = \frac{1}{4} \int d^4 x\, F^a_{\mu\nu}\, F^a_{\mu\nu} \,,$$

with

$$F^a_{\mu\nu} = \partial_\mu A^a_\nu - \partial_\nu A^a_\mu + g\, C_{abc}\, A^b_\mu\, A^c_\nu \,.$$

In order for the functional integration to be finite and gauge invariant the functional integration measure $d[A]$ is to be defined $a\ la$ Faddeev-Popov, i.e. as

$$d\,[A] = \prod_{\mu=1}^{4} \prod_a d\,A^a_\mu\, \delta(\chi^a)\, \Delta_\chi \,,$$

where Δ_χ is the Faddeev-Popov determinant which depends on the gauge fixing function $\chi^a = \chi^a\,(A_\mu)$. It has the form:

$$\Delta_\chi = \det\left(\frac{\partial \chi^a}{\partial \Omega^b} \right) \,,$$

where $\Omega^b\,(x)$ is the infinitesimal gauge transformation parameter.

The problem of finding stochastic variables is that of defining, in a given gauge, three more field variables N^a_i such that:

(i)   the action $I(A)$ becomes Gaussian in the N^a_i

$$I(A) \sim \sum_{i=1}^{3} \int d^4 x\, N^a_i\, N^a_i \,,$$

(ii) the functional measure becomes trivially

$$d[N, \chi] = \prod_{i=1}^{3} d N_i^a \, d\chi^a \, \delta(\chi^a) .$$

If (i) and (ii) can be fulfilled, the correlation functions of the N_i^a variables do become those of a free theory, i.e. δ-functions. In order to solve the theory it is then sufficient to express the A_μ^a variables in terms of the variables N_i^a, χ^a.

It has been known for some time[6] that a set of variables satisfying (i), up to surface terms, is given by:

$$N_i^a = f_i^a = F_{0i}^a + \frac{1}{2} \epsilon_{ijk} F_{jk}^a .$$

One is thus led to study the Jacobian of the transformation from $d[A_\mu]$ to $d[f_i]d[\chi]$.

To this purpose, it is convenient to work in the basis given by:

$$f_\pm = f_1 \pm i f_2 ; \qquad A_\pm = A_1 \pm i A_2 , \qquad A_{R,L} = A_0 \pm A_3 ,$$

in terms of which one has

$$
\begin{vmatrix} df_+ \\\\ 2df_3 \\\\ df_- \\\\ d\chi \end{vmatrix}
=
\begin{vmatrix}
-D_L & D_+ & 0 & 0 \\\\
D_- & D_R & -D_L & -D_+ \\\\
0 & 0 & -D_- & D_R \\\\
\dfrac{\partial \chi}{\partial A_+} & \dfrac{\partial \chi}{\partial A_L} & \dfrac{\partial \chi}{\partial A_R} & \dfrac{\partial \chi}{\partial A_-}
\end{vmatrix}
\begin{vmatrix} dA_+ \\\\ dA_L \\\\ dA_R \\\\ dA_- \end{vmatrix} ,
$$

where D_μ represents the covariant derivative in the adjoint representation.

It is amusing to watch what happens if we take $\partial\chi/\partial A$ to have just one non-zero entry in this basis. Take for instance $\chi = \chi(A_L)$. Clearly

$$\det\left(\frac{\partial^3 f \, \partial\chi}{\partial^4 A}\right) = \det\left(\frac{\partial\chi}{\partial A_L}\right) \det(-D_L) \det \not{D}_{adj} ,$$

where $\not{D} = D_\mu \sigma_\mu$ and $\sigma_\mu = (1, \sigma_{Pauli})$. The first two terms give the Faddeev-Popov determinant:

$$\det\left(\frac{\partial\chi}{\partial A_L}\right) \det(+D_L) = \det \frac{\partial\chi}{\partial\Omega} = \Delta_\chi ,$$

so that the original volume becomes $(\chi = \chi(A_L)$ or $\chi(A_+)...)$

$$d[A] = d^3 f_i \, d\chi \, \det^{-1} \frac{\partial^3 f_i \, d\chi}{\partial^4 A} \, \delta(\chi) \Delta_\chi$$

$$= \frac{d^3 f_i \, d\chi \, \delta(\chi)}{\det \slashed{D}_{adj}} \quad .$$

This is our basic result. The quantum theory has become Gaussian in the f_i variables except for the $(\det \slashed{D})^{-1}$ factor in the functional measure.

Is there a way to compensate for this extra factor? The answer is clearly yes. It is enough to add to the theory a set of Majorana fermions $\lambda_\alpha^a (\alpha = 1,2)$ in the adjoint representation. Their contribution to the action is $\bar\lambda \, \slashed{D}_{adj}\lambda$ which, by functional integration over $\lambda, \bar\lambda$ gives precisely the desired factor.

On the other hand adding λ to the ordinary Yang-Mills theory is known[4] to yield its supersymmetric extension. The fact that a supersymmetry has emerged is hardly surprising in view of the general Parisi-Sourlas arguments.

Furthermore we have seen that the theory is stochastic in gauges of a (generalized) light-cone type of which the simplest example is the usual $(A_L = 0)$ gauge. The problem of extending this result to other gauges and of finding possible deviations from a Gaussian action is presently the subject of investigation by several groups.[7,8] A clear-cut answer is still not available.

The possible special role of the light-cone gauge can also be seen by trying to derive directly the trival correlations of the f_i variables in the super Yang-Mills theory. Indeed the f's are supersymmetric variations δ_s of the λ's. Naively one would then expect that

$$\langle f(x)f(y)\rangle = \langle \delta_s\lambda(x)f(y)\rangle \overset{?}{=} -\langle\lambda(x)\delta_s f(y)\rangle \quad .$$

If the above equation is correct one can proceed further and observe that

$$\delta_s f(y) = \frac{\delta I}{\delta \lambda(y)} \quad ,$$

i.e. that $\delta_s f$ is the equation of motion for $\bar\lambda$. From this it would immediately follow that the $<f\text{-}f>$ correlation is a δ-function.

The trouble with the previous argument is that the gauge fixing condition does break supersymmetry in general and one is not allowed to use the corresponding Ward identities. In a generic $\chi = 0$ gauge, since $\delta_s\chi \neq 0$ for any non-trivial δ_s, supersymmetry is completely broken.

It has been known[9] for some time, however, that in the light-cone gauge a non-trivial subset of supersymmetry transformations is preserved. This

"half supersymmetry" was exploited in Ref. 1 in order to offer an alternative derivation of the results obtained by the direct Nicolai method.

In concluding we should also recall that this unique gauge[10] has other virtues, especially in connection with the ultraviolet behaviour of its Feynman diagrams.[9] It would be nice, of course, to see whether this further property of the light-cone gauge could allow one to go further into the analysis of the non-perturbative properties of the $N = 1$ super Yang-Mills theory for which a number of results have been already obtained.[11]

It is a pleasure to thank D. Amati and S. Fubini for discussions on the material presented here.

References

1. V. de Alfaro, S. Fubini, G. Furlan and G. Veneziano, *Phys. Lett.* **142B**, 399 (1984); CERN preprint – TH.4021/84.

2. H. Nicolai, *Phys. Lett.* **89B**, 341 (1980); *Nucl. Phys.* **B176**, 419 (1980).

3. G. Parisi and N. Sourlas, *Phys. Rev. Lett.* **43**, 244 (1979); *Nucl. Phys.* **B206**, 321 (1983).

4. For a review see for instance P. Fayet and S. Ferrara, *Phys. Reports* **5**, 249 (1977).

5. S. Cecotti and L. Girardello, *Ann. Phys.* (N.Y.) **145**, 81 (1983).

6. See for instance H. Nicolai, *Phys. Lett.* **117B**, 408 (1982).

7. O. Lechtenfeld, Bonn preprint HE-84-9 (1984); K. Dietz and O. Lechtenfeld, Bonn preprint HE-84-26 (1984); M. Claudson and M. B. Halpern, Berkeley preprint LBL-18355 (1984).

8. D. Amati, S. Fubini and G. Veneziano, in progress; G. C. Rossi, private communication; A. Bassetto and R. Soldati, private communication; R. Floreanini and G. Furlan, private communication.

9. S. Mandelstam, *Nucl. Phys.* **B213**, 149 (1983); L. Brink, O. Lindgren and B. Nilsson, *Phys. Lett.* **123B**, 323 (1983).

10. W. Kummer, *Acta Physica Austr.* **41**, 315 (1975). For some recent developments, see G. Leibbrandt and S. L. Nyeo, *Phys. Lett.* **140B**, 417 (1984); D. M. Capper, J. J. Dulwich and M. J. Litvak, *Nucl. Phys.* **B241**, 463 (1984); A. Bassetto, M. Dalbosco, I. Lazzizzera and R. Soldati, University of Trento preprint UTF 110 (1984).

11. E. Witten, *Nucl. Phys.* **B188**, 513 (1981); **B202**, 253 (1982); G. Veneziano and S. Yankielowicz, *Phys. Lett.* **113B**, 321 (1982); V. A. Novikov, M. A. Shifman, A. I. Vainshtein and V. I. Zakharov, *Nucl. Phys.* **B229**, 407 (1983); E. Cohen and C. Gomez, *Phys. Rev. Lett.* **52**, 237 (1984).

COMMENTS ON HEAVY QUARK DECAYS AND CP VIOLATION

Ling-Lie Chau

Because of the severe suppression of quark mixing with the third generation, implied from the recent b-decay measurements, the two-by-two quark-mixing matrix of the first and second generations becomes essentially unitary. In the limit of SU(3) symmetry, this result implies that in the charm meson decays, the number of contributing weak-decay quark amplitudes has been reduced from six to four. Many relations among different charm meson decays can be obtained, and serve as a basis for studying SU(3) breaking and final-state interactions.

For short-lived heavy neutral meson decays, like D^0, $\bar{D}^0$, B^0, $\bar{B}^0$, the usual methods of measuring CP violation by isolating K_L and regenerating K_S cannot be easily done. It is pointed out that it is possible to do time-integrated experiments to separately measure the mass-matrix CP-violating parameters, such as $2\,\mathrm{Re}\ \bar{\epsilon}/(1+|\bar{\epsilon}|^2)$, and the decay amplitude CP violating quantities, such as $|A|^2 - |\bar{A}|^2/(|A|^2 + |\bar{A}|^2)$, without isolating states like K_L, K_S. Feasible experiments are pointed out in e^+e^- and $\bar{p}p$ reactions.

1. Heavy Quark Decays

It has been established[1,2] that all weak decays of meson states can be classified according to six quark diagrams (see Figs. 1.1 and 1.2), the external W-emission diagram a, the internal W-emission diagram b, the W-exchange diagram c, the W-annihilation diagram d, the horizontal W-loop diagram e, and the vertical W-loop diagram f. This classification is independent of the strong interaction schemes, and can incorporate any specific strong-interaction model calculations. Thus all the strange, charm, beauty and truth particle decays can be expressed in terms of these six types of quark diagrams and the quark mixing matrix. Tables in the literature list amplitudes for the decays of a pseudoscalar meson to two pseudoscalar mesons[1,2] ($P_0 \rightarrow P_1 P_2$), and to one pseudoscalar meson and one vector meson[3] ($P_0 \rightarrow P_1 V_1$), in the limit of SU(3) symmetry and no final-state interaction. Such a general classification provides a useful framework in which to do model calculations and to seek out ways to test results. For example, for F^+ decay, the quark-diagram classification gives[2]

$$A(F^+ \rightarrow \eta_8 \pi^+)/A(F^+ \rightarrow \eta_0 \pi^+) = -\sqrt{2}\,(a-d)/(a+2d)\ , \quad (1.1a)$$

$$A(D^0 \rightarrow \bar{K}^0 \eta_8)/A(D^0 \rightarrow \bar{K}^0 \eta_0) = (1/\sqrt{2})\,(b-c)/(b+2c)\ . \quad (1.1b)$$

From perturbative QCD calculations, the amplitudes c and d are small compared with amplitude a. The quark-diagram classification suggests that the

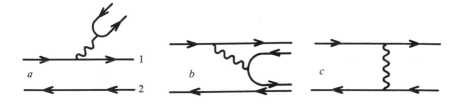

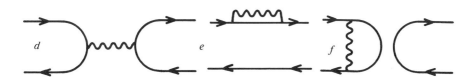

Fig. 1.1 The six quark diagrams for inclusive meson decay.

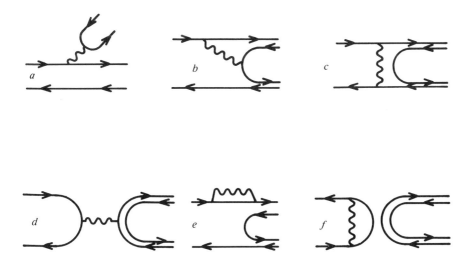

Fig. 1.2 The six quark diagrams for a meson decaying to two mesons.

measurement of the ratio as shown in Eqs. (1.1a,b) can provide a sensitive test of such a model. Another use of such a classification, complementary to model calculations, is to determine these amplitudes and the quark-mixing matrix by comparing them with experiments. This was difficult to achieve for the strange particle decays, due to the small number of channels available. However with the numerous channels available in the charm and beauty decays, such a systematic study can be possible, e.g., there are nearly twenty channels in the $P_0 \rightarrow P_1 P_2$ decays of D^0, D^+, D^-, F^+ (not including the mixing-matrix doubly suppressed ones). First, one should see if such a classification, in the limit of SU(3) and ignoring final-state interactions, can fit experimental results. For example, the ratio given by the general classification,

$$|A(D^0 \rightarrow \bar{K}^0 \pi^0)/A(D^0 \rightarrow \bar{K}^0 \eta_8)|^2 = 3 , \quad \text{and} \tag{1.2a}$$

$$A(F^+ \rightarrow \pi^+ \pi^0) = 0 , \tag{1.2b}$$

are good to test SU(3) and final-state interactions. The ratio

$$|A(D^+ \rightarrow \pi^0 \pi^+)/A(D^+ \rightarrow \bar{K}^0 \pi^+)|^2 = (1/2)|V_{cs}/V_{cd}|^2 , \tag{1.3}$$

can be used to determine $|V_{cs}/V_{cd}|^2$, since $\pi^0 \pi^+$, $\bar{K}^0 \pi^+$ are both exotic and thus free of final-state interactions. If this does not work, one learns about SU(3) breaking and final-state interactions. Step-by-step one can learn the mixing matrix and the dynamics for the amplitudes, i.e. the quark-diagram classification serves as a basis for dynamical calculations, and for incorporating SU(3) breaking and final-state interaction effects.

Recently our knowledge of the quark-mixing matrix[4] has dramatically improved owing to the b-lifetime measurement[5,6] and the branching ratio bound $\Gamma(b \rightarrow u)/\Gamma(b \rightarrow c) < 0.05$ from the $b \rightarrow \ell^- X$ measurements,[7] which indicated that X is mainly made out of states with charm. At present the errors on the b-lifetime are still rather large. Here we use $\tau_b = 10^{-12}$ sec as an example. In the following, we list all the mixing-matrix elements that have so far been determined directly from experiment:

$$|V_{ud}| = 0.9737 , \quad \text{from nuclear } \beta \text{ decays;}[8]$$

$$|V_{us}| = 0.228 , \quad \text{from strange particle decays;}[8]$$

$$|V_{cb}| = 0.059 , \quad \text{from } \tau_b = 10^{-12} \text{ sec;}[6,9]$$

$$|V_{ub}| \lesssim 0.0082 , \quad \text{from } \Gamma(b \rightarrow u)/\Gamma(b \rightarrow c) < 0.05.[7-9] \tag{1.4}$$

Following the convention that these matrix elements are positive, using unitarity from Eq. (1.4) we obtain the following full quark-mixing matrix (ignoring the imaginary part for the time being)

$$
V = \begin{array}{ccc} d & s & b \\ \end{array}
$$

$$
V = \begin{pmatrix} 0.9737 & 0.228 & \lesssim 0.0082 \\ -0.23 & 0.98 & 0.059 \\ 0.01 & -0.06 & 1 \pm 0(10^{-2}) \end{pmatrix} \begin{array}{c} u \\ c \\ t \end{array} .
$$

$$(1.5a)$$

The matrix elements obtained from unitarity, not directly from experimental measurements, are underscored with dashed lines. It is still important to compare these numbers directly with the results of future experiments.

To include the phase in the matrix, we can adapt the convention of Ref. (9) in which the imaginary parts of the matrix elements appear only to the order of 10^{-3}:

$$
V = \begin{array}{ccc} d & s & b \\ \end{array}
$$

$$
V = \begin{pmatrix} 0.9737 & 0.228 & V_{ub} \lesssim 0.0082\, e^{i\phi} \\ -0.23-0.059\, V_{ub} & 0.98 & 0.059 \\ 0.01-V_{ub} & -0.06+0.228\, V_{ub} & 1 \pm 0(10^{-2}) \end{pmatrix} \begin{array}{c} u \\ c \\ t \end{array} .
$$

$$(1.5b)$$

Note that V_{ub} cannot be zero in order to explain CP violation from the phase ϕ, as defined in Ref. 9. Actually one can show that in order to give CP violation none of the off-diagonal element can be zero, i.e., the vanishing of any single off-diagonal element can lead to a null CP-violating effect. This one can check from all three known parameterizations, Refs. 4 and 9. Therefore the analysis of CP violation can give an estimate of the lower bound on V_{ub}.

It is interesting to note that owing to the severe suppression of the off-diagonal element in the third column and row, the upper left two-by-two matrix is almost unitary, i.e.,

$$
V_{cd}/V_{cs} = -V_{us}/V_{ud} \approx -s_1/c_1 . \tag{1.6}
$$

With such a well-determined mixing matrix, the unknown quantities remaining in the classification for all meson decays are the six amplitudes. An interesting result of this is the prediction from Eq. (1.3):

$$|A(D^+ \to \pi^0\pi^+)/A(D^+ \to \bar{K}^0\pi^+)|^2 = (1/2)(s_1/c_1)^2 = 0.028 .\qquad (1.7)$$

It is very important to measure this quantity.

Equation (1.6) has another very striking implication for the charm meson decays, i.e., in the SU(3) limit, the W-loop diagram contributions are negligible owing to the cancellation between the strange and the down quark contributions in the loop, and the b-quark contribution was small to begin with. This means that in the tables for charm meson decays, we can drop all the e and f amplitudes.[11] So for all the charm meson decays, there are only four unknown amplitudes a, b, c, d. The inclusive and the exclusive $P_0 \to P_1P_2$ and $P_0 \to P_1V_1$ decays for D^0, D^+, F^+ are now listed in Tables I, II, and III.

Table I. Inclusive Charm Meson Decays in the Limit
of $V_{us}V_{cs}^* \approx -V_{ud}V_{cd}^* = s_1c_1 = 0.22$

$$
\begin{aligned}
D^0 &\to \text{hadrons} \quad (c_1)^2(a+b+c)\\
D^+ &\to \text{hadrons} \quad (c_1)^2(a+b) + s_1c_1(d)\\
F^+ &\to \text{hadrons} \quad (c_1)^2(a+b+d)
\end{aligned}
$$

Table II. Charm Meson Decays into Two Pseudo Scalars in the
Limit of $V_{us}V_{cs}^* \approx -V_{ud}V_{cd}^* = s_1c_2 = 0.22$

II. a. D^0 decays

K^-	π^+		$(c_1)^2$	$(a+c)$
$\bar{K}^0$	π^0	$(1/\sqrt{2})$	$(c_1)^2$	$(b-c)$
$\bar{K}^0$	η_8	$(1/\sqrt{6})$	$(c_1)^2$	$(b-c)$
$\bar{K}^0$	η_0	$(1/\sqrt{3})$	$(c_1)^2$	$(b+2c)$
K^-	K^+		s_1c_1	$(a+c)$
π^+	π^-		$-s_1c_1$	$(a+c)$
K^0	$\bar{K}^0$		0	
π^0	π^0	$\{\sqrt{2}\}\cdot(1/2)$	s_1c_1	$(b-c)$
η_8	η_8	$\{\sqrt{2}\}\cdot(-1/2)$	s_1c_1	$(b-c)$
π^0	η_8	$(-1/\sqrt{3})$	s_1c_1	$(b-c)$
π^0	η_0	$(-1/\sqrt{2})$	s_1c_1	$(b+2c)$
η_8	η_0	$(-1/\sqrt{2})$	s_1c_1	$(b+2c)$
η_0	η_0		0	
K^+	π^-		$-(s_1)^2$	$(a+c)$
K^0	π^0	$(-1/\sqrt{2})$	$(s_1)^2$	$(b-c)$
K^0	η_8	$(-1/\sqrt{6})$	$(s_1)^2$	$(b-c)$
K^0	η_0	$(-1/\sqrt{3})$	$(s_1)^2$	$(b+2c)$

II. b. D^+ decays

$\bar{K}^0$	π^+		$(c_1)^2$	$(a+b)$
$\bar{K}^0$	K^+		s_1c_1	$(a-d)$
π^0	π^+	$(1/\sqrt{2})$	s_1c_1	$(a+b)$
η_8	π^+	$(-1/\sqrt{6})$	s_1c_1	$[(a+b)+2(b+d)]$
η_0	π^+	$(-1/\sqrt{3})$	s_1c_1	$(a+2d)$
K^0	π^+		$-(s_1)^2$	$(b+d)$
K^+	π^0	$(1/\sqrt{2})$	$(s_1)^2$	$(a-d)$
K^+	η_8	$(-1/\sqrt{6})$	$(s_1)^2$	$(a-d)$
K^+	η_0	$(-1/\sqrt{3})$	$(s_1)^2$	$(a+2d)$

II. c. F^+ decays

$\bar{K}^0$	K^+		$(c_1)^2$	$(b+d)$
π^0	π^+		0	
η_8	π^+	$(-\sqrt{2}/\sqrt{3})$	$(c_1)^2$	$(a-d)$
η_0	π^+	$(1/\sqrt{3})$	$(c_1)^2$	$(a+2d)$
K^0	π^+		$-s_1c_1$	$(a-d)$
K^+	π^0	$(-1/\sqrt{2})$	s_1c_1	$(b+d)$
K^+	η_8	$(-1/\sqrt{6})$	s_1c_1	$[2(a+b)+b+d]$
K^+	η_0	$(1/\sqrt{3})$	s_1c_1	$(a+2d)$
K^0	K^+		$-(s_1)^2$	$(a+b)$

Table III.   Charm Meson Decays into Vector and Pseudo-Scalar Bosons in the Limit of $V_{us}V_{cs}^* \approx -V_{ud}V_{cd}^* = s_1c_1 = 0.22$

III. a. D^0 decays

ρ^+	K^-		$(c_1)^2$	$(a'+c)$
K^{*0}	π^0	$(1/\sqrt{2})$	$(c_1)^2$	$(b'-c)$
K^{*-}	π^+		$(c_1)^2$	$(a+c')$
ρ^0	$\bar{K}^0$	$(1/\sqrt{2})$	$(c_1)^2$	$(b-c)$
K^{0*}	η_8	$(1/\sqrt{6})$	$(c_1)^2$	$(b'+c'-2c)$
ϕ	$\bar{K}^0$		$(c_1)^2$	(c')
ω	$\bar{K}^0$	$(1/\sqrt{2})$	$(c_1)^2$	$(b+c)$
$\bar{K}^{*0}$	η_0	$(1/\sqrt{3})$	$(c_1)^2$	$(b'+c'+c)$
K^{*-}	K^+		s_1c_1	$(a+c')$
K^{*+}	K^-		s_1c_1	$(a'+c)$
ρ^-	π^+		$-s_1c_1$	$(a+c')$
ρ^+	π^-		$-s_1c_1$	$(a'+c)$
$\bar{K}^{*0}$	K^0		s_1c_1	$(c'-c)$
K^{*0}	$\bar{K}^0$		s_1c_1	$(c-c')$
ρ^0	π^0	$(+1/\sqrt{2})$	s_1c_1	$(b+b'-c-c*)$
ρ^0	η_8	$(\sqrt{3}/\sqrt{6})$	s_1c_1	$(-3b+b'+c+c')$
ρ^0	η_0	$(1/\sqrt{6})$	s_1c_1	$(b'+c'+c)$
ω	π^0	$(1/2)$	s_1c_1	$(b-b'+c+c')$
ω	η_8	$(1/\sqrt{12})$	s_1c_1	$(-3b-b'-c-c')$
ϕ	π^0	$(1/\sqrt{2})$	s_1c_1	(b')
ϕ	η_8	$(1/\sqrt{6})$	s_1c_1	$(b'-2c-2c')$
ϕ	η_0	$(1/\sqrt{3})$	s_1c_1	$(b'+c+c')$
ω	η_0	$(-1/\sqrt{6})$	s_1c_1	$(b+c+c')$
ρ^-	K^+		$(s_1)^2$	$(a+c')$
ρ^0	K^0	$(1/\sqrt{2})$	$(s_1)^2$	$(b-c')$
K^{*+}	π^-		$(s_1)^2$	$(a'+c)$
K^{*0}	π^0	$(1/\sqrt{2})$	$(s_1)^2$	$(b'-c)$
ω	K^0	$(1/\sqrt{2})$	$(s_1)^2$	$(b+c')$
ϕ	K^0		$(s_1)^2$	(c)
K^{*0}	η_8	$(1/\sqrt{6})$	$(s_1)^2$	$(b'+c-2c')$
K^{*0}	η_0	$(1/\sqrt{3})$	$(s_1)^2$	$(b'+c+c')$

III. b. D^+ decays

K^{*0}	π^+		$(c_1)^2$	$(a+b')$
ρ^+	$\bar{K}^0$		$(c_1)^2$	$(a'+b)$
ρ^0	π^+	$(1/\sqrt{2})$	s_1c_1	$(a+b'+d-d')$
ρ^+	π^0	$(1/\sqrt{2})$	s_1c_1	$(a'+b-d+d')$
K^{*+}	$\bar{K}^0$		s_1c_1	$(a'-d')$
K^{*0}	K^+		s_1c_1	$(a-d)$
ω	π^+	$(-1/\sqrt{2})$	s_1c_1	$(a+b'+d+d')$
ρ^+	η_8	$(-1/\sqrt{6})$	s_1c_1	$(a'+3b+d+d')$
ρ^+	η_0	$(-1/\sqrt{3})$	s_1c_1	$(a'+d+d')$
ρ^+	K^0		$(s_1)^2$	$(b+d')$
ρ^0	K^+	$(1/\sqrt{2})$	$(s_1)^2$	$(d'-a)$
K^{*+}	π^0	$(1/\sqrt{2})$	$(s_1)^2$	$(d-a')$
K^{*0}	π^+		$(s_1)^2$	$(b'+d)$
ω	K^+	$(1/\sqrt{2})$	$(s_1)^2$	$(a+d')$
ϕ	K^+		$(s_1)^2$	(d)
K^{*+}	η_8	$(1/\sqrt{6})$	$(s_1)^2$	$(a'+d-2d')$
K^{*+}	η_0	$(1/\sqrt{3})$	$(s_1)^2$	$(a'+d+d')$

III. c. F^+ decays

ρ^+	π^0	$(1/\sqrt{2})$	$(c_1)^2$	$(d-d')$
ρ^0	π^+	$(1/\sqrt{2})$	$(c_1)^2$	$(d-d')$
K^{*+}	$\bar{K}^0$		$(c_1)^2$	$(b+d')$
K^{*0}	K^+		$(c_1)^2$	$(b'+d)$
ρ^+	η_8	$(1/\sqrt{6})$	$(c_1)^2$	$(-2a'+d+d')$
ϕ	π^+		$(c_1)^2$	(a)
ω	π^+	$(1/\sqrt{2})$	$(c_1)^2$	$(d+d')$
ρ^+	η_8	$(1/\sqrt{3})$	$(c_1)^2$	$(a'+d+d')$
ρ^+	K^0		s_1c_1	$(-a'+d')$
K^{*0}	π^+		s_1c_1	$(-a+d)$
ρ^0	K^+	$(1/\sqrt{2})$	s_1c_1	$(b'+d')$
K^{*+}	π^0	$(1/\sqrt{2})$	s_1c_1	$(b+d)$
K^{*+}	η_8	$(1/\sqrt{6})$	s_1c_1	$(-2a'+3b+d-2d')$
ω	K^+	$(1/\sqrt{2})$	s_1c_1	$(-b'+d')$
ϕ	K^+		s_1c_1	$(a+b'+d)$
K^{*+}	η_0	$(1/\sqrt{3})$	s_1c_1	$(a'+d+d')$
K^{*+}	K^0		$(s_1)^2$	$(a'+b)$
K^{*0}	K^+		$(s_1)^2$	$(a+b')$

From Table IIa we see that all the decays of D^0 to two pseudoscalars are given by three independent quark-diagram combinations, $(a+c)$, $(b-c)$, and $(b+2c)$; and many relations among decay amplitudes follow:

$$(a+c) = \frac{1}{(c_1)^2} A(D^0 \to K^- \pi^+) ,$$

$$= \frac{1}{s_1 c_1} A(D^0 \to K^- K^+) = \frac{-1}{s_1 c_1} A(D^0 \to \pi^+ \pi^-) ,$$

$$= \frac{-1}{s_1^2} A(D^0 \to K^+ \pi^-) ; \qquad (1.8)$$

$$(b-c) = \frac{\sqrt{2}}{(c_1)^2} A(D^0 \to \bar{K}^0 \pi^0) = \frac{\sqrt{6}}{(c_1)^2} A(D^0 \to \bar{K}^0 \eta_8) ,$$

$$= \frac{\sqrt{2}}{s_1 c_1} A(D^0 \to \pi^0 \pi^0) = \frac{-\sqrt{2}}{s_1 c_1} A(D^0 \to \eta_8 \eta_8)$$

$$= \frac{-\sqrt{3}}{s_1 c_1} A(D^0 \to \pi^0 \eta_8) ,$$

$$= \frac{\sqrt{2}}{(s_1)^2} A(D^0 \to K^0 \pi^0) = \frac{-\sqrt{6}}{(s_1)^2} A(D^0 \to K^0 \eta_8) ; \qquad (1.9)$$

$$(b+2c) = \frac{\sqrt{3}}{(c_1)^2} A(D^0 \to \bar{K}^0 \eta_0) ,$$

$$= \frac{-\sqrt{2}}{s_1 c_1} A(D^0 \to \pi^0 \eta_0) = \frac{-\sqrt{2}}{s_1 c_1} A(D^0 \to \eta_8 \eta_0) ,$$

$$= \frac{-\sqrt{3}}{(s_1)^2} A(D^0 \to K^0 \eta_0) . \qquad (1.10)$$

Note that $A(D^0 \to K^0 \bar{K}^0) = 0$ or not, will be an important test of such a scheme from the cancellation between the loop amplitudes involving the strange quark and involving the down quark, since

$$A(D^0 \to K^0 \bar{K}^0) = s_1 c_1 [(c+2f)_s - (c+2f)_d] . \qquad (1.11)$$

From Table IIb, and c we see that all the decays of D^+, F^+ to two pseudoscalars are given by four quark-diagram combinations, i.e., $(a+b)$, $(a-d)$, $(a+2d)$, and $(b+d)$; and many relations among amplitudes follow:

$$(a+b) = \frac{1}{(c_1)^2} A(D^+ \to \bar{K}^0 \pi^+) ,$$

$$= \frac{\sqrt{2}}{s_1 c_1} A(D^+ \to \pi^0 \pi^+) ,$$

$$= -\frac{1}{(s_1)^2} A(F^+ \to K^0 K^+) ; \qquad (1.12)$$

$$(a-d) = \frac{1}{s_1 c_1} A(D^+ \to \bar{K}^0 K^+) ,$$

$$= \frac{\sqrt{2}}{(s_1)^2} A(D^+ \to K^+ \pi^0) = \frac{-\sqrt{6}}{(s_1)^2} A(D^+ \to K^+ \eta_8) ,$$

$$= \frac{-\sqrt{3}/\sqrt{2}}{(c_1)^2} A(F^+ \to \eta_8 \pi^+) ,$$

$$= \frac{-1}{s_1 c_1} A(F^+ \to K^0 \pi^+) ; \qquad (1.13)$$

$$(a+2d) = \frac{-\sqrt{3}}{s_1 c_1} A(D^+ \to \eta_0 \pi^+) ,$$

$$= \frac{-\sqrt{3}}{(s_1)^2} A(D^+ \to K^+ \eta_0) ,$$

$$= \frac{\sqrt{3}}{(c_1)^2} A(F^+ \to \eta_0 \pi^+) ,$$

$$= \frac{\sqrt{3}}{s_1 c_1} A(F^+ \to K^+ \eta_0) ; \qquad (1.14)$$

$$(b+d) = \frac{-1}{(s_1)^2} A(D^+ \rightarrow K^0 \pi^+) \; ,$$

$$= \frac{1}{(c_1)^2} A(F^+ \rightarrow \bar{K}^0 K^+) \; ,$$

$$= \frac{-\sqrt{2}}{s_1 c_1} A(F^+ \rightarrow K^+ \pi^0) \; ; \tag{1.15}$$

$$[a+b+2(b+d)] = \frac{-\sqrt{6}}{s_1 c_1} A(D^+ \rightarrow \eta_8 \pi^+) \; ; \tag{1.16}$$

$$[2(a+b)+b+d] = \frac{-\sqrt{6}}{s_1 c_1} A(F^+ \rightarrow K^+ \eta_8) \; . \tag{1.17}$$

Note that all these relations are independent of any dynamical model. The only assumptions used are the SU(3) symmetry and the absence of final-state interactions. It will be very interesting to analyze these relations with respect to experimental results. Much can be learned about SU(3) breaking and final-state interactions.[12]

From perturbative QCD calculations, the amplitudes c and d are negligible. Comparisons of reactions in Eqs. (1.9) and (1.10), and comparisons of reactions in Eqs. (1.13) and (1.14) can test in a model independent way the importance of amplitudes c and d, respectively.

We now discuss the implications of the recent charm decay data from the Mark III experiment:[13]

$$\frac{\Gamma(D^0 \rightarrow K^- K^+)}{\Gamma(D^0 \rightarrow \pi^+ \pi^-)} = \frac{(12.5 \pm 1.8 \pm 1.0)}{(3.8 \pm 1.0 \pm 0.5)} \; . \tag{1.18}$$

We see that this is not consistent with Eq. (1.8). Thus the breaking of SU(3) and final-state interaction effects must be important. It can come from large SU(3) breaking of the form of Eq. (1.11), besides the effect due to $f_K / f_\pi = 1.26 \, M_\pi / 0.94 \, M_\pi$, since the same term is contributing with opposite sign with respect to $(a+c)$, i.e.,

$$A(D^0 \rightarrow K^+ K^-) = s_1 c_1 [(a+c) + (e+2f)_s - (e+2f)_d] \; , \tag{1.19a}$$

$$A(D^0 \rightarrow \pi^+ \pi^-) = s_1 c_1 [-(a+c) + (e+2f)_s - (e+2f)_d] \; . \tag{1.19b}$$

A possible source of final-state interaction effects is the following: in the c amplitude for $D^0 \to K^- K^+$, the intermediate states are $s\bar{s}$, while for $D^0 \to \pi^- \pi^+$ the intermediate states are $d\bar{d}$. These two intermediate states may have very different behavior of final-state interactions.

Another interesting ratio is

$$\Gamma(D^+ \to \bar{K}^0 K^+) / \Gamma(D^+ \to \bar{K}^0 \pi^+) = (29.4 \pm 7.4 \pm 5.1)\% ,$$

$$= (s_1/c_1)^2 \, |(a-d)/(a+b)|^2$$

$$= 0.055 \, |(a-d)/(a+b)|^2 ,$$

$$(1.20)$$

which can be taken as an indication that amplitude d is important so that $|a-d| \gg |a+b|$. Similar discussions can be made for a charm meson decaying into a vector meson plus a pseudoscalar meson. (Note that only amplitudes of the same letter in the same Table I, II, or III are of the same value.)

Whether the amplitudes c and d are important or not compared with amplitudes a and b will have important implications in the partial-rate-difference CP violating effects in the charm and beauty particle decays (see Ref. (19)). There is an indication of the importance of amplitude d from the measurements of the F^+ lifetime,[14] which is close to that of D^0 (use Table I).

In conclusion, with the quark-mixing matrix being well determined, we are entering a new era in which the nonleptonic decay dynamics may be studied systematically via the many channels available in heavy quark decays.

2. Phenomena of CP Violation

It has been twenty years since the first observation[15] of CP violation of $K_L \to 2\pi$, and later the difference of $K_L \to \pi^\pm e^\mp \bar{\nu}_e$. So far they are still the only ones observed. Both phenomena have the same CP violating origin, i.e., the $K^0 \leftrightarrow \bar{K}^0$ transition in the mass matrix. CP-violating effects can also be due to complexity in the weak decay amplitudes (with the strong interaction phase excluded). A non-zero ϵ' would be such an effect. Unfortunately $\triangle I = \frac{1}{2}$ dominance gives a suppression of a factor 20, compared with ϵ, so that $|\epsilon'| < |\epsilon|/20$.

Recently, another type of CP-violating effect has received attention, i.e. partial decay-rate differences in particle and antiparticle decays.[2,16] Partial decay-rate differences in charged mesons or baryon particle decays are purely decay-amplitude effects. The KM scheme provides a definite mechanism for them, e.g.

$$\frac{|A(\Lambda \to \pi^- p)|^2 - |A(\bar{\Lambda} \to \pi^+ \bar{p})|^2}{|A(\Lambda \to \pi^- p)|^2 + |A(\bar{\Lambda} \to \pi^+ \bar{p})|^2} = \frac{s_2 s_3 s_\delta \, \mathrm{Im}(A_S^* A_P)}{|A_S|^2 + |A_P|^2}$$

$$\sim 10^{-3} \cdot 10^{-2} \, . \qquad (2.1)$$

The first factor[17] is from the phase interference in weak interactions, a universal factor[9] in the KM scheme now determined to be 10^{-3}; the second factor is from the interference from strong interactions. In $\Lambda \to \pi N$ decay, because of the small phase space available, the p-wave amplitude is strongly suppressed, giving the second small factor in Eq. (2.1). Current experiments carried out at LEAR,[18] CERN, have a sensitivity for Eq. (2.1) close to 10^{-4}. Seeing a partial rate difference of Eq. (2.1) greater than 10^{-5} is clear evidence of a non-KM CP-violating mechanism. Recent analyses in the Kobayashi-Maskawa (KM)[4] scheme of CP violation have shown that such CP-violating effects from the decay amplitudes, giving partial decay-rate differences among charged particles and their antiparticles, can be significant.[19] To check such partial rate differences may require about tens or hundreds of reconstructed B's of some specific channels. Such partial rate differences certainly can also lead to inclusive partial rate differences in B decays. Thus experimentally an easy way to see this is to measure

$$\frac{\sigma(e^+ e^- \to B^- \bar{B}^+ \to \ell^- \bar{D} X) - \sigma(e^+ e^- \to B^- \bar{B}^+ \to D \ell^+ X)}{\sigma(e^+ e^- \to B^- \bar{B}^+ \to \ell^- \bar{D} X) + \sigma(e^+ e^- \to B^- \bar{B}^+ \to D \ell^+ X)}$$

$$= \frac{|A(B^- \to \ell^- X)|^2 \, |A(\bar{B}^+ \to \bar{D} X)|^2 - |A(\bar{B}^+ \to \ell^+ X)|^2 \, |A(B^- \to D X)|^2}{|A(B^- \to \ell^- X)|^2 \, |A(\bar{B}^+ \to \bar{D} X)|^2 + |A(\bar{B}^+ \to \ell^+ X)|^2 \, |A(B^- \to D X)|^2} \, ,$$

$$(2.2)$$

where X stands for everything else inclusively. A statistically significant non-zero result of Eq. (2.2) is an indication of CP violation. (Later we shall show that Eq. (2.2) also holds for neutral B's, i.e. replacing $B^- \bar{B}^+$ by $B^0 \bar{B}^0$.)

For the neutral meson case, Nature has provided us with a very interesting quantum-mechanical system, the K_S, K_L. The K_L lives about six hundred times longer than the K_S owing to the fact that the three-pion masses are very close to the K mass. With its 5×10^{-8}-sec lifetime, K_L can travel quite a few meters before it decays. It provides a beautiful entity for the study of K^0, $\bar{K}^0$ mixing and CP violations through regeneration of K_S from K_L. However heavier quark states have short lifetimes: charm particles a few $\times 10^{-13}$ sec, t quark particles, less than 10^{-19} sec. Even with the b-lifetime of 10^{-12}

sec, it's not so easy to do K_L, K_S-type experiments. So time-integrated cross sections have to be considered. Another difference between the heavier quark state and the K states is that the K decays are dominated by $K \rightarrow 2\pi$; however, the decays of heavy quark states have many equally important channels. Under these circumstances, can we still measure the CP violating and mixing quantities as defined in the K system?

First we shall briefly review and clarify some concepts about CP violation using the K systems as an example. Because of the K^0, $\overline{K}^0$ transition in the presence of weak interactions, K^0, $\overline{K}^0$ are no longer physical eigenstates. After diagonalizing the mass matrix one finds the physical eigenstates,[20]

$$|K_{S,L}\rangle = N_{\overline{\epsilon}}[(1 + \overline{\epsilon})|K^0\rangle \pm (1 - \overline{\epsilon})|\overline{K}^0\rangle] , \qquad (2.3a)$$

where $N_{\overline{\epsilon}} = [2(1 + |\overline{\epsilon}|^2)]^{-\frac{1}{2}}$. Note that $\overline{\epsilon}$ is not entirely a physical quantity since it depends on the phase convention of $|K^0\rangle$ and $|\overline{K}^0\rangle$, which however cannot be fixed. First we adopt the phase convention that $CP|K^0\rangle = |\overline{K}^0\rangle$, and $CP|\overline{K}^0\rangle = |K^0\rangle$. Let's see how $\overline{\epsilon}$ changes to $\overline{\epsilon}'$ as we adopt a different phase convention $CP|K^0\rangle' = e^{i\xi}|\overline{K}^0\rangle'$ and $CP|\overline{K}^0\rangle' = e^{-i\xi}|K^0\rangle'$. Then the states in the two conventions are related by $|K^0\rangle' = e^{-i\xi/2}|K^0\rangle$, $|K^0\rangle' = e^{-i\xi/2}|\overline{K}^0\rangle$. The latter is fixed by the requirement $CP(CP|K^0\rangle) = |K^0\rangle$. Following the same diagonalization procedure for the mass matrix in the bases of $|K^0\rangle'$, $|\overline{K}^0\rangle'$ states, we find again, (see p. 10 of Ref. 2),

$$|K_{S,L}\rangle' = N_{\overline{\epsilon}'}[(1 + \overline{\epsilon}')|K^0\rangle' \pm (1 - \overline{\epsilon}')|\overline{K}^0\rangle'] , \qquad (2.3b)$$

where $N_{\overline{\epsilon}'} = [2(1 + |\overline{\epsilon}'|^2)]^{-\frac{1}{2}}$. Comparing Eqs. (2.3a) and (2.3b) and the relation of the two states, we find $(1 + \overline{\epsilon}')e^{i\xi/2} = (1 + \overline{\epsilon})$; $(1 - \overline{\epsilon}')e^{-i\xi/2} = (1 - \overline{\epsilon})$; and $N_{\overline{\epsilon}'} = [|1 + \overline{\epsilon}'|^2 + |1 - \overline{\epsilon}'|^2]^{-\frac{1}{2}} = N_{\overline{\epsilon}}$. Since physical quantities should be independent of phase convention, they should be only functions of $|1 + \overline{\epsilon}|$, $|1 - \overline{\epsilon}|$. Because of the normalization factor of $N_{\overline{\epsilon}}$, we shall find that all physical quantities are functions of

$$\eta \equiv |1 - \overline{\epsilon}| / |1 + \overline{\epsilon}| . \qquad (2.3c)$$

The deviation of η from being one is an indication of such mass-matrix CP violation. A simple corollary is that pure imaginary $\overline{\epsilon}$ gives $\eta = 1$, thus no mass-matrix CP violation. The $K^0 \leftrightarrow \overline{K}^0$ transition mass-matrix terms M_{12}, Γ_{12} enter into four other physical quantities: Δm, $\Delta\Gamma$, $\overline{\epsilon}$ with its real and imaginary parts:

$$(\Delta m - i\Delta\Gamma/2)/2 = [(M_{12} - i\Gamma_{12}/2)(M_{12}^* - i\Gamma_{12}^*/2)]^{\frac{1}{2}} , \qquad (2.4a)$$

$$(1 - \overline{\epsilon})/(1 + \overline{\epsilon}) = 2(M_{12}^* - i\Gamma_{12}^*/2)/(\Delta m - i\Delta\Gamma/2) , \qquad (2.4b)$$

As mentioned before $\eta \equiv |1 - \bar{\epsilon}|/|1 + \bar{\epsilon}|$ is the only physically measurable quantity, and $\eta \neq 1$ is an indication of mass-matrix CP-violating effect. The appearance of a non-zero Δm and $\Delta \Gamma$ is a physical consequence of $K^0 \leftrightarrow \bar{K}^0$ mixing, that can occur even without CP violation.

Theories which give $K^0 \leftrightarrow \bar{K}^0$ in first order interactions are called super weak theories.[21] Thus they give only the mass-matrix CP violation, but no decay-amplitude CP violation.

A direct measurement of mass-matrix CP-violating effects is to measure the lepton charge asymmetry in K_L decays[22]

$$\delta_\ell = \frac{A(K_L \to \pi^- \ell^+ \overleftarrow{\nu}) - A(K_L \to \pi^+ \ell^- \overrightarrow{\nu})}{A(K_L \to \pi^- \ell^+ \overleftarrow{\nu}) + A(K_L \to \pi^+ \ell^- \overrightarrow{\nu})}$$

$$= \frac{2 \operatorname{Re} \bar{\epsilon}}{(1 + |\bar{\epsilon}|^2)} = \frac{(1 - \eta^2)}{(1 + \eta^2)} = (3.3 \pm 0.12) \times 10^{-3} . \quad (2.5)$$

Historically, the first measured CP-violating quantities were[15] the absolute values of

$$\eta_{+-} = \frac{A(K_L \to \pi^+ \pi^-)}{A(K_S \to \pi^+ \pi^-)}$$

$$= \frac{(1 + \bar{\epsilon}) A(K^0 \to \pi^+ \pi^-) - (1 - \bar{\epsilon}) A(\bar{K}^0 \to \pi^+ \pi^-)}{(1 + \bar{\epsilon}) A(K^0 \to \pi^+ \pi^-) + (1 - \bar{\epsilon}) A(\bar{K}^0 \to \pi^+ \pi^-)}$$

$$= \frac{A_{+-}/\bar{A}_{+-} - p/q}{A_{+-}/\bar{A}_{+-} + p/q} = \epsilon + \epsilon' , \quad (2.6a)$$

$$\eta_{00} = \frac{A_{00}/\bar{A}_{00} - p/q}{A_{00}/\bar{A}_{00} + p/q} = \epsilon - 2\epsilon' , \quad (2.6b)$$

where $A_i = A(K \to f_i)$, $A_i = A(K \to f_i)$, and $p = 1 - \bar{\epsilon}$, $q = 1 + \bar{\epsilon}$; ϵ is the CP-violating parameter of the amplitude of isospin zero of the two pions; and $\bar{\epsilon}'$, of the isospin two.[20] Here both the mass-matrix and the decay amplitude CP violations are involved. In the ratios $A_{+-}/\bar{A}_{+-}$, $A_{00}/\bar{A}_{00}$ the strong-interaction phase cancels. Without decay-amplitude CP violation in weak interactions, any phases in $A_{+-}/\bar{A}_{+-}$ and $A_{00}/\bar{A}_{00}$ can be simultaneously taken away by choosing a proper phase convention so that $\bar{A}_{+-}/$

$\overline{A}_{+-} = A_{00}/\overline{A}_{00} = 1$, thus $\eta_{+-}/\eta_{00} = 1$. The reverse is also true, i.e., if $\eta_{+-}/\eta_{00} = 1$, then $A_{+-}/\overline{A}_{+-} = A_{00}/\overline{A}_{00}$, and $|A_{+-}/\overline{A}_{+-}| = |A_{00}/\overline{A}_{00}| = 1$, (the second relation must also be true is due to the fact that the K^0, $\overline{K}^0$ to two pions are a closed system and the CPT theorem applies, $\Gamma(K^0 \rightarrow \pi^+\pi^-) + \Gamma(K^0 \rightarrow \pi^0\pi^0) = \Gamma(\overline{K}^0 \pi^+\pi^-) + \Gamma(\overline{K}^0 \rightarrow \pi^0\pi^0)$. Therefore if $|A_{+-}/\overline{A}_{+-}| < 1$, then $|A_{00}/\overline{A}_{00}| = |A_{\pm}/\overline{A}_{+-}| > 1$. We cannot have a situation $|A_{+-}/\overline{A}_{+-}| = |A_{00}/\overline{A}_{00}| \neq 1$). There are decay-amplitude CP violations if $|A/\overline{A}| \neq 1$, or even when both $|A_{+-}/\overline{A}_{+-}| = |A_{00}/\overline{A}_{00}| = 1$, but no phase convention can be found such that $A_{+-}/\overline{A}_{+-}$ and $A_{00}/\overline{A}_{00}$ are both real. Therefore $\eta_{+-}/\eta_{00} \neq 1$, i.e. $\epsilon \neq 0$ is a necessary and sufficient indication of decay-amplitude CP violation. Such decay-amplitude CP violating effects can be measured[23] directly in K^0, $\overline{K}^0 \rightarrow \pi^+\pi^-$, and $\pi^0\pi^0$ reactions. Such experiments are being carried out at LEAR,[18] tagging K^0, $\overline{K}^0$ by $P\overline{P} \rightarrow K^+\pi^-\overline{K}^0$, $K^-\pi^+K^0$. Partial decay rate differences in neutral mesons can result from both the mass-matrix and decay-amplitude CP violations, which we shall discuss in detail later.

There are two classes of experiments where the phase of η_{+-} can be measured. First is by generating a coherent state $|K_L > + \rho|K_s>$, where ρ is the regeneration parameter.[24,25] Its time evolution can be written as

$$|A[(K_L + \rho K_S) \rightarrow f](\tau)|^2$$

$$= |A(K_S \rightarrow f)|^2 \left[|\rho|^2 e^{-\Gamma_S\tau} + |\eta_f|^2 e^{-\Gamma_L\tau} \right.$$

$$\left. + 2|\rho||\eta_f|e^{-\tilde{\Gamma}\tau}\cos(\tau\Delta m + \phi_\rho - \phi_f) \right] , \qquad (2.7)$$

where $\rho = |\rho|e^{i\phi_\rho}$ is the regeneration parameter, $\eta_f = |\eta_f|e^{i\phi_f}$ is defined the same way as in Eq. (2.6), $\Delta m \equiv m_S - m_L$, $\tilde{\Gamma} \equiv (\Gamma_S + \Gamma_L)/2$. The regeneration parameter ρ, can be determined by measuring time-dependent semileptonic decays, in which $A(\overline{K}^0 \rightarrow \pi^-\ell^+\nu) = 0$, $\eta_{\ell^+} = +1$ and we define $A(K^0 \rightarrow \pi^-\ell^+\nu) \equiv A$; similarly $A(K^0 \rightarrow \pi^+\ell^-\nu) = 0$, $\eta_{\ell^-} = -1$, and $A(\overline{K}^0 \rightarrow \pi^+\ell^-\nu) \equiv \overline{A}$. The time dependent evolution from Eq. (2.7) becomes

$$|A[(K_L + \rho K_S) \rightarrow \pi^\mp \ell^\pm \nu](\tau)|^2 = \left\{ \begin{array}{l} |2N_{\overline{e}}(1+\overline{\epsilon})|^2 |A|^2 \\ |2N_{\overline{e}}(1-\overline{\epsilon})|^2 |\overline{A}|^2 \end{array} \right\}$$

$$\cdot \left\{ |\rho|^2 e^{-\Gamma_S\tau} + e^{-\Gamma_L\tau} \pm 2|\rho|e^{-\tilde{\Gamma}\tau}\cos(\tau\Delta m + \phi_\rho) \right\} . \qquad (2.8)$$

Therefore ρ can be determined from Eq. (2.8) by measuring the time evolution of various $(K_L + \rho K_S) \rightarrow$ f; then one can measure η_f. Any measurement of a difference in η_f for different f is an indication of the existence of a decay-amplitude CP violation, a deviation from the super weak CP violation.

The second way of measuring the phases of η_{+-}, η_{00} is to do the so-called vacuum regeneration experiment, where K^0 and $\bar{K}^0$ are generated incoherently in a hadronic reaction

$$|A(K^0 \to f)(\tau)|^2 + n |A(\bar{K}^0 \to f)(\tau)|^2$$

$$= |2N_{\bar{\epsilon}}|^{-2} |A(K_S \to f)|^2 \{ (|1 + \bar{\epsilon}|^{-2} + n |1 - \bar{\epsilon}|^{-2})$$

$$\cdot (e^{-\tilde{\Gamma}_S \tau} + |\eta_f|^2 e^{-\tilde{\Gamma}_L \tau})$$

$$+ (|1 + \bar{\epsilon}|^{-2} - n |1 - \bar{\epsilon}|^{-2}) 2 |\eta_f| \cos(\tau \Delta m - \phi_f) \} \ . \qquad (2.9)$$

By doing these time evolution regneration experiments $|\eta_f|$, ϕ_f can be measured.[26] The results are[22]

$$|\eta_{+-}| = (2.274 \pm 0.022) \times 10^{-3} \ ; \quad \phi_{+-} = (44.6 \pm 1.2)^{\circ} \ ,$$

$$\phi_{00} = (54.5 \pm 5.3)^{\circ} \ .$$

Clearly a better measurement of ϕ_{00} is urgently needed. To be complete, the recent measurements of

$$|\eta_{00}/\eta_{+-}|^2 - 1 = -6 \times \begin{cases} -0.0046 \pm 0.0053 \pm 0.0024, [27] \\ +0.0017 \pm 0.0082, [28] \end{cases}$$

are also given here.

Recently a new type of experiment has been considered: the time-evolution[18] of K^0 and $\bar{K}^0$, e.g. $P\bar{P} \to K^- \pi^+ K^0$, $K^+ \pi^- \bar{K}^0$.

$$\left. \begin{matrix} |A(K^0 \to f)(\tau)|^2 \\ \\ |A(\bar{K}^0 \to f)(\tau)|^2 \end{matrix} \right\} = \left\{ \begin{matrix} |2N_{\bar{\epsilon}}(1 + \bar{\epsilon})|^{-2} \\ \\ |2N_{\bar{\epsilon}}(1 - \bar{\epsilon})|^{-2} \end{matrix} \right\} |A(K_S \to f)|^2$$

$$\cdot [e^{-\Gamma_S \tau} + |\eta_f|^2 e^{-\Gamma_L \tau} \pm 2 |\eta_f| e^{-\tilde{\Gamma}\tau} \cos(\tau \Delta m - \phi_f)] \ , \qquad (2.10)$$

and the difference and the sum

$\overline{A}_{+-} = A_{00}/\overline{A}_{00} = 1$, thus $\eta_{+-}/\eta_{00} = 1$. The reverse is also true, i.e., if $\eta_{+-}/\eta_{00} = 1$, then $A_{+-}/\overline{A}_{+-} = A_{00}/\overline{A}_{00}$, and $|A_{+-}/\overline{A}_{+-}| = |A_{00}/\overline{A}_{00}| = 1$, (the second relation must also be true is due to the fact that the K^0, $\overline{K}^0$ to two pions are a closed system and the CPT theorem applies, $\Gamma(K^0 \rightarrow \pi^+\pi^-) + \Gamma(K^0 \rightarrow \pi^0\pi^0) = \Gamma(\overline{K}^0 \pi^+\pi^-) + \Gamma(\overline{K}^0 \rightarrow \pi^0\pi^0)$. Therefore if $|A_{+-}/\overline{A}_{+-}| < 1$, then $|A_{00}/\overline{A}_{00}| = |A_{\pm-}/\overline{A}_{+-}| > 1$. We cannot have a situation $|A_{+-}/\overline{A}_{+-}| = |A_{00}/\overline{A}_{00}| \neq 1$). There are decay-amplitude CP violations if $|A/\overline{A}| \neq 1$, or even when both $|A_{+-}/\overline{A}_{+-}| = |A_{00}/\overline{A}_{00}| = 1$, but no phase convention can be found such that $A_{+-}/\overline{A}_{+-}$ and $A_{00}/\overline{A}_{00}$ are both real. Therefore $\eta_{+-}/\eta_{00} \neq 1$, i.e. $\epsilon \neq 0$ is a necessary and sufficient indication of decay-amplitude CP violation. Such decay-amplitude CP violating effects can be measured[23] directly in K^0, $\overline{K}^0 \rightarrow \pi^+\pi^-$, and $\pi^0\pi^0$ reactions. Such experiments are being carried out at LEAR,[18] tagging K^0, $\overline{K}^0$ by $P\overline{P} \rightarrow K^+\pi^-\overline{K}^0$, $K^-\pi^+K^0$. Partial decay rate differences in neutral mesons can result from both the mass-matrix and decay-amplitude CP violations, which we shall discuss in detail later.

There are two classes of experiments where the phase of η_{+-} can be measured. First is by generating a coherent state $|K_L> + \rho|K_s>$, where ρ is the regeneration parameter.[24,25] Its time evolution can be written as

$$|A[(K_L + \rho K_S) \rightarrow f](\tau)|^2$$

$$= |A(K_S \rightarrow f)|^2 [|\rho|^2 e^{-\Gamma_S \tau} + |\eta_f|^2 e^{-\Gamma_L \tau}$$

$$+ 2|\rho||\eta_f| e^{-\widetilde{\Gamma}\tau} \cos(\tau \Delta m + \phi_\rho - \phi_f)] , \qquad (2.7)$$

where $\rho = |\rho|e^{i\phi_\rho}$ is the regeneration parameter, $\eta_f = |\eta_f| e^{i\phi_f}$ is defined the same way as in Eq. (2.6), $\Delta m \equiv m_S - m_L$, $\widetilde{\Gamma} \equiv (\Gamma_S + \Gamma_L)/2$. The regeneration parameter ρ, can be determined by measuring time-dependent semileptonic decays, in which $A(\overline{K}^0 \rightarrow \pi^-\ell^+\nu) = 0$, $\eta_{\varrho^+} = +1$ and we define $A(K^0 \rightarrow \pi^-\ell^+\nu) \equiv A$; similarly $A(K^0 \rightarrow \pi^+\ell^-\nu) = 0$, $\eta_{\varrho^-} = -1$, and $A(\overline{K}^0 \rightarrow \pi^+\ell^-\nu) \equiv \overline{A}$. The time dependent evolution from Eq. (2.7) becomes

$$|A[(K_L + \rho K_S) \rightarrow \pi^\mp \ell^\pm \nu](\tau)|^2 = \left\{ \begin{array}{c} |2N_{\overline{e}}(1+\overline{\epsilon})|^2 |A|^2 \\ |2N_{\overline{e}}(1-\overline{\epsilon})|^2 |\overline{A}|^2 \end{array} \right\}$$

$$\cdot \left\{ |\rho|^2 e^{-\Gamma_S \tau} + e^{-\Gamma_L \tau} \pm 2|\rho| e^{-\widetilde{\Gamma}\tau} \cos(\tau \Delta m + \phi_\rho) \right\} . \qquad (2.8)$$

Therefore ρ can be determined from Eq. (2.8) by measuring the time evolution of various $(K_L + \rho K_S) \rightarrow f$; then one can measure η_f. Any measurement of a difference in η_f for different f is an indication of the existence of a decay-amplitude CP violation, a deviation from the super weak CP violation.

The second way of measuring the phases of η_{+-}, η_{00} is to do the so-called vacuum regeneration experiment, where K^0 and $\overline{K}^0$ are generated incoherently in a hadronic reaction

$$|A(K^0 \to f)(\tau)|^2 + n|A(\overline{K}^0 \to f)(\tau)|^2$$

$$= |2N_{\overline{\epsilon}}|^{-2}|A(K_S \to f)|^2 \{(|1 + \overline{\epsilon}|^{-2} + n|1 - \overline{\epsilon}|^{-2})$$

$$\cdot (e^{-\widetilde{\Gamma}_S \tau} + |\eta_f|^2 e^{-\widetilde{\Gamma}_L \tau})$$

$$+ (|1 + \overline{\epsilon}|^{-2} - n|1 - \overline{\epsilon}|^{-2}) 2|\eta_f| \cos(\tau \Delta m - \phi_f)\} \quad . \tag{2.9}$$

By doing these time evolution regneration experiments $|\eta_f|$, ϕ_f can be measured.[26] The results are[22]

$$|\eta_{+-}| = (2.274 \pm 0.022) \times 10^{-3} \; ; \quad \phi_{+-} = (44.6 \pm 1.2)° \; ,$$

$$\phi_{00} = (54.5 \pm 5.3)° \; .$$

Clearly a better measurement of ϕ_{00} is urgently needed. To be complete, the recent measurements of

$$|\eta_{00}/\eta_{+-}|^2 - 1 = -6 \times \begin{cases} -0.0046 \pm 0.0053 \pm 0.0024,^{(27)} \\ +0.0017 \pm 0.0082,^{(28)} \end{cases}$$

are also given here.

Recently a new type of experiment has been considered: the time-evolution[18] of K^0 and $\overline{K}^0$, e.g. $P\overline{P} \to K^- \pi^+ K^0$, $K^+ \pi^- \overline{K}^0$.

$$\left. \begin{array}{c} |A(K^0 \to f)(\tau)|^2 \\ \\ \\ |A(\overline{K}^0 \to f)(\tau)|^2 \end{array} \right\} = \left\{ \begin{array}{c} |2N_{\overline{\epsilon}}(1 + \overline{\epsilon})|^{-2} \\ \\ \\ |2N_{\overline{\epsilon}}(1 - \overline{\epsilon})|^{-2} \end{array} \right\} |A(K_S \to f)|^2$$

$$\cdot [e^{-\Gamma_S \tau} + |\eta_f|^2 e^{-\Gamma_L \tau} \pm 2|\eta_f| e^{-\widetilde{\Gamma} \tau} \cos(\tau \Delta m - \phi_f)] \; , \tag{2.10}$$

and the difference and the sum

$$|A(K^0 \to f)(\tau)|^2 - |A(\bar{K}^0 \to f)(\tau)|^2 = |2N_{\bar{\epsilon}}|^{-2} |A(K_S \to f)|^2$$

$$\cdot 2\left\{[-2\operatorname{Re}\bar{\epsilon}/(1+|\bar{\epsilon}|^2)] X(\tau) + Y(\tau)\right\} , \tag{2.11a}$$

$$|A(K^0 \to f)(\tau)|^2 + |A(\bar{K}^0 \to f)(\tau)|^2 = |2N_{\bar{\epsilon}}|^{-2} |A(K_S \to f)|^2$$

$$\cdot 2\left\{X(\tau) - [2\operatorname{Re}\bar{\epsilon}/(1+|\bar{\epsilon}|^2)] Y(\tau)\right\} , \tag{2.11b}$$

where $X(\tau) = e^{-\Gamma_S \tau} + |\eta_f|^2 e^{-\Gamma_L \tau}$, $Y(\tau) = 2|\eta_f| e^{-\tilde{\Gamma}\tau} \cos(\tau \Delta m - \phi_f)$.

From the time integrated difference and sum, we simply use integrated X_I, Y_I

$$X_I(\tau_1) \equiv \int_0^{\tau_1} d\tau \, X(\tau)$$

$$= (1 - e^{-\Gamma_S \tau_1})/\Gamma_S + |\eta_f|^2 (1 - e^{-\Gamma_L \tau_1})/\Gamma_L , \tag{2.11c}$$

$$X_I(\tau_1 = \infty) = 1/\Gamma_S + |\eta_f|^2/\Gamma_L ; \tag{2.11d}$$

$$Y_I(\tau_1) = \int_0^{\tau_1} d\tau \, Y(\tau)$$

$$= 2|\eta_f| \left\{ \Delta m \left[\sin\phi_f - e^{-\tilde{\Gamma}\tau_1} \sin(\phi_f - \Delta m \, \tau_1) \right] \right.$$

$$+ \tilde{\Gamma} \left[\cos\phi_f - e^{-\tilde{\Gamma}\tau_1} \cos(\phi_f - \Delta m \, \tau_1) \right] \right\}$$

$$\cdot [(\Delta m)^2 + (\tilde{\Gamma})^2]^{-1} , \tag{2.11e}$$

$$Y_I(\tau_1 = \infty) = 2|\eta_+| [\Delta m \sin\phi_f + \tilde{\Gamma} \cos\phi_f]$$

$$\cdot [(\Delta m)^2 + (\tilde{\Gamma})^2]^{-1} ; \tag{2.11f}$$

The partial rate differences are defined to be

$$\Delta(K^0, \bar{K}^0 \to f)(\tau) \equiv \frac{|A(K^0 \to f)(\tau)|^2 - |A(\bar{K}^0 \to f)(\tau)|^2}{|A(K^0 \to f)(\tau)|^2 + |A(\bar{K}^0 \to f)(\tau)|^2}$$

$$= \frac{[-2\,\mathrm{Re}\,\bar{\epsilon}/(1+|\bar{\epsilon}|^2)] + Y(\tau)/X(\tau)}{1 - [2\,\mathrm{Re}\,\bar{\epsilon}/(1+|\bar{\epsilon}|^2)]\,Y(\tau)/X(\tau)} \ ,$$

$$(2.12a)$$

$$\Delta_I(\tau_1) \equiv \frac{\displaystyle\int_0^{\tau_1} d\tau\,|A(K^0 \to f)(\tau)|^2 - \int_0^{\tau_1} d\tau\,|A(\bar{K}^0 \to f)(\tau)|^2}{\displaystyle\int_0^{\tau_1} d\tau\,|A(K^0 \to f)(\tau)|^2 + \int_0^{\tau_1} d\tau\,|A(\bar{K}^0 \to f)(\tau)|^2}$$

$$= \frac{[-2\,\mathrm{Re}\,\bar{\epsilon}/(1+|\bar{\epsilon}|^2)] + Y_I(\tau_1)/X_I(\tau_1)}{1 - [2\,\mathrm{Re}\,\bar{\epsilon}/(1+|\bar{\epsilon}|^2)]\,Y_I(\tau_1)/X_I(\tau_1)} \ . \qquad (2.12b)$$

$[2\mathrm{Re}\bar{\epsilon}/(1+|\bar{\epsilon}|^2)]Y/X$ is in general negligible compared with 1 and can be ignored in the denominator, then

$$\Delta(\tau) \approx -2\,\mathrm{Re}\,\bar{\epsilon}/(1+|\bar{\epsilon}|^2) + Y(\tau)/X(\tau) \ , \qquad (2.13a)$$

$$\Delta_I(\tau_1) \approx -2\,\mathrm{Re}\,\bar{\epsilon}/(1+|\bar{\epsilon}|^2) + Y_I(\tau_1)/X_I(\tau_1) \ . \qquad (2.13b)$$

Note that $\Delta(\tau)$ and $\Delta_I(\tau_1)$ are from both effects of mass-matrix CP violation and $K^0 \leftrightarrow \bar{K}^0$ mixing.

Another interesting final state to study is the time dependent $K^0, \bar{K}^0 \to \ell^+ X$. In this case $\eta_{\varrho^+} = +1$, i.e. $\phi_{\varrho^+} = 0$, since $\bar{K}^0 \not\to \ell^+ X$ at the moment when it is tagged as $\bar{K}^0$. In this case $X_I(\tau_1 = \infty) = 2\tilde{\Gamma}/\Gamma_S\Gamma_L$, $Y_I(\tau_1 = \infty) = 2\tilde{\Gamma}[(\Delta m)^2 + (\tilde{\Gamma})^2]^{-1}$ in Eqs. (2.11d,f). The time integrated fractional difference between $K^0, \bar{K}^0 \to \ell^+ X$ becomes,

$$\Delta_I(K^0, \bar{K}^0 \to \ell^+ X, \tau_1 = \infty)$$

$$= \frac{-[2\,\mathrm{Re}\,\bar{\epsilon}/(1+|\bar{\epsilon}|^2)] + \Gamma_S\Gamma_L[(\Delta m)^2 + (\tilde{\Gamma})^2]^{-1}}{1 - [2\,\mathrm{Re}\,\bar{\epsilon}/(1+|\bar{\epsilon}|^2)]\,\Gamma_S\Gamma_L[(\Delta m)^2 + (\tilde{\Gamma})^2]^{-1}}$$

$$\approx -\frac{2\,\mathrm{Re}\,\bar{\epsilon}}{1+|\bar{\epsilon}|^2} + \frac{\Gamma_S\Gamma_L}{(\Delta m)^2 + (\tilde{\Gamma})^2} \quad, \text{ for either } K^0 \text{ or } \bar{K}^0 \ .$$

$$(2.14)$$

For $K^0, \bar{K}^0 \rightarrow \ell^- X, \eta_{\ell^-} = -1$, i.e. $\phi_{\ell^-} = \pi$,

$$\Delta_{\mathrm{I}}(K^0, \bar{K}^0 \rightarrow \ell^- X, \tau_1 = \infty)$$

$$= \frac{-[2\,\mathrm{Re}\,\bar{\epsilon}/(1+|\bar{\epsilon}|^2)] - \Gamma_S\Gamma_L[(\Delta m)^2 + (\tilde{\Gamma})^2]^{-1}}{1 - [2\,\mathrm{Re}\,\bar{\epsilon}/(1+|\bar{\epsilon}|^2)]\,\Gamma_S\Gamma_L[(\Delta m)^2 + (\tilde{\Gamma})^2]^{-1}}$$

$$\approx -\frac{2\,\mathrm{Re}\,\bar{\epsilon}}{1+|\bar{\epsilon}|^2} - \frac{\Gamma_S\Gamma_L}{(\Delta m)^2 + (\tilde{\Gamma})^2} \quad, \text{ for either } K^0 \text{ or } \bar{K}^0 \ .$$

$$(2.15)$$

so by taking the sum and difference

$$\Delta_{\mathrm{I}}(K^0, \bar{K}^0 \rightarrow \ell^+ X, \tau_1 = \infty) + \Delta_{\mathrm{I}}(K^0, \bar{K}^0 \rightarrow \ell^- X, \tau_1 = \infty)$$

$$= \frac{-4\,\mathrm{Re}\,\bar{\epsilon}/(1+|\bar{\epsilon}|^2)}{1 - [2\,\mathrm{Re}\,\bar{\epsilon}/(1+|\bar{\epsilon}|^2)]\,\Gamma_S\Gamma_L[(\Delta m)^2 + (\tilde{\Gamma})^2]^{-1}}$$

$$\approx \frac{-4\,\mathrm{Re}\,\bar{\epsilon}}{1+|\bar{\epsilon}|^2} = 2\frac{1-\eta^2}{1+\eta^2} \ ; \qquad (2.16)$$

$$\Delta_{\mathrm{I}}(K^0, \bar{K}^0 \rightarrow \ell^+ X, \tau_1 = \infty) - \Delta_{\mathrm{I}}(K^0, \bar{K}^0 \rightarrow \ell^- X, \tau_1 = \infty)$$

$$= \frac{2\Gamma_S\Gamma_L[(\Delta m)^2 + (\tilde{\Gamma})^2]^{-1}}{1 - [2\,\mathrm{Re}\,\bar{\epsilon}/(1+|\bar{\epsilon}|^2)]\,\Gamma_S\Gamma_L[(\Delta m)^2 + (\tilde{\Gamma})^2]^{-1}}$$

$$\approx \frac{2\Gamma_S\Gamma_L}{(\Delta m)^2 + (\tilde{\Gamma})^2} \quad, \qquad (2.17)$$

thus without isolating K_L^0, the same CP-violation parameters, as measured in $K_L \to \pi^\pm e^\mp \bar{\nu}$, Eq. (2.5) can be measured through these time integrated measurements. Note that this result is independent of whether the intrinsic amplitudes, (defined at the moment K^0 and $\overline{K}^0$ are identified), $A \equiv A(K^0 \to \ell^+ X)$ is equal to $\overline{A} \equiv A(\overline{K}^0 \to \ell^- X)$ or not. In this way we can measure the mass-matrix CP-violation and the mixing parameters separately.[29]

For the $K^0, \overline{K}^0$ system, the measurement of such semileptonic decays at LEAR $\overline{P}P \to \pi^- K^+ \ell^\pm X$, $\overline{P}P \to \pi^+ K^- \ell^\pm X$ can provide another independent measurement of these parameters. For heavy quark states, it may not be possible to isolate any P_S^0, P_L^0 states (here we use P^0 to denote any zero charged mesons), Eqs. (2.16, 2.17) can serve as a way to measure the mass-matrix CP-violating parameters and the $P^0 \leftrightarrow \overline{P}^0$ mixing parameters separately. For example, $e^+ e^- \to \psi(4160, 4415) \to D^0 \pi^+ D^- \to \ell^\pm X \pi^+ D^-$ or $\overline{D}^0 \pi^- D^+ \to \ell^\pm X \pi^- D^+$ can be used for such studies. Actually for D^0, $2\mathrm{Re}\bar{\epsilon}_D/[1 + |\bar{\epsilon}_D|^2]$ can be as large as a few percent.[30]

Another interesting case to study is $A(P^0 \to f X)(\tau)$, $A(\overline{P}^0 \to \bar{f} X)(\tau)$, where $\overline{P}^0 \not\to f X$, $P^0 \not\to \bar{f} X$ when P^0, $\overline{P}^0$ are tagged, e.g,

$$f = \ell^+ \text{ for } K^0; \quad f = \ell^+, \overline{K} \text{ for } D^0; \quad f = \ell^-, D \text{ for } B^0 . \qquad (2.18)$$

In this case, using equations Eq. (2.10) and substituting $A(P_S^0 \to f) = N_{\bar{\epsilon}}(1 + \bar{\epsilon})A$, $\eta_f = +1$; $A(P_S^0 \to \bar{f}) = N_{\bar{\epsilon}}(1 - \epsilon)A$. $\eta_{\bar{f}} = -1$, and we have

$$\Delta(\tau) = \frac{|A(P^0 \to f X)(\tau)|^2 - |A(\overline{P}^0 \to \bar{f} X)(\tau)|^2}{|A(P^0 \to f X)(\tau)|^2 + |A(\overline{P}^0 \to \bar{f} X)(\tau)|^2}$$

$$= \frac{|A|^2 - |\overline{A}|^2}{|A|^2 + |\overline{A}|^2} , \qquad (2.19)$$

independent of the proper time τ. Here $A \equiv A(P^0 \to f X)$, $\overline{A} \equiv A(\overline{P}^0 \to \bar{f} X)$ at the time P^0, $\overline{P}^0$ are tagged. This method provides a direct measure of decay-amplitude CP violation, just as for studying charged meson decays into their charge conjugated states.

Another interesting situation is that of the charge-conjugation eigenstates created naturally[28,29] in $e^+ e^- \to \gamma_v \to P^0 \overline{P}^0 + n(\gamma) + m(\pi^0)$, e.g. for $n(\gamma) = $ even (odd) the state $P^0 \overline{P}^0$ has odd (even) charge conjugation. We denote them by $(P^0 \overline{P}^0)^-$, $(P^0 \overline{P}^0)^+$ states. It is interesting to note that

$$(P^0 \overline{P}^0)^- = |P^0 \overline{P}^0\rangle - |\overline{P}^0 P^0\rangle$$

$$= [2N_{\bar{\epsilon}}(1 + \bar{\epsilon})]^{-1} [2N_{\bar{\epsilon}}(1 - \bar{\epsilon})]^{-1} [|P_S^0 P_L^0\rangle - |P_L^0 P_S^0\rangle] , \qquad (2.20a)$$

$$(P^0 \, \bar{P}^0)^+ = |P^0 \, \bar{P}^0 \rangle + |\bar{P}^0 \, P^0 \rangle$$

$$= [2N_{\bar{\epsilon}}(1 + \bar{\epsilon})]^{-1} [2N_{\bar{\epsilon}}(1 - \bar{\epsilon})]^{-1} [|P_S^0 \, P_S^0 \rangle - |P_L^0 \, P_L^0 \rangle] \ .$$

$$(2.20b)$$

If the neutrals are not specified in $e^+ e^- \to \gamma_v \to P^0 \bar{P}^0$ + neutrals, the $P^0 \bar{P}^0$ will be an incoherent sum of $(P^0 \bar{P}^0)^+$, $(P^0 \bar{P}^0)^-$ states. Similarly, in a proton antiproton annihilation experiment $p\bar{p} \to P^0 \bar{P}^0$ + neutrals, $P^0 \bar{P}^0$ is always in an incoherent mixed state of $(P^0 \bar{P}^0)^+$ and $(P^0 \bar{P}^0)^-$. From Eqs. (2.20), these neutral reactions become an incoherent source of P_S's and P_L's with an intensity ratio of 1 to 1. Here we give its time evolution in decaying into any two final states f_1, f_2,

$$\sigma[(P^0 \, \bar{P}^0)^+ \to f_1 f_2] (\tau_1, \tau_2)$$

$$= (\dots) |A(P_S \to f_1) A(P_S \to f_2)|^2$$

$$\cdot \left\{ e^{-\Gamma_S(\tau_1 + \tau_2)} + |\eta_1|^2 |\eta_2|^2 \, e^{-\Gamma_L(\tau_1 + \tau_2)} \right.$$

$$\left. - 2|\eta_1| |\eta_2| e^{-\tilde{\Gamma}(\tau_1 + \tau_2)} \cos[\Delta m(\tau_1 + \tau_2) - \phi_1 - \phi_2] \right\},$$

$$(2.21)$$

where

$$(\dots) \equiv |2N_{\bar{\epsilon}}(1 + \bar{\epsilon})|^{-2} |2N_{\bar{\epsilon}}(1 - \bar{\epsilon})|^{-2} \ ,$$

and its time integrated probability,

$$\sigma[(P^0 \, \bar{P}^0)^+ \to f_1 f_2]_I (\tau_1 = \infty)$$

$$= (\dots) |A(P_S \to f_1) A(P_S \to f_2)|^2$$

$$\cdot \left\{ 1/\Gamma_S^2 + |\eta_1|^2 |\eta_2|^2 (1/\Gamma_L^2) \right.$$

$$\left. - 2|\eta_1| |\eta_2| \left(\frac{\cos(\phi_1 + \phi_2)}{[(\Delta m)^2 + (\tilde{\Gamma})^2]} + \frac{2\Delta m \tilde{\Gamma} \sin(\phi_1 + \phi_2)}{[(\Delta m)^2 + (\tilde{\Gamma})^2]} \right) \right\} ;$$

$$(2.22)$$

and similarly

$$\sigma[(P^0 \bar{P}^0)^- \to f_1 f_2] (\tau_1 \tau_2)$$

$$= (\ldots) |A(P_S \to f_1) A(P_S \to f_2)|^2$$

$$\cdot \left\{ |\eta_1|^2 e^{-\Gamma_L \tau_1} e^{-\Gamma_S \tau_2} + |\eta_2|^2 e^{-\Gamma_L \tau_2} e^{-\Gamma_S \tau_1} \right.$$

$$\left. - 2|\eta_1||\eta_2| e^{-\tilde{\Gamma}(\tau_1 + \tau_2)} \cos[\Delta m (\tau_1 - \tau_2) - \phi_1 + \phi_2] \right\},$$

$$(2.23)$$

and its time integrated cross section,

$$\sigma[(P^0 \bar{P}^0)^- \to f_1 f_2]_I (\tau_1 = \infty)$$

$$= (\ldots) |A(P_S \to f_1) A(P_S \to f_2)|^2$$

$$\cdot \left\{ (|\eta_1|^2 + |\eta_2|^2)/\Gamma_S \Gamma_L \right.$$

$$\left. - 2|\eta_1||\eta_2| \cos(\phi_1 - \phi_2) / [(\Delta m)^2 + (\tilde{\Gamma})^2] \right\} \quad . \quad (2.24)$$

So by measuring various f_1, f_2 states, one can measure the mixed CP-violating effects both in the decay amplitudes and in the mass matrix.

An interesting case is $(P^0 \bar{P}^0)^\pm \to f_1 f_2$ where f_1 and f_2 represent states defined in Eq. (2.18). One can show that

$$\Delta(\tau) = \frac{\sigma[(P^0 \bar{P}^0)^\pm \to f_1 f_2 X] - \sigma[(P^0 \bar{P}^0)^\pm \to f_{\bar{1}} f_{\bar{2}} X]}{\sigma[(P^0 \bar{P}^0)^\pm \to f_1 f_2 X] + \sigma[(P^0 \bar{P}^0)^\pm \to f_{\bar{1}} f_{\bar{2}} X]}$$

$$= \frac{|1 + \bar{\epsilon}_P|^4 |A_1 A_2|^2 - |1 - \bar{\epsilon}_P|^4 |\bar{A}_1 \bar{A}_2|^2}{|1 + \bar{\epsilon}_P|^4 |A_1 A_2|^2 + |1 - \bar{\epsilon}_P|^4 |\bar{A}_1 \bar{A}_2|^2} ,$$

$$= \frac{\sum_{i=\pm} \left\{ \sigma[(P^0 \bar{P}^0)^i \to f_1 f_2 X] - \sigma[(P^0 \bar{P}^0)^i \to f_{\bar{1}} f_{\bar{2}} X] \right\}}{\sum_{i=\pm} \left\{ \sigma[(P^0 \bar{P}^0)^i \to f_1 f_2 X] + \sigma[(P^0 \bar{P}^0)^i \to f_{\bar{1}} f_{\bar{2}} X] \right\}} .$$

$$(2.25)$$

Here actually the time dependence cancels out. The last equality in Eq. (2.25) says that we do not have to trigger $(P^0\bar{P}^0)^+$ or $(P^0\bar{P}^0)^-$ states, as long as they are the incoherent sum of $(P^0\bar{P}^0)^{\pm}$, such as in $e^+e^- \to P^0\bar{P}^0 +$ neutrals, or $p\bar{p} \to P^0\bar{P}^0 +$ neutrals.

For $f_1 = f_2 = \ell^+$, $f_{\bar{1}} = f_{\bar{2}} = \ell^-$, in the KM model $A_\ell = \bar{A}_\ell$, so Eq. (2.26) becomes

$$\frac{\sigma[\ell\,\ell\,X] - \sigma[\bar{\ell}\,\bar{\ell}\,X]}{\sigma[\ell\,\ell\,X] + \sigma[\bar{\ell}\,\bar{\ell}\,X]} = \frac{|1+\bar{\epsilon}_P|^4 - |1-\bar{\epsilon}_P|^4}{|1+\bar{\epsilon}_P|^4 + |1-\bar{\epsilon}_P|^4}$$

$$= \frac{1 - \eta_P^4}{1 + \eta_P^4} \,. \tag{2.26}$$

measures pure mass-matrix CP-violation effects, a rather well known equation.

Another interesting case is $(P^0\bar{P}^0)^{\pm} \to f_1 f_2$, where f_1, f_2 represents states in Eq. (2.18),

$$\frac{\sigma[(P^0\,\bar{P}^0)^{\pm} \to f_1 f_{\bar{2}}\, X] - \sigma[(P^0\,\bar{P}^0)^{\pm} \to f_{\bar{1}} f_2\, X]}{\sigma[(P^0\,\bar{P}^0)^{\pm} \to f_1 f_{\bar{2}}\, X] + \sigma[(P^0\,\bar{P}^0)^{\pm} \to f_{\bar{1}} f_2\, X]}$$

$$= \frac{|A_1|^2\,|\bar{A}_2|^2 - |\bar{A}_1|^2\,|A_2|^2}{|A_1|^2\,|\bar{A}_2|^2 + |\bar{A}_1|^2\,|A_2|^2}$$

$$= \frac{\displaystyle\sum_{i=\pm 1} \left\{\sigma[(P^0\,\bar{P}^0)^i \to f_1 f_{\bar{2}}\, X] - \sigma[(P^0\,\bar{P}^0)^i \to f_{\bar{1}} f_2\, X]\right\}}{\displaystyle\sum_{i=\pm 1} \left\{\sigma[(P^0\,\bar{P}^0)^i \to f_1 f_{\bar{2}}\, X] + \sigma[(P^0\,\bar{P}^0)^i \to f_{\bar{1}} f_2\, X]\right\}} \,.$$

$$\tag{2.27}$$

Bigi and Sanda[28] have discussed the case of $(B^0\bar{B}^0)^{\pm} \to \ell^- f, \ell^+ f$, where f is a state both B^0, $\bar{B}^0$ can go to. We can easily use the general formula given in Eqs. (2.21) and (2.22) to obtain Δ_f of their results. The interesting point here is that if Δ_f is different for different states f, it is a proof of decay amplitude CP violation. However such experiments are much harder to do.

In conclusion, it is possible to measure separately the mass-matrix CP violating effects, $2\mathrm{Re}\bar{\epsilon}/(1 + |\bar{\epsilon}|^2) = (1 - \eta^2)/(1 + \eta^2) \neq 0$, and the decay-amplitude CP-violating effects $(|A|^2 - |\bar{A}|^2)/(|A|^2 + |\bar{A}|^2) \neq 0$ via time-integrated experiments without isolating the K_S, K_L type of states. One type is tagged P^0 or $\bar{P}^0$, e.g. in $e^+e^-\ \pi^\pm\ P^\mp \bar{P}^0$ or $e^+e^-\ \pi^\pm\ P^\mp\ P^0$ by reconstructing the other states then Eq. (2.16a) gives purely the mass-matrix CP violating $\eta \neq 1$ effect (note that the mixing effect is given by Eq. (2.16b)); Eq. (2.17) gives the $P^0 \leftrightarrow \bar{P}^0$ mixing effects independent of CP violation; Eq. (2.19) gives the decay amplitude effects; other types of experiments are $e^+e^- \rightarrow P^0\bar{P}^0$ + neutrals, or $p\bar{p} \rightarrow P^0\bar{P}^0$ + neutrals, then Eq. (2.26) gives the pure mass-matrix $\eta \neq 1$ CP-violating effects, and Eq. (2.27) gives the pure decay-amplitude CP-violating effect. One can generalize these results to the most sophisticated ones of reconstructing specific decay channels, as well as to the crudest of simply detecting the difference of inclusive production in e^+e^- or $p\bar{p}$ of a particle and its antiparticle. A non-zero difference is an indication of CP violation, however in general it is a mixed mass-matrix and decay amplitude CP-violating effects.

Acknowledgement

It was a heart warming experience to be with Geoff and his family and his many friends and students at the Jubilee. Geoff's passion for physics, and his inspiration to his friends are an example for us all. I would like to thank Carleton DeTar for organizing the Jubilee, and for reading this manuscript and making many suggestions which have greatly improved the presentation of the manuscript.

I would like to thank H.-Y. Cheng, W.-Y. Keung, and W.M. Morse for many discussions on the subject. I have also benefited greatly from stimulating discussions and visits with physicists at various laboratories, the High Energy Physics Institue (Beijing), SLAC, DESY and Cornell, where the physics of charm and beauty are being carried out.

References

1. L.-L. Chau, talk in the *Proceedings of the 1980 Quangzhou Conference* (Jan. 5–10, 1980), Science Press, Beijing, Reinhold Comp., China; Van Nostr.
2. L.-L. Chau, *Phys. Reports,* Vol. 95, #1 1983.
   There are quite a few errors in Table 2.5 of this reference: $b+2e$ in $D^0 \rightarrow \bar{K}^0X^0$ should read $b-2c$; $-b-c+2e$ in $D^0 \rightarrow \eta^0X^0$ should read $-b-4c+2e$; $b+c$ in $D^0 \rightarrow K^0\eta^0$ should read $b-c$; $b+c$ in $D^0 \rightarrow K^0X^0$ should read $b+2c$; $a+d$ in $D^+ \rightarrow K^0\pi^+$ should read $b-d$; in the second to the last line of Table 2.5b D^+ to $K^0\pi^+$ should read $K^0\eta^0$ and $b-d$ should read $a-d$; in $D^+ \rightarrow K^+X^0$ $a+d$ should read $a+2d$; there should be an overall negative sign for $F^+ \rightarrow \eta^0\pi^+$; in $F^+ \rightarrow X^0\pi^+$ $V_{ud}V_{cs}^*\,(a+d)$ should read $V_{ud}V_{cs}^*\,(a+2d)$.
3. Table for charm meson decays, see Refs. 1 and 2, for Charm P $\rightarrow$ PV see also M. Gorn, *Nucl. Phys.* **B191**, 269 (1981) X.-Y. Li, S-.F. Tuan (to be submitted to *Zeits. für Physik C*).

4. M. Kobayashi and T. Maskawa, *Prog. Theor. Phys.* **49**, 652 (1973).

5. For recent developments in the subject, see talks in *Proceedings of Flavor Mixing in Weak Interactions,* Europhysics Conference, March 5-10, 1984, Erice, Italy, ed. L.-L. Chau (Plenum, New York, 1985).

6. For the b-lifetime, E. Fernandez, *Phys. Rev. Lett.* **51**, 1022 (1983); N. S. Lockyer *et al., Phys. Rev. Lett.* **51**, 1316 (1983); for more up-to-date information see talks by W. T. Ford, and G. H. Trilling in Ref. 5.

7. For Γ(b → u)/Γ(b → c), C. Klopfenstein *et al., Phys. Lett.* **103B**, 444 (1983); A. Chen *et al., Phys. Rev. Lett.* **111B**, 1084 (1984); and talks by J. Lee-Franzini, and P. Avery in Ref. 5.

8. For earlier fits to find V_{ud}, V_{us}, R. Shrock, and L.-L. Wang, *Phys. Rev. Lett.* **41**, 1972 (1978); more recent fits, see J. F. Donoghue and B. R. Holstein, *Phys. Rev.* **D25**, 2015 (1982); A. Garcia and P. Kielanowski, *Phys. Lett.* **110B** (1982) 498; and the most recent fits, WA2 experiment at CERN, M. Bourquin *et al., IV. Tests of the Cabbibo Model,* CERN preprint (1983); see talk by H. W. Siebert in Ref. 5.

9. L.-L. Chau and W.-Y. Keung, *Phys. Rev.* **D29**, 592 (1984); *Phys. Rev. Lett.* **53**, 1802 (1984).

10. L. Wolfenstein, *Phys. Rev. Lett.* **51**, 1945 (1984).

11. L.-L. Chau, Invited talk at the *First Workshop on Colliding Beam Physics in China,* Beijing, PRC, June 12-21, 1984.

12. General discussions incorporation SU(3) breaking and final-state interactions will be given elsewhere.

13. R. Schindler, talk given at the *XXIInd Int. Conf. on High Energy Physics,* Leipzig, July 1984. D. Hitlin, talk given at the SLAC Summer Institute, July 23 - August 3, 1984.

14. N. Ushida, *et al., Phys. Rev. Lett.* **51**, 2362 (1983).

15. J. H. Christenson, J. W. Cronin, V. L. Fitch and R. Turlay, *Phys. Rev. Lett.* **13**, 138 (1964).

16. M. Bander, D. Silverman and A. Soni, *Phys. Rev. Lett.* **43**, 242 (1979); J. Barnabeu and C. Jarlskog, *Z. Phys.* **C8**, 233 (1981); L. L. Chau Wang, AIP Conf. Proc. No. 72, Particle and Fields, Subseries No. 23, Virginia Polytechnic Inst. 1980, eds. G. B. Collins, L. N. Chang and J. R. Ficenec; L.-L. Chau, *Proceedings of 8th International Workshop on Weak Interactions and Neutrinos,* Javea, Spain, Sept. 5-11, 1983.

17. L.-L. Chau and H. Y. Cheng, *Phys. Lett.* **131B**, 202 (1983); T. Brown, S. F. Tuan and S. Pakvasa, *Phys. Rev. Lett.* **51**, 1823 (1983).

18. *Physics at LEAR with Low-Energy Cooled Antiprotons,* edited by U. Gastaldi and R. Klapisch, Ettore Majorana Int. Sci. Series, ed. A. Zichichi (Plenum), P. Pavlopoulos, talk in Ref. 5. G. Backenstoss *et al.,* CERN/PSCC/83-28/ PSCC/I65 (1983).

19. L. L. Chau and H.-Y. Cheng, *Phys. Rev. Lett.* **53**, 1037 (1984).

20. T. D. Lee, R. Oehme and C. N. Yang, *Phys. Rev.* **106**, 340 (1957). T. T. Wu and C. N. Yang, *Phys. Rev. Lett.* **13**, 380 (1964).

21. L. Wolfenstein, *Phys. Rev. Lett.* **13**, 562 (1964); and in *Theory and Phenomenology in Particle Physics,* ed. A. Zichichi (Academic Press, New York, 1969), p. 218.

22. See *Rev. Mod. Phys.* **56** No. 2, Part II, pp. S1-S304 (1984).

23. For discussion partial rate differences in K decays, see Sect. 3.2.2 of Ref. 2; L.-L. Chau, talk at Erice Conference on *Electroweak Effects at High Energies,* Feb. 1–12 1983; C. Kounnas, A. B. Lahanas and P. Pavlopoulos, *Phys. Lett.* **127B**, 381 (1983); C. Avilez, *Phys. Rev.* **23**, 1124 (1981); H.-Y. Cheng, *Phys. Lett.* **129B**, 357 (1983).

24. For a review of CP violation in the K system see, K. Kleinknecht, *Ann. Rev. Nucl. Sci.* **26**, 26 (1976); for some general discussions of CP violations in charm and beauty particles, see A. Pais and S. B. Treiman, *Phys. Rev.* **D12**, 2744 (1975); L. B. Okun, V. I. Zakharov and B. M. Pontecorvo, *Lett. Nuovo Cim.* **13**, 218 (1975).

25. A. Gsponer *et al., Phys. Rev. Lett.* **42**, 13 (1979).

26. J. H. Christenson *et al., Phys. Rev. Lett.* **43**, 1209 (1979).

27. Chicago, Stanford, Saclay collaboration 1984, K. Nishikawa, talk given at the *XXIIInd Int. Conf. on High Energy Physics,* Leipzig, July 1984.

28. BNL-Yale collaboration, *Measurement of the CP-Violating Parameters ϵ'/ϵ'',* J. K. Black *et al.,* Nov. 1984, submitted to *Phys. Rev. Lett.*

29. M. B. Wise, J. Hagelin, *Nucl. Phys.* **B189**, 87 (1981); J. Hagelin **B193**, 123 (1981). Here the following quantity was proposed:

$$\frac{\int_0^\infty d\tau\, S_-}{\int_0^\infty d\tau\, S_+} = \frac{P_{\varrho^+} - P_{\varrho^-}}{2 + P_{\varrho^+} + P_{\varrho^-}} ,$$

where

$$S_{\mp} = |A(P^0 \to \ell^+ X)|^2 + |A(\bar P^0 \to \ell^+ X)|^2$$
$$\mp |A(P^0 \to \ell^- X)|^2 \mp |A(\bar P^0 \to \ell^- X)|^2$$

and

$$P_{\varrho^+} \equiv |(1+\bar\epsilon)/(1-\bar\epsilon)|^2 |A/\bar A|^2 \cdot [(\Delta m)^2 + (\Delta\Gamma/2)^2]$$
$$\cdot [(\Delta m)^2 - (\Delta\Gamma/2)^2 + 2(\tilde\Gamma)^2]^{-1} ,$$

$$P_{\varrho^-} \equiv |(1+\bar\epsilon)/(1-\bar\epsilon)|^2 |\bar A/A|^2 \cdot [(\Delta m)^2 + (\Delta\Gamma/2)^2]$$
$$\cdot [(\Delta m)^2 - (\Delta\Gamma/2)^2 + 2(\tilde\Gamma)^2]^{-1} ,$$

but even in the case of $A = \bar A$, it is still a rather complicated mixture of effects in $\bar\epsilon$, and $\Delta m, \Delta\Gamma$.

30. L.-L. Chau, W.-Y. Keung, M. D. Tran, *Phys. Rev.* **D27,** 2145 (1983).
31. M. Goldhaber, T. D. Lee, C. N. Yang, *Phys. Rev.* **112,** 1796 (1958); M. Goldhaber, C. N. Yang in *Estratto da Evolution of Particle Physics,* ed. M. Conversi (Academic Press, New York, 1969).
32. M. Goldhaber, J. L. Rosner, *Phys. Rev.* **D15,** 1254 (1977).
33. I. I. Bigi and A. L. Sanda, *Nucl. Phys.* **B193,** 81 (1981). L. Wolfenstein, *CP Violation in B^0 - $\bar{B}^0$ Mixing,* Santa Barbara preprint, NSF-ITP-83-146.

"COUPS DE FOUDRE ET PASSIONS" OF TWELVE LIVELY YEARS WITH GEOFF

Denyse M. Chew

*"Our todays are the tomorrows
I used to dream about."*

Ever since I learnt that Geoff's students and collaborators were planning to celebrate his birthday, I have hoped to welcome them to our home, some for the first time — those who have not been in Berkeley since I married Geoff almost 13 years ago. Having been involved with Geoff for such a period of time, I feel as if I owe his friends the tale of some of these moments, some of Geoff's passions for physics and life as well.

Our life "together" started with a very romantic encounter, the stage for which was beautifully set by Prof. Zichichi in one of the summer schools he organizes each year in Erice, Sicily. At the School of High Energy Physics I attended, I was "looking for Chew" since, as a postdoc at CERN the previous summer, I had been given the task of performing a "Chew-Low extrapolation." In fact, had it been Francis Low lecturing, I would have attended for the same reason the school which was to last three weeks in July 1971. My plans were then to visit this mysterious country, just discovered by me through that magnificent Visconti movie, *The Leopard* — watched one month earlier in an enlarged-screen theater on the Champs-Élysées.

I had just returned from the Amsterdam Conference of High Energy Physics, when I boarded a plane in Paris to Rome, before travelling in a much smaller one to Palermo, Sicily. I landed there late in the afternoon. The air was still warm and full of Mediterranean scent and I could not help remembering that Sicily was one of the last European bastions before reaching Africa. I was pulled out of my reveries by the chauffeur of the School whose duty was to collect the latest arrivals including myself.

We climbed through the mountains which were parallel to the north coast of the Island, until we arrived at the town and harbour of Trapani. We then took the road to the top of a "sugarcone" where Erice sits, a delightful little town, formerly a place of worship to Venus in the Roman times. Its still marble-paved streets would be our daily promenade to reach one of the dozen restaurants where we were supposed to eat. Arriving so late, I figured that I would not attend the opening lecture — even if it were by Chew: he would be giving the next ten morning classes; besides there was always a discussion session in the afternoon and it would be surprising if I could not grab the "spirit" of his opening lecture to the school.

So I went to that first afternoon session. I sat far back, in order not to be spotted as a new student, and observed a very American-looking and behaving Professor: he was sitting on top of the table, one knee in hand, surrounded by all the morning students. All questions and answers were quite theoretical; being myself an experimentalist, I would not suffer too much from my lack of attendance. Suddenly I focused. There was a deep silence when everyone seemed to hold his breath. A question had been asked and the Oracle seemed to be thinking. Suddenly "he" spoke and I stopped being amused. I had most clearly heard "I don't know." And that was it. As a European, I could not believe that simple "cry of the heart", so sincere. Yet was he? I looked at Geoff for the first time. I noticed a sad look on his face (I learnt later from the students that he had recently lost his wife from a tragic illness). He seemed to be drifting away. Perhaps these facts were his excuses for admitting his limited knowledge? From now on, I would be curious about the real Geoff.

Every day, the classes took place in a long room with, at one end, a large blackboard, a lecturing podium, a lecturing desk, and a magnificent wooden piece in front painted with what could have been one of the adventures of "Orlando Furioso", the Arioste version of the story of Charlemagne's nephew, Roland, so popular in Sicily. Facing this imposing ensemble, was a no less imposing row of wide armchairs — for the Professors who wished to attend some lectures — in front of the tables and chairs for the students. I was one of them and nearsighted. The following morning, I made an effort to arrive early enough so I could sit close to the front row of students. I listened to Geoff's talk. During the following lecture my attention wandered for a few minutes to the view outside. All of Sicily seemed to be displayed at the foot of the sugarcone. A light heat haze already showed. I noticed a few clouds coming in from the Bay of Trapani and I distracted my German neighbor by commenting then "It was just like Berkeley, when at the height of summer the clouds seem to rush through the Golden Gate..." (I had spent a summer there when I had been given a NATO fellowship as a student, a few years earlier.) Apparently I spoke loud enough so that the Berkeley Professor turned around; I was innocent and looked away but he did not give up and looked and looked... I suddenly felt very warm as I eventually blushed.

From then on, we engaged in reciprocal questioning. But although I kept Geoff at "arms-length" by calling him "Professor" in the most European traditional way and joked all the time — I used to "defend" myself rather well — I took all Geoff's questions seriously from the beginning. However, light conversations were a "must" as we were never alone. Among the students, I remember Philip Mannheim and Niels Tornquist and Fumiyo Uchiyama; we would go and eat and make excursions together. Surrounding Geoff were Don Tow ('71) and Tom Neff. Geoff asked me once for dinner, when his daughter Beverly had arrived — whether for my sake or hers, I did not know. Nevertheless, little by little I would hear some personal news. One of them was his concern for his daughter. I felt compassion for this little 18-year old girl who had just lost her mother. I therefore gave Bev my home address, so I could help her if she came to study in Paris. But with Bev around, exchanges between Geoff and myself were scarce: neither of us wished to disturb his daughter further.

However, I was in the back seat of Geoff's rented car when he and Bev left Erice to go to Palermo on the Sunday morning of the end of the School. Geoff and Beverly had plans to spend a week in Europe, first at CERN and at the Summer School of Physics, Les Houches in the French Alps; Maurice Jacob, a long time collaborator and friend would welcome them in Geneva. Then they were to finish their European tour in London visiting one of Geoff's cousins, Elsa Dunbar. The trip to Palermo was long and wound along the mountains. We kept the conversation light like the air in that very early and sunny morning. The car stopped by the sea, along the Palermo promenade. I left quickly: Geoff's plane could not wait. Yet Geoff was also out of the car and his "I believe we will meet again" did not quite sound like a new School of Physics appointment. Filled with confusion, I sat on the beach until I thought his plane had gone. I was going to be so busy that I would not think any more of Geoff than of those beautiful puppets one sees in Sicily. In fact, buying a puppet was the first thing I did coming out of the Cathedral that morning after the visit to the Cloister: across the street, I got myself a magnificent friend of Orlando as the knight object of my attention.

I then proceeded to finish organizing the tour I was about to start around Sicily with other students, through the Greek temples and theaters of Selinunte, Agrigento and Syracuse, the Roman city of Piazza Armerina in the southern mountains, the flowery town of Taormina, Etna, the 3000-meter high volcano that we would climb one freezing night to observe the hot lava before flying from Catania to Naples, Capri and Pompei. We all had a marvelous week buried in these antique civilizations which gave us an appropriate measure of our own life: I had plenty of distractions to fill my attention. I remember so vividly the Byzantine frescoes of Montreale and those Roman mosaics in Pompei. I was in love with what I saw. Yet "was not there someone missing?..."

After a week of such visual gorging I landed back in Paris deserted by everyone I knew and loved: it was August then and vacation time. And rather than starting another quieting journey through the Parisian museums, I decided to prepare to work by checking my mail in my University laboratory. A surprise awaited me — a letter from Geoff. The first letter I did not even dream about. Of course, along with the other students, he had my working address. It took me a whole Sunday — and many re-writings — to answer all the questions Geoff had asked, before I strolled along the streets of Paris to the post office. I was surprised to find a second letter the next morning, in a completely different tone: light, light, light, so different from Geoff's whole style that I could not believe it. Only on checking the envelopes did I realize that, while both letters had been mailed from England, the latter just before his departure to the States, the former had a stamp more than a week old and the return address of his London cousin. It looked as if Geoff had been expecting an answer for a week. Of course I felt at peace since I had answered as soon as possible. Two weeks or so later a third letter came with Geoff's answer to my first letter: obviously he had had a hard time waiting and was relieved that he had heard from me at last. All his thoughts were now as deep as I wished and I just had to answer yes, yes, yes... but for a few practical conditions. Geoff agreed to all of them as long as I agreed to marry him. He had two weeks before teaching again in the fall. Could he fly over so we could get engaged?

It was during that following month that I read about Geoff's dearest beloved ones: of course about his twin children, Bev and Berkeley, already in College at Bryn Mawr and Princeton. But also about the warm affection which surrounded him while he was growing up as the youngest of four children. I heard about his enterprising mother — she was one of the first English suffragettes while still a bachelor teacher; about his generally bad-tempered father never raising his voice to his "pet son"; about his oldest sister Audrey enough his senior to mother him for a long time and telling him stories (she obtained a PhD in English and taught in a college before marrying a Los Alamos optical engineer — a move that cost her her career); about his kindly protective brother Bernard; of his other sister Ruth who had already written a dozen or so "witchy" Halloween stories for children.

Geoff arrived in Paris in mid-September and after picking up our luggage we departed. It was all so natural to meet again and for Geoff to ask about my present, past, family, friends and colleagues. It was fall in Paris, but sunny and decorative, when the trees had started to change color and no strong wind had yet blown away the leaves. We strolled along; from the University to the cozy banks of the Seine River, from the Jardins du Louvre and its statues by Maillol to the Tuileries, from his hotel and my apartment to my mother's place. We got engaged amidst my family and friends. We also departed for a one-week trip through France "A La Recherche Du Temps Perdu..." of my past. In my small car we reached and met, in Sens, my grandmother's cousin; in Vezelay and the Morvan Mountains and La Pierre-qui-vire and Nevers, my youth; in Moulins, my grandmother; in Vierzon, one uncle; in Saint-Etienne, my father's tomb; in Valence and the mountains of Vercors, my other grandmother. The roads along the vineyards of Burgundy and Vallee du Rhone were lovely and there were long drives when we conversed endlessly. The weather became real "fall" at times but no storm prevented us from sharing our thoughts. And this is how I heard about Geoff's friends in physics — his students, collaborators and colleagues — and all those who had influenced Geoff's life from an early age.

While still an undergraduate at the George Washington University, Geoff had encountered Gamow, so instrumental in recommending Geoff for a job in Los Alamos though he himself was not allowed to work there in 1944. I heard about Edward Teller, Geoff's boss in Los Alamos, then of Fermi, Geoff's PhD advisor in Chicago from whom Geoff learned that "if it is true, it can be proved." While sharing the same office, Geoff made many friends — some collaborators subsequently: I heard of the Argos, Harold and Mary and of their everlasting friendship since Los Alamos; then at the University of Chicago, there were "Murph" Goldberger and his wife Mildred, Chen Ning Yang, and Jack Steinberger and Owen Chamberlain. Later came younger Tsung-Dao Lee. Geoff was moved as he spoke of all these friends of early times. In 1949, when Geoff was first appointed to the Berkeley faculty, time flew quickly as he had only one wish: to be left in peace so he could work. He refused to allow his precious time to be disturbed by controversy at Berkeley over the oath and he accepted an offer at the University of Illinois, in Champaign-Urbana. It turned out for his own good; it was there that he met Francis Low and that started their fruitful collaboration as well as another everlasting friendship. In 1957, however, Geoff was back in Berkeley and Francis was at MIT, and although there were summer contacts, it became more difficult with family settlement on the opposite coasts to continue their work — but at least their friendship continued intact: Francis was one of Geoff's first friends to welcome me in the US when he made a trip to Fermilab, in May 1972. In Berkeley, there would be Stanley Mandelstam, Henry Stapp, Ken Watson — all names I had quoted in my PhD thesis and that my mother still remembers typing. Also Geoff's first Berkeley students and postdocs since his return there: Bill Frazer ('59), Jim Ball ('60) and Jose Fulco, followed by Steve Frautschi, all friends ever since. Then there were all of Geoff's students and postdocs whom I would meet as they visited Berkeley, or as we visited Chicago, Fermilab or London for High Energy Physics Conferences. I believe it was in that first summer in Berkeley that started my own friendship with Carleton DeTar ('70) and his family, when he was getting ready to go and help his archeologist wife dig in the Nevada Desert. At the FNAL Conference which took place in September 1972, I met a delightful and enthusiastic Ling-Lie Chau ('66): she would be in Berkeley on many of her trips to China — or rather *from* China as her Chinese souvenirs to Geoff reminded us. And it was in London, at the beginning of July 1974, that Geoff would meet for the first time an Austrian bootstrapper, Fritjof Capra, soon to become famous for his book *The Tao of Physics*. In Europe we would keep "bumping" into Chung-I Tan ('68) and his family during some of Chung-I's visits to his collaborators in Tran Thanh Van's group in Orsay. Also, in Paris and at CERN, we encountered often Keiji Igi, one of Geoff's close collaborators in the early sixties and a friend since, whom I first knew in Berkeley during the summer of 1972. There are very few names I was not already familiar with as I read the list of guests today.

But I am anticipating my story: Geoff returned to Berkeley after our engagement trip in September 1971. Two weeks later, his sister Ruth and her husband "Buck" Silver were in Paris to check on me and "make sure that I would not give up the idea of marrying Geoff." I never convinced her of my real feelings — Ruth was quite sorry that Geoff and I would not see each other until I landed in San Francisco on Christmas day. There I met Beverly again and her brother, Berkeley, already a very sophisticated young man with a hippyish hairstyle. It was with all my heart that I kissed a balloon of hair handled in a very grand and welcoming manner. Although not so dramatically, Beverly had also been very thoughtful and worked to prepare a warm welcome home. Both had been sweetly lectured while well taken care of by another dear English cousin, Betty Foucar, who was then finishing her stay in Berkeley. She left during the following days and I changed name in a home civil wedding ceremony — with memorable colored pictures skillfully taken by Berkeley and with Dave and Barbara Jackson as witnesses. Soon, besides meeting all the high energy physicists here in two memorable parties, organized respectively by the Rosenfelds and the Jacksons, we had elegant dinners at the MacMillans and at the Trillings. We then proceeded to visit Jose Fulco and his family in Santa Barbara. The day of our return, we took our civil certificate to the French Consulate where our marriage was made official and I left for my job in Paris early in January 1972.

In April, Geoff came to Paris and we were religiously married surrounded by our families and many of our European friends: Geoff's sister Ruth and her husband flew in from New York, while his cousin Elsa as well as some of my English friends came from London. We took off for a week's honeymoon in Greece before Geoff flew back alone to Fermilab. A month later, I was ready — or so it seemed — and met him and some of his family in Washington, D.C., in particular, his mother who offered me hospitality in the same home where Geoff grew up. I was moved finding Geoff's early letters still lying around in the cupboard of the bedroom he shared with his older brother, Bernard. Geoff's mother reminded me of my little southern grandmother and we immediately developed a warm relationship. Perhaps she realized I loved her son in her same dear and true way. I was delighted also to meet Geoff's kind brother and his wife Betty, as Bernard had been the witness of Geoff's most precious childhood souvenirs, when they would play baseball together or while he taught Geoff golf and driving.

We settled down in May and June 1972 at Fermilab with the kindest help of Ned Goldwasser and Lizie, his wife, before visiting — again from Geoff's past — the Physics Department of Champaign-Urbana where I met all Geoff's friends gathered at a memorable dinner so elegantly given by

David and Susie Pines — a huge crowd, but everyone was seated at a table. We also visited Purdue University where Louis Balázs ('62) welcomed us — the beginning of another long friendship. At Argonne, we saw Ed Berger — often met since at CERN — and became friends also with the Lipkins from Israel.

In July 1972, after crossing Idaho and visiting the Badlands, the Rushmore Monument, Yellowstone and the Grand Teton National Park, we arrived one evening in Buffalo, Wyoming, where we met by accident Russ Huson and his wife Joyce, friends I had known ever since I had been a NATO fellowship student in Berkeley: Russ had given me — second-hand — my first "S-matrix classes by a certain G. F. Chew" (who was then, I discovered, on a sabbatical in Europe). We had met the Husons at length while at Fermilab and now found ourselves in their homeland where they were visiting their parents who lived in neighboring ranches. I watched my first rodeo that same evening. A few days later we were home in Berkeley, at last! And I began to settle in my new country, fortunately with Geoff.

I met Georgella Perry, the LBL Theory Group administrative assistant so helpful to Geoff ever since his arrival in Berkeley. I made acquaintance with sweet Chih Kwan Chen ('72), Chun Fai Chan ('72) and Cris Sorensen ('72) as well as with Geoff's three current students Ghassan Ghandour, Joel Koplik and Ramamurti Shankar, who all graduated with their PhD's in June 1974. Shankar even proposed an explanation of results from an experiment on which I was working and became one of our dearest friends.

In the spring of 1973, Geoff took me with him on a delightful trip to Virginia where he was invited by Arndt ('65) and to New Orleans and Baton Rouge where he was to give talks. In September 1973, our first son Pierre-Yves arrived just on the day when my mother landed back in Paris after a six-week stay with us. But Geoff was due in Paris in December as one of the PhD examiners for a physicist there. So we presented our offspring to our French family after a stop on the East Coast where we again met all Geoff's family. Our three weeks in Europe and Morocco — where we visited my aunt and many of her friends — were a very happy time and it was therefore only logical that we should plan a European summer 1974.

Geoff elected CERN and there took place an important event in his encounter with Veneziano who immediately proceeded to explain one of the embryonic ideas for the topological bootstrap — an approach to particle theory which has dominated Geoff's work ever since. The early form of this approach came to be known as "Dual Topological Unitarization" or DTU — after the contribution had been recognized of Veneziano (for the "Topological Expansion") and Chan Hong Mo (for "Dual Unitarization"). Gabriele Veneziano was interested then in Geoff's reaction as well as in an offer to come to Berkeley which followed after Geoff had returned to Berkeley in the fall. But with his family in Italy and Israel, Gabriele preferred the appointment that he was subsequently offered at CERN. Fortunately (for Geoff), before leaving Israel Veneziano had, working with him, a post-doc from Berkeley, Carl Rosenzweig, who immediately started to work with Geoff after his and Geoff's return in the fall of 1974. Four students joined them, Phil Lucht and George Weissmann who were already working with Geoff, Jaime Millan and Jean-Pierre Sursock — who came in spring 1975 and the following fall. Also in this early effort was Fritjof Capra who was now in Berkeley.

In summer 1976, we were back in Europe, Geoff in Stockholm to speak on baryoniums before joining me at CERN where we spent the summer, apart from his attendance at a DTU Oxford workshop organized by Chan Hong Mo. Back in Berkeley in the fall of 1976, Geoff and Carl soon started to write the DTU review article suggested by Maurice Jacob, editor of *Physics Reports*, with many references to the theses of J. Millan ('77) and Phil Lucht ('78). Geoff hosted the first Berkeley workshop on DTU in July 1977; Veneziano and Chan Hong Mo — whose workshop of 1976 was the model — were both present, and, of course, Henry Stapp and Fritjof Capra. Also the present students of Geoff named above and some former students who had joined this field of research: Louis Balázs, Ed Jones ('64) and Jerry Finkelstein ('67). Plus some other physicists who had worked in the field in recent years such as Jan Kwiecinski, who was later, on two occasions, to be our host in Poland.

As our second son, Jean-Francois, was born in June 1975 and our daughter, Pauline, in December 1976, we planned some quiet holidays for two weeks in August 1977. It was in a rented cabin by Lake Tahoe that Geoff polished his part of the Review Report on DTU which was published the following spring. In spring 1978, both George Weissmann and Jean-Pierre Sursock got their PhDs; we were almost ready to leave for a sabbatical year at CERN. However a fortunate event happened in that same spring.

On a sunny April Sunday morning, Geoff was happily whistling while gardening and thinking about a paper then in preparation with Jerry, George and Jean-Pierre, when one of our neighbors, Prof. Leon Henkin of the Mathematics Department heard him and enquired as to the reason for such a joyful tune. Geoff explained to Leon the new track of research his collaborators and he were on and Leon asked if Geoff would give a talk in the Math Department. Geoff accepted but the day following this departmental talk he received two phone calls: one from a senior topologist and one from Prof. David Goldschmidt, both with the same purpose: to convince Geoff that deductions made with diagrams emphasized by the new paper would be more powerful "if he would just make use of topology with a closed surface embedding these diagrams." In fact, Prof. Goldschmidt was so convinced that he gave Geoff time to discuss his questions. Geoff visited him in his office on the campus a couple of times, enough to convince himself that 2-dimensional topology was the mathematical structure necessary for future bootstrap development. In fact, Geoff had already played with such thoughts many years earlier — long before the diagrams of Rosner — and some books on topology could be found at home. But nothing had come of the earlier flirtation.

Geoff was to spend one month with the theorists of Saclay before our year at CERN. In Paris, in his first talk, he explained his frustration about lack of sufficient background in topology. He was immediately consoled by his French colleagues: they all knew Prof. Poénaru from the University of Paris XI and École Polytechnique, who in fact had just performed a remarkable job collaborating in solid state physics with a bright physicist of École Normalé. Geoff phoned "Poe" and immediately started a collaboration which broadened into a wonderful friendship, Geoff and Poe complementing each other at each step of the developments during these last six years.

While at CERN, Geoff enlarged his collaboration with Poe by correspondence — they started a heavy exchange of letters when they could not meet — and worked with Henry Stapp who spent a few months overlapping with us. It was after his return to Berkeley that Henry would become responsible for key bootstrap developments involving spin and chirality, with Ed Jones helping back in Nebraska. During that year 1978–1979 a continuing relationship began with Basarab Nicolescu, Vinh-Mau and the University of Paris — where Geoff was to be invited for an extended visit five years later, in 1983–1984. Meanwhile, Basarab and one of his Parisian colleagues, Pierre Gauron, focused on phenomenological applications which led later to the discovery of hadronic supersymmetry.

Geoff felt very busy after coming back from Europe in the fall of 1979: he now had to teach at the same time as continuing the research that was occupying a large place of his thoughts — how would he be able to continue his research? In front of the TV one evening in the fall he reflected "that with the children to help prepare for school departure he had inadequate time left for research." I remembered Geoff telling me that early morning was the time when he was the most energetic and that he would not mind getting up early. I suggested that he cut the TV short and go to bed at 9 pm if necessary. From then on, Geoff did all his research from 5 am, sometimes 4:30 am... and skipped TV.

In 1980 there took place the second Berkeley workshop, the subject now called "Topological Bootstrap". New participants included Poenaru, Nicolescu and current students, Mark Levinson and Raul Espinosa. During this workshop the junction line achieved a firm place in bootstrap theory as a result of observations by Jerry Finkelstein and Julian Uschersohn. Geoff was extremely excited by this development and greatly relieved when Poe declared the new ingredient to be legitimate.

Following the workshop Geoff leaned heavily on Jerry and inveigled him into an extensive collaboration which still continues. Jerry quickly proposed a topologization of electric charge that has stood up not only to Poe but to experiment. In 1981 the next workshop was organized in Paris and Geoff travelled there alone working afterward with Poe on the first effort to topologize leptons. In the fall of 1982, his present student Dieter Issler joined in the effort to extend the bootstrap beyond hadrons. Jerry, Dieter and Poe have been instrumental in the most recent developments included in the book Geoff wrote during the Paris sojourn of 1983–84. This book integrates all bootstrap developments that have occurred during the 12 lively years I have here recounted and, with Geoff's characteristic optimism, includes guesses about the years to come.

TOPOLOGICAL THEORY OF STRONG AND ELECTROWEAK INTERACTIONS

Jerome Finkelstein

1. Introduction

During the past several years Geoff Chew has, along with several collaborators, been developing a program which has become known as the "topological theory". Since I have been privileged to participate in some of these developments, this volume in honor of Geoff is an appropriate place to record a few comments about them. This is in no way intended to be a systematic review of the topological program — the reader interested in such a review may consult the paper by Capra listed as Ref. 1.

Some time ago it was argued by Veneziano[2] that a good first approximation to hadronic scattering amplitudes would consist of those contributions whose Harari-Rosner duality diagrams[3] were planar; these were said to constitute the "planar amplitudes". The idea of the topological expansion was that all of the corrections to this planar approximation (namely those contributions whose duality diagrams required surfaces of greater topological complexity) could at least in principle be obtained from iterations of the planar amplitudes. Originally, the existence of baryons and of particle spin could not be treated seriously by this expansion; the program to be discussed in this paper (which is the program that began with the work of Ref. 4) is an extension of the topological expansion to include the effects of spin and of the existence of baryons. By virtue of this extension, what began as, at best, a toy model of the strong interactions, has become a candidate for a theory of all particle interactions.

The comments I make in this paper concern two developments that have arisen from the topological program: these are, first, that predictions could be made for quantities such as the number of hadron generations, and second, that the theory could be extended so as to encompass the electroweak interactions. It is perhaps somewhat surprising that topological theory should have anything at all to say on these subjects, since it developed from a model for strong interactions in which it seemed that any number of generations could be equally well accommodated. I address the questions of how these predictions and extensions could arise from topological theory, and to what extent they should be considered to be integral parts of that theory.

2. How the Number of Generations is Determined

Among the predictions of topological theory are the number of quarks in a baryon (3, which implies that the number of colors is also 3 because the baryon is a color singlet), the maximum number of quarks and antiquarks in an elementary hadron (4, in baryonium), and the number of hadron generations (4, giving a total of 8 flavors). In this section I discuss, as an example of these predictions, the determination of the number of hadron generations in the topological theory of Ref. 4.

It is certainly possible to represent the generation quantum numbers by means of labels that accompany the quark lines of duality diagrams: one merely asserts that each such quark line carries a label that specifies the generation of that particular quark, and by postulating that this label never varies along a given quark line, one assures the conservation of each generation. This labelling was used in Ref. 3 (and implictly in Ref. 2) and it certainly does allow one to accommodate within the topological expansion the existence of any number of conserved generations.

However, in the theory of Ref. 4 there is another way to represent generation conservation which is at the same time more restrictive and more natural. In this theory, quarks are represented by triangles, which each share two of their edges with a quark in another particle participating in the same reaction. If one imagines that these shared edges are oriented (i.e. are directed line segments), then one obtains restrictions on which quarks can share edges with others; it turns out that these restrictions imply conserved internal quantum numbers that can be identified as generations (the flavor degree of freedom *within* a generation being represented separately). The number of generations is then simply determined: any given quark has two edges to share with others, each of which can be oriented in one of two ways, so there are $2 \times 2 = 4$ different quark generations, each of which is separately conserved.

Thus the argument that there are four hadron generations is really an esthetic one: it is certainly possible, by attaching labels to quark lines, to define a topological expansion for any number of generations; however, there is a more natural and more elegant way to represent generations, which only makes sense if there are exactly four generations. How compelling this argument is found to be depends on one's taste. My own feeling is that it is sufficiently compelling so that, if it were to be discovered that the number of generations were different from four (admittedly not a likely development in the near future, even if the supposition be true), the whole topological program would appear considerably less attractive.

3. Extension of Topological Theory to Electroweak Interactions

Since the topological expansion was originally developed as a model for the purely strong interactions, one may wonder how the electroweak interactions could fit in. One possible point of view is that they are entirely apart from the topological expansion. According to this viewpoint, one might in principle determine the lowest-order approximation to the topological expansion, and then proceed to add to it all of the higher-order terms; one would then have an expression for strong-interaction amplitudes, to which electroweak effects would still have to be added. Thus although the topological expansion might imply some constraints on the electroweak interactions (since not every conceivable electroweak interaction might be compatible with the strong interactions), one could not discover just by studying the topological expansion any reason for the electroweak interactions to exist at all. One way to restate this point of view is to say that the topological expansion could in principle be summed, and would yield well-defined scattering amplitudes which (because they lacked electroweak effects) simply do not correspond to the answers that nature has given us.

A second possible point of view is that the electroweak interactions are completely contained in the topological expansion. Again one assumes that the topological expansion converges, and thus gives well-defined amplitudes, but now one supposes that the amplitudes so obtained are the correct ones, including all electroweak as well as strong effects (but probably excluding gravitational effects?). It is rather hard to imagine how certain regularities of the lowest-order approximation (such as parity invariance) could be lost by the rest of the topological expansion, but I am not aware of any way of rigorously ruling out this possibility.

It is, however, a third point of view that is suggested by the program discussed in this paper. This point of view assumes that if one tried to sum the topological expansion one would encounter some pathology, some divergence perhaps, that would prevent the amplitudes as constructed from this expansion from being well defined, unless some additional piece were added, and that one could identify this additional piece with the electroweak interactions. Thus the electroweak interactions, while strictly speaking lying outside the topological expansion, would be required by it. This point of view was advanced in a remarkably bold paper by Chew,[5] in which he accused the "naked cylinder" term of being the part of the topological expansion that required fixing, and suggested that this repair would also determine the value of the fine structure constant.

At the present time, this suggestion of a dynamical origin of the electroweak interaction from within the topological expansion remains conjectural. What *has* been shown is that the electroweak interaction can be represented in a fairly natural way by the same topological construction that was used for the strong interactions, but that this representation implies a very particular model of the electroweak interactions.

This model is particularly restrictive for the spectrum of vector gauge bosons and for their coupling to leptons.[6] There are predicted to be four charged vector bosons (left- and right-handed $W^{\pm}$) and four neutral vector bosons (the photon and three Z_0's). The four least-massive of these bosons (the photon, the left-handed $W^{\pm}$, and one Z_0) have the same coupling to leptons as is implied by the standard (Weinberg-Salam) model, if in that model one sets the Weinberg angle θ_w to 30°. Thus any effects in the interaction of gauge bosons and leptons that in the standard model would be ascribed to a departure of θ_w from 30° would in the topological model have to be explained by invoking the higher-mass bosons. One striking prediction of the topological model that is unchanged even by the higher-mass bosons is that the vector coupling of the massive neutral boson(s) to charged leptons vanishes. This coupling can be determined from measurements of the charge asymmetry in $e^+e^- \rightarrow \mu^+\mu^-$; since the standard model (with $\theta_w \neq 30°$) predicts a small but non-zero value for this coupling, in principle we have a way to decide between the two models, but presently available data are not sufficiently accurate to do so.

This extension of the theory of Ref. 4 to the electroweak interactions could be considered to be a separate theory that might stand or fall independently. However, the same sort of esthetic considerations that led from the theory of Ref. 4 to the prediction of the number of hadron generations lead also to the particular electroweak model mentioned above. For this reason I would consider it a great blow to all of topological theory if this electroweak model were found to be incorrect, and conversely a great triumph for topological theory if it were found to be correct.

Acknowledgement

I wish to acknowledge the hospitality of the Lawrence Berkeley Laboratory. This work was supported by the National Science Foundation under Grant No. PHY-8405415, and by the Director, Office of Energy Research, Office of High Energy and Nuclear Physics, Division of High Energy Physics of the U.S. Department of Energy under Contract DE-AC03-7600098.

References

1. F. Capra, *Surveys in High Energy Physics* **4**, 127 (1984).

2. G. Veneziano, *Nucl. Phys.* **B74**, 365 (1974).

3. H. Harari, *Phys. Rev. Lett.* **22,** 562 (1969); J. L. Rosner, *Phys. Rev. Lett.* **22,** 689 (1969).

4. G. F. Chew and V. Poénaru, *Phys. Rev. Lett.* **45,** 229 (1980); *Zeit. Phys.* **C11,** 59 (1981).

5. G. F. Chew, *Phys. Rev.* **D27,** 976 (1983).

6. G. F. Chew and J. Finkelstein, *Phys. Rev. Lett.* **50,** 795 (1983).

DEDUCING T, C, AND P INVARIANCE FOR STRONG INTERACTIONS IN TOPOLOGICAL PARTICLE THEORY

C. Edward Jones

It is shown here how the separate discrete invariances [time reversal (T), charge conjugation (C), and parity (P)] in strong interactions can be deduced as consequences of other S-matrix requirements in topological particle theory.

It is a special privilege for me to be able to salute my friend and teacher Geoff Chew on this memorable occasion. To those of us who have worked around and with him, he is a superb role model both as a physicist and as a human being. He has always been at the center of exciting new ideas and developments in particle physics. And his co-workers always seem to enjoy a high level of research productivity as a result of his influence.

Geoff has an incredible talent for working with research students. He assigns interesting and stimulating problems to his students and generously shares his counsel and encouragement throughout the project. Students never doubt his genuine interest in them and their careers.

For many years Chew has held a bold vision of the fundamental role of self-consistency as a basic aspect of nature's laws. I think that philosophy made an indelible impression on all his students and co-workers whether they still work on bootstrap physics or not. The idea that the "final theory" should contain essentially no adjustable parameters is an influential concept regardless of the context in which one works.

One conviction of Chew's has been that the symmetries of particle physics should be a consequence of self-consistency just as much as the particle masses and couplings. It is some recent work along this line that I wish to describe here.

Over twenty years ago Henry Stapp[1] presented a proof within the context of S-matrix theory that scattering amplitudes are invariant under the product of the three discrete symmetries T, C, and P. Previous proofs of this result had been accomplished using field theory. However, Stapp's proof[1] assumed only fundamental properties about S-matrix elements, such as unitarity, analyticity and crossing symmetry.

The recent work I discuss here by Finkler and myself[2] is concerned with *separate* T, C, and P invariance in strong interactions and is carried out within the framework of topological bootstrap theory. This modern version of S-matrix theory[3,4] has not yet become well appreciated but to those who have followed its development, it is certainly more promising and sophisticated than any of the versions of bootstrap theory that have preceded it. New insight into the discrete symmetries is just one of the intriguing aspects of the new theory. I summarize here several of the characteristics of this modern bootstrap theory which are particularly relevant for this discussion of discrete symmetries in strong interactions:

(i)   Spin variables[4] are incorporated into the problem at the outset and the bootstrap requirements influence the form of the spin dependence at a fundamental level.

(ii)   The bootstrap problem[3] is localized at the simplest level of topological expansion — the so-called zero entropy level, where the analyticity structure of amplitudes is planar.

(iii)   It is possible to unambiguously identify the topological zero-entropy level of the problem as associated with strong interactions only.[5] Electroweak effects come into the theory only at higher levels of topological complexity[6-8] corresponding to non-zero entropy.

Since it is possible to identify terms in the S matrix that are associated exclusively with strong interactions, such terms (actually sums of terms) should presumably exhibit separate invariance under T, C and P transformations. The question then becomes whether such discrete symmetries should be put in by hand or whether they, in fact, come out automatically as a consequence of self-consistency. Stapp's original work on this subject[4] showed that the sum of zero-entropy terms could have the invariances T, C and P. This raised the question: could a self-consistent zero-entropy bootstrap exist without these invariances? As we now discuss, the answer to the question is tied to the issue of the relative phases of the zero-entropy terms which are summed in the topological expansion.

The zero-entropy amplitudes are representable as graphs constructed out of quark and diquark lines. The two basic types of quark lines entering into such diagrams and their associated Lorentz invariant spin dependences[2,4] are indicated in Fig. 1.

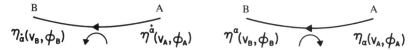

Fig. 1a.   Spin dependence of an ortho quark.   Fig. 1b.   Spin dependence of a para quark.

In Fig. 1, the η's are two-component spinors with Lorentz transformation properties corresponding to either dotted or undotted representations;[4] the symbols v denote a four-vector velocity associated with the particle of which the quark is a constituent; the two-component spinors ϕ denote the rest-frame spin state of the quark. The head of an arrow B in Fig. 1 indicates an out-quark or an in-antiquark, and the tail of the arrow B an in-quark or out-antiquark. The small arrows either in agreement or disagreement with the direction of the quark line arrow are embellishments which indicate topologically either dotted or undotted indices. The quark in Fig. 1a is called an "ortho" quark, the one in Fig. 1b a "para" quark.

Stapp[4] emphasized that spin dependence of the type indicated in Fig. 1 is self-reproducing. In particular, if either ortho or para quark lines are cut in the middle, the sum over intermediate spin states gives:

$$\sum_i \eta^{\dot{\beta}}(v, \phi_i)\, \eta_{\dot{\alpha}}(v, \phi_i) = \delta^{\dot{\beta}}_{\dot{\alpha}} \quad ,$$

$$\sum_i \eta_{\beta}(v, \phi_i)\, \eta^{\alpha}(v, \phi_i) = \delta^{\alpha}_{\beta} \quad , \tag{1}$$

where the ϕ_i denote a complete set of rest-frame spin states. Such a spin dependence for quark lines then leads to the construction of particle amplitudes which possess at the lowest (zero-entropy) level a completely factorized self-reproducing spin dependence. In such amplitudes each quark can be either of the ortho or para type and these possibilities are summed over in the topological expansion, since the ortho-para degree of freedom is not measurable.

In Fig. 2 is depicted an example of a simple topological diagram (zero-entropy) corresponding to a three-point amplitude in which one meson (A) is in the initial state and two mesons (B and C) are in the final state. The spin dependence of each quark line is that previously indicated in Fig. 1. The remaining momentum dependence for the graph in Fig. 2 is given by a multiplicative invariant scalar function and the flavor dependence is another multiplicative factor. Also there is an important phase factor which must be included in evaluating the diagram. As mentioned above, the graph in Fig. 2 must be summed with other graphs having other arrangements of ortho and para quarks. There are eight different graphs of this type.

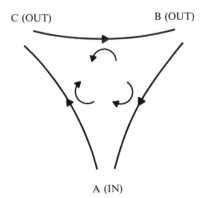

Fig. 2.   Three-meson zero-entropy amplitude.

We shall illustrate the question of discrete symmetries by considering the parity transformation P. At issue is the relationship between the amplitude for the diagram in Fig. 2 and the amplitude for the same process in which all three-momenta have been reversed and all spin states are unchanged. It can be shown that the effect of this transformation is to replace each ortho quark in Fig. 2 with a para quark and *vice versa*. The invariant scalar function of momenta and the flavor dependence are unchanged by this transformation. Clearly the diagram of Fig. 2 is not invariant under a parity transformation since ortho and para quarks are interchanged.

We recall that Fig. 2 must be summed with seven other terms one of which will be Fig. 3, in which each quark line has the opposite ortho-para

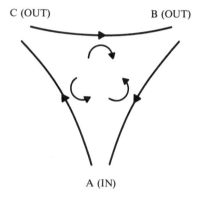

Fig. 3.   Three-meson zero-entropy amplitude with ortho and para quarks reversed with respect to Fig. 2.

structure to that in Fig. 2. It might seem obvious now that parity invariance will hold in the theory because the eight terms which must be summed consist of four pairs analogous to Fig. 2 and Fig. 3 having opposite ortho-para structures, and therefore being invariant under the interchange of ortho and para quarks. However, this conclusion is not warranted for two reasons:

(i)   Since each term in the sum has a multiplicative phase associated with it in addition to the spin, flavor and momentum dependence, it is not clear that the relative phase between two terms such as Fig. 2 and Fig. 3 will be unchanged after the ortho-para quark interchange.

(ii)   Even if the relative phase between the terms in each of the four pairs of terms in our example is unchanged, parity invariance will not hold for the entire sum of eight terms unless the relative phases between the four pairs are themselves unchanged, a necessary condition for the parity invariance of the entire sum.

Thus to discover whether parity invariance holds for the sum of eight zero-entropy terms, it is necessary to understand the properties of the phases which multiply each of these terms. It is, of course, possible that the phases — in particular, the relative phases between the individual terms in the sum — possess a degree of arbitrariness which can be removed by requiring that the discrete transformations T, C, and P are invariances of the zero-entropy sum — a sum which is associated exclusively with strong interactions.

A careful study of the problem of the phases of zero-entropy amplitudes[9] shows that the relative phases of these amplitudes are severely constrained by the fundamental S-matrix theory requirements of pole factorization, crossing symmetry, hermitian analyticity, plus the requirement that the zero-entropy amplitudes satisfy a non-linear bootstrap equation.

Assuming a factorized form for the phases associated with each quark line, these requirements determine the form of the relative phase factor between amplitudes of the type being considered which differ only by the presence of a different distribution of ortho and para quarks. For the process in Figs. 2 and 3 this phase factor has the form:[9]

$$e^{i\phi} = (-1)^{N_{LP}} \ ,$$
(2)

where N_{LP} is the number of para quark lines whose heads and tails are either both in-states or both out-states and which therefore represent incoming or outgoing para quark-antiquark state. The relative phase (2) also holds for more general processes where baryons and mesons are present. When baryons and baryonia are both present the phase (2) may be multiplied by another factor[9] slightly generalizing its form but this generalization does not alter the validity of the discrete invariances.

Applying (2) to the example we are considering leads to the result that each of the diagrams among the eight having a para quark connecting the B and C mesons has a phase of minus one relative to those having an ortho quark connecting the B and C mesons. This relative phase leads at once to the parity invariance of the above sum of eight terms. In fact it shows that the sum evaluated with all three-momenta reversed is minus the original sum. This can be interpreted as indicating that the mesons have negative intrinsic parity.

Although we have only indicated how the P-invariance is deduced for the special case of the three-meson amplitude, by applying (2) and its generalization, we find that the conclusion holds for any zero-entropy process, including those involving baryons and baryonia. Again this follows because the relative phases of the amplitudes determined by self-consistency in S-matrix theory[9] in the sum of zero-entropy terms are just such as to give the same amplitude up to a phase when the three-momenta are reversed and spins left unchanged. When baryons are included one shows that baryon-antibaryon pair can be assigned a negative intrinsic parity.

The derivation of time reversal invariance in the zero-entropy sum follows the same pattern as in the case of parity, in the sense that pairs of terms having opposite ortho-para structures are found to be invariant under T. However, the details of the argument for T-invariance are quite different from the parity case since "in" and "out" states as well as spin and momenta must be reversed under time reversal. All relative phases will work out just right to give T-invariance, but this is by no means obvious *a priori*.

Charge conjugation invariance is deduced in the zero-entropy sum also, where each individual term is found to be separately invariant under C. Again the relative phases between terms must be checked to verify that the entire sum is also C-invariant, which, indeed, it turns out to be.

Thus Chew's vision of a nature whose symmetries and whose particle properties are determined by self-consistency appears to have been brought closer to realization. It remains to be seen whether the other quantitative details of this approach will work out as well as a complete theory of electroweak processes. Whatever happens, Chew's innovative view of nature as based fundamentally on self-consistency has made a deep impression on the physics of the last half of the twentieth century.

Acknowledgement

This work was supported in part by the National Science Foundation.

References

1. H. P. Stapp, *Phys. Rev.* **125,** 2139 (1962).

2. C. E. Jones and P. Finkler, Nebraska preprint.

3. C. F. Chew and V. Poénaru, *Zeit. Phys.* **C11,** 59 (1981).

4. H. P. Stapp, *Phys. Rev.* **D27,** 2445 and 2478 (1983).

5. G. F. Chew, *Phys. Rev. Lett.* **47,** 764 (1981).

6. G. F. Chew and J. Finkelstein, *Phys. Rev. Lett.* **50,** 795 (1983).

7. G. F. Chew and V. Poénaru, *Zeit. Phys.* **C14,** 233 (1982).

8. G. F. Chew, J. Finkelstein, R. M. McMurray Jr. and V. Poénaru, *Phys. Lett.* **100B,** 53 (1981) and *Phys. Rev.* **D24,** 2287 (1981).

9. P. Finkler and C. E. Jones, Nebraska preprint.

FROM BARYONIUM TO HEXONS

B. Nicolescu and V. Poénaru

After a short summary of the theoretical status of fermionic and bosonic constituents of hadrons in the topological bootstrap, two distinctive predictions of this approach — narrow-width baryonia and very high-mass hexons — as well as the relevance of the di-quark concept are discussed. In particular, the hexons are expected to reveal a new (TeV) scale of strong interactions.

1. Introduction

It is, of course, a pleasant but redoubtable task to discuss here some of the recent ideas of Geoff Chew, realized in collaboration with some of us. Given the limited amount of space and time at our disposal, we will not attempt to present a review of the new approach to particle physics known under the name of "topological bootstrap" (or "topological self-consistency"). In particular, we will not describe the impressive work done in the framework of electroweak interactions by Geoff, in collaboration mainly with Dieter Issler. In fact, a comprehensive review of the present status of the topological bootstrap will be available soon in the form of a book written by Geoff himself.[1]

We have chosen instead to discuss a particular subject in the topological bootstrap — the baryonium problem — which, we hope, will allow us to present some basic ideas of the new approach and, at the same time, to connect with experiment.

2. Short History of the Baryonium idea

As has happened several other times, the new fashion started with a new name, invented by Geoff and adopted very fast by the physics community. This name — "baryonium" — which "tends to ring helpful bells in the mind",[2] was coined by Geoff in 1976 in order to designate diquark-anti-diquark states whose coupling to baryon-antibaryon channels is much stronger than the coupling to channels involving usual mesons.[2]

In fact, the concept itself of baryonium is older. It appeared in the framework of duality, in 1968, in connection with the so-called "Rosner paradox",[3] whose resolution implies the existence of new q̅q̅qq states in baryon-antibaryon scattering. One year later Freund, Rosner and Waltz invented *ad hoc* selection rules[4] in order to explain the paradoxical proper-ties of the baryonium states (these selection rules are true ancestors of the topological rules which will be discussed here). Finally, in 1970, Mandula, Weyers and Zweig[5] showed that the duality equations ask for the existence of these "exotic" states. (Freund proposed to call them "gallons", simply because there are four quarts in a gallon; this suggestion was followed by Rosner.[6]

However, in the period 1968–1976, there was no experimental evidence for these new states, in spite of the fact that duality had a more and more impressive overall phenomenological success. The situation was so frustrating that Freund, who was very active in that period in analyzing their dynamics,[7] exclaimed at the Purdue Conference on Baryon Resonances in 1973, "... give us our exotics or take our illusions away!"[8] As we will see, his prayer was soon heard but in a rather vicious manner.

It was in 1976 that a sudden experimental proliferation of baryonium states occurred. This true experimental explosion stimulated, of course, a rich theoretical activity, mainly in the framework of the dual topological unitarization (DTU) approach (as illustrated, e.g., by the work of Veneziano,[9] of the bag models (e.g. Jaffe[10] and Chan[11] or of the potential approach (e.g. Vinh Mau[12]). The enthusiasm concerning the multiquark states was so great in that period that Chan[11] even dreamt about a possible "color chemistry".

However, with the passing of time, it became apparent that baryonium did not play a fundamental role in many theoretical approaches. In particular, if no baryonium states were observed QCD would still remain valid, even though QCD-inspired models, like the bag models, present persuasive arguments about the existence of multiquark states. But in contrast, it became more and more obvious that baryonium plays a fundamental role in DTU. The history of the topological bootstrap, born on the rich soil of DTU,[13] is interlocked with the evolution of the baryonium concept, even if the baryonium problem *per se* is only one of many new intriguing aspects of particle physics which emerged in the topological bootstrap.

When one of us (B.N.) was at LBL during the academic year 1976–1977, the topological bootstrap was at its very beginning, through parallel work of Geoff, in collaboration with Finkelstein, Sursock and Weissmann[14] and of Stapp.[15] At that moment we thought topology could be viewed as a source of new selection rules and we looked for their phenomenological manifestations by considering baryonium as t-channel exchanges in the pure exotic (phaneroexotic) $I = 2$ and $3/2$ and $S = -2$ channels.[16] We obtained in such a way clean, but of course indirect, phenomenological evidence for the existence of baryonium.

In 1978–1979 Geoff came to CERN and wrote an article[17] which marks, in our opinion, the clean-cut conceptual transition between DTU and the topological bootstrap. Soon after, he visited us in Paris and, in a paper written in collaboration with Nicolescu, Uschersohn and Vinh Mau,[18] we underlined, for the first time, the interest of baryonium states *under* the NN̄ threshold which could be very narrow (in contrast, bag models predict only broad states under this threshold). This visit constituted also the opportunity of starting a long-term collaboration with Poénaru which led, in a first stage, to a rigorous topological treatment of hadrons, including baryons,[19] an essential distinguishing feature of the topological bootstrap when compared with the old DTU.

In the meantime, the experimental status of baryonium arrived at the zenith of its glory. However already in June 1979, when we organized in Orsay a "workshop on baryonium and other unusual states",[20] polemical statements concerning the very existence of narrow baryonium states began to be heard. These polemical statements developed into a fast decline of the experimental status of baryonium: the narrow baryonium states began to disappear one after the other. The situation was so sad that already the $\bar{p}$ Bressanone Conference in 1980, Kalogeropoulos felt the need to announce that the narrow baryonium was dead.

Paradoxically enough, during its long *'traversée du désert'* (1980–1984?), baryonium achieved a more and more important status on the theoretical side. For example, in 1983 we computed, in collaboration with Balázs, hadron masses at the planar level of the topological bootstrap and predicted at least four baryonium states under the $N\bar{N}$ threshold.[21]

Recently the LEAR experiment PS183 reported a very narrow state at 1620 MeV[22] and Dover[23] showed that this state corresponds probably to $I = 2$, $J^P = 1^+$, in agreement with our predictions.[21] If this new C (Cordelia) state is not another mirage, it signifies a possible revival of baryonium.

The last theoretical surprise occurred a few months ago when, in a collaboration with Geoff and Issler, we realized that the topological bootstrap implies a new (TeV) scale for strong interactions.[24] This scale is connected with the existence of a new class of hadrons — the "hexons" — whose masses are in the TeV range. The hexons have the same number of constituents as baryonium but the quantum numbers associated with fermionic constituents are different from those in the baryonium case. We think that hexons are a source of novel phenomena destined to be observed at TeV accelerators.

In any case, baryonium and hexons represent a crucial test for the topological bootstrap.

3. Topological Constituents (fermions and bosons) from the Topological Bootstrap

The topological bootstrap emerged from the idea that *topological self-consistency* will provide the key to understanding the basic particle properties.

The topological bootstrap considers embellished momentum-carrying Feynman graphs, where topology represents the flow of all particle properties. The *events* are associated with the *graph vertices*, the *elementary particles* with *embellished Feynman lines*, and the *topological amplitudes* with the *graphs* themselves. The infinite superposition of topological amplitudes constitutes the *topological expansion*, unitarity being satisfied order by order. The *physical particles* correspond to divergences (poles) of the full topological expansion. The relation between elementary particles and physical particles is provided by a given set of conserved *quantum numbers*. The *quantum numbers* are described in the topological bootstrap by the *orientations* of Feynman graph embellishments.

a)   Halves, antihalves and topological constituents

A Feynman graph, which is a 1-dimensional entity, is embedded in a 2-dimensional multi-piece surface Σ_c, called the *classical surface*, because the classical observables reside there. The *complexity* of the event pattern is characterized by complexity integers, corresponding to the topology of a 2-dimensional manifold. The topological expansion corresponds to a sequence of events of increasing complexity.

The classical surface Σ_c is *globally oriented* and *bounded*.

The ends of a Feynman graph lie along the boundary of Σ_c, thereby defining boundary segments. A *fermion line* is a boundary segment belonging to a single smooth piece of Σ_c. It carries spin $1/2$ through local orientations. An example of a classical surface with its corresponding Feynman graph is given in Fig. 1. In Fig. 1 two equivalent descriptions of Σ_c are shown.

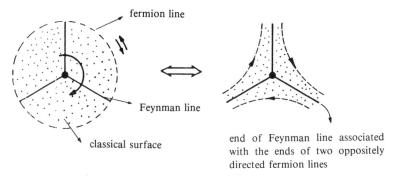

fermion line

Feynman line

classical surface

end of Feynman line associated with the ends of two oppositely directed fermion lines

Fig. 1. Example of classical surface Σ_c.

As seen from the example shown in Fig. 1, any elementary particle is divided by its Feynman line into a *half* and *antihalf*: in this sense, any elementary particle is *composite*.

The global orientation of Σ_c is maintained at all levels of the topological expansion. Therefore: (1) particle halves and antihalves forever maintain separate identities; (2) the induced boundary orientation is perpetuated; (3) the continuity of oriented fermion lines is always maintained. One concludes that each fermion line transports one unit of a conserved *fermion number* ($f = \pm 1$).

Σ_c is generally *feathered*, i.e., Σ_c is locally a bounded smooth surface but with a finite number of junction lines (see Fig. 2). In fact, unitarity requires Σ_c to be 3-feathered.[19] Three "feathers" join along a junction line so that their separate orientations consistently induce a *single orientation* of the junction line. In this way the entire Σ_c, even though multisheeted, carries a single global orientation.

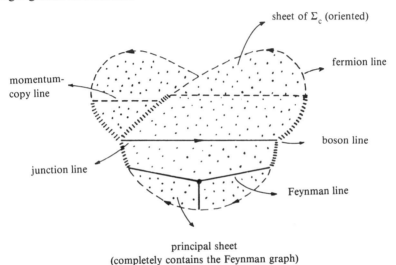

principal sheet
(completely contains the Feynman graph)

Fig. 2. A 3-feathered classical surface Σ_c.

As seen from Fig. 2, a new type of topological line — *the boson line* — has to be considered in the topological bootstrap. The boson line (see Fig. 3) is an oriented multi-piece line which begins and ends at a Feynman line end and includes a junction line.

Fig. 3. Topological boson line.

The boson line does not carry spin, but it is continuous and oriented. One concludes that each boson line transports one unit of a conserved *boson number* ($b = \pm 1$). The boson lines never cross Feynman lines. In such a way, the half-antihalf division of elementary particles is preserved.

Let us make two important remarks:

(1) In Feynman loops (Fig. 4), each closed fermionic strip brings a (-1)

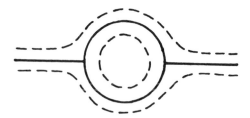

Fig. 4. A Feynman loop.

factor, while each closed bosonic strip brings a $(+1)$ factor. Unitarity requires the presence of both signs,[19] therefore there is no consistent world of only mesons: baryons are required to exist in the topological bootstrap. This is the deep reason why Σ_c has to be odd-feathered (bosonic halves have to be introduced).

(2)   Boson and fermion numbers are separately conserved and hence any linear combination between them is also conserved. In particular, one identifies the *baryon number B* and the *lepton number L* as corresponding to the following linear combinations[1] of b and f:

$$B = \tfrac{1}{2}f + \tfrac{1}{2}b \ , \tag{1}$$

$$L = \tfrac{1}{2}f + \tfrac{3}{2}b \tag{2}$$

One therefore obtains the striking prediction that *the proton is stable*.

The (f,b) and (B,L) quantum numbers corresponding to halves and antihalves of elementary particles are indicated in Tables Ia) (hadrons) and Ib) (nonhadrons).

Table Ia. (f,b) and (B,L) quantum numbers of halves and antihalves of elementary hadrons.

	Fermionic				Bosonic			
	f	b	B	L	f	b	B	L
Half	1	0	1/2	1/2	−2	1	−1/2	1/2
Antihalf	−1	0	−1/2	−1/2	2	−1	1/2	−1/2

By taking all possible combinations between halves and antihalves one obtains the following states: mesons, baryonia, baryons and antibaryons in the hadron sector (see Table IIa) and electroweak bosons, H-bosons, leptons and antileptons in the non-hadron sector (see Table IIb).

Table Ib. (f,b) and (B,L) quantum numbers of halves and antihalves of elementary non-hadrons.

	Fermionic				Bosonic			
	f	b	B	L	f	b	B	L
Half	1	0	1/2	1/2	0	1	1/2	3/2
Antihalf	−1	0	−1/2	−1/2	0	−1	−1/2	−3/2

Table IIa. Elementary states in the hadron sector.

States	Topological constituents	f	b	B	L
mesons	$f\bar{f}$	0	0	0	0
baryonia	$\bar{f}\bar{f}\,bb\,\bar{f}\bar{f}$	0	0	0	0
baryons	$fff\bar{b}$	3	−1	1	0
antibaryons	$\bar{f}\bar{f}\bar{f}b$	−3	1	−1	0

Table IIb. Elementary states in the non-hadron sector.

States	Topological constituents	f	b	B	L
electroweak bosons	$f\bar{\bar{f}}$	0	0	0	0
H-bosons	$b\bar{b}$	0	0	0	0
leptons	$\bar{f}b$	−1	1	0	1
antileptons	$f\bar{b}$	1	−1	0	−1

By contemplating Tables I and II, one can note several differences with the standard theory:

(1)   baryons correspond to *four* topological constituents;

(2)   baryonia, which appear on the same footing as mesons and baryons, correspond to *six* topological constituents;

(3)   the electroweak states are all *composite*;

(4)   there is a new class of electroweak bosons — the H-bosons.

One can recognize two levels of "compositeness": (i) the level of halves and antihalves (which can be themselves "composite"); (ii) the level of topological fermions and bosons. In fact, all states are built from topological fermions and bosons.[25]

It is interesting to note that the halves and antihalves (see Tables Ia and Ib) carry *at the same time* $B \neq 0$ and $L \neq 0$: we have here a manifestation of the *unifying* character of topological fermions and bosons which act, in this sense, like *topological preons*. However one has to remember that there is no momentum attached to topological fermions and bosons but a *single* momentum for each elementary particle (the topological constituents *are not* particles).

Once the particle spectrum is identified, one can proceed to the description of unitarity products which correspond topologically to *connected sums* of two different Σ_c via particle "plugs". These connected sums are performed along the boundary of the two Σ_c. It is therefore easy to realize that any Σ_c boundary is a *closed* graph composed of the *I and Y units* shown in Fig. 5.

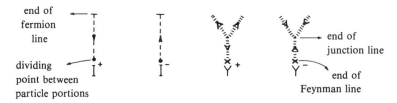

Fig. 5. *I* and *Y* units of the boundary of the classical surface Σ_c.

Table III. The topological content of elementary particles.

States	Topological constituents
mesons	$(I^+)\,(I^-)$
baryonia	$(I^-I^-\,Y^+)\,(Y^-I^+I^+)$
baryons	$(I^+)\,(Y^-I^+I^+)$
electroweak bosons	$(I^+)\,(I^-)$
H-bosons	$(Y^+)\,(Y^-)$
leptons	$(I^-)\,(Y^+)$

These I and Y units are the topological manifestation of the previously discussed fermion (I) and boson (Y) constituents. In terms of this new notation the content of Table II is transcribed in Table III.

Elementary particles appear as connected collections of boundary units together with the contained Feynman end.

One can note the dual role of the fermion constituent I : I is a part of a topological line that describes the *interaction* between particles and, at the same time, it is a *constituent* of an individual particle.

One has also to note a problem with the Y-plugs. Feynman-graph continuity allows us to pick out one of the three legs of a Y^+ to be identified with a corresponding Y^- (see Fig. 5). The problem is how to pair the remaining Y legs; one needs to introduce a cyclic order for the legs of Y. This is achieved by thickening the hadronic boundary portions, i.e. by embedding them in a new locally-oriented 2-dimensional transverse surface — the *quantum surface* Σ_Q (the reason for this name will be made obvious in § 3b). The local orientation of Σ_Q gives a cyclic order to any hadron Y. An equivalent statement is that one can assign a *3-valued* topological index $\mathscr{C}$ to each $I^\pm$ constituent: one can define $\mathscr{C}$ as being #1 when I touches the hadron Feynman end and #2 or #3 in the other cases (see Fig. 6).

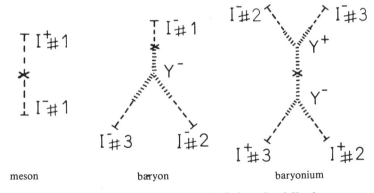

Fig. 6. Elementary hadron states as built from I and Y units.

There is a 2-3 $\mathscr{C}$-symmetry in strong interactions, which is broken by the electroweak interaction of hadrons.[1] This new degree of freedom, as well as the chirality (for hadrons), are *inaccessible* degrees of freedom (a summation is made over them). On the contrary, the boson and fermion constituents' content is accessible via the baryon and lepton numbers.

b) Zero-entropy dynamics and the multiplicity of the topological constituents

The complexity of each hadronic event is quantified, in the topological bootstrap, via *entropy indices*, higher-order patterns being connected sums of lower-order patterns.

There are four strong-interaction entropy indices in the topological bootstrap. The first two, g_1 and g_2 were already introduced in DTU[9,13]:

$$g_1 = \text{genus of the thickened Feynman graph} , \tag{3}$$

and

$$g_2 = b + g_1 - 1 , \tag{4}$$

where b is the number of boundary components of Σ_c that contain ends of Feynman lines. The extensively studied *planar* amplitudes of DTU correspond to

$$g_2 = 0 \quad (g_1 = 0 \text{ implied}) . \tag{5}$$

The new entropy indices g_3 and g_4 are the following:

$$g_3 = \text{number of fermionic chiral}^{\text{a}} \text{ switches} , \tag{6}$$

and

$$g_4 = \text{number of } \mathscr{C}\text{-switches} . \tag{7}$$

Every one of these four indices possesses an "entropy" property: that they never decrease in connected sums, i.e. either

$$g(\gamma) \geqslant g(\gamma') + g(\gamma'') , \tag{8}$$

or at least

$$g(\gamma) \geqslant \max(g(\gamma'), g(\gamma'')) , \tag{9}$$

(here γ labels an embellished Feynman graph).

The zero-entropy level corresponds to

$$g_1 = g_2 = g_3 = g_4 = 0 . \tag{10}$$

It is easy to increase g_3 and g_4 in connected sums, so in general $g_3 = 0$ or $g_4 = 0$ is not a good approximation to physical amplitudes.

An apparent exception concerns ratios of hadron amplitudes deduced from $g_2 = 0$, $g_4 = 0$ (no $\mathscr{C}$-switches) counting rules.[26] Certain of the $g_4 = 0$ cross section sum rules are the same as those obtained in the usual duality

---

diagram studies (only $g_2 = 0$); however $g_4 = 0$ implies new sum rules in the case of inclusive reactions, e.g.

$$\sigma_{K^-p \to \pi^+X} - \sigma_{K^+p \to \pi^+X} = 0 \ , \qquad (11)$$

while the usual duality diagrams anticipate the difference in the left-hand side of Eq. (11) to be different from zero. The experimental data agree with our prediction (11).

The planar level ($g_1 = g_2 = 0$) has generally been found to be a good approximation to physical amplitudes, as illustrated by the extensive and successful phenomenological studies of Capella and Tran Thanh Van in reproducing experimental data from low energies to collider energies.[27]

From a theoretical point of view zero-entropy has a central role in the topological bootstrap. Topologies at zero-entropy are *self-determining*: they cannot be built from topologies with nonzero entropy.

An essential and distinctive feature of the topological bootstrap is the *principle of contraction*, which gives a rigorous status to the familiar notion of duality. Contractions do not change entropy and thereby have an intimate relation with the notion of zero-entropy (see Appendix).

Only at the level of zero-entropy are all topologically conceivable contractions actually possible. The bootstrap notion that each hadron is a bound state of other hadrons is fully effective precisely at the zero-entropy level.

The principle of contraction represents another facet of topological self-consistency: it is a powerful constraint, allowing arbitrariness to be avoided. It determines the spectrum of elementary hadrons and the patterns of events which these particles mediate. All components of the topological expansion correspond to fully contracted embellished Feynman graphs.

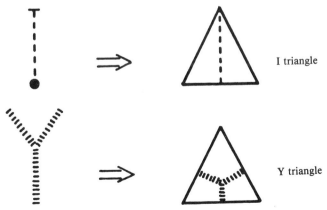

Fig. 7. The I and Y-triangles on the quantum surface Σ_Q associated with the I and Y units on the classical surface Σ_c.

Interesting information concerning the topological constituents is obtained from the zero-entropy quantum surface Σ_Q, which is a triangulated sphere. The I and Y units on Σ_c are associated with I and Y-triangles on Σ_Q (see Fig. 7). A complete definition of I and Y constituents is, in such a way, obtained.

The compositeness of elementary hadrons in terms of I and Y-triangles is shown in Fig. 8.

| meson | baryon | baryonium |

Fig. 8. The elementary hadrons as built from I and Y triangles.

One can note the distinctive role of I and Y-triangles.

The I-triangles appear on the hadron *perimeters*: they forge connecting interhadron links. Hence the I-triangle content of hadrons controls the strong interaction selection rules. From this point of view there is a similarity between the fermionic I constituents and the standard fermions (quarks).

In their turn the Y-triangles act like a "core" of strong interactions: they are "invisible", their role being revealed only when electroweak interactions are introduced.[1]

The I-constituents are doublets of charge (there is an I_c constituent corresponding to $Q = +1$ and an I_n constituent corresponding to $Q = 0$), while the Y constituents are always charged in strong interactions (Y_c corresponding to $Q = +1$).

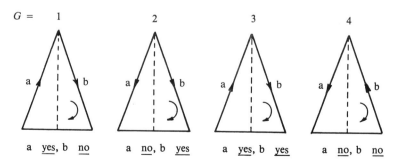

Fig. 9. The generation G topological degree of freedom.

It is seen from Fig. 8 that I-triangles have two edges along the hadron perimeters (while Y-triangles have none). Their orientations correspond to a new topological degree of freedom G which has 4 values (see Fig. 9). One can therefore identify *four generations* of I-triangles. The G number of mated triangles has to match and hence the quantity.

$$N_G \equiv N_G^{I+} - N_G^{I-} ,\tag{12}$$

is a conserved quantum number in strong interactions.

The orientation structure and plugging rules for the quantum surface automatically insure conservation laws for discrete quantum numbers (see Appendix).

From the above considerations it is clear why the name "quantum surface" was introduced. In many ways the couple (Σ_c, Σ_Q) act like a space similar to those considered in Kaluza-Klein type theories.[28]

It is important to note that, unlike in the standard theory, different quantum numbers are carried *independently* by different parts of the topological structure. Therefore one obtains a big multiplicity associated with the fermionic I constituents, namely

$$32 = 2 \text{ spins} \times 2 \text{ chiralities} \times 2 \text{ charges} \times 4 \text{ generations},\tag{13}$$

while there is just one Y constituent.

It is easy to understand that this induces a huge multiplicity of elementary hadrons. Of course, in the GeV range there is no sign of such a big multiplicity of hadrons. However, as we will argue in the following section, the TeV range can present unexpected surprises.

Let us close this section by mentioning a basic property of zero-entropy — *the topological supersymmetry* — recognized by Gauron, Nicolescu and Ouvry.[26] At zero-entropy there is a degenerate supermultiplet of elementary hadrons (spins 0, $\frac{1}{2}$, 1, $\frac{3}{2}$, 2) of mass m_0. A crucial distinctive feature of our theory is that self-consistency of spin-parity structure at the zero-entropy level implies a *non-zero* m_0. This mass m_0 sets the scale for the entire topological expansion. Also, all vertices at zero-entropy are expressible through the same coupling constant g_0, which can be estimated by the bootstrap condition (see Fig. 10):

$$g_0 \simeq \frac{g_0^3}{16\pi^2} N_0 ,\tag{14}$$

where N_0 is the difference between the number of two I loops and the number of one I loops,

$$N_0 = (32)^2 - 32 .\tag{15}$$

One deduces[29] that g_0 is a very small number

$$g_0 \simeq e . \tag{16}$$

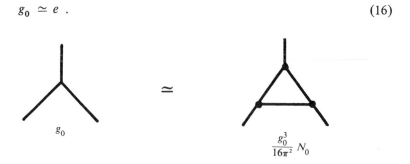

Fig. 10. Bootstrap condition for g_0.

The highly nonlinear zero-entropy dynamics has not yet been solved. However, the models of Espinosa[30] and of Balázs, Gauron and Nicolescu[31] calculate g_0 and verify the relation (16).

4. Hexons and the TeV Scale of Strong Interactions

We have shown recently that the big multiplicity (32) of fermionic constituents induces unexpected experimental consequences.[24]

Each fermionic loop brings a factor of 32. It is therefore natural to organize the graphs in three classes: (i) graphs involving *no* fermion loops per Feynman loop; (ii) graphs involving *one* fermion loop per Feynman loop; (iii) graphs involving *two* fermion loops per Feynman loop. As we will argue in the following these three classes of graphs correspond to *three scales* for strong interactions: (i) the MeV scale (the nuclear physics domain), (ii) the GeV scale (the familiar strong-interactions domain); (iii) the TeV scale (a new scale for strong-interactions).

Of course, the graphs involving two fermion loops per Feynman loop are the dominant contributions. A necessary condition for such a graph is to be representable by a planar topology with a *boson-line loop* inside each Feynman loop.

In order to visualise such *maximal planar* graphs (i.e. involving two fermion loops per Feynman loop) let us first introduce the shorthand notation for elementary hadrons shown in Fig. 11.

The shorthand notation of Fig. 11 is analogous with the 't Hooft representation of planar graphs in the large N_c approximation of QCD.[32] The difference is that, in standard theory, there are no bosonic constituents and the multiplicity of fermionic lines is hence smaller than in our case.

An example of a maximal planar graph, using the notation of Fig. 11, is shown in Fig. 12.

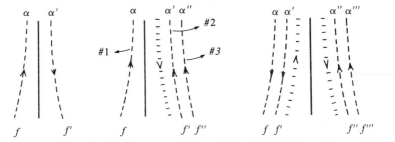

Fig. 11. Shorthand notation for elementary hadrons (α is a 4-valued Dirac index and f is a flavor index).

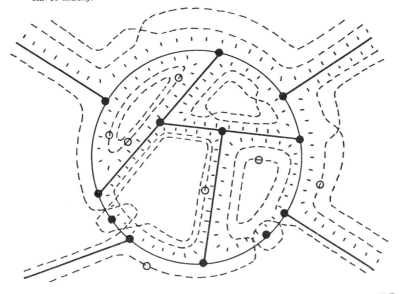

Fig. 12. Example of maximal planar graph (o denotes a chiral switch while ⌐⌐⌐ᐳ⋖⌐⌐ denotes a $\mathscr{C}$-switch).

In the maximal planar approximation to the topological expansion one recognizes a notion of *valence fermion line* (see Fig. 11), i.e. a fermion line which is not a part of a closed loop and which passes all non-trivial Feynman-perimeter vertices on the outside of the graph.

The graphs in the maximal planar approximation correspond to *6-constituent fishnets*.

Using standard ladder physics arguments one can show that the infinite sum of ladder graphs diverges at isolated values of p^2,

$$(m_1^{(2)})^2, \qquad (m_1^{(4)})^2 \quad \text{and} \quad (m_1^{(6)})^2, \tag{17}$$

where m_1 designates a "bare" mass and the number between parenthesis indicate the total number of constituents in the corresponding state.

At this level of the topological expansion the topological supersymmetry is *broken* because the "switching (spin-chiral or $\mathscr{C}$) potential" *differs* for different numbers of constituents. One can understand this fact by considering the valence fermion lines, which are allowed to cross the Feynman perimeter before reaching the next rung of the ladder. Such excursions are impossible for any valence fermion line accompanied by a valence boson line (boson lines cannot cross Feynman lines). Therefore no such crossing is possible in the case of 6-constituent states (see Fig. 13a) while they can occur in the case of 4- or 2-constituent states (see the example shown in Fig. 13b).

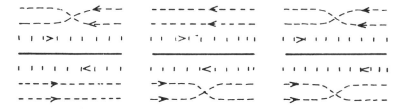

Fig. 13a. $\mathscr{C}$-switches in the case of 6-constituent states.

Fig. 13b. Example of $\mathscr{C}$-switch in the case of baryons.

One concludes that the topological supersymmetry has to be broken at the maximal planar level of the topological expansion.

In the absence of a rigorous calculation, we argue, on phenomenological grounds,[24] that:

$$m_1^{(2)}, \; m_1^{(4)} \ll m_0, \; m_1^{(6)} \; ; \quad m_0, \; m_1^{(6)} \gtrsim 1 \text{ TeV} \; . \tag{18}$$

The new hadrons with masses in the TeV range will be called, in the following, *hexons*, in order to stress that they are *6-constituent* states.

Here are several phenomenological arguments[24] justifying the relations (18):

(1)   The experimental information on the top-quark mass[33] indicates that the difference between the lowest and the highest baryon or meson m^2 is $\gtrsim 10^4$ GeV^2. But in the topological bootstrap, flavor symmetry breaking is realized by the electroweak interaction of hadrons and has to

occur at the 1% level. So, in order to understand the observed degree of symmetry breaking one concludes that

$$m_0^2 \gtrsim 10^6 \text{ GeV}^2 \quad (\text{or } m_0 \gtrsim 1 \text{ TeV}) \ . \tag{19}$$

(2)   Let us now consider the observed $\sim$ 100 GeV mass for[34] W and Z and the existing bounds ($\gtrsim$ 400 GeV) for the right-handed boson masses.[35] In the topological bootstrap, the coupling of massless elementary electroweak bosons to two fermion-1 boson ("diquark") halves breaks parity and SU(2) isospin symmetry;[36] mass is given in such a way, without any need for Higgses, to all electroweak bosons except the photon. In this mixing between electroweak bosons and hexons, the hexons "attract" the electroweak bosons, because they are more numerous. One concludes that hexon masses must exceed the electroweak boson masses, i.e.

$$m_1^{(6)} \gtrsim 1 \text{ TeV} \ . \tag{20}$$

(3)   The success of QCD-parton models in describing GeV-range electroweak-hadron data by considering fractional (2/3, $-$1/3) quark charges is understandable in the topological bootstrap if bare hexons are suppressed by their large mass, i.e. if

$$m_1^{(2)}, m_1^{(4)} \ll m_1^{(6)} \ . \tag{21}$$

(4)   The success of QCD-parton models in describing purely strong-interaction GeV data[37] is understandable in the topological bootstrap by considering renormalized Feynman graphs with lines corresponding to bare mesons and bare baryons with masses

$$m_1^{(2)}, m_1^{(4)} \lesssim 1 \text{ GeV} , \tag{22}$$

but with no bare hexon lines.

(5)   The lack of evidence for hexons in data from the CERN pp collider,[38] indicates that hexon masses $\lesssim$ 200 GeV are unlikely.

(6)   The Centauro cosmic-ray events[38,39] with multiplicity $\sim$ 100 but with very few π^0's could be understood as due to the production and decay of hexons with TeV masses.

The hexon could be *produced* in a soft collision of a high-energy baryon with another hadron. A valence bare-baryon constituent of the physical baryon emits a hexon before colliding with the other hadron (see Fig. 14). The impact parameter being controlled by the bare-baryon mass, the cross-section can reach the mb range.

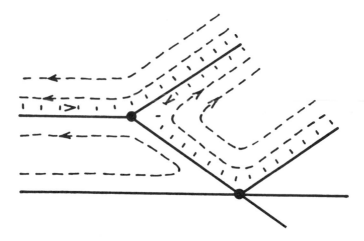

Fig. 14. Hexon production.

The *decay* of hexons occurs first into two bare baryons (see Fig. 15) and subsequently results in a cascade development of two large jets. This cascade *favors* physical baryons over physical mesons, due again to the big multiplicity (32) of fermion lines.

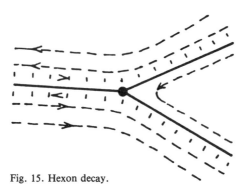

Fig. 15. Hexon decay.

Parallel to the hexons in the TeV scale of strong interactions, there are also baryonia which are part of the GeV-scale of strong interactions. The GeV-scale physics corresponds to renormalized planar ·graphs where all nonperimeter Feynman lines whose masses are much greater than 1 GeV are contracted (bare hexon lines disappear). A 6-constituent-baryonium potential can be generated by graphs such as the one shown in Fig. 16.

The spectrum of the baryonium states was computed by Balázs and Nicolescu.[21] The states they predict under the $N\bar{N}$ threshold are shown in Fig. 17. The Cordelia meson seen recently at LEAR in[22] $p\bar{p} \rightarrow \pi^{\pm} X^{\mp}$ has a mass of 1620 ± 1 MeV and a very narrow width ($\Gamma < 5$ MeV). The assignment

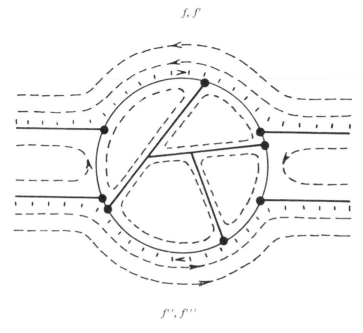

Fig. 16. Example of graph corresponding to a baryonium potential.

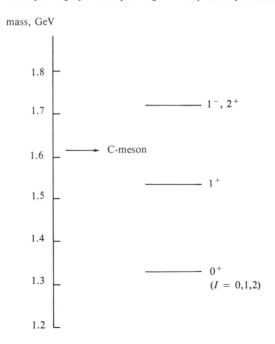

Fig. 17. Prediction of baryonium states under the NN̄ threshold (Ref. 21).

advocated by Dover[23] for this (still controversial) state is $J^P = 1^+$, $I = 2$, in agreement with the prediction of Ref. 21.

One can wonder why baryonium is different from the hexons in spite of the fact that they have the same "genetic" content (6 topological constituents). The answer lies in the fact that the quantum numbers associated with fermionic constituents are different in the two cases. Let us describe briefly the argument leading to this property.

The three values of the topological index $\mathscr{C}$ have the following association with electric charge and isospin[1]:

$$\#1 \quad \Longrightarrow \quad \begin{cases} Q = +1, & I_3 = +\frac{1}{2} \\ \\ Q = 0, & I_3 = -\frac{1}{2} \end{cases}$$

$$\#2 \text{ and } \#3 \quad \Longrightarrow \quad \begin{cases} Q = +\frac{1}{2}, & I_3 = +\frac{1}{2} \\ \\ Q = -\frac{1}{2}, & I_3 = -\frac{1}{2} \end{cases} \tag{23}$$

The "abnormal" association in the case of $\#2$ and $\#3$ is essentially due to the proximity of the corresponding fermion lines to the boson line, which has a frozen orientation (see Figs. 2, 6 and 11).

Now, each of the flavors belonging to a bare meson, baryon or baryonium spends equal portions of its line history in each of the three values of the topological index $\mathscr{C}$. Therefore, the valence fermions have (from (23)) fractional charges

$$Q = \frac{2}{3}, \quad I_3 = +\frac{1}{2}$$

$$Q = -\frac{1}{3}, \quad I_3 = -\frac{1}{2}, \tag{24}$$

like the standard fermions.

The situation is different for hexons, which are associated with the 2-loop, 6-constituent fishnets: each of the four flavours spends equal portions of its line history in the values $\#2$ and $\#3$, but *none* in $\#1$. Therefore (again from (23)), the valence fermions are, in this case, *exotic* — they have

$$Q = +\frac{1}{2}, \quad I_3 = +\frac{1}{2}$$

$$Q = -\frac{1}{2}, \quad I_3 = -\frac{1}{2}. \tag{25}$$

In other words, there are exotic fermions in hexons, while in baryonia there are standard fermions.

5. Conclusions

The familiar baryons are still mysterious from the theoretical point of view. This rarely acknowledged circumstance can be recognized both in the standard theory and in the topological bootstrap.

QCD, in its large N_c realization, is merely a theory of mesons. The baryons were only recently associated, in this meson theory, with solitons (skyrmions) with a non-zero topological charge, identified with baryon number.[40]

In the topological bootstrap baryons appear to have not only fermionic constituents but also a new bosonic constituent. Baryonia and hexons have an even richer content in terms of the bosonic constituents. This fact is not postulated in an arbitrary manner, but is a result of *topological self-consistency*.

These new bosonic constituents have several important consequences on both theoretical and experimental sides.

For example, in the topological bootstrap, both the fractional charges of standard fermions and the breaking of $SU(2)$ symmetry are consequences of the existence of topological boson lines.

On the experimental side we can quote some of the predictions intimately connected with the presence of the topological boson lines:

(1) The possibility of very narrow baryonium states under the $\overline{\text{NN}}$ threshold.[21] In contrast, the low-mass baryonium states in bag models are generally broad.

(2) At present energies, we expect the bosonic half — the diquark in the standard terminology — to play a pre-eminent dynamical role. For example, in pp collisions at high energies we expect not only to have a much more abundant production of protons at large p_T as compared with antiprotons, but also that the production rates are governed by the existence of diquarks. Recent ISR data[41] seem to be in a qualitative agreement with such a prediction. Again, the diquark notion is a result of topological self-consistency. In the standard theory, even by accepting the skyrmion interpretation of baryons, we do not see the reason why two quarks must have the tendency of clustering in a diquark. The identification of baryons in future high-energy experiments would be therefore of great interest.

(3) We expect a large collection of novel events (e.g. Centauro-like events) to appear at TeV accelerators. A new class of hadrons — the hexons — is predicted, with masses in the TeV range. The hexon dynamics is likely to induce new phenomena not only in the realm of strong interactions but also in that of electroweak interactions.

Appendix — The Quantum Surface

In this Appendix we will focus on some aspects of the zero-entropy hadronic bootstrap.

Let us start by recalling that in classical DTU as well as in its subsequent generalization — the topological bootstrap — a connected part of the S matrix M_{fi} (where i, f designate sets of ingoing and outgoing elementary particles together with momenta and spins) is expanded with respect to a topological index τ of increasing entropy (complexity)

$$M_{fi} = \sum_{\tau, k} M_{fi}^{\tau, k} \ . \tag{A.1}$$

The symbol k in (A.1) describes the association of the elementary particles in channels f and i with the topological structure τ.[19]

One has, for (τ, k), a notion of Landau connected sum

$$(\tau', k') \underset{L}{\#} (\tau'', k'') = (\tau, k) \ , \tag{A.2}$$

with non-decreasing complexity, so that *zero-entropy is the only self-reproducing level*

$$(\text{zero entropy}) \underset{L}{\#} (\text{zero entropy}) = (\text{zero entropy}) \ . \tag{A.3}$$

Moreover, the topological expansion (A.1) gives rise to an infinite set of discontinuity formulae

$$\text{disc}_L M^{\tau, k} = \sum_{(\tau', k') \# (\tau'', k'') \# \ldots \ (\tau, k)} = \int dp_L M^{\tau', k'} M^{\tau'', k''} \ldots$$

$$\tag{A.4}$$

where all the *non-linearity* is concentrated at the zero-entropy level.

The topological index τ includes a Landau graph L, which is eventually embellished into a bounded, feathered classical surface Σ_c (containing L, and such that $\partial L \subset \partial \Sigma_c$). To begin with, a *feathered* classical surface is imposed by unitarity considerations (see text).

So, topological self-consistency asks for *junction lines* embedded in the classical surface, where several feathers should meet. The necessity of the *threeness* of the feathered surface will become transparent only later. But let us notice already that the junction lines will turn out to be bosonic; some hadrons will have bosonic *halves*.

But now that the feathers of Σ_c have made their appearance, a subsequent constraint emerges: in order to have unambiguous plugging rules, the feathers along a given junction line have to be cyclically ordered, like for instance in Fig. A1.

A natural way to achieve this is to further embellish Σ_c by giving a thickening of $\partial \Sigma_c$ into a smooth orientable 2-dimensional surface. By capping off every boundary component of this thickening with a 2-disk, we get a *closed* 2-dimensional surface which, after some more embellishments, will become our *quantum surface* Σ_Q. It should already be clear that the Σ_c

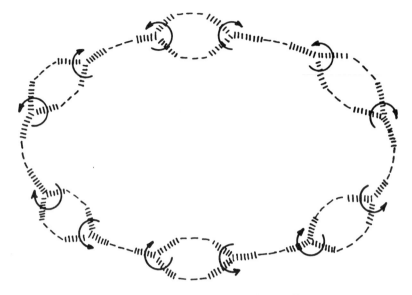

Fig. A1. Cyclically ordered feathers on Σ_c.

plugs will have to be accompanied by Σ_Q (possibly multi-plugs) *connected sums*. Let us remind the reader that if S_1, S_2 are two connected oriented surfaces, one defines their single-plugged connected sum

$$S \equiv S_1 \# S_2 \ , \tag{A.5}$$

by considering two disks $D_1 \subset S_1$, $D_2 \subset S_2$, by glueing D_1 to D_2 with mismatched orientations and by erasing from the union the interiors of D_1, D_2. In this way one gets a new *connected*, smooth, naturally oriented surface S.

It is already natural to guess that, for a zero-entropy amplitude, Σ_Q should be (topologically speaking, and other embellishments not withstanding) a 2-dimensional sphere; the 2-sphere is the *only* surface satisfying the self-reproducing condition

$$S^2 \# S^2 = S^2 \ , \tag{A.6}$$

which one should compare with (A.3).

Once we have gone this far let us list some of the general requirements which zero-entropy quantum spheres will have to fulfill, for a self-consistent topological bootstrap to be possible, at all:

(a) Σ_Q will be covered by *particle areas* which will cut the belt $\partial \Sigma_c \subset \Sigma_Q$ into the various pieces which have already been recognized as representing the elementary particles (constituting i, f) on $\partial \Sigma_c$.

(b) Since any *sub*-collection of particles has to be able to participate in a

Landau collected sum, the union of the corresponding particle areas has to be invariably a 2-disk $D^2 \subset S^2 = \Sigma_Q$.

(c) Corresponding to the in $\leftrightarrow$ out distinction, particle areas will carry their own clockwise $\leftrightarrow$ anticlockwise local orientation. (Remember that Σ_Q is globally oriented; this global orientation is itself assured by a combination of local Σ_Q orientations, together with local $\pm$ signs induced on Σ_Q from Σ_c, but all these considerations are too long and technical to be recorded here. Let us only add that these refinements become indispensable when we move to the electroweak sector.)

(d) If (τ',k'), (τ'',k'') are zero-entropy components of the topological expansion, then any single-plug connected sum which preserves zero-entropy

$$(\tau', k') \# (\tau'', k'') = (\tau, k), \tag{A.7}$$

should be *uniquely* defined (notice, for instance, that rotational symmetry could, *a priori,* put this kind of uniqueness into danger).

(e) In a formula like (A.2), if (τ,k) is zero entropy, then so are also (τ',k'), (τ'',k'').

(f) Every channel disk is uniquely contractible (in the sense of Harari[42] and Rosner[43]) to a particle disk completely determined by the perimeter. In particular, any zero-entropy Σ_Q is completely contractible into a propagator.

(g) Once the topology is specified, there must be no ambiguity about where one particle area ends and another begins.

These, as well as other natural requirements are explained in detail in Refs. 1 and 19.

It turns out that *all* these requirements can be very naturally met by a certain *triangulation* pattern of Σ_Q. This pattern is the only survivor of an extended search and we indeed do believe that it is the unique self-consistent solution for our problem.

Let us anyway mention right away that introduction of n-gons with $n > 3$ into the patch-structure of Σ_Q would immediately introduce inconsistencies.[19] So we are left only with *triangles* and hence only with 3-feathers and not more, along any junction line.

The whole structure of the zero-entropy Σ_Q is explained in detail in Refs. 1 and 19, where it is also shown how the requirements a),..., g) are fulfilled. Let us just mention here some features of this structure:

(a) Triangles are each independently (locally) oriented and they occur in "mated" pairs of opposite orientation. Y-triangles (Fig. 7) will always be mated with Y-triangles.

(b) The particle areas turn out to be those of Fig. 8 (see text).

Let us notice already some nice consequences of these considerations. For each particle disk there is an additively-conserved quantity (at zero-entropy level, and hence via plugs at *all* levels):

#(anticlockwise Y-triangles) − #(clockwise Y-triangles) .   (A.8)

This quantity is related to baryon number as explained in Fig. A2.

E > 0 out elementary baryon   E < out elementary antibaryon
E > 0 in elementary antibaryon   E < in elementary baryon

Fig. A2. Topological interpretation of baryon number.

Let us note that this topological interpretation of baryon number is completely adequate in the purely hadronic sector and consistent with a more general interpretation of baryon *and* lepton number.[1]

An *orientable* Σ_Q automatically insures the conservation of any discrete quantum number represented by local orientation of the *edges* of a particle area. Only *I*-triangles can appear along the particle-perimeter and therefore *four* possible *generations* can be introduced (see text and Fig. 9). Taking into account that *I*-triangles carry a 2-valued charge (see §3b) of the main text) one obtains *eight flavors.*

Each of these flavors is conserved as long as one starts with our zero-entropy Σ_Q's and obtains the other topological components by Landau plugs. Flavor violation requires introduction of *non-orientable* Σ_Q's, which cannot any longer be generated by plugs from zero-entropy.

References

1. G. F. Chew, *Topological Bootstrap Theory of Particles,* book in preparation.
2. G. F. Chew, in *Proceedings of the 3rd European Symposium on Anti-nucleon-Nucleon Interactions,* Stockholm (1976), eds. G. Ekspong and S. Nilsson, (Pergamon Press, New York, 1977), p. 515.
3. J. L. Rosner, *Phys. Rev. Lett.* **21**, 950 (1968).
4. P. G. O. Freund, J. L. Rosner and R. Waltz, *Nucl. Phys.* **B13**, 237 (1969).
5. J. Mandula, J. Weyers and G. Zweig, *Ann. Rev. Nucl. Sci.* **20**, 289 (1970).
6. J. L. Rosner, *Phys. Reports* **11**, 189 (1974).
7. P. H. Frampton and P. G. O. Freund, *Nucl. Phys.* **B24**, 453 (1970); S. Ellis, P. H. Frampton, P. G. O. Freund and D. Gordon, *Nucl. Phys.* **B24**, 465 (1970).

8. P. G. O. Freund, in *Proceedings of the Conference on Baryon Resonances,* Purdue University (1973).
9. G. Veneziano, *Phys. Lett.* **52B,** 220 (1974); *Nucl. Phys.* **B74,** 365 (1974); G. Veneziano, "Color Symmetry and Quark Confinement", in *Proceedings of the XIIth Rencontre de Moriond,* ed. J. Tran Thanh Van (Editions Frontières, Paris, 1977), p. 113; G. C. Rossi and G. Veneziano, *Nucl. Phys.* **B123,** 507 (1977).
10. R. L. Jaffe, *Phys. Rev.* **D15,** 267, 281 (1977); R. L. Jaffe, "Phenomenology of Quantum Chromodynamics", in *Proceedings of the XIIIth Rencontre de Moriond,* ed. J. Tran Thanh Van (Editions Frontières, Paris, 1978), p. 257.
11. Chan Hong-Mo, in "Phenomenology of Quantum Chromodynamics", *op. cit.,* p. 237; Chan Hong-Mo and H. Høgaasen, *Phys. Lett.* **72B,** 121 (1977); *Nucl. Phys.* **B136,** 401 (1978).
12. R. Vinh Mau, in "Phenomenology of Quantum Chromodynamics", *op. cit.,* p. 273; M. Lacombe, B. Loiseau, B. Moussallam and R. Vinh Mau, *Phys. Rev.* **C29,** 1800 (1984).
13. G. F. Chew and C. Rosenzweig, *Phys. Reports* **41,** 263 (1978).
14. G. F. Chew, J. Finkelstein, J. P. Sursock and G. Weissmann, *Nucl. Phys.* **B136,** 493 (1978).
15. H. P. Stapp, *Phys. Rev.* **D27,** 2445, 2478 (1983).
16. B. Nicolescu, *Nucl. Phys.* **B134,** 495 (1978); B. Nicolescu, in "Phenomenology of Quantum Chromodynamics", *op. cit.,* p. 339.
17. G. F. Chew, *Nucl. Phys.* **B151,** 237 (1979).
18. G. F. Chew, B. Nicolescu, J. Uschersohn and R. Vinh Mau, CERN Report TH 2635 (1979).
19. G. F. Chew and V. Poénaru, *Zeit. Phys.* **C11,** 59 (1981).
20. *Proceedings of the Workshop on Baryonium and other Unusual States,* I.P.N. Orsay, June 21-22, 1979, eds. B. Nicolescu, J. M. Richard and R. Vinh Mau.
21. L. A. P. Balazs and B. Nicolescu, *Phys. Rev.* **D28,** 2818 (1983).
22. G. Smith *et al.,* LEAR experiment PS183, results reported by K. Kilian, *Proceedings of the 4th Topical Workshop on Proton-Antiproton Collider Physics,* Bern, Switzerland, March 5-8, 1984, CERN Report 84-09, ed. H. Hanni and J. Schacher, p. 324; A. Angelopoulos *et al.,* CERN Report EP/84-47 (1984).
23. C. B. Dover, Orsay Report IPNO/TH 84-40 (1984).
24. G. F. Chew, D. Issler, B. Nicolescu and V. Poénaru, in "New Particle Production", *Proceedings of the XIXth Rencontre de Moriond,* ed. J. Tran Thanh Van (Editions Frontières, Paris, 1984), p. 143.
25. G. F. Chew, J. Finkelstein, B. Nicolescu and V. Poénaru, *Zeit.Phys.* **C14,** 289 (1982).
26. P. Gauron, B. Nicolescu and S. Ouvry, *Phys. Rev.* **D24,** 2501 (1981).
27. A. Capella and J. Tran Thanh Van, *Zeit.Phys.* **C23,** 165 (1984) and references quoted therein; see also A. Capella, U. Sukhatme, C. I. Tan and J. Tran Thanh Van, *Phys. Lett.* **81B,** 68 (1979).
28. E. Witten, *Nucl. Phys.* **B186,** 412 (1981); A. Salam and J. Strathdee, *Ann. Phys.* **141,** 316 (1982).
29. G. F. Chew, *Phys. Rev. Lett.* **47,** 764 (1981).
30. R. Espinosa Marty, "Topological Zero-Entropy Bootstrap", Ph.D. thesis, University of California, Berkeley, 1983.

31. L. A. P. Balázs, P. Gauron and B. Nicolescu, *Phys. Rev.* **D29**, 533 (1984); see also B. Nicolescu, in *Proceedings of the XIVth International Symposium on Multiparticle Dynamics,* eds. P. Yager and J. F. Gunion (World Scientific, Singapore, 1984), p. 835.
32. G. 't Hooft, *Nucl. Phys.* **B72**, 461 (1974); **B75**, 461 (1976).
33. UA1 Collaboration, CERN Report EP/84-135, Invited talk given by C. Rubbia at the *XIth International Conference on Neutrino Physics·and Astrophysics,* Nordkirchen near Dortmund, 11-16 June 1984.
34. UA1 Collaboration, G. Arnison *et al., Phys. Lett.* **129B**, 273 (1983); UA2 Collaboration, results presented by J. Schacher, in *Proceedings of the 4th Topical Workshop on Proton-Antiproton Collider Physics, op. cit.,* p. 142.
35. R. N. Mohapatra, Lectures delivered at the *NATO Summer School on Particle Physics,* September 4-18, 1983, Munich, West Germany, University of Maryland preprint (1983).
36. G. F. Chew and V. Poénaru, *Phys. Rev.* **D30**, 1579 (1984).
37. A. H. Mueller, *Phys. Reports* **73**, 237 (1981); G. Altarelli, *Phys. Reports,* **81**, 1 (1982).
38. N. Yamdagni, Talk at the *International Workshop on Very High Energy Interactions in Cosmic Rays,* University of Pennsylvania, Philadelphia, Penn., U.S.A., 22-24 April 1982; this reference also contains a critical discussion of the Centauro events.
39. C. Lattes, Y. Fujimoto and S. Hasegawa, *Phys. Reports* **65**, 151 (1980).
40. E. Witten, Princeton Report (1984) and references quoted therein, in *Proceedings of the Workshop on Solitons in Nuclear and Elementary Particle Physics,* eds. A Chodos *et al.* (World Scientific, Singapore, 1984), p. 306.
41. A. Breakstone *et al., Phys. Lett.* **147B**, 237 (1984); see also CERN Courrier, vol. 24, no. 7, September 1984, p. 281.
42. H. Harari, *Phys. Rev. Lett.* **22**, 562 (1969).
43. J. L. Rosner, *Phys. Rev. Lett.* **22**, 689 (1969).

PHYSICS REPORTS:
AN EDITORIAL EXPERIMENT

Maurice Jacob

Launching a new journal is a bootstrap operation. In order to receive good papers, one needs to have published some already. Yet it may work.

Foreword

In the course of 1985, I shall be leaving the Editorial Board of *Physics Reports* after having served on it for nearly 15 years, in effect since the birth of the journal in 1971. *Physics Reports* shares some features with other review journals, yet it is also somewhat unique in several ways. As things developed with time, I practically became responsible for the particle physics section of the journal, which has altogether represented about 30% of the articles so far published. This has been a very interesting experience which I certainly leave with regret at present; nevertheless, I am now no longer able to devote the same attention to it. Furthermore I have the firm belief that, after these first 15 years, others should take over and bring to the journal new ideas and new contacts. As I leave this editorship, I thought it appropriate to try to summarize in a short essay my present views about *Physics Reports,* bringing together a few facts and a few numbers in which readers of the journal may find interest and even some fun.

I started working on *Physics Reports* in 1971, which was also the year during which I left *Physics Letters B.* At that time I also wrote some memoirs, put together under a very similar title. The style was that of a physics article and it was even accepted for publication, but by a journal which sadly enough never appeared. Attempts at launching a European brother to *Physics Today* have indeed not yet been successful. The *Physics Letters B* memoirs are lost. Here are now somewhat similar memoirs covering another editing experiment, this time with *Physics Reports.* They are organized as follows.

Section 1 is written somewhat as a testimony, insofar as it is a personally biased historical survey of the development of the journal but, to be honest, mainly of the part for which I was directly responsible. It goes from conception to the present time. It remains at a qualitative level as I try to give the reasons for the different options taken with, occasionally, some interesting crossings of swords on the Editorial Board. Section 2 is a more quantitative survey which brings together some data about the particle physics section of *Physics Reports*. Section 3 discusses the so-called "Bulk Order Scheme", through which reprints have become financially accessible to many readers. It also discusses the side venture of the reprint volumes. In Section 4, I try to conclude with a few general remarks.

1.   The Conception, Birth and Youth of *Physics Reports*; A Recollection

It was in 1969, at the Lund Conference in Sweden, that I first heard about the intention of North-Holland to publish a journal of review articles which would appear as a special section of *Physics Letters*. I was then the editor for theoretical physics of *Physics Letters B,* and J. Hamilton, who had already discussed the idea with the management of North-Holland, asked me to collaborate in it. The editors of this new section were indeed expected to include a large subset of the editors of *Physics Letters A and B.* At that time, the general plan was to put together a journal of review articles aimed at presenting new developments in topical domains of physics, so that non-specialist physicists could thus collect rather detailed information about what was happening in other corners of their discipline. It was recognized that a letter journal such as *Physics Letters* was read mainly by specialists focusing on new papers in their own particular field, readers of the *B* section hardly venturing into the *A* section, and *vice versa.* It was felt that a new section, the *C* section, was needed in order to propagate efficiently the information between subfields of physics. In a nutshell, the idea was to provide material where the colleague down the corridor could learn something about what was so interesting at present for his/her colleagues a few offices away in the Physics Department building.

An original and interesting format was considered for publication. Each article would correspond to a separate issue of the journal, with a typical size of 60–70 printed pages. Issues would be distributed to subscribers and available separately as reprints.

This was certainly a worthwhile endeavour. Nevertheless, I remember having had some reservations at that time. I thought that most of my physicist colleagues would, in general, find little time to enter into details which would take them much beyond the level of information already available in excellent articles currently appearing in *Annual Reviews, Physics Today,* let alone in *Scientific American.* The clever few who knew how to combine ideas originating in different subfields of physics in their own research already knew their way through the original literature, and would not *a priori* resort much to such reviews for general and somewhat delayed, though more easily accessible, information. I was then worried that since the need for a new set of such reviews was not clear, it would be too difficult to convince very active physicists, who would be the best potential authors, to invest the necessary time and effort in their writing. Credit would be limited and the much-required incentive would not be compelling enough. I now realize that these reservations were to a large extent due to my being a particle physicist at CERN, where emphasis on particle physics is overwhelming and where information is just dumped on you. In any case, I did agree to participate, since I have long incubated an editorial virus, but argued for more technical reviews, which would be rather aimed at dedicated readers willing to enter a new domain of research, and who would thus be ready to invest some effort in their reading.

As far as I was concerned, things remained at this stage for one year. A year later, in 1970, W. H. Wimmers, director of North-Holland, was still somewhat reluctant to start a new journal: the preprint grinder, which was at that time strongly advocated by some of the editors of *Nuclear Physics*. The main motivations, as I saw it at that time, were as follows. Research physicists had to face an increasing number of preprints. Some were good and even excellent. Some were not very good and sometimes misleading, in particular for the relatively isolated readers. Fishing out the few gems from this extending and unevenly distributed preprint literature was becoming difficult to many, while it was felt that it was at that stage that information had to be collected in order neither to miss nor to catch an exciting new venture too late. This was, of course, particularly the case in theoretical particle physics, which is by essence a frontier domain where promising lines of research may suddenly appear and quickly develop. As the editor for theoretical physics of *Physics Letters B,* I was naturally brought into the debate.

The preprint grinder was, in the mind of its promoters, going to cover some of the new topical developments in physics through a critical analysis of the relevant preprints which had recently become available. A preprint grinder which would thus conduct its readers through the apparently treacherous maze of preprint literature certainly appeared worthwhile. Nevertheless, and probably again because of my personal bias being at CERN, I was not immediately convinced of its usefulness. My main objection, however, was, as I remember it, of a different kind. Having been the close witness of some clashes over priority as editor of *Physics Letters,* and the receiver of many preprints which were never published, I felt that a preprint should not be considered as an actual publication, from which an author could claim some unambiguous credit and priority. Indeed, it is not very infrequent to see several preprints leading eventually to one publication, and preprints leading to none at all. Discussing, let alone mentioning the key points of a preprint in a regular journal, would automatically give it some — I felt undeserved — official status. Furthermore, if negative points were to be raised against a preprint, the author had to be granted some right of response in the journal. This could sometimes lead to the publication of material which would have been better left unnoticed to most. While I certainly realized that the most useful information which one may obtain from preprints is accessible only with great difficulty to many, I felt that giving too much official status to preprints — before the relevant manuscripts had been refereed and accepted for publication — would cause more harm than good.

I mentioned all this in some detail because *Physics Reports,* as it grew up in the seventies, was actually just a (happy, I should say) compromise between the original proposal of a review journal at a rather general level and the stillborn proposal of a preprint grinder. It was launched as a journal covering rather technical reviews of topical domains of physics. When I say *Physics Reports,* I should rather say those articles in *Physics Reports* covering particle physics since, almost from the start, in the winter of 1970–1971, the different subdisciplines turned out to follow somewhat different editorial policies. The reasons having earlier led to the split between *Physics Letters A* and *Physics Letters B* must have presented an insurmountable problem. Indeed, it later took a lot of goodwill to avoid a split of *Physics Reports* according to the respective specializations of *Physics Letters A* and *B*. This could, happily, be done, adiabatically only, with the one- and two-diamond markings, which first appeared a few years ago on each issue.

As far as particle physics is concerned, the journal was definitely conceived as a journal of rather technical and topical reviews, providing information to the dedicated reader willing to get involved or, in any case, ready to invest some effort. It thus also appeared as a manageable substitute for the preprint grinder area. As I remember it, *Physics Reports,* with the format it took, was born in Copenhagen in August 1970 during a meeting with L. Rosenfeld. I had come to Copenhagen with W. Wimmers. At stake was the future of the proposal already discussed a year ago under the name of *Physics Reports,* and the future of the preprint grinder with some of its proponents on the *Nuclear Physics* staff in Copenhagen. Within an afternoon of discussions, the preprint grinder was set aside but, as a compensatory measure, it was decided that *Physics Reports,* at least in theoretical particle physics, where the grinder was almost ready to start its activity, would tend somewhat to the technical side in some of the issues, in order to provide the type of guidance for specialists which the grinder was supposed to give, though in a far more acceptable and general way than that offered by the critical discussion of specific preprints.

I felt very satisfied with the decision and set myself to work. I knew that Gerry Brown and Harry Lipkin, whom I deeply respected as my senior colleagues in this endeavour, were in agreement with this general line of approach. I learned only later that this was, however, not uniformly shared on the Editorial Board which was going to launch the journal. My view of a typical *Physics Reports* article at that time was that of a review which could have corresponded to a series of lecture notes at a Summer School. The Les Houches Summer School, with which I have been closely associated in various capacities for many years, ·was of course what I had in mind, with its long and thorough survey of topical domains by distinguished physicists. The particular format of *Physics Reports* was especially appropriate. Each review article could be considered as a particular issue of a regular journal (six issues, say, making a volume), but also as a monograph to be used as a small book. This format certainly contributed to the success of the journal.

By the summer of 1971, the Editorial Board met for the first time in Amsterdam. A few articles had already appeared, most of them in theoretical particle physics. This was my first meeting with Dik ter Haar, and I got a cold shower. I had certainly been over-enthusiastic and persuasive enough with authors, since particle physics represented 60% of the first five volumes. The emphasis on particle physics and the rather technical nature of the first papers were not at all to ter Haar's liking. I tried to hold my line with my deep belief that the articles which I had commissioned and brought to the journal were at least of high scientific quality, but I still remember ter Haar's quiet voice issuing devastating criticisms. I must say that the discussion was not made any easier by the fact that the two sides of *Physics Letters, A* and *B* were actually facing each other in that meeting. With *Physics Letters B,* I was somewhat the involuntary heir to a dispute with *Physics Letters A* which had developed up to an acute level much before my time, and had led to two separate editorial boards. It took the kindness and conciliary attitude of W. Wimmer to reach a "wait and see" conclusion, everyone pledging to do his best for the success of the new journal, which was then seen as an experiment by North-Holland. Its association with *Physics Letters* did allow for an easy try. It went automatically to subscribers, together with *Physics Letters.* One had to wait for their response, which had to carry much weight. We took note of the different opinions expressed on the Editorial Board.

This rather cold meeting was followed by a fairly quiet period. At that time I had to look for a job. I left *Physics Letters B* after nearly three years as editor for theoretical physics, which had taken a big toll on my time, probably too much for someone with a fixed-term position, and I left CERN for the United States.

My initial flare of enthusiasm at convincing colleagues to write review articles quieted down somewhat. Other editors started bringing numerous articles to the journal. By the end of 1972, when I came back to CERN, the fraction of articles in particle physics had practically reached the level which it was going to keep, with rather small fluctuations, over a full decade, a level of the order of 30%.

By that time I was convinced that the journal had a clear need to meet and was already doing so to some extent. It could be a substitute for the quickly-diminishing number of postgraduate series of lectures the world over. After the big boom of the sixties, physics was then experiencing its first difficulties with job openings and funding. This readily led to a de-

crease of the number of doctoral students and, by the same token, of the number of topical postgraduate courses, once given simultaneously on many campuses. New topics, which used to be taught through special series of lectures, were no longer presented that way in many graduate schools. Nevertheless, there remained a wide but geographically scattered audience for detailed discussions of topical fields. *Physics Reports,* by making available to many a topical series of lectures given at a particular place, or the equivalent thereof compiled as a thorough review by a leading physicist, could supply the needed material to physicists willing to learn about the new developments thus covered. The format of the journal, each article being circulated separately, could help a great deal. This was the direction in which I then wanted to push the journal. The leading figure among such papers is certainly the article *Gauge Theories,* by E. S. Abers and B. W. Lee, which appeared as Volume 9, No. 1, in 1973, and which has remained for many years the "best-seller" of the bulk order scheme, which I shall discuss later. This is the article through which many physicists the world over have taught themselves gauge theories over several years. Many other articles, though not quite reaching the same level of fame, have also been extremely useful to many readers, as the sales on the bulk order scheme readily show.

By the mid-seventies *Physics Reports* had come of age. It was clear that the response met by the new journal was positive enough for it to live on its own. By 1978, formal ties with *Physics Letters* were severed, the *C* appearing next to each number being dropped as a last measure. Subscription to *Physics Reports* could be entered independently of those to *Physics Letters.* The journal had reached a good steady state in terms of subscriptions (close to 1800) and output (about 12 volumes per year). However, the balance between different fields of physics was not yet satisfactory, the usefulness and reputation of the journal among physicists of different fields being rather uneven.

As things went on, I soon took responsibility for almost all the articles published in particle physics; it is worth mentioning at this stage, however, the few but all excellent papers commissioned by H. Lipkin. I started with theoretical high energy physics only in mind but, after a short while, the need for experimental physics reviews was felt and, with the agreement of C. Rubbia, I started commissioning some and eventually became, to a large extent, the editor-in-charge of particle physics as a whole. By 1976, the ratio among articles in theoretical particle physics and in experimental physics had reached a value close to three which it has kept since, though of course with some large fluctuations on a volume-to-volume basis. Practically all the articles published were commissioned from authors or originated from discussions which I was able to have with the author(s) before work on the article actually started. Indeed, in order to get a good review article on a topical field, one should rely on a very active author who is in essence "overbooked". It follows that launching an article may require a fair amount of convincing, and friendship ties are sometimes instrumental. I take here the opportunity to express my gratitude to the many authors who wrote for *Physics Reports* and who made the journal what it became. Their kind understanding and co-operation was all the time very deeply appreciated. If one wishes to have an important job done well, one has to ask someone who is already too busy. This popular saying took on a very deep meaning indeed. Following such an attitude may, of course, lead at the same time to some delays, which one has to accept, and I must now express my thanks to the publishers for having accepted proposed dates of submission which turned out to be far too hypothetical. This philosophy may also lead to a rather casual attitude with respect to the actual presentation of the manuscript. One cannot bother a very busy author with too many technical details or favour those who write (or can have typed) better English. I must now express my gratitude to the Desk Editor, K. Korswagen and the people working with her, for the beautiful job which she and they did with manuscripts which happened to be in a really pitiful technical shape when they reached her office. The reader could not see the difference.

As I mentioned already, complete harmony did not always prevail on the Editorial Board whenever it met, which was probably too infrequently to develop efficient contacts. It came close to a fencing match in 1975, when Dik ter Haar and some of the editors associated with the *A* section of *Physics Letters* called for a limitation of the number of papers appearing in particle and nuclear physics. This would have brought them to a frequency level closer to that found with journal publications in physics at large. The editors on the *Physics Letters B* side (as far as fields of interest are concerned) had, however, a united front and argued that quality was to be insisted upon as opposed to a careful weighting of fields, and that emphasis on some particular domains of physics was very acceptable insofar as the correspondingly more numerous reviews remained of a high scientific standard. Bringing to the journal a 30% share located almost solely in particle physics, I of course got a good fraction of the heat. It again took all of W. Wimmers' kind understanding and diplomacy to ease things and avoid a split between the two sections along the dividing line between *Physics Letters A* and *B*. All this did eventually lead to some separation, though of a rather adiabatic type (the one- and two-diamond marking). It was recognized that different fields of physics could require different types of coverage and it was thus deemed acceptable that different editors would choose different editorial policies, insofar as each of them was rather closely associated with some particular domain(s), within the same journal. This went a long way towards ending the arguments which had started in 1971 and reached a peak in 1975, as the two sections thereupon went their own way to a large extent. After many years, I think that Dik ter Haar must still think of me as something of a *Don Quixote* of particle physics. He would certainly be right, since I entered these debates with too much green enthusiasm when more sense of measure would have been appropriate. I think, however, that the journal still needs some strengthening, in quality as well as in quantity in some domains, and in particular some of these associated with the *A* section of *Physics Letters*.

I learned much from these meetings of the Editorial Board, which turned out to be quite fruitful but reaching the proper conclusion certainly made great demands on the patience of W. Wimmers and later of P. Bolman.

In 1981, the two-diamond marking which was covering particle and nuclear physics, where similar editorial policy prevailed, was extended to astrophysics as D. Schramm became editor-in-charge of that particular domain. *Physics Reports* was then recognized as one of the world's leading review journals in physics. It had found its style and its stance.

2. Physics Reports, A Few Figures

The vitality of a journal can be assessed through the amount of material published per year. Figure 2.1 shows the number of volumes published every year since 1971. Each volume carries about 400 pages (an average of six issues) and the numbers entered in Fig. 2.1 are those corresponding to the publication dates actually appearing on the covers. Publishers and subscribers may sometimes count differently, considering volumes as attributed to each yearly subscription. The curve corresponds to my personal prejudices. One sees the starting period when the new journal was actually "carried" by *Physics Letters*. Next to this rapid rise, one may see a maturing period, as a relatively high and rather steady state has been reached. In between the two, the "*C*-marking" (the formal association with *Physics Letters*) had been removed (1978) as the new journal continued on its own. I think that the time evolution should be considered with such theoretical prejudices in mind when venturing an extrapolation. The authors' goodwill, let alone library budgets, may indeed resist the mere extrapolation of a best fit straight line giving an average but misleading growth rate!

Contributions in particle physics had an overwhelming role at the very start but, healthily so, they quickly fell in relative, if not in absolute, amount. Figure 2.2 gives the fraction of issues in particle physics per year. By 1973, it had practically reached a constant level with an average value of $1/3$ of all the published articles. Reading the relative importance of particle physics from Fig. 2.2 puts, however, too much emphasis on the first two years during which, while the fraction was high, the global number of published issues remained rather small. It is therefore better to consider the fraction of particle physics by calculating it per volume (or rather per five volumes, in order to partly smear out fluctuations). This is shown in Fig.

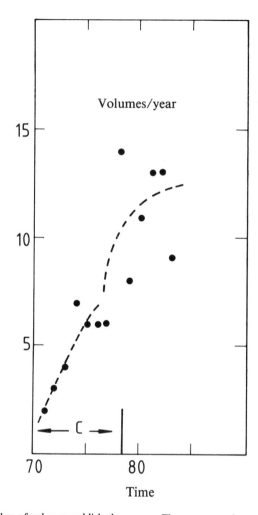

Fig. 2.1. Number of volumes published per year. The curve translates personal prejudices.

2.3. Only the first data point now acknowledges my initial over-enthusiasm and, from the fifth volume onwards, one finds a relatively steady behaviour with an average ratio of 0.29 for particle physics. Are some fluctuations meaningful? I am tempted to say yes, as I can clearly associate the dips in 1978 and in 1982 to my being in charge of the LEP Summer Study (1978) and to my becoming TH Division Leader (1982), activities which, at least for a while, readily moved *Physics Reports* down the priority list. This shows how triggering new projects is important.

I started with theoretical physics reviews only but, after two years, began commissioning papers in experimental particle physics. Figure 2.4 shows the number of articles in theoretical (full dots) and experimental (open dots)

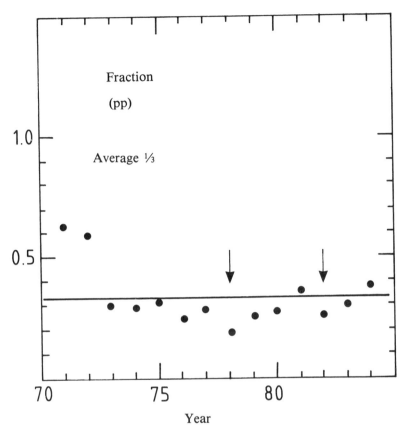

Fraction

(pp)

1.0

Average ⅓

0.5

70   75   80

Year

Fig. 2.2. Fraction of the published issues covering particle physics as a function of time. The straight line corresponds to the average value.

particle physics published per five volumes as a function of volume number. There are large fluctuations. Nevertheless, it is meaningful to mention an average of one experimental paper for 2.5 theoretical ones, the early points having to be disregarded. It should be said that it is always more difficult to obtain an experimental review article than a theoretical one. When presenting recent and often very topical data, various opinions within the collaboration to which he/she belongs may easily present touchy problems for the author. Reviewing data from other groups, when one wishes to cover progress in a whole domain of physics, may easily generate still more difficult questions. It is therefore understandable that busy experimentalists are a bit reluctant to embark on an enterprise which may represent some amount of diplomatic work together with a very large quantity of technical work. I am therefore all the more grateful to all those who contributed to the success of the journal by timely and comprehensive reviews of impor-

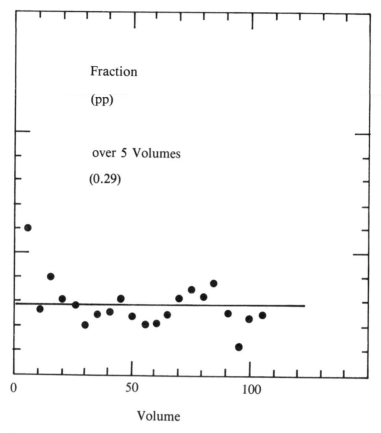

Fig. 2.3. Fraction of the issues in every five volumes covering particle physics. The straight line corresponds to the average value (0.29).

tant developments at SLAC, Fermilab, CERN and DESY over the past ten years. Each review represented a great deal of work, but quickly became a gold mine of information and references. Should one then say that there are perhaps relatively too many theoretical articles? I would certainly have liked to bring to the journal more experimental reviews and I must admit that I failed to be convincing, persuasive or clever enough to obtain timely reviews of important developments. I hopefully followed tracks which eventually vanished, but, on the whole, I should not complain at all and rather be thankful to those who did write excellent papers. On the other hand, the numerous theoretical papers have been generally well received, as is shown by the bulk order scheme sales list and, even if some duplication may be pointed out in some cases, I think that the quality of the reviews justified it. It would have been a pity to restrict their number greatly.

Physics Reports had, from the start, the ambition to be a world journal

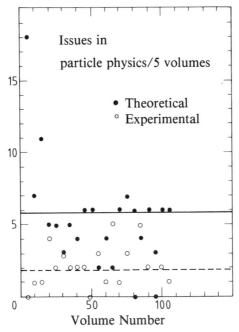

Fig. 2.4. Number of issues per five volumes in theoretical particle physics (full dots) and experimental particle physics (open dots). The two lines correspond to the average values.

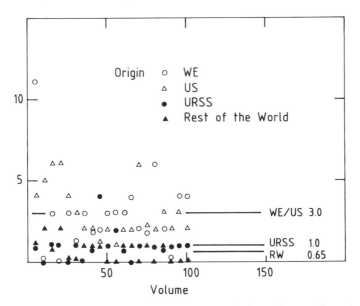

Fig. 2.5. Regional distribution of the articles in particle physics. Values per five volumes for Western Europe (o), the United States (△), the Soviet Union (•) and the rest of the world (▲). The lines are average values.

despite the dominantly European affiliation of its Editorial Board. This actually changed with time as more non-European editors were gradually associated to the Board. However, the geographical location of the editor may not introduce too strong a bias. Figure 2.5 shows the distribution of the published articles per region. The values given are for five volumes, separating articles originating from Western Europe, the United States, the Soviet Union and the rest of the world. One sees that, fluctuations notwithstanding, contributions from Western Europe and America appear on an equal footing (three issues per five volumes in each case). There is a strong, steady contribution from the Soviet Union (one issue per five volumes). The contributions from the rest of the world are at a lower level (0.65 per five volumes only). In particle physics this may, however, be deemed a reasonable distribution.

3.   The Bulk-Order Scheme

North-Holland publications are rather expensive. However, I have always found a very co-operative attitude on the part of the North-Holland management when discussing schemes which could ease financially the access to publications for individual buyers. A very successful outcome of such discussions was the "bulk order scheme".

It was recognized that the journal, which over a few years had developed into one of the leading review journals for various branches of physics, had to be regarded primarily as a "library journal" by virtue of the fact that the publisher was obliged to charge a relatively high price for a single issue, owing to the individual postage, handling and invoicing charges involved. In order to enable the research worker or graduate student to buy his own copy of a particular report, the following scheme was devised. The publisher agreed to make single issues of *Physics Reports* available to individuals only at a price of a few US dollars (depending on the number of pages), provided that combined orders of at least US$50 would be placed with them. In effect, this meant that a group of people could combine their separate orders, as long as the collective order amounted to US$50 or more.

This became effective in 1976 and has been quite successful since. This is illustrated by Fig. 3.1, which shows the number of issues in particle physics sold every year through the bulk order scheme. Next to a very high point, followed by a relatively low one, both expected of a starting period (1976–1977) during which many readers could choose among the numerous reports already available, one sees a relatively steady rise with time which at present gives a value of the order of 2000 per year (full dots). Also shown are the sales values of what has been the best-selling article so far: the paper of Abers and Lee, *Physic Reports* **9**, No. 1 (1973), which has been at the top of the sales list for many years. Articles in particle physics have represented a

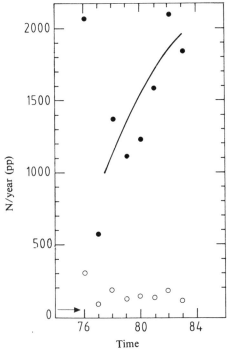

Fig. 3.1. The number of issues in particle physics sold every year through the bulk order scheme (full dots) and the sales values of the best-seller so far: the Abers and Lee article on gauge theories.

practically constant fraction (2/3) of the articles requested through the bulk order scheme. This is shown in Fig. 3.2 and, I think, reflects the vitality of particle physics, a frontier domain where many physicists are willing to learn new developments. A relatively large fraction of the bulk order sales (Fig. 3.2) is indeed contributed by a moderate fraction (Fig. 2.3) of the total output. If one now considers those papers most in demand (over 50 times per year and over 100 for 1976), one finds about 60 titles, sometimes repetitive and all falling under the general category of "particles and fields". The articles by Wilson and Kogut, *Physics Reports* **12**, No. 2 (1974), Politzer, *Physics Reports* **14**, No. 4 (1974), Marciano and Pagels, *Physics Reports* **36**, No. 3 (1978), Eguchi, Gilkey and Hanson, *Physics Reports* **66**, No. 6 (1980) and van Nieuwenhuizen, *Physics Reports* **68**, No. 4 (1981) have thus been much in demand, next to the clear first Abers and Lee article. It may then even seem surprising that excellent experimental physics reviews did not appear high on the bulk order scheme list. One may give two reasons for that. The first one is that reviews in experimental physics usually originate from large laboratories with an associated emission of preprints which are even more cheaply available than issues ordered through the bulk

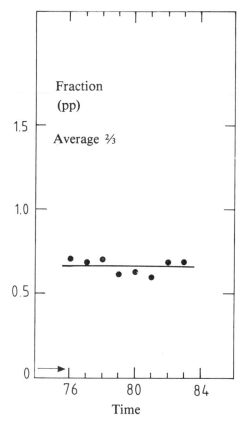

Fig. 3.2. The fraction of all the issues sold through the bulk order scheme which belong to particle physics.

order scheme. The second, and more serious one, which is my conclusion from analyzing the titles most in demand, is that the issues which are most frequently requested are those which provide a self-teaching course, which readers have to consult in full and over a reasonable period of time, even scribbling on pages where necessary. The best-sellers are actually the working tools. Papers carrying very useful information and of easier reading are merely being photocopied in part from the library shelves and do not appear very high in the bulk order scheme sales.

The bulk order schemes turned out to be very useful, as Fig. 3.1 shows. The results eased somewhat the discussions on the Editorial Board previously alluded to. The publishers must be thanked for having maintained prices in dollars (the only easy unit) at a time of wild currency fluctuations, and also for having kept them at a level which did not follow the average inflation rate. Services to the physics community carry their importance, and North-Holland has been very co-operative in that matter.

Another venture worth mentioning next to the bulk order scheme is the publication of reprint volumes.

Attempting to provide a detailed survey of topical questions in physics, *Physics Reports* quickly offered several issues discussing closely interrelated development, or covering at successive intervals a rapidly-changing field. It was then deemed appropriate to group together several issues into a reprint volume which would start with a general introduction written by a leading expert. The understanding was that, since these volumes would contain mainly reprints from *Physics Reports,* thus published at no extra costs but mere material ones, they could be sold at a relatively modest price and hence be available to individual physicists. The publishers agreed to it and, in the course of time, five such reprint volumes have already been published, four of them in particle physics. One must say that in contradistinction to what happened with the bulk order scheme, the success in this case was rather mediocre.

The first volume, published in 1974, was on *Dual Theory,* the second one published in 1978 was on *Gauge Theory and Neutrino Physics.* The third one was published on the occasion of the 25th Anniversary of CERN and carried articles almost entirely devoted to research done at CERN. Its title is *CERN — 25 Years of Physics.* The fourth one, published in 1982, was on *Perturbative Quantum Chromodynamics.* Each volume contains four to six *Physics Reports,* which altogether offer a fairly complete survey of the corresponding topic. It is clear that, but for specific and valuable introduction and some updating additions, these volumes merely reproduced material which libraries already had. It was thought, however, that individual physicists may be tempted, the price of the volumes being kept relatively low (for North-Holland publications). The sales were, however, not considered encouraging; but I must say that if I had not been deeply involved in the matter, I would not have had, except by chance, any knowledge of their existence. It seems that World Scientific Publishing Company, which has now taken up such reprint publications, has indeed had an encouraging success with the first one which they published: *Non-Linear and Collective Phenomena in Quantum Physics.* This volume puts together the proceedings of the Paris topical meeting of 1975 and that of two specialized sessions of the Les Houches Centre of Physics in 1978 and 1980 respectively. These papers altogether provide a survey of the most interesting developments of common interest to particle and condensed matter physics. One may thus still try another one in 1985, which will then be on *Supersymmetry and Supergravity.*

In all these cases, one can find several *Physics Reports* articles which describe a particular topical domain at different times through its rapid and important evolution, and/or at different levels of technicality, whether addressing a rather general audience or a more specialized one. I still think that, for the first four, the publisher ought perhaps to have made more effort to announce them and clearly aimed their price at the individual market.

4. A Few Editorial Comments

I much enjoyed my work as an editor and relations with the many authors and with the publishers have been very agreeable, at least as my personal experience goes. While it took a toll on my time, it also helped me much in my work as a research physicist.

Practically all the articles published in particle physics have been invited, this meaning that some discussion took place before the review article was actually written. I already said that, as I see it, good papers require busy authors and a certain amount of convincing may thus be needed, the editor having to make the first approach. Through many contacts, listening to others and eavesdropping, one may however often find the proper time to approach the proper authors. My being at CERN, with extended visits to the large American laboratories, and in particular to Fermilab in the seventies, certainly helped a lot. The steady stream of very good articles from the Soviet Union shows, however, that one can also develop acceptable, though far less effective, contacts through the mail or through its substitutes. I was very happy when I eventually received the first article from China in 1980. Patient efforts were thus rewarded.

Physics Reports articles are refereed, but I felt that refereeing was to be more a service provided to the author(s), assuring them that their paper had been read by a specialist, bringing up in many cases suggestions and advice for improvements, than a critical examination of the work, leading to its acceptance or rejection. Most authors. must indeed be trusted and encouraged to write an article, and they are actually formally invited by the publisher before the paper is written. It would then be somewhat embarrassing not to reach an eventual acceptance. For that reason, I preferred on several occasions to put author and referee openly in contact when the article was still in a draft version, so that the referee's comments could be used fruitfully before the paper was given its final form. I did not receive any bitter complaints.

Authors invited to write a *Physics Reports* article are usually well-known specialists and therefore often senior physicists. I was, however, extremely happy to trust several junior physicists to write a *Physics Reports* before they eventually became well known. This is a very satisfactory feeling for an editor.

The typical article has been described in Section 1. Nevertheless, there have been many atypical ones, sometimes corresponding to experiments which were deemed appropriate, though I must confess that they involved strong personal prejudices which could well not be universally shared.

There is general agreement among the editors that *Physics Reports* should not publish Conference Proceedings. This should not belong to a regular journal subscribed to on a long-term basis. However, all rules are meant to suffer some exceptions. The only one I considered worthwhile making, though, was to take the proceedings of the 1975 topical conference, held at ENS, Paris, and of the three specialized spring sessions organized by the Les Houches Centre of Physics in 1978, 1980 and 1983 respectively. They all appeared as a set of contributions preceded by a general introduction, bound together as one issue of *Physics Reports*. These meetings covered in great depth the development of the very interesting interface between particle and condensed matter physics. Over the past ten years, this domain has developed quickly with many interesting results. It was thus deemed appropriate to provide a large number of people with reviews of these developments, presented by experts in a commanding, if of course often in a rather technical way. The response to the bulk order scheme where the first three already made the best-sellers' list (over 50 requests per year), showed that the exception was indeed worthwhile.

Some issues included contributions by a rather large number of authors. Nevertheless, the organization of the material was highly structured with a general pedagogical introduction, so that the issues could be used as a self-teaching monograph. A few issues covered the research programme of large laboratories rather than physics topics proper. I had mixed feelings about it and the corresponding series has had only three numbers so far. I have to confess that in some cases I have used the journal to provide a monograph in a domain which I felt deserved coverage while still hardly existing. In such cases, I would ask several experts to write short reviews of different potential facets which would then be put together as an issue of *Physics Reports*. Subjects thus covered included lifetime measurements in the 10^{-13} sec range, the use of synchroton radiation in nuclear physics as it can be considered at LEP, quark matter formation and heavy ion collisions,... I hope that their role in triggering interest may one day justify such ventures In these cases, I have to be particularly thankful to the authors because some time co-ordination was essential.

It seems that there is a widespread and genuine interest in the recent history of physics, and I was happy to obtain approval for a few *Physics Reports* articles (at most one a year, say, in particle physics), which would review particularly interesting periods in the development of physics. I am extremely happy that E. Amaldi agreed to write the first one. Its title is *From the Discovery of the Neutrino to the Discovery of Nuclear Fission*. It will appear in 1984; others will certainly follow.

Several lines of research in theoretical physics have had a rapid and fascinating development, and series of *Physics Reports* could follow them at a yearly interval. This was, for instance, the case for *Dual Theory* in the early seventies and *Quantum Chromodynamics* in the middle and late seventies. It was very interesting to embark on such ventures as an editor, and I am very grateful to the many authors who responded so well.

This has altogether been a very interesting experience and a venture which I am sure others will now develop further and better, with new ideas and much enthusiasm.

A PASSION FOR PHYSICS

Marvin L. Goldberger

Since I stopped doing physics completely in 1978 I felt it was necessary for me to take up another, at least part-time, profession. These are not so easy to come by, especially if you insist on a certain amount of ego gratification. However, I have found one that will satisfy me for a few years until I can find something else. Namely, I do gigs at my physics friends' 60th-birthday parties.

Let me explain how the ego thing comes about. You are asked to give the after-dinner speech for an old friend's 60th-birthday worship. There is often a scientific program associated with the celebration, but since you have nothing of any scientific interest whatsoever to say, you are relieved not to have to fake something or talk about "my life in physics", etc., and still grateful that people remember you and invite you to the party. That's the first reason to feel good. Next, you have an opportunity to wallow in the nostalgia of your youth. Nostalgia, you know, is edited amnesia. This, too, is very satisfying. The honoree is beginning, like you, to lose his memory and will believe anything about the "good old days that never really were" so long as you flatter him (there are very few hers in our generation) enough. The young attendees don't know anything, and by the time the after-dinner speech comes, they are either drunk or asleep; and anyhow, they don't matter very much. They can wait for their own time to come.

The last part of the process is the most gratifying. It is where you talk about your long, personal association with the birthday boy, your history of scientific collaboration and its profound bearing on whatever distinction your great old friend and co-worker has attained. You do this all in such a way that the perceptive listener wonders why they even bothered to come to a party for such an unworthy person. This must be done with taste and tact so that the 60 year-old boob doesn't know it's happening.

I should probably not have revealed all this in advance, but having done so makes it more of a challenge to see if I can pull it off one more time.

I've entitled this talk for Geoff, *A Passion for Physics*. I don't think that anyone who knows him could deny that he has a real thing about physics.

In spite of the fact that we've known each other for nearly forty years, I don't know how this spark was kindled. But it was clearly apparent when we first met in the spring of 1946 at Chicago. Geoff came from Los Alamos where he had been on the Manhattan Project, a protégé of Edward Teller and Emil Konopinski. I had been on the project in Chicago and I was interviewed by Edward for suitability to be a graduate student. Admission to graduate school was a little more cavalier in those days than it is now.

Geoff and I met, as I recall, as students in Edward's course on quantum mechanics. The course was a disaster. Edward never prepared a lecture and had as a backup teacher Maria Mayer, one of the all-time rotten lecturers. Occasionally, Bob Christy, who lived in Edward's garage, gave a reasonable lecture. Frank Yang, who even then was terribly precocious, was the grader for the course. But the fact that that particular course was bad, or the one we took in solid state physics from Clarence Zener was in its own way even more grotesque, was not particularly important. The really important thing was that we were a part of a small, but unusually talented group of students, most of whom had been working for two or three years as real physicists and were thus far more knowledgeable and sophisticated than normal first year graduate students.

It was truly a remarkable time. We had been working side by side with the very best scientists in the world: Fermi, Wigner, Bohr, Teller, Weisskopf, Bethe, Alvarez, Peierls, Serber, Oppenheimer, Segre, Urey, Seaborg, Christy, Kistiakowsky, Rabi — even spies like Hans Fuchs and Alan Nun May. These people were all shockingly young — middle thirties, early forties — in retrospect it's hard to imagine anyone taking such whippersnappers seriously. But we worked with and were on a first-name basis with all of these people. And, we were wild about physics and bursting to get going.

We were unusually close as students at Chicago. We shared offices on the fourth floor of Eckhart Hall and we ate together, studied together and taught each other physics. I remember many things about the learning process — like field theory — Wentzel's book had just appeared in German and we struggled to understand it.

As we gradually established ourselves in the pecking order as students are wont to do, it quickly became clear that Geoff was very close to the top. He was not always the quickest or the most articulate or glib, but somehow or other he always got the homework done and exuded an air of quiet confidence.

For the most part the graduate students were married and our families became quite close. I was the only one who had a car and I recall many expeditions with the Chews, the Chamberlains and the Wattenbergs in that miserable 1936 Plymouth. We were also all extremely poor, but it didn't matter. We were young and full of beans.

Geoff and I began scurrying around for some kind of thesis problem in summer and fall of 1947 under the general aegis of Edward Teller. Teller, however, was so preoccupied with weapons work and concerned over the future of Los Alamos that he suggested that Geoff and I approach Fermi and ask him if he would take us on. Fermi had not ever had any theoretical students before, but much to our pleasure he agreed to accept us. After a number of false starts we finally got into serious thesis work. Fermi had a very refreshing view about Ph.D. theses: He said "You don't have to show your thesis to your grandchildren." His own thesis had consisted of something like putting an iron cross in an electron beam and observing the shadow on a flourescent screen. At any rate, we did get through, I doing a Monte Carlo calculation of neutrons passing through a nucleus, and Geoff working on neutron-deuteron scattering.

We got finished and began the process of thinking about jobs. We both ended up going to the Radiation Laboratory at Berkeley. I know how I made the decision to go there — an extraordinarily interesting story — but quite irrelevant to this occasion, and I no longer remember why Geoff made his decision. However made, it was an exciting environment for both of us to be in Bob Serber's theoretical group. Bob, overshadowed for a time by the glamorous Oppenheimer, was a brilliant physicist who could talk equally well with theorists and experimentalists. Berkeley was where it was at in high energy physics, and Geoff and I quickly became involved in a series of interesting projects related to nucleon-nucleon scattering — a preoccupation of the times — and had our introduction to applied field theory trying to understand photo-meson production.

We were both offered assistant professorships at Berkeley; and Geoff, in fact, accepted. He was unfortunately swept into the maelstrom of the loyalty oath issue at UC and, along with many others, left after a rather turbulent year. After an interlude at Brookhaven he went to Illinois and I went to Chicago. I mention this because we began collaborating again by telephone and by frequent visits, a practice which continued until I left for Princeton in 1957.

It was at Illinois that Geoff started a mode of doing physics that I always envied. He had, at any given time, a program. He became interested in the static model of pion-nucleon interactions and he just studied the hell out of it. There never seemed to be any indecision about what he would be working on next week, next month, or next year. I don't mean to imply that Geoff was immune to new ideas, but that there never seemed to be any ambiguity for him about what he would be doing at $t + \triangle t$.

The Illinois years were very good for Geoff. He had a tremendously fruitful collaboration with Francis Low who is, of course, much older than Geoff and me, and at whose 60th-birthday worship I had the honor of working, too. I can save some time and agony for the audience by referring to my brilliant speech recorded in Francis' festschrift instead of telling once again about the profoundly important work the three of us did in plasma physics and in collaboration with Nambu, on pion-nucleon and photo-pion production.

We all fled the mid-west at about the same time — Francis to MIT, I to Princeton, and Geoff to Berkeley. I think Geoff's return to Berkeley was a very important thing for that University. He had left in protest, had been very active as head of the Federation of American Scientists during the McCarthy era, and had obviously not abandoned his principles. He totally revitalized the high energy theory group that had been decimated by the loss of Serber and Wick. He captured Stanley Mandelstam, embarked on a big program of exploitation of Stanley's double dispersion relations, and began a real production line of outstanding graduate students, many of whom are now grown-ups and are here tonight to honor their inspirational teacher.

Let me interrupt the beautiful continuity of this narrative to remark that Geoff had an uncanny ability to extract the best from his collaborators and his students. His positive mental attitude had a great deal to do with this, in my opinion. His natural inclination was to say yes, to be enthusiastic and to look for redeeming virtue in things people said. He was never a nay-sayer and his general attitude was very supportive.

It was around this time in the very early sixties that Geoff became enamoured with the work of Regge and with Steve Frautschi, and made important observations about the relation of poles in the angular momentum plane to elementary particles. This work led to the concept, long championed by Geoff, of nuclear democracy, the idea that none of the observed long-lived particles should be regarded as more fundamental than any others; that everything is part of an incestuous mess. These notions led him to a rejection of quantum field theory to the extent that such theories appeared to contain arbitrary parameters and to the belief that an S-Matrix theory could be constructed based on concepts of unitarity and analyticity of various kinds that would be unique and have no free parameters. I don't know what Geoff's present position on these issues is.

At any rate, Geoff and I continued to interact scientifically, albeit less frequently. One summer, 1968, Geoff, Francis and I got together in Aspen and worked on a Regge-exchange model of the old multiperipheral model of Amati, Fubini and Stanghellini. Geoff insisted at one time in describing this work in a terribly erudite and complicated way he had been taught by his student Carleton DeTar which I recall Francis and I had a terrible time understanding. Perhaps I'm being unfair to Francis — I can certainly say it for myself. Geoff and I came together again in Princeton in 1969-70 where, with Henry Abarbanel and Leslie Saunders, we wrote a number of papers on multiperipheral things, pomerons, etc. This was a year of terrible tragedy for Geoff when his wife Ruth was struck down by a massive stroke. His inner strength, and I believe in part his dedication to physics, carried him through this unbelievably difficult period. He had the enormous good fortune to meet Denyse at a critical time in his life.

In the ensuing years I have drifted further away from physics and have had fewer opportunities to interact with Geoff and I have not kept up with his work. I will therefore conclude by returning briefly to the title of this talk, *A Passion for Physics*.

Aside from the fact that Geoff really wanted to be a professional baseball player and was frustrated in this desire by a bad back, in all of my experience with him, physics seemed to be the dominant force in his life. Of course, he was terribly involved in the world around him in a variety of ways. I'm sure he even read books other than Goldberger and Watson — though why would one need anything more? But it was physics with a capital F, as our friend Bernardini used to say, that was and still seems to be Geoff's obsession. There are worse kinds of infatuations, I've noticed. Perhaps if my own passion had been greater I wouldn't now have to be dealing with 275 faculty maniacs, all of whom think they know how to do my job better than I.

I have to say that I'm glad that Geoff had that back problem. I can't really see him (he was a catcher) as a WASP Yogi Berra chewing tobacco and screaming at umpires — perhaps a Gary Cooperesque Lou Gehrig character. But baseball's loss was physics' gain. I became a much better physicist, indeed a better human being because of Geoff, as I know did all of his collaborators. The world is much richer for his deep contributions to our field. Eugene Wigner used to occasionally ask the question, "What is so-and-so's second fault?" I can answer this about Geoff. He's too good to be true. It's also his first fault, his third fault, etc.

Happy 60th Birthday, Geoff.

PART II

BOOTSTRAP PHYSICS: A CONVERSATION WITH GEOFFREY CHEW

Fritjof Capra

I. Introduction

For Geoff Chew, the year 1984 is a double jubilee. It is the year of his sixtieth birthday and, at the same time, the twenty-fifth anniversary of his celebrated bootstrap hypothesis. It seemed therefore appropriate to review the history, present status, future potential, and philosophical implications of the bootstrap approach to particle physics. The present paper is the transcript of a wide-ranging conversation about these topics between Chew and the author, which took place in July 1983. The text of the transcript has been edited only minimally in order to preserve the spontaneity of the conversation, and it has been organized as follows.

II.   The Bootstrap Idea

III. History of the Bootstrap
    A.   Fermi's Influence
    B.   Collaboration With Low; Analyticity and Pole-Particle Correspondence
    C.   Collaboration With Mandelstam; Origin of Bootstrap
    D.   Regge Poles; Chew-Frautschi Plot
    E.   Recognition of S Matrix
    F.   Emergence of Bootstrap Philosophy
    G.   Break With Convention
    H.   Decline of Bootstrap in Late Sixties

IV. Philosophical Influences

V.   Recent Advances in the Bootstrap Program
    A.   Topological Expansion; Ordered S Matrix
    B.   Topology — The Language for a New Science?
    C.   Achievements of Topological Bootstrap Theory

II. The Bootstrap Idea

CAPRA: Geoff, I would like to begin by asking you: What is the bootstrap? What does it say?

CHEW: The idea tends to evolve in time, and the way I describe it now will probably be different from how I would have described it five or six years ago, or from how I would describe it five or six years in the future. The key notion certainly is consistency; the idea that the laws of nature are controlled by consistency and are not arbitrary. From a bootstrap standpoint, one is not content to see any arbitrary aspect in a theory.

CAPRA: Arbitrary meaning what? Do you mean by that, for example, that the mass of the proton has its reasons?

CHEW: Yes, that is certainly the sense in which I mean it. However, when you actually apply the bootstrap idea, you always accept certain ideas, you have to, and within the context of these accepted ideas you then try to remove arbitrariness as much as possible. For example, in the beginning we simply accepted the idea of particles, the idea of an S matrix, which brings with it the ideas of energy, momentum, superposition, and also the Poincaré group and ideas of analyticity. All these ideas were accepted as the basis of our thinking about consistency.

CAPRA: They were part of your scientific framework, part of your language.

CHEW: Yes, and within that framework an effort was made to understand the properties of the hadrons, just the strongly interacting particles. That was what we operationally called the bootstrap. But then, as time went on, we became more demanding, and we asked: could we also understand the electroweak particles? And this evolved to the feeling that one needs also to understand the origin of space-time, the Poincaré group, probably; ultimately also superposition, the presence of complex numbers, analyticity, all these things.

CAPRA: The presence of complex numbers?

CHEW: Yes, why complex numbers are appropriate to understanding physics. There are lots of other formalisms you might think of. No matter how far you go, because of human limitations you will always have to accept, at any stage, a certain set of ideas.

CAPRA: But apart from those ideas, which are provisionally accepted as fundamental, you don't accept anything arbitrary in your theory. You want to derive everything from overall self-consistency.

CHEW: Yes, that's the idea.

CAPRA: Now, what would you say about the nature of the bootstrap idea? Is it a scientific hypothesis, which has now, maybe, turned into a theory? Is it a philosophy? How would you characterize it?

CHEW: Well it is certainly a philosophy, and I think operationally it has turned into a scientific program. I suppose this scientific program has now enough substance to call it a theory. It is very hard to say when you make these transitions from one category to another.

CAPRA: It is also something like a principle, something like Occam's razor, for example.

CHEW: Yes, or like Mach's principle.

CAPRA: However, there seems to be one problem with this notion of self-consistency. One could say that it is a fundamental principle of an approach which does not accept fundamental principles.

CHEW: That's right. That's the ultimate paradox.

CAPRA: Does that bother you?

CHEW: Well, it disturbs me vaguely, but I don't expect to get to the bottom of the whole thing in my lifetime anyway... All is relative; it's a matter of making a certain amount of progress.

CAPRA: I have sometimes worried about this problem, and I have thought that one could maybe put this principle of self-consistency together with the scientific framework, with the scientific language. It is certainly an important aspect of science that you don't want to be inconsistent, which is again related to the way human beings think and the way we observe.

CHEW: Yes, that would be a way to talk about it.

CAPRA: The notion of self-consistency brings to mind the celebrated paradoxes of quantum mechanics. How do you see the role of these paradoxes?

CHEW: I think that this is one of the most puzzling aspects of physics, and I can only state my own point of view, which I don't think is shared by anybody else. My feeling is that the principles of quantum mechanics, as they are stated, are not satisfactory and that the pursuit of the bootstrap program is going to lead to a different statement. I think that the form of this statement will include such things as: you should not try to express the principles of quantum mechanics in an *a priori* accepted space-time. That is the flaw in the present situation. Quantum mechanics has something intrinsically discrete about it, whereas the idea of space-time is continuous. I believe that if you try to state the principles of quantum mechanics after having accepted space-time as an absolute truth, then you will get into difficulties. My feeling is that the bootstrap approach is going to eventually give us simultaneous explanations for space-time, quantum mechanics, and the meaning of reality. All these will come together, somehow, but you will not be able to begin with space-time as a clear, unambiguous basis and then put these other ideas on top of it.

CAPRA: By the way, I know that some people are confused when they hear you use the term "reality". Whenever you say "reality," you mean Cartesian reality, right?

CHEW: Oh yes, I'm sorry, I should always use "objective reality" or "Cartesian reality".

CAPRA: You don't mean to say that the quantum reality, or the reality of emotions, or of the spiritual realm are any less real?

CHEW: No, no, no! I am just being careless. I mean objective reality, the explicate order, as David Bohm calls it.

CAPRA: Coming back to quantum mechanics, you are saying, in fact, that these paradoxes exist, as Bohr and Heisenberg already emphasized, because we are talking about atomic phenomena in a language which is inappropriate. They were referring to the Cartesian language of classical physics, and what you seem to be saying is that space-time is still a remnant of the classical way of thinking.

CHEW: Absolutely. I don't think the meaning of space-time has ever been separate from classical notions. Somehow, we are trying to grasp the connection between the real world and the quantum principles, and we have to understand that space-time is part of the real world and not something that pre-exists before quantum principles are stated.

CAPRA: I would now like to discuss with you the general significance of the bootstrap idea. I have recently been more and more impressed by the idea that the major shift and the deepest change in our thinking may be the shift from an architectural metaphor of a building, with firm foundations upon which one builds, to the metaphor of a network, which has no foundations but represents a web of interrelated events and, correspondingly, consists of a web of concepts to describe these events. That seems to be the major shift. The notion of a basis, of fundamental concepts, building on strong foundations, etc. — all that runs through Western science and philosophy. Descartes wrote that the knowledge of his time was built on sand and mud and that he was going to build new firm foundations for a new science; and three hundred years later Einstein wrote that the foundations of classical physics, that is of this very edifice of Descartes, were shifting and that he did not see any firm ground upon which he could build a theory. I think, maybe, since the bootstrap, it is now the first time in Western science that we are not looking for firm ground and solid foundations anymore.

CHEW: I think that is true, and it is also true that because of the long tradition of Western science the bootstrap approach has not become reputable yet among scientists. It is not recognized as science precisely because of its lack of a firm foundation. The whole idea of science is, in a sense, in conflict with the bootstrap approach, because science wants questions which are clearly stated and which can have unambiguous experimental verification. Part of the bootstrap scheme, however, is that no concepts are regarded as absolute and you are always expecting to find weaknesses in your old concepts. The bridge, however, between standard science and the bootstrap approach lies in the commonly shared awareness of the approximate nature of all experiments. Even people who are dedicated traditional scientists recognize that no measurement can be completely precise.

CAPRA: But these are two things, the approximate nature of measurement and the approximate nature of concepts.

CHEW: Right, and both are recognized.

CAPRA: By the way, do you have any idea when the appreciation of the approximate nature of scientific theories emerged in the history of science?

CHEW: I don't know for sure, but I suspect that it came along with quantum mechanics. I suspect that in the 19th century people might well have believed that theories like Newton's could have absolute validity.

CAPRA: Anyway, now the approximate nature of science is generally accepted.

CHEW: Yes, but in spite of that, the traditional point of view in science is that at any given stage of activity, there is supposed to be a consensus about certain principles whose validity has not yet been disproved or even challenged. All scientists are supposed to conduct their activities within this framework of accepted principles until some measurement comes along which is accurate enough to show that some principle has to be abandoned. The bootstrap approach recognizes from the start that the principles used are not going to be absolute, that everything is approximate. Nevertheless, it is incumbent upon a bootstrap theorist to get an understanding of the degree of approximation.

CAPRA: But now you have said more or less the same thing about bootstrap science and orthodox science.

CHEW: Well, that's why it is possible for them to coexist. Psychologically, however, there is a difference which causes great misunderstanding. Let me give you an example. At the present time, the overwhelming majority of the theorists working in high energy physics accept an absolute notion of local fields. They do this because it is to them the only known way of combining the quantum principles with the space-time continuum. They accept the space-time continuum as an absolute and accept quantum superposition as an absolute, and they only know one way to put these two things together, which is through the local quantum field, and so they take for granted that whatever the description of natural phenomena is going to be, it will be done through local fields. Now, if you get them in a philosophical discussion such as this one, and if you push them, the more talented ones will agree that probably local quantum fields do not represent absolute truth. But they would say, "So far that has not been shown."

CAPRA: So they would think it *might* be the absolute truth?

CHEW: I suspect that if you took *the* most talented ones — people like t'Hooft, Gell-Mann, Weinberg, or Salam — when they are in a philosophical mood they would probably agree that local fields are not the ultimate truth. But they are guessing that within their own lifetime nobody is going to go beyond the capacity of the local field to describe high-energy phenomena. Somehow or other I have come to the belief that it is not too soon to go beyond local fields. What that means is that in trying to develop a theory I don't start with a local quantum field. I start with other ideas, and all these people find this incomprehensible. They say, "Why don't you use local fields? They have never been shown to be wrong." Now, the reason why I don't like them is because they bring in an inherent arbitrariness. Nobody has ever found a way to use local quantum fields without introducing an unpleasant arbitrariness.

III. History of the Bootstrap

CAPRA: Geoff, I would now like to turn to the history of the bootstrap idea. A little while ago you said, "Somehow or other I came to the belief..." Since the shift from orthodox physics to bootstrap physics is so radical, I am extremely curious to know how you developed these ideas and to what extent you appreciated their radical nature.

A. Fermi's Influence

CHEW: I made an attempt not long ago to reconstruct some of these developments, and I believe that the beginning came right at the time of my Ph.D. thesis with Fermi. Now there is an irony here, because Fermi was an extreme pragmatist who was not really interested in philosophy at all. He simply wanted to know the rules that would allow him to predict the results of experiments. I remember him talking about quantum mechanics and laughing scornfully at people who spent their time worrying about the interpretation of the theory, because he knew how to use those equations to make predictions. But Fermi suggested as a thesis problem for me an extension of an approximation which he had discovered in connection with the scattering of slow neutrons by molecular systems. He had realized that the molecular binding was important in this process but that nevertheless the interaction of the neutron with the nuclei was overwhelmingly strong compared to its interaction with the rest of the system. While the neutron was interacting with the nucleus you could ignore the molecular forces. It was a very subtle thing which, eventually, became called the impulse approximation. Fermi's idea was that the nuclei behave in response to the atomic forces until the neutron arrives; then, when the neutron is in contact with a particular nucleus, the nucleus forgets that it has any other things around it, until the neutron departs when, once again, it responds to its environment. Now, all of this is done quantum-mechanically, so it's not trivial. But it led Fermi to a certain set of formulas, a recipe of how to know the molecular wave functions, and then all you had to know in addition was the scattering amplitude of the neutron by the nucleus, as if the nucleus were free. And then you could put these two things together to do your computations.

CAPRA: So that was what Fermi had done.

CHEW: Fermi had done that and he suggested that I extend the same idea to scattering of neutrons by nuclei, where you think of the nucleus as being made up of neutrons and protons. The point of the idea was that if the neutron was moving very fast, there might again be something like a neutron interacting with a single nucleon. What Fermi had done here was really to make a practical application of an S-matrix idea. He did not recognize that, but he intuitively understood that there was a complex number which characterizes the scattering of the neutron, which you can measure, and you can use that number in computations. You don't have to say that there is a potential between the neutron and the nucleus; you don't have to go through the apparatus of the Schrödinger equation. All you have to know is that one number, which is an S-matrix element. So that idea got into my head.

CAPRA: And you worked it out?

CHEW: I worked it out for the case of scattering of neutrons by deuterons and various other things.

CAPRA: And it worked?

CHEW: It worked, and it also persuaded me that it was not necessary to have a Schrödinger equation and a potential. Previously, people had always thought that when you computed something you had to have a detailed microscopic interaction between the particles together with a Schrödinger equation.

CAPRA: In other words, you had to have a temporal sequence for the wave function.

CHEW: That's right. Fermi simply produced formulas. You saw no time; you saw no Schrödinger equation. He simply worked directly with amplitudes.

CAPRA: And he did this because he was a pragmatist.

CHEW: That's right. He somehow knew intuitively what he had to do. Now, he did not describe it that way. He described it in ways that very much obscured the S-matrix interpretation. But nevertheless I began to think that a large part of what we normally associate with the Schrödinger equation is simply done by S-matrix principles, and you don't need all this microscopic space-time.

CAPRA: But these S-matrix principles were not formulated at that time.

CHEW: No.

CAPRA: Was the S matrix itself known?

CHEW: Yes. John Wheeler had identified it, I think, in 1939. Heisenberg had written papers about certain of its properties in the mid-forties, and he had actually called it the S matrix. Then Christian Møller wrote some review papers which propagated Heisenberg's thinking.

CAPRA: Were you familiar with these papers at that time?

CHEW: Well, that's a very funny thing. I had Fermi's idea, and I knew about the S matrix abstractly, but I did not connect the two; not for a long time. It's very strange. I found the S-matrix theory at that time kind of forbidding. It used an apparatus that was difficult, and I simply did not connect it to those other ideas. But I did become aware of the S matrix while I was a graduate student.

After I left Chicago, I continued to work on this impulse approximation for a couple of years, but it was done within sort of a bastard framework. It wasn't S-matrix theory, it was something in between. I was picking up Fermi's intuition and trying to generalize it, and I produced a series of papers in which Murph Goldberger and Giancarlo Wick were also involved. Then I went to the University of Illinois in 1950 and started thinking about π-mesons which had been discovered not long before that. For some reason — I wish I could recall that precisely — I was completely persuaded that the idea of local fields was inappropriate for describing π-mesons. Up until then, people had been dominated by the idea of Yukawa, which was that π-mesons were the analogue of photons. Yukawa had said that the electromagnetic force, which is due to the exchange of photons, was the analogue to the nuclear force due to the exchange of π-mesons. So people were writing down equations just like electromagnetic equations, except that they would have fields associated with the π-mesons.

Now I had been in contact with the early experiments on π-mesons, and it was clear to me that these were particles just like any other nuclear particle, like neutrons or protons, and it seemed silly to me to use fields to describe them. The kinds of experiments you were trying to describe were just like any other nuclear reaction. You didn't use fields in connection with nuclear physics before that; why should you use fields for the π-mesons when they were just another kind of nuclear particle? But people said, π-mesons are not nuclear particles; they are field quanta; they are like photons. It is very strange when you look back now to understand that psychology. So in 1950, when I went to the University of Illinois, I decided to try to make a little model to describe scattering of π-mesons by protons, based on the same idea that Fermi had. I said to myself, suppose the proton is some kind of a structure that contains π-mesons within it and then we shoot π-mesons at it from the outside... Although I did not know that the word S matrix was relevant at that time, it was a model in the spirit of S-matrix theory. It was a model in which you did not use the Schrödinger equation; you just used the superposition of amplitudes. Looking back now I can see that it had much of the Feynman idea that you can build amplitudes by superposition.

B.   *Collaboration with Low; Analyticity and Pole-Particle Correspondence*

CHEW: The model had a certain amount of success, and then Francis Low came to the University of Illinois, and after a year or so we started to work together. He had made a certain discovery in axiomatic field theory and for some reason either he, or I, or both of us, recognized that his discovery might be relevant to this model that I had developed. So we started to work together on it, and I was so pleased to have somebody of Low's talent to work with that I put aside my feelings about the nature of my model and tried to re-express the content of it in field-theory language. It turned out that, to a large extent, this was possible. Then we wrote a paper together, which many more people could understand. Not so many people could understand the thing I had written at first, but when it was re-expressed in the language of field theory it could be appreciated by many more people. The mathematical structure that came along with it was, in fact, much improved, so that we could see a lot more things.

Now Francis understood that the additional content was, in fact, of a general nature associated with analyticity. It was at that point that I began to be aware of analyticity as a principle. Francis and I had, somehow, come upon the notion that analytic continuation is very powerful. We still did not think of it as S matrix; we thought of it as analyticity suggested by field theory. But, in fact, what we did was to sort of forget the field theory at a certain point and start working with analytic functions. Most of the content of what we did was just based on analytic functions. We started to recognize the complex plane explicitly at that point.

CAPRA: Did the S-matrix framework, as it existed at that time, have analyticity in it, or was this your discovery?

CHEW: I am not quite sure what the honest answer to that is, but I'll tell you what Landau said to me. He was a very dramatic person, very outspoken with no hesitation to express his views about anything. In 1959, at a meeting in Kiev, he expressed annoyance to me about the work that I was doing with Mandelstam on the π-π dynamics. He said we wasted our time with approximations, dealing with a system that was incomplete. He was partly right, but through our effort we discovered general things which we would not have discovered had we not made that effort. In any case, in the course of criticizing me for putting so much effort into this π-π dynamics, Landau said, "You know, you have discovered an absolutely crucial point, which is that particles correspond to poles, that the S matrix is an analytic function, and that the poles of the S-matrix are the particles." He attributed that discovery to me. I didn't think of that as my discovery, but when I look back and ask myself, who was it who first really appreciated that particles correspond to poles, maybe it was me; I am not sure. It was an idea that was floating; it occurred in various special forms here and there, but somehow the generality was not recognized. For example, a few people, such as Wigner, had come to the idea that the notion of an unstable atomic state could be associated with a complex pole in something or other, and that the imaginary part of the pole location was associated with its lifetime.

CAPRA: Was that the Breit-Wigner resonance?

CHEW: The Breit-Wigner resonance formula was an example. It's hard to tell how general Breit and Wigner thought these concepts were. At that time, such ideas were always presented as if they could be derived from perturbation theory, but at least Fermi knew very well that they had to be general; they couldn't rest on perturbation theory.

CAPRA: Now, what about the analyticity of the S matrix?

CHEW: Well, the S matrix itself was not a well-recognized notion.

CAPRA: It seems that what you contributed, then, was the emphasis on analyticity which put the whole notion of a pole in a different context. Without even mentioning the S matrix, it was nevertheless a step in that direction.

CHEW: That's right; that's true. I certainly contributed something, but it's hard to say exactly what it was. I remember being puzzled at the time that there weren't lots of people recognizing these points, and I felt there must be something the matter with me, because it seemed so evident to me that we were dealing with an analytic function which has poles. But nobody else... and then Landau! That was a tremendous thing. Here I go to Russia, and here comes Landau and congratulates me for exactly recognizing this. Then there was one other place that I know of where I was given credit. This was in a paper by a Berkeley mathematician who was studying the abstract mathematical problem of how to extrapolate a function which you only know incompletely. He was focusing on the use of the idea that the function had poles with known locations, and he attributed the use of this information for the extrapolation of an incompletely known function to me. In presenting the history of this problem, he referred to a paper of mine, which might be the first paper in which a definite statement about the association of particles with poles is made. This was a paper on the problem of deducing the pion-nucleon coupling constant from nucleon-nucleon scattering data, which I had written in 1958.[1]

Just as Francis Low and I were doing that work, Gell-Mann and Goldberger had started to develop their dispersion relations, which had a big influence on me. They believed the relationships that they employed were all based on field theory, but I remember I was quite convinced that it was analyticity that counted and that field theory was not really necessary. I still did not make the connection with the term S matrix. It's very strange; that was already in 1955–56.

C. Collaboration with Mandelstam; Origin of Bootstrap

CHEW: I left Illinois in 1957 and came here to Berkeley, and then I met Stanley Mandelstam, who had discovered double dispersion relations and had thereby solved a problem I had been struggling with for a long time. I had become aware of the fact that analytic continuations in energy needed to be extended to an angle — that you had to continue both in energy and angle. I could not figure out quite how to do it, but Mandelstam did.

CAPRA: He developed that whole framework of the s and t variables, didn't he?

CHEW: Yes, that's right. Well, I got Mandelstam to come to Berkeley and we worked together. He was at Columbia and had gotten his Ph.D. at Birmingham with Peierls. At Columbia nobody knew what he was doing; nobody paid any attention to him. I heard him give a talk at the Washington meeting of the American Physical Society, and I remember that I said to myself when I heard his talk, "Oh, this young guy, he doesn't know how hard his problem is. He thinks he solved it, but I'm sure he hasn't solved it because he doesn't know this difficulty and that difficulty, and so on." And I thought, in kindness to him I'll point out some of these difficulties after his talk. But when I started to ask him questions he just answered every question. I was totally overwhelmed; he had really solved the problem! So I persuaded him to come out to Berkeley, which he happily did, and we collaborated on two papers extending the whole idea to π-π scattering. Up until then it had always been πN scattering, but now that Mandelstam had extended the analytic continuation, it was possible to think about π-π scattering.

We did not get a satisfactory theory, of course, because the pion is not the end of the story, although at that time we thought it was. It is funny to look back at this now. We thought, somehow, that the π-meson was the key, and if you could understand how pions interacted with pions, you really got it. But we discovered that something was loose; the system did not close.

CAPRA: In all this there was no S matrix yet, and of course no bootstrap?

CHEW: That's right, but this was where the idea came into my head, and in 1959 the word "bootstrap" appeared in print for the first time, although rather casually. Mandelstam and I had pushed our π-π analysis to the point where we could see that there might be a solution of the following character. The pions would interact to produce either a bound state or a pseudo-bound state, and that bound state by crossing would then constitute a force which would be the agent for making a bound state in the first place. We could see this possibility quite clearly in the way the coefficients of the equations arose.

CAPRA: Had the crossing property been identified at that time?

CHEW: Yes, crossing had been discovered by Gell-Mann and Goldberger, but it had not been used in the sense of dynamics to make a theory of forces. It was understood that ingoing particles became outgoing antiparticles by crossing, but the crossing property had not been applied to talk about forces in the cross channel. Somehow it needed Mandelstam's representation to do that. Well, Mandelstam and I figured those things out, and in 1959 there was that conference in Kiev at which I was a rapporteur. When I reported on our work, together with the work of others, I used the term "bootstrap" for the first time in the text of this report, referring to that possibility that we had noticed. Now, you have to realize that the ϱ-meson had not been discovered at that time; Mandelstam and I thought of a bound state of two pions being simultaneously, through its exchange, the force that holds the pions together. A corresponding particle was not yet experimentally known. So all this was very tentative. Nevertheless, we had noticed this possibility and we described this as a kind of bootstrap dynamics.

CAPRA: "We" meaning Mandelstam and you?

CHEW: I said it. I don't think Mandelstam would have used the term, but it certainly came out of our joint work. I think in discussions with Mandelstam I had used the term "bootstrap". Stanley never endorsed it but, being a very mild person, he did not fight it, and the term also appeared in one of our papers.[2] What happened then was that a number of other people, in particular Zachariasen and Zemach, and some others, used the term once they had grasped the idea. Going along with it was an approximation called the N/D approximation, in which you use S-matrix principles to do computations within the framework of scattering amplitudes, which you analytically continue without using the Schrödinger equation. If you think of Mandelstam's subsequent interests, he never picked up the bootstrap idea. He allowed me to use it in one of our joint papers, but he never felt comfortable with it. Stanley is a beautiful example of the kind of physicist I was talking about earlier. He feels a need for something fundamental. I think he always believed that he had firm ground under his feet.

CAPRA: Even though you could say that his double dispersion relations were really the first tool that pulled out the firm ground from under you.

CHEW: That's right, that's right; that's exactly right!

CAPRA: If you disperse in one channel, and then you turn everything around and disperse in the other channel, that is very much connected with that whole network idea that was later to emerge.

CHEW: That's right, but Stanley thought that it was based on field theory. By the way, Francis Low's earlier work was of somewhat similar status. Low did the same thing in one variable, and then Mandelstam did it in two variables.

D. Regge Poles; Chew-Frautschi Plot

CAPRA: Where did Frautschi come in?

CHEW: Frautschi came a year or so after that, in 1960. Mandelstam and I had been frustrated in our N/D calculations by a certain divergence that appeared in these equations. It turned out to be impossible to avoid this with the methods that we were aware of. This was associated with a power behavior that goes along with the spin 1 of the ϱ-meson. We had to use the spin 1 in order for anything interesting to happen, and then we got into this difficulty in connection with asymptotic behavior. I was furious because I felt intuitively that there should not be any divergence. The ϱ-meson was not an elementary particle, it was coming out as a composite, and it was ridiculous that it should produce a divergence just like in field theory. It was most irritating to have a difficulty characteristic of field theory just because the ϱ-meson had spin 1. When Frautschi came — now this is a very important historical question — somehow or other we became aware of a paper by Tullio Regge. I forgot who told us about that paper, maybe it was Mandelstam. I am not sure, but it was probably Mandelstam. Anyway, somebody told us about the paper by Regge, which seemed to have something to do with our difficulty of the spin-1 asymptotic behavior. So we tried to read Regge's paper. In the beginning we did not understand it very well, but we did grasp the idea of an angular momentum which depends on energy. Regge somehow made an analytic continuation away from the integer angular momentum so as to make it smooth.

CAPRA: Was this one of his basic papers on complex angular momentum?

CHEW: It was practically the only one. As far as I know, he just wrote one paper, and he did it in the context of potential scattering. Frautschi and I, in frequent consultation with Mandelstam, came to the belief that this kind of behavior was general, that it would apply to the relativistic problem. I remember that Mandelstam was not very keen on this at first. We had long, long arguments about this question, which went on into 1961, I think. Frautschi was enthusiastic, and he and I worked together and developed some phenomenological applications before we understood clearly what was going on. Strangely, Murray Gell-Mann played a big role in this. He got interested, and it was Gell-Mann, I think, who said you should call these things Regge poles. He thought it was a big joke, because Regge himself did not have a clue as to what we were doing with them. He had simply written that one paper, and from his point of view it was mathematics based on the Schrödinger equation, and there was no connection with a more general'problem.

CAPRA: Did you see the relevance of crossing to Regge's formalism at that time?

CHEW: Yes, we certainly did. There was a confused period there, in which we were sure we had come upon something of generality and importance, but we weren't clever enough to get it really straight. We kept talking to other people about it and getting their advice, and gradually a number of other people became interested in the development. Gell-Mann certainly did; he was very enthusiastic about it; also Goldberger and some other people. Then Frautschi and I wrote a paper applying the idea. There were just enough baryon masses that had been measured at that point, so you could begin to see a Regge trajectory developing. But my real interest, and I suppose also Frautschi's, was to apply this to the bootstrap idea. We wanted to take the equations that Mandelstam and I had developed and apply this Regge boundary condition to them, so that we would get away from that divergence. Well, there was progress made in that respect, but in retrospect you can see that the understanding of Regge behavior still did not close the problem. During that period we worked up a lot of enthusiasm for the bootstrap notion, and other people picked it up and started to work on it from a variety of standpoints. So in the early sixties the term ''bootstrap'' was very widely spread, and a lot of different approaches to it were developed.

CAPRA: It seems that there were a number of simultaneous developments that generated great interest and enthusiasm at that time: the bootstrap, Regge poles, S-matrix theory, and all that.

E.   Recognition of S Matrix

CHEW: That reminds me of the time when the S matrix finally became recognized. It was not until I tried to write a book in 1961. I wrote a little book for the Benjamin series, *S-Matrix Theory of Strong Interactions*.[3] When I prepared that book and a talk for a conference that was held in La Jolla I said to myself: After all these years of pretending that what I was doing was field theory, I finally want to be honest and say that I don't really believe in it; that what is important is analytic continuation. I kept looking for a word to contrast it with field theory, and suddenly I became aware that the S matrix was the point. It was not until 1961 that I really grasped that this was the concept Wheeler and Heisenberg had discovered twenty years before. I think at that talk in La Jolla I used the term "S matrix", and I certainly did in the book, and from then on I kept using it. Henry Stapp provided amplification very quickly by extending the idea to the description of spin.

CAPRA: When was the axiomatic work by Stapp, Iagolnitzer, and others done?

CHEW: That was somewhat later, but in 1962, and probably starting in 1960/61, Henry worked on the problem of spin.

CAPRA: What about Polkinghorne? He and some others wrote a book about S-matrix theory.[4]

CHEW: That's a tricky business. There was a team of four authors: Polkinghorne, Eden, Olive, and Landshoff. They had been working on dispersion relations and analytic continuation, and their book, which finally appeared around 1966, comes actually in two parts. Part of it is sort of straight S-matrix theory, which was mainly written by David Olive, and the other part is Feynman diagrams. I remember, at the time I didn't like that. I thought the book ought to be just on straight S-matrix theory, that they should not spend all this effort on Feynman diagrams. Well, subsequently I've changed my mind; what they were doing was very relevant.

CAPRA: Around the mid sixties, then, the S-matrix framework was more or less established.

CHEW: Yes.

CAPRA: This was the time when you wrote *The Analytic S Matrix*.[5] So that must have represented the culmination of your ideas at that time.

CHEW: At that time, it did. Yes.

CAPRA: Did you have any new insights while working on this book? You said that while working on the first book you really recognized the S matrix for the first time. Was there anything like that connected with the second book?

CHEW: I think there was a good deal less. As I remember, the book was a disappointment to me, because it was not able to move past two-particle channels. When Mandelstam and I developed our techniques we knew how to discuss poles and we knew how to discuss the two-particle branch points, but that was it. We did not know how to discuss anything higher — and we still don't! This impasse has never really been overcome. Essentially, what the second book did was to add the Regge theory in a good deal more detail.

CAPRA: And I suppose you also presented things in a more systematic way.

CHEW: Yes.

F. Emergence of Bootstrap Philosophy

CAPRA: Now what about the philosophical side of the bootstrap idea? First of all, it seems that the bootstrap idea was always tied to S-matrix theory, even before you knew that you were dealing with S-matrix theory.

CHEW: Yes, that's right.

CAPRA: It seems that the whole idea emerged out of a pragmatic position and in a sort of technical way.

CHEW: Right.

CAPRA: You did not sit down to think how the world was built; you did not entertain general philosophical thoughts?

CHEW: No.

CAPRA: So when did the whole bootstrap philosophy emerge?

CHEW: I think it was during my collaboration with Mandelstam. I particularly remember one item in those discussions, which focused the issue. In developing the equations for the π-π system with Mandelstam, we not only encountered the possibility of the ϱ-meson being generated as a bound state and also producing the force necessary to sustain the bound state; we encountered a parameter in connection with the s-wave scattering, which Mandelstam wanted to associate with a standard field-theoretical parameter. In standard scalar field theories there is a $\lambda\phi^4$ term in the Lagrangian, which corresponds to an s-wave interaction for spin-0 particles. The parameter which showed up in our equations could be interpreted as such a coefficient in a Lagrangian. That's how Mandelstam wanted to interpret it. We had long arguments about this, and I don't remember exactly how the paper was finally written, but I didn't like that at all. I couldn't believe this system was going to admit a fundamental parameter of that character. It seemed absurd to me that it would. Mandelstam felt this was just a representation of field theory, and he thought λ was the fundamental parameter and that the ϱ-meson would then, somehow, emerge driven by that parameter. Our equations did not indicate that; they indicated that the ϱ-meson was driving itself. There was no real connection between that parameter and the ϱ-meson. The parameter was just dangling out there, and subsequently it has been understood that it is no more fundamental than anything else. Nowadays one would not dream of referring to λ as a fundamental parameter. Because of that particular aspect of our theory I was forced to think hard about fundamental parameters. In this example it seemed clear that λ could not be a fundamental parameter. And I said to myself: But here is Mandelstam who believes that it's fundamental. Why? Because he believes in a Lagrangian. So, at that point I said: there is something sick about the whole Lagrangian idea that causes people to think there have to be parameters sitting there, which you are not going to be able to understand. I think in trying to defend myself, in trying to find a language that would express my idea, somehow the term "bootstrap" was helpful. I tried to explain to people why I felt that way. That parameter should not be there, because this was a bootstrap system which would not allow such things. I am pretty sure that up until then I had been vague; I had been rather unclear in my own head as to what I believed concerning fundamental parameters, elementary particles, and the like. At that point I had somehow crossed the bridge.

CAPRA: The fact that you should be able to derive the masses, or rather the mass ratios of particles seems to be much more intrinsic to the bootstrap framework, crossing, and all that. Didn't you feel that?

CHEW: Yes, but you know it is remarkably hard to put aside ideas you grew up with. When I was a student it was accepted that neutrons and protons were fundamental particles, and nobody dreamed of explaining their masses. I was aware that the logic of the bootstrap said you had to be able to determine them, but still, because nobody believed that you could determine them, the possibility was hard to accept. But then Frautschi and I were led to make our Regge plot, and — my God! — there was the proton sitting on the same curve with these other things. That was, somehow, a real punch — to see the mass of the proton in what was clearly a dynamical context.

CAPRA: So the Regge formalism really helped you to work out your philosophy.

CHEW: Oh, yes, tremendously! When you see the mass of the proton sitting on the same curve with a lot of other things, that tends to dissolve prejudices.

G. Break with Convention

CAPRA: Now the bootstrap idea is extremely radical compared to the whole scientific tradition. Was this radical nature apparent to you, and was there a struggle? You know, when you read Heisenberg and Bohr, you realize that they struggled like hell. Did you go through a similar phase?

CHEW: I remember going through something like that before that conference in La Jolla, asking myself: do I really believe this? Am I really prepared to back up this position? I went over all the developments that I had been exposed to until then, and I could only come to one conclusion, and that was the idea of nuclear democracy. None of the nuclear particles really could be said to have a fundamental status; they all had to be bound states of each other. It's true I was aware this was a radical idea, but nothing else made sense to me at that point. I couldn't see any alternative. The fact that the Schrödinger equation was not to be taken as a fundamental statement of dynamics had been working gradually on me over these years. I had seen how much the S matrix could do. Mandelstam, by the way, drove the final nail into that coffin, because he explicitly showed, using his double disperson relations, how you could recapture the Schrödinger equation as an approximation. So I had no feelings any longer that one needed an equation of motion.

CAPRA: Several years ago you told me that this was very crucial in your thinking, because in giving up the equation of motion you also give up the notion of "things". When you have an equation of motion there is a thing that moves.

CHEW: That's correct.

CAPRA: I have heard people refer to a talk of yours where you were very enthusiastic and very radical. You said, "From now on you can forget about Lagrangians", and things like that. Was that the La Jolla talk?

CHEW: Yes, that was the La Jolla talk in 1961. I suspect there was a lot of emotional stress associated with preparing that talk and giving it. Up until then I had continued to operate as if I accepted field theory, even though I didn't believe it. I felt torn and dishonest, but I was so anxious to get problems solved that I didn't want to let arguments with my colleagues get in the way of solving these technical problems. But for some reason I decided...

CAPRA: ...to come out of the closet, as they say these days.

CHEW: That's right (laughs), and having done that I was probably more inclined to think about philosophical questions. Once you have said to yourself: conventional wisdom does not have to be accepted, that's a big psychological break. I guess I was sort of expecting that as a result of that talk somebody would come and give me an overwhelming argument to the contrary. But they didn't. They didn't like what I said; they were furious, but there was no counter statement that was substantial. I remember a story about Arthur Wightman, who was doing axiomatic field theory at that time. He was furious at my La Jolla talk, but he also had a sense of humor. He put up a sign at his office door in Princeton, which said "Closed by order of G. F. Chew."

H.   Decline of Bootstrap in Late Sixties

CAPRA: During the late sixties, there was a decline of the bootstrap idea, probably because of the difficulties you mentioned before, the inability to go beyond two-particle channels and to find the right kind of approximation.

CHEW: Yes, right!

CAPRA: At the same time the quark idea gained momentum. How did you feel in those years? You must have been disappointed, of course, but did you actually have doubts as to whether the bootstrap program could be carried out?

CHEW: I did not have doubts about the ultimate story; I certainly had doubts about the time scale, about whether I was going to see any significant part of it. I resisted the quark business very strongly at the beginning, because I felt that it was abandoning the whole bootstrap idea.

CAPRA: In those days people thought of quarks as particles, I suppose.

CHEW: Well, there was a confused period at the beginning, from 1962 to 1966 or so, in which Gell-Mann played a very big role. He did not call them particles.

CAPRA: He was talking about mathematical quarks, I remember.

CHEW: That's right; he didn't think they were particles. Then gradually naive but phenomenologically successful models were developed, by Dalitz for example, and, I guess, when people discovered the color concept to resolve the difficulty of the symmetry of the baryon wave function, they started to be less inhibited about calling the quarks particles. Then, finally, when QCD was invented, they lost all their inhibition.

CAPRA: So what was your attitude in those years?

CHEW: I resisted the quark idea for quite a number of years, but I began to be more receptive when the dual models began to show up.

CAPRA: So that was quite late.

CHEW: That's right; 1968–69.

CAPRA: Did you sense then that there was something behind the quark idea other than quarks as particles?

CHEW: I certainly resisted the idea of quarks as particles. I have never been able to swallow that, and I couldn't fit the quark idea into anything that made sense to me until the dual models appeared.

CAPRA: There is an interesting coincidence here. I remember you giving a talk at a conference in Irvine in 1969. I thought that this was a very pessimistic talk, very subdued. Actually, it was the only pessimistic talk that I have ever heard you give. At that time you must have been at the end of a long stretch of years where there did not seem to be much hope for the bootstrap.

CHEW: Yes.

CAPRA: And yet, it was at that very conference that the Harari-Rosner diagrams were also discussed. So that was the lowest point, and from then on it went uphill.

CHEW: Yes, I think that's about right.

CAPRA: However, at the same time you wrote two general, more philosophical articles about the bootstrap,[6] one of them called *Hadron Bootstrap — Triumph or Frustration?* In these two articles you expressed, basically, a positive outlook. Now, what made you keep your faith?

CHEW: I think, by that time there were so many philosophical elements in the picture which seemed to be stronger than the difficulties. I always felt that the difficulties were just lack of imagination. It wasn't that the bootstrap idea itself was wrong; it was just that we were without a good technique for pursuing it. I never really changed from that attitude. But, you know, when you are speaking at a meeting of physicists, and you haven't got anything to present...

CAPRA: That's not much fun.

CHEW: That's right. It is much easier to write a philosophical article and express your enthusiasm.

CAPRA: It is interesting that by that time, by the end of the sixties, the philosophy had become so strong that you could actually do that. In 1961, say, you couldn't have done it.

CHEW: Right, that's true.

IV.   Philosophical Influences

CAPRA: Given the radical nature of this bootstrap philosophy, I have always been very curious about your philosophical background. You are obviously a very philosophical person in the way you do science. Were you always interested in philosophy?

CHEW: No, I was not aware of being interested in philosophy. I tended to model myself after Fermi. I find this paradoxical in retrospect, but for a long time I tried to think that I was going to behave as much as possible in the spirit of Fermi. As a matter of fact, I recall that during the period of collaboration with Francis Low, one day we were riding in a car back from a conference, and Francis brought up the question of whether quantum mechanics was really understood, and we began discussing some of the crazy things about quantum mechanics. And I remember feeling what a waste of time this was to think about such things. I couldn't respond to Francis' arguments, but I was still very much a student of Fermi at that point, and I just didn't believe that scientists should spend their time worrying about issues like that.

CAPRA: You know, it's interesting that the S-matrix approach does have this pragmatic aspect, and it also has a very deep philosophical aspect. It's a very curious mixture.

CHEW: That's absolutely right. The S-matrix idea is the clearest expression of the Copenhagen interpretation.

CAPRA: You must have been interested, though, in the whole mystery of quantum mechanics, the Bohr-Einstein debates, and so on.

CHEW: No, I wasn't. I think I appreciated that there was a difference between quantum mechanics and the Schrödinger equation. Fairly early on I knew that quantum mechanics really meant the S matrix. So my war at that point was with the Schrödinger equation or, if you like, with the use of the space-time continuum as the underpinning. I felt that the S matrix was completely capable of doing everything that needed to be done, and I didn't worry very much about the philosophical significance of that position. It really was only a good deal later, when I had to write and give talks, that I started to think about that.

CAPRA: This is very difficult for me to imagine. I met you in 1969, when I was at UC Santa Cruz, and I remember that you came and gave a talk about the significance of small parameters from the bootstrap point of view. I was very impressed, already then, by your way of presenting things and by the depth of your thinking. So I have always known you as a very deep thinker and a very philosophical person. Did you turn into that at some stage?

CHEW: Hmm! (smiles)

CAPRA: You see, this is really a surprise to me that you say you weren't interested in philosophy, not even in the philosophical aspects of physics.

CHEW: Well, somewhere in the 1960s, I guess, there must have been... Well, okay, I can remember, when I was in England in 1963, that I was asked to give a lecture. I was beginning to become more philosophical during that year. I remember that in addition to this big lecture, which had a certain amount of philosophy in it, I also gave a small lecture to a Cambridge college, in which I tried to persuade them that there was no absolute truth in science. I remember that this was a pretty radical thing to do, at that point, in Cambridge.

CAPRA: You see, I always had the idea that there must be something in your interest — some philosophical tradition, some religious tradition, or something in the world of art — something that influenced your thinking. We know that Niels Bohr was influenced by Kierkegaard and by William James, that Heisenberg was reading Plato. Some of the ideas from these traditions influenced them and helped them in their conceptual crisis. But there doesn't seem to be anything of that kind in your life.

CHEW: I can't identify anything like that. That's quite true.

CAPRA: Maybe that just means that you are really an original thinker.

CHEW: No, I don't think so. The influence was there, coming in various ways that were not so obvious. Let's see, maybe I can identify a few roots. You know, Edward Teller was somebody who had a substantial influence on me in addition to Fermi. Fermi was not interested in philosophical questions, but Teller really was. When I was a student at the University of Chicago, Teller made me aware, either in formal lectures or in private conversations, of some of the great philosophical issues associated with quantum mechanics. In particular he told me a few things which somehow stuck. I haven't thought about this for a long time, but either Teller or somebody else made the point that the quantum theory of electromagnetism, which had been analyzed by Bohr and Rosenfeld and which implied some extremely puzzling aspects in connection with electric charge, measurement, and so on, that all this only made sense because of the zero mass of the photon. You could understand the known facts about electromagnetism and also the presence of quantum principles only because of the zero mass of the photon. There was an approximation involved that had to do with the dimensions of the measuring apparatus, and you couldn't expect the notion of a local quantum field to have any final, definite meaning. I guess I've never forgotten that. So I got this idea early on that we really depend on approximations. And not only do we depend on approximations, but the nature of the theories that we construct depends on certain physical parameters. There is a remark, along the same line, attributed to Bohr, which I recall. If the fine-structure constant were not small, our whole way of looking at quantum mechanics and the real world would be totally different. It is very, very important that the fine-structure constant be a small number in order for matter to be involved in a way that allows us to think about it the way we do. We depend on the smallness of $1/137$ very, very much. I found it troubling that most physicists, when they carry out their activities, ignore those considerations, that they never stop to think about the significance of the parameters.

Also, George Gamow had an influence on me. I met Gamow extremely early, when I was only 18 years old, at George Washington University. His courses were anecdotal and not very systematic; he picked out the spectacular and glamorous aspects of physics. You know that he also wrote a series of popular books.

CAPRA: Yes, of course.

CHEW: From him, I guess, I must have learned some of these peculiarities of quantum mechanics very early. And those were things you could not grasp within the traditional view. That's right. When you put your finger on it, the fact that quantum mechanics makes sense has a strong bootstrap implication. If the parameters were not right, it wouldn't make sense. I believe that Gamow might have gotten that across in his discussions of some of the paradoxes that arise when you suppose that quantum principles govern the phenomena of our ordinary world. In discussing these examples he must have taken the parameters of the real world and shown that some very good approximation was involved. So that idea that approximation was crucial and that parameters were always important must have come very early.

CAPRA: So all these philosophical influences on you really came from scientists. There was no parallel influence, apparently, from any school of philosophy.

CHEW: Well, I am certainly not aware of any. I realize, when I talk to philosophers, that I know so little about philosophy, it is embarrassing.

V.   Recent Advances in the Bootstrap Program

A.   *Topological Expansion; Ordered S Matrix*

CAPRA: Now I would like to come to the recent history of the bootstrap. What was the decisive advance, and when did you become aware of it?

CHEW: There were many steps which impressed me, and the cumulative effect is a little hard to break up into pieces. I became seriously interested in the new developments in 1974 when I ran into Veneziano at CERN and learned about his notion of a planar approximation. He identified the idea that there was a level in something like a topological expansion, which was topologically planar, where some remarkably simple things happened and the bootstrap became really very much clearer and simpler to understand. Not only that, there were also experimental facts which supported the usefulness of this topological expansion. Shortly thereafter Carl Rosenzweig showed up here in Berkeley. He had been in contact with Veneziano and we started to work together and wrote a few papers which looked quite promising. We were also in touch with a fair number of other people who worked on related things, and then in 1977 we undertook to write a review of those new developments.[7] In the course of getting ready for this review we discovered the concept of what we then called the ordered S matrix. It was a formalization of Veneziano's thinking, but I remember that, when it was presented to Veneziano, he was quite clear in saying that this was something new, that it was something added to his ideas. Again, it is a little hard to say in which way it added, but he did make that statement. Certainly in my own thinking, seeing the concept of the ordered S matrix appear was a big support. It meant that there was a mathematical area which was suitable for bootstrap theory. Up until that point there were a lot of vague statements floating around and we didn't know how to convert them into something that was really a discipline.

CAPRA: Now I want to backtrack a little bit. In the years between 1969 and 1974, in those five years, there were a lot of ideas which were precursors of the new development — duality, the Veneziano model, etc. Did you recognize those as being relevant to the bootstrap?

CHEW: That's a good question. Between 1969 and 1974 I was aware of these dual models and very interested in them, but I didn't know how to take them and do something with them in terms of the S-matrix framework.

CAPRA: These models were very much associated with quarks.

CHEW: That's right, but it was apparent to me that they were not field theory. There was something else that was going on. Unfortunately, from my standpoint, people succeeded in translating a lot of that into something that was called a string model. The string model has a funny in-between status, which just threw a fog over everything. It is not field theory, but it is Lagrangian theory with arbitrary parameters and uses the space-time continuum as a base. I was quite confused and put off by all the activity that went into string models; it did not seem the right thing one ought to be doing.

CAPRA: In a sense this seems to be a parallel to the early history of S-matrix theory, where people were doing something that would later turn out to be relevant to a new development in S-matrix theory but were doing it from a field-theory perspective.

CHEW: Yes, that's right. So I listened to what people were saying about the string model, but I didn't work on it. What I did during those years was work related to the concept of the pomeron. There were several papers with Pignotti and Snyder on trying to clarify the status of the pomeron, and that set me up for the influence of Veneziano in 1974. What I became sensitive to in those years was the fact that this phenomenon that was called the pomeron had a lot of simplicity to it, but that there was a mysterious weakness associated with it. This was perplexing to me because it seemed to contradict one of the assumptions of bootstrap theory, which was that strong interactions were self-generating. Here was a piece that had clearly strong interactions with some very simple properties but with a strength that was very weak. I was puzzled; where could this small number come from? I think I wrote several papers in which I made an effort to understand what it was that made the pomeron weak. Well, in 1974, when I went to CERN and talked to Veneziano, that was the thing that really hit me. His topological expansion didn't have the pomeron at the planar level. The pomeron was a correction, and that immediately appealed to me as a natural explanation for its weakness. You see, that was kind of symbolic of the whole new development. Even though strong interactions are strong, nevertheless it is profitable, via the topological expansion, to make some sort of a classification of different levels of strength. I think that was for me a very, very big step; to get over the idea that all of strong interactions need to be understood at the same time. Maybe we could do bootstrap but nevertheless have hierarchies.

CAPRA: At that time you must have felt a tremendous surge of enthusiasm, after these ten years or so of "crossing the desert", as it were.

CHEW: Yes, that's absolutely right. Of course, the enthusiasm did not suddenly come in 1974. It began, and then, as Rosenzweig and I started to work, it built up as we saw more and more things that wanted to emerge.

B.   *Topology — The Language for a New Science?*

CAPRA: So the really new development was the recognition of order as a new ingredient in particle physics; and topology, of course, is very closely related to order.

CHEW: Right.

CAPRA: From the most general point of view you could say that, when you have that philosophy of "no foundation", you deal with relationships and topology seems to be the language of relationships *par excellence*. Therefore, it would seem to be the language most appropriate for this whole web philosophy and for the bootstrap idea. I really see a tremendous potential here. Topology could really be the mathematical language for a new science.

CHEW: Yes, I agree. That's my feeling about it. I tried to say that while David Bohm was here. Bohm has emphasized the importance of language, and I suggested to him that in this problem of getting beyond explicate order, as he calls it, the order of the ordinary real world, our language is extremely prejudicial, because so much of the language that we use is based on explicate order. Bohm knows this and he tries hard to get around it. So what I was proposing to him is that the language of topology, and in particular of graphs, seems very suitable. It is my feeling that in the future some extremely deep questions are going to be approached using the language of graphs.

CAPRA: Now, topology and graph theory are two distinct even though closely related languages. Topology seems the more general framework.

CHEW: I have asked myself that question many times, and I am not sure. I have also asked Poénaru and he is not very definite on this subject. Certainly, graphs without "thickening" are not sufficient, but what I don't grasp is whether this thickening of a graph is all of topology or whether it is only a teeny bit of topology. At the moment I find it still a puzzling feature of the topological bootstrap theory that there is so much redundancy. Sometimes we find it appropriate to talk about graphs, sometimes about surfaces, and the two are so interlocked that it's hard to know...

CAPRA: Coming back to the problems of language, you have mentioned several times in discussions we had over the years that the question-and-answer framework of ordinary scientific investigation will be found unsuitable when we want to go beyond the Cartesian framework. Have you given that any more thought?

CHEW: Well, I have come to believe that topological language is a very good candidate for going beyond the question-and-answer framework. The way our theory has developed in the last few years, we quite typically don't know what question to ask. We don't get into the posture of saying: Here is the question; let's try to answer that question! We simply...

CAPRA: ...sort of muddle along...

CHEW: ...muddle along and use consistency as the guide. Each increase in the consistency then suggests something that is incomplete, but it rarely takes the form of a well-defined question. We are constantly downgrading concepts that in the recent past would have been considered fundamental and would have been used as the language for questions. You see, when you formulate a question you have to have some basic concepts that you are accepting in order to formulate the question. This is also related to something that you and I have already discussed. The description of our subject can begin at a great variety of different places.

There isn't any clear starting point. So it's very hard to say, when you are writing about this business, that this is the problem that is being attacked and then go from there.

CAPRA: Right. Since the whole system represents a network of relationships without any well-defined foundation, you can start at almost any arbitrary point.

C.   Achievements of Topological Bootstrap Theory

CAPRA: Geoff, I would now like to ask you to give an assessment of the topological bootstrap, sort of a summary of the results achieved so far.[8] Which puzzles, actually, did it really solve? Where were the most important achievements?

CHEW: I am almost sure that what I am going to say will not be what I would say a year hence, because this is a subjective question. As a matter of fact, some of the things that impressed me a number of years ago no longer impress me now, because I have gotten so used to them. Let me see if I can overcome that.

One of the important developments has been the explanation of the distinction between strong and nonstrong interactions. The connection of this distinction with the topological expansion has been, I think, a big success. I believe that in the future it will also illuminate the meaning of space-time, because the notion of a continuum, which has some connection with space-time, does not emerge until you get to the electroweak level. The ingredient that characterizes the strong interactions qualitatively is the contraction idea, which goes with zero entropy and which is also very much connected with inaccessible degrees of freedom. We can now see not only how these things cause the strong interactions to be strong; we also understand the order of magnitude of the observed strength. I think that's an enormous step forward. However, it will take further development of the theory to convince other people of this.

We also understand why the machinery of quantum electrodynamics with its reliance on space-time should work and why strong interactions can co-exist without having any such underpinning. All interactions share the S matrix — the analyticity properties, unitarity — all these notions co-exist, and yet we get separation between strong and electroweak interactions.

CAPRA: Now let's talk about the strong interactions themselves. I think the understanding of the nature of quarks would have to be counted as one of the big successes there.

CHEW: Oh yes, and going into more detail I would say the meaning of the mysterious color degree of freedom has been exposed and the meaning of quark generation tentatively brought out, although we are still not completely sure about quark generation.

CAPRA: With respect to electroweak interactions, of course, the whole theory is still changing.

CHEW: That's right.

E. Skepticism of Orthodox Physicists

CAPRA: Now, if the topological bootstrap has been so successful in hadron physics, why is there such tremendous skepticism among orthodox physicists? Why do they hesitate so much to accept it and what will convince them?

CHEW: I think there are various ingredients in the answer. One is that QCD was very successfully sold as *the* theory of strong interactions. Although the deficiencies of QCD are recognized by many people, there is this prevailing sense that it is the correct theory. Some of the things that it doesn't explain and which the topological theory explains would be, for example, the origin of quarks, the origin of three colors, the origin of all these quantum numbers which you simply have to put into QCD. But people have gotten used to putting things in, and they have forgotten that one needs to answer questions about why such ingredients are there in the first place. At some point they *will* come around to thinking about that. Part of the problem, Fritjof, is that the topological theory has not been presented in any easily understandable way. You wrote a review and I wrote a review,[8] but in neither of these reviews did we go into any detail about Feynman rules.

CAPRA: In other words, nobody can apply the theory.

CHEW: Nobody can apply it, that's right. I think there are lots of young people around who would do things with it if they could get their hands on it. Maybe I made a mistake in not sticking with the strong interactions; I became deeply involved in this problem of the electroweak interactions.

CAPRA: So what happens is that practically all the people working on the topological theory work on the fundamental development of the theory, and nobody worries too much about applications.

CHEW: Well, there are some who do, like Nicolescu.

CAPRA: Yes, but since the entire number is very small those are just one or two.

CHEW: That's right. On the other hand, given the state of QCD at the moment, I think that people are subconsciously aware that QCD is not doing the job, but without an alternative they are not recognizing this explicitly.

CAPRA: And you think the feeling that QCD is not living up to the expectations is spreading?

CHEW: Well, my best measure is the graduate students here. During this last year I repeatedly found graduate students who were not satisfied with

QCD; there was a lot of interest in the topological approach at the level of graduate students.

F.   QCD and Weinberg-Salam Theory

CAPRA: Maybe, at this point, I could ask you to summarize your criticism of quantum field theory, that is both of QCD and of the Weinberg-Salam theory.

CHEW: My position derives from the way the topological theory has been evolving and from the fact that it makes so much sense. What has developed is that you can associate with both weak and strong interactions a Feynman expansion. That goes somewhat beyond what we used to say. We used to think that strong interactions would be pure S matrix and would not admit an off-shell continuation. The way the theory has evolved, there is an off-shell continuation. This was painful to accept; we did not really want it; we thought that it was contrary to the S-matrix spirit, but after long discussions we came to the conclusion that you really had to extend off-shell and that this did not upset the essential ideas. More importantly, the theory tells you how to go off-shell; it isn't something that is left open. But this extension does not imply a field theory. This is the strange thing. For a long time people said: if you go off-shell this is equivalent to field theory. That's not true.

CAPRA: So you don't have local interactions?

CHEW: You don't have local interactions, even though you have Feynman rules. The big difference is that the vertices for strong interactions are not simple polynomials in momentum.

CAPRA: Because of contraction?

CHEW: Because of contraction. Each hadronic vertex represents the contraction of an infinite number of topologies, so that the function associated with the vertex has an infinite sequence of singularities. This is qualitatively different from what you get in ordinary field theory. If you Fourier-transform a topological vertex function you will not get a local space-time interaction. This is the situation for the strong interactions. Now, the extension to electroweak interactions, right from the beginning, has not admitted contractions. The logic of this situation has never been explored as carefully as would be appropriate. Next year I hope to start writing a complete and systematic account of the whole thing, and then I will try to work out why the electroweak topologies do not admit contractions. There are all sorts of indications that they should not admit contractions; therefore the vertices for their Feynman rules are local if you Fourier-transform.

CAPRA: So then you do have local fields.

CHEW: Yes, we think that you can define local fields. There is a tricky point here. The locality really is not a property of a single field; it's a property of their interactions; for example, you have three fields interacting at the same point in space-time with each other. So it's a little bit misleading to talk about just local fields individually; it's a matter of the Lagrangian.

CAPRA: And this locality is a feature of the electroweak topologies?

CHEW: Right. Without having insisted on locality, it seems that the non-contraction associated with the electroweak interactions implies that the interactions are local.

CAPRA: Regarding your criticism of the orthodox theories, there seem to be two key issues involved then, the locality and the arbitrariness.

CHEW: That's right, and the two are connected, because it was contractions that eliminated the arbitrariness for the strong interactions, where the zero-entropy level is completely controlled by contractions. Now, you can then ask: what is it that makes the electroweak theory non-arbitrary if you don't have contractions. Here we are in a fuzzy area, but there are at least two recognized sources of non-arbitrariness for electroweak theory. Firstly, segments of surface boundary are building blocks of *all* elementary particles. They control strong interactions and you use the same objects to build electroweak particles. If you just said that, however, there would still be a fair amount of arbitrariness.

CAPRA: Well, the other link would be via the "naked cylinder".

CHEW: That's right, but I think it's probably true that I am the only one so far who has paid much attention to this. Of course, the argument is not tight; it has been loose. Finkelstein and Poénaru have been sympathetic to my reasoning, but...

CAPRA: This is probably because they came in later, after you had worked out the whole cylinder business. So you probably have a better feeling for it.

CHEW: That's probably true. We were talking before about this strange period between 1969 and 1974, when I was working on pomeron theory. Now that was all cylinder! So later, when the electroweak stuff came along, I immediately saw it as cylindrical. It was always cylindrical, right from the beginning.

CAPRA: So the arbitrariness is reduced, or even eliminated, by that link to the naked cylinder.

CHEW: I think that it will eventually be eliminated, but it is reduced already.

CAPRA: So what, then, is your assessment of QCD and the Weinberg-Salam theory on the basis of the topological theory?

CHEW: I can see Weinberg-Salam as basically O.K. It's a question of what the full group is; what they have done is to identify the dominant low-energy subgroup. The idea of using a gauge field theory for describing the electroweak interactions seems to be supported by the topological approach.

CAPRA: So you expect the Weinberg-Salam theory to be recuperated more or less completely by the topological approach.

CHEW: Yes, it almost has been already. We have come close to recapturing the whole thing. What we are doing now is trying to figure out the part of the story that has not already been guessed by Weinberg and Salam.

CAPRA: And what about QCD?

CHEW: QCD is a local field theory, which treats strong interactions exactly the same way as electroweak. It is a naive extension of Weinberg-Salam; you take Weinberg-Salam and you replace SU(2) by SU(3). Otherwise, you do very little to it.

CAPRA: Which means, you ignore the fundamental difference between strong and electroweak interactions.

CHEW: Right.

CAPRA: They would argue, of course, that this is justified by the phenomenon of asymptotic freedom.

CHEW: Yes, they say that there is another scale at which these things are unified, but there are qualitative differences beyond that. The degree of freedom associated with SU(2) is isospin, or electric charge, which is an observable degree of freedom labeling the particles. The analogous degree of freedom for SU(3) is color, which is not observable. Now that is a clear qualitative difference between these two situations, and there isn't any logical explanation why you should get confinement in the one case and not in the other. They set up the two theories in completely parallel fashion, and then they just say you get confinement in one case and not in the other.

CAPRA: Now, in the topological theory, can you relate confinement to contraction?

CHEW: Yes. We are talking here about color confinement, which in topological theory means that color is an inaccessible degree of freedom, similar to the cyclic order of lines around a vertex. It is another kind of order which you sum over. Now, if you don't have contractions, you don't have inaccessible degrees of freedom either. The inaccessible degrees of freedom and the idea of contraction go together. There are no contractions without inaccessible variables and in electroweak interactions all variables are accessible.

CAPRA: That is an interesting connection.

CHEW: Yes, it is tremendously interesting. This is one of the things I am going to try hard to get straight next year.

CAPRA: Coming back to QCD, do you think that it will be thrown away entirely?

CHEW: Yes, as a fundamental theory, because it is fundamentally wrong. As a phenomenological theory for GeV-scale physics, part of QCD will survive. It gets certain things right, such as energy-momentum conservation and Lorentz invariance, and people have put in by hand the right number of degrees of freedom. They looked at experiment and said, we see there are three colors, and there are two spins on the quark, and they inserted these features, so the theory is bound to have phenomenological utility, but it's profoundly wrong.

CAPRA: Now if QCD is wrong, then the grand unification schemes will have no future either.

CHEW: No, they will not. By the way, topological bootstrap theory predicts absolute stability for the proton, in contrast to most grand unification schemes.

VI.   Outlook

A.   *Space-time Continuum and Electromagnetism; Gravity*

CAPRA: I would now like to talk about future developments, and to begin with I would like to discuss the concept of the space-time continuum with you. During the course of our conversation you have repeatedly been critical of the use of a space-time continuum, and you have also said that the paradoxes of quantum mechanics arise, in your view, because in the framework of quantum mechanics atomic phenomena are embedded in a continuous space-time. Now, evidently, atomic phenomena *are* embedded in space-time. You and I are embedded in space-time, and so are the atoms we consist of. Space-time is a concept that is extremely useful, so what do you mean by the statement that one should not embed atomic phenomena in space-time?

CHEW: Well, first of all, I take it as obvious that the quantum principles render inevitable the idea that objective Cartesian reality is an approximation. You cannot have the principles of quantum mechanics and, at the same time, say that our ordinary ideas of external reality, the explicate order, are an exact description. You can produce examples showing how a system subject to quantum principles begins to exhibit classical behavior when it becomes sufficiently complex. That is something which people have repeatedly done. You can show how classical behavior emerges as an approximation to quantum behavior. The WKB approximation is a famous example, and there are lots of others.

CAPRA: Well, more generally, you can derive the basic laws of Newtonian physics from quantum physics...

CHEW: ...as approximations, when things become adequately complex. So the classical Cartesian notion of objects, and all of Newtonian physics are approximations. I don't see how they can be exact. They have to depend on the complexity of the phenomena which are being described. If the phenomena become too simple, the classical description won't work.

CAPRA: So you have a quantum level at which there are no solid objects and at which those classical concepts do not hold; and then, as you get to higher and higher complexity, the classical concepts somehow emerge.

CHEW: Yes.

CAPRA: And you are saying, then, that space-time is such a classical concept.

CHEW: That's right. It emerges along with the classical domain and you should not accept it at the beginning.

CAPRA: And now you have also some ideas about how space-time will emerge at high complexity.

CHEW: Right. The idea, actually, was present in a qualitative form long before and probably goes back right to my graduate-student days. When you learn quantum field theory, you learn that the quantum fields are introduced as operators, just like the operators in standard quantum mechanics, but they don't correspond to observables.

CAPRA: Except for the electromagnetic field.

CHEW: Except for the electromagnetic field; that's right! That's the only exception. And that just hit me like a bomb. Why should the electromagnetic field be different? I never forgot that, and I was constantly amazed that my colleagues, who did field theory, never seemed to pay any attention to that. It never fell out of my consciousness that there had to be some very special feature connected with the electromagnetic field.

  In my student days the idea was put into my head that the possibility of the electromagnetic field being an actual observable, in the same sense, as say, momentum, was associated with the zero photon mass. It is actually associated with more than that, but I remember being told that zero mass was the essential ingredient. And as time went on and I began to think about the S matrix in connection with strong interactions, I was much impressed by the fact that electromagnetic fields which could be described classically would not tolerate an S-matrix description. There was a funny complementarity. The zero photon mass, which allowed the electromagnetic field to have the status of a classical observable, also means that you cannot describe photons by the S matrix.

CAPRA: Is this statement still true in view of the recent successes of topological electroweak theory?

CHEW: It is still true because of the infrared phenomenon. At our present level of understanding, we have to think of the electroweak particles as massless, and that leaves this very important infrared problem still to be faced.

CAPRA: And we might have to go beyond the S matrix to solve it?

CHEW: I am sure. Henry Stapp has already taken the first step in that direction by showing how you can start, basically, with an S-matrix approach but then, when you are faced with these zero-mass particles, have to change the basis from the asymptotic states which are based on counting individual numbers of particles to asymptotic states where you superpose coherently different numbers of particles. Now, when you are superposing states containing differing numbers of particles you are not, strictly speaking, going outside the S-matrix idea, because the S matrix allows superposition, but it is not the way we normally use the S matrix. The idea that these states are then measureable as superpositions, that's where you get into a new area. What is it you are measuring when your apparatus is sensitive to a superposition of states with an indefinite number of particles? But that is exactly what a classical apparatus does. When you get to the classical level, you are using the fact that soft photons are coming in whose number is not well-defined.

I want to emphasize again that the idea of the S matrix implies such an extension should be possible. The statement that the S matrix is unitary is based on the idea that you can superpose the basic states. You can always give a meaning to an arbitrary superposition. In fact, you can't prove unitarity unless you assume that an arbitrary superposition of states is possible. That means also states of different numbers of particles. It is not a notion that you normally use in S-matrix theory, but it really is implied by unitarity. The thing which is perhaps qualitatively new is this idea that the superposition should involve states of arbitrarily large numbers of particles.

CAPRA: So the very special nature of electromagnetism stayed in the back of your mind during all those years while you were developing the S-matrix framework?

CHEW: Oh yes. Because the zero mass kept electromagnetism out of the standard framework and because it allowed the status of a classical observable for the electromagnetic field, I have always been very much impressed by the importance of electromagnetism, and you will find occasional references to it in my papers, here and there.

CAPRA: I know. In fact, I would like to read to you a passage from a paper you wrote in 1971:[9]

> *Electromagnetism is deeply mysterious and its origin unlikely to be explained within our current scientific framework because the unique attributes of this interaction are inextricably enmeshed with the framework itself.*

In view of the recent progress, have your views changed since you wrote this passage?

CHEW: No.

CAPRA: But you expect now to unravel a little more of that mystery don't you?

CHEW: That's right, but we *are* departing from the scientific framework. That's one of our problems of communication, because in challenging the standards of space-time we are off into the unknown, to some extent. Now we can conceal it when we publish papers and talk to people, and people won't know that we are really...off the deep end (laughs). But the fact is, you *are*, as soon as you say that the meaning of space-time is coming from the graphs and not vice versa.

CAPRA: So your statement still stands, and you are saying the more we learn about electromagnetism the more we are forced to give up the standard scientific framework. It is at that expense that we can learn about electromagnetism.

CHEW: That's correct.

CAPRA: Now we got into this discussion of electromagnetism by talking about space-time.

CHEW: I know. You see the understanding of what a measurement is, of what space-time is, of what an observer is, of what electromagnetism is — all these are tied together. The language that is useful for discussing this is the language of graphs, and the key notion is the idea of gentle events.[10] This idea is uniquely associated with photons. What it means is that in the Feynman graphs there is a special kind of vertex where two of the lines are very closely connected — what is carried in on one line is almost exactly carried out on the other line — and the third line is the photon, which is bringing almost nothing in or out.

CAPRA: That is, a very slight disturbance.

CHEW: Very slight disturbance, and it is in the analysis of why this is possible that you understand the special features of the photon. It has to have zero mass, and it also turns out that it has to have spin 1. It has to flip the chirality, that's the strange thing. Connected with spin 1, furthermore, is the attraction of unlike charges and the repulsion of like charges, which produces the effect of large clumps of matter that are almost electrically neutral. That is necessary for the appearance of classical reality. A classical object is recognizable as such, partly, because it doesn't carry an enormous electric charge.

CAPRA: So there are these gentle events, and they pile up.

CHEW: Yes, and they pile up coherently, and these coherent superpositions of photons generate the classical fields.

CAPRA: And how is this connected with space-time?

CHEW: Well, from the point of view of a quantum starting point, everything is discrete in the beginning; there is no continuum, and the discreteness is represented by the vertices of graphs. The graphs have no metric associated with them; there is no meaning to the distance between two vertices. These vertices I would call the "hard" vertices, and they are interspersed with all the "gentle" or "soft" photon vertices. There will be an infinite number of superpositions of these gentle vertices, whereas the hard vertices will remain finite and discrete. What Stapp showed, in order to solve the infrared problem — the specific mathematical problem associated with the zero mass of the photon — is that you are led to certain particular superpositions which, in effect, approximately localize the hard vertices. So after you have added this infinite coherent superposition of soft photons a hard vertex, which to begin with had no sense of space-time localization, acquires an approximate localization.

CAPRA: And the more soft vertices you have, the more precise the localization?

CHEW: Well, it doesn't ever localize beyond a certain limit.

CAPRA: You mean the limit given by the uncertainty principle?

CHEW: Yes. You don't ever get arbitrary localization, but you discover that you get as much localization as you expect in order to have a classical interpretation.

CAPRA: Now, you are saying that you could *derive* the uncertainty principle from that?

CHEW: Oh sure. You can derive the uncertainty principle *and* you can derive space-time. The idea of deriving space-time, of course, is really the more striking.

CAPRA: So what emerges is the notion of continuity and the notion of approximate localization.

CHEW: Right.

CAPRA: And with it the uncertainty principle.

CHEW: Yes. And, I would say, with it a meaning for measurement.

CAPRA: I see. All these steps are still tentative, though.

CHEW: That's right. But out of this will also come, at the same time, the capacity for recognizing certain patterns of events as representing an observer looking at something. Once you have the gentle-photon idea in the picture, you can begin to do that. In this sense, I would say, you can hope to make a theory of objective reality. But the meaning of space-time will come at the same moment. You will not start with space-time and then try to develop a theory of objective reality.

CAPRA: Now what about the dimensions of space-time? That does not follow from the gentle events.

CHEW: No. I think that comes out of the topology, and we are getting some very, very strong hints about that right now. The fact that momentum has four components is associated with a 2×2 matrix, and we suspect very much that this matrix is related to these pairs of two-valued orientations, that is to the apparent twoness inherent in the nature of elementary particles. So it seems that these topological notions can be translated into the statement that momentum must be a four-component object.

CAPRA: What about the conservation of energy and momentum?

CHEW: Well, that is something we don't have such a specific idea about, but I have a conjecture about it. Momentum appears to be built from indices which are closely connected to spin indices, and the same kind of topological symmetry that gives rise to SU(2) isospin invariance also seems to give rise to SU(2) spin invariance, which is rotational invariance and means angular momentum conservation. So the topology does definitely promise to explain why angular momentum is conserved. Now, if spin and momentum are built basically from the same topological indices and you can get conservation of angular momentum, it seems to be very plausible that you are also going to get conservation of linear momentum and energy. I feel that sooner or later we will understand that.

CAPRA: Now I have another question. Considering that you envisage deriving the basic properties of space-time, what about the constancy of speed of light? Will that be derived too?

CHEW: Well, that somehow just comes along with the Lorentz invariance. If you can get rotational invariance, the analytic continuation of the rotation group will lead you to the Lorentz group, and the Lorentz group effectively contains this notion of the speed of light.

CAPRA: So you foresee that all this could really come out of the topology.

CHEW: Oh yes. I don't think that's implausible.

CAPRA: You have often said that you expect gravity, too, to emerge together with continuous space-time in the high-complexity limit.

CHEW: Yes, that's true.

CAPRA: If so, then what about gravitons?

CHEW: From the topological standpoint you don't start with gravitons; you don't have gravitons on the same footing with the elementary particles. Gravitation is expected to emerge as a manifestation of extremely high complexity, *beyond* the level at which space-time becomes recognizable. If gravitation has meaning only at a classical level, there may be no gravitons.

B.   Extending the S-Matrix Framework

CAPRA: Looking into the future, I am curious about the necessity of either extending or abandoning the S-matrix framework.

CHEW: We have already extended it in two ways, actually. We have extended it off-shell and also by changing the basis in connection with the infrared problem.

CAPRA: It seems now that this extended framework of the S matrix is appropriate for all of particle physics.

CHEW: If it is understood in the sense of being supplemented by a topological expansion, I do think so. However, there is something else. When you say "*the* S matrix is the basis for understanding everything," I would object and say that the S matrix is defined in terms of momentum. But the whole notion of momentum, as we have been discussing in the last ten or fifteen minutes, promises not to be something you have to accept on an *a priori* basis, but will come from somewhere else. Now where does it come from? In the end, the meaning of momentum has to come from large-scale objective reality. The striking point about momentum is that in order to measure it precisely, you need large-scale apparatus. The more accurately you measure momentum, the bigger is the apparatus you are using. And the fact that high complexity is involved is somehow essential. So there is some elusive quality to the conceptual structure.

There is another dimension which should also be mentioned, and that is cosmology. It is the aspect of the story which says that the ideas of physical phenomena and physical laws are somehow localized in time. That also has to be an approximation. Any sophisticated cosmological approach will tell you that the conditions which lead to our sense of Cartesian reality don't necessarily always exist.

CAPRA: So there is no abstract, eternal validity of the laws of nature?

CHEW: No, I think we are surely making an approximation.

CAPRA: Now, coming back to the bootstrap program, in the past you have often expressed the idea of a mosaic of interlocking models. This idea has been of tremendous value for people outside physics. I know many people who have been inspired by it. But it seems now that in particle physics it might no longer be necessary.

CHEW: Well, let me think whether I agree with that or not... I think there are two considerations to bear in mind. One of them is that already at the level of the zero-entropy bootstrap one may not be able to find an exact solution. One may always have to use some kind of model. So the notion of a mosaic of models could be relevant right there at zero entropy. For example, Espinosa has been doing just that in his thesis. He is making models which are appropriate to certain portions of the zero-entropy space.

CAPRA: So what you felt would apply to the entire hadron physics applies now to the nonlinear part, which is confined to zero entropy.

CHEW: Could be. It may that we shall be condemned to always understand zero entropy in a piecemeal fashion.

The other point is that somewhere consciousness has to enter the picture. So far I have been talking about using soft photons to develop an understanding of space-time, objective reality, and the Cartesian-Newtonian view. But you know that in this domain of high complexity there is something else which, in a vague way, people describe by this term "consciousness," and which has an actual impact. The fact that I am raising my hand to gesticulate...

CAPRA: Of course, but there is much more to it. There is the hand itself, which you will not explain in the S-matrix framework. There is the whole world of living organisms.

CHEW: That's right. But that has to affect the accuracy of our description of the physical world. You can't have a completely accurate description of the physical world which leaves out consciousness, because it is clear that consciousness interacts with the physical world. How can I possibly have a complete description of the physical world if I don't include consciousness in the story? At the moment we work with a model that neglects consciousness; it's an approximation.

CAPRA: It's obvious that the inclusion of consciousness would give a more complete picture, but will this actually be necessary to make progress in our understanding of physical phenomena?

CHEW: Eventually, surely.

CAPRA: At what point do you think that we will be forced to go into this domain?

CHEW: I don't have well-developed views about at what level consciousness will be necessarily the concern of physical scientists, but I feel sure that the time has to come. It is clear that if you push your desire for complete understanding far enough, eventually you will have to bring it in.

References

1. G. F. Chew, *Phys. Rev.* **112**, 1380 (1958).

2. G. F. Chew and S. Mandelstam, *Nuovo Cimento* **19**, 752 (1961).

3. G. F. Chew, *S-Matrix Theory of Strong Interactions,* Benjamin, New York, 1962.

4. R. J. Eden, P. V. Landshoff, D. I. Olive and J. C. Polkinghorne, *The Analytic S Matrix,* Cambridge U.P., 1966.

5. G. F. Chew, *The Analytic S Matrix,* Benjamin, New York, 1966.

6. G. F. Chew, *Science* **161**, 762 (1968); *Physics Today* **23**, 23 (1970).

7. G. F. Chew and C. Rosenzweig, *Phys. Rep.* **41C**, No. 5 (1978).

8. See also G. F. Chew and V. Poenaru, *Z. Phys.* **C11**, 59 (1981); F. Capra, *Surveys in High Energy Phys.* **4**, 127 (1984).

9. G. F. Chew, *Phys. Rev.* **4D**, 2334 (1971).

10. See G. F. Chew, Zygon **20**, No. 2, 159 (1985).

LIST OF CONTRIBUTORS

Louis A.P. Balázs
Physics Department
Purdue University

James S. Ball
Department of Physics
University of Utah

A. Capella
Laboratoire de Physique Théorique et
  Hautes Energies
Université de Paris XI, Orsay

Fritjof Capra
Lawrence Berkeley Laboratory

Ling-lie Chau
Department of Physics
Brookhaven National Laboratory

Owen Chamberlain
Lawrence Berkeley Laboratory and
  Department of Physics
University of California

Denyse Chew
Lawrence Berkeley Laboratory
University of California

Carleton DeTar
Department of Physics
University of Utah

Duane A. Dicus
Center for Particle Theory
University of Texas

J. Finkelstein
Department of Physics
San Jose State University

Steven Frautschi
Division of Physics, Mathematics and
  Astronomy
California Institute of Technology

William R. Frazer
  Vice President
University of California

Marvin L. Goldberger
  President
California Institute of Technology

David J. Gross
Joseph Henry Laboratories
Princeton University

Maurice Jacob
Theory Division
CERN, Geneva

C. Edward Jones
Behlen Laboratory of Physics
University of Nebraska-Lincoln

Francis E. Low
Center for Theoretical Physics
Massachusetts Institute of Technology

Stanley Mandelstam
Department of Physics
University of California, Berkeley

Michael J. Moravcsik
Department of Physics and Institute
for Theoretical Science
University of Oregon

Al Mueller
Department of Physics
Columbia University

Basarab Nicolescu
Division de Physique Théorique
Institut de Physique Nucléaire, Orsay
and LPTPE
Université Pierre et Marie Curie, Paris

Georgella Perry
Kensington, California

V. Poénaru
Départment des Mathématiques
Université de Paris-Sud, Orsay and
Institut des Hautes Études
Scientifiques

John Polkinghorne
Canterbury, England

Carl Rosenzweig
Department of Physics
Syracuse University

John H. Schwarz
Division of Physics, Mathematics, and
Astronomy
California Institute of Technology

Uday Sukhatme
Department of Physics
University of Illinois, Chicago

Chung-I Tan
Physics Department
Brown University

Vigdor L. Teplitz
Strategic Affairs Division
U.S. Arms Control and Disarmament
Agency and
Physics Department
University of Maryland

J. Tran Thanh Van
Laboratoire de Physique Théorique et
Hautes Energies
Université de Paris XI, Orsay

Gabriele Veneziano
Theory Division
CERN, Geneva

R. Vinh-Mau
Division de Physique Théorique
Institut de Physique Nucléaire, Orsay
and LPTPE
Universite Pierre et Marie Curie, Paris

Steven Weinberg
Department of Physics
University of Texas

PUBLICATIONS OF GEOFFREY F. CHEW

1. G. F. Chew, "Comparison of Data on the Scattering Cross Sections of Carbon and Hydrogen," LADC-918 (AECD-3157), March 14, 1944; declassified April 19, 1951.

2. E. Greuling, H. Argo, M. Argo, G. F. Chew, M. Frankel, *et al.,* "Theory of Water-Tamped Water Boiler," LA-399, September 1945.

3. E. Greuling, H. Argo, G. F. Chew, M. Frankel, E. Konopinski, *et al.,* "Critical Dimensions of Water-Tamped Slabs and Spheres of Active Material," LA-609, August 6, 1946.

4. G. F. Chew, "Production of Cosmic-Ray Mesons," *The Physical Review* **73,** 1128 (1948).

5. G. F. Chew and M. L. Goldberger, "High Energy Neutron-Proton Scattering," *The Physical Review* **73,** 1409 (1948).

6. G. F. Chew, "Elastic Scattering of High Energy Nucleons by Deuterons," *The Physical Review* **74,** 809 (1948).

7. G. F. Chew and M. L. Goldberger, "Nuclear Reactions Produced by High Energy Neutrons," *The Physical Review* **75,** 1456 (1949).

8. G. F. Chew and M. L. Goldberger, "Analysis of Low Energy Proton-Proton Scattering Experiments," *The Physical Review* **75,** 1466 (1949).

9. G. F. Chew and M. L. Goldberger, "On the Analysis of Nucleon-Nucleon Scattering Experiments," *The Physical Review* **75,** 1637 (1949).

10. G. F. Chew and M. L. Goldberger, "The Production of Fast Deuterons in High Energy Nuclear Reactions," *The Physical Review* **77,** 470 (1950).

11. G. F. Chew and T. B. Taylor, "Energy and Angular Distribution of

π-Mesons Produced by 350-MeV Protons," *The Physical Review* **78**, 86 (1950).

12. G. F. Chew and J. L. Steinberger, "The Positive-Negative Ratio of π-Mesons Produced in Complex Nuclei," *The Physical Review* **78**, 86 (1950).

13. G. F. Chew and J. L. Steinberger, "Positive-Negative Ratio of π-Mesons Produced Singly in Collisions of Nucleons with Complex Nuclei," *The Physical Review* **78**, 497 (1950).

14. G. F. Chew and B. J. Moyer, "Collisions of High-Energy Nuclear Particles with Nuclei," *American Journal of Physics* **19**, 17 (1951).

15. G. F. Chew, "The Inelastic Scattering of High Energy Neutrons by Deuterons According to the Impulse Approximation," *The Physical Review* **80**, 196 (1950).

16. G. F. Chew and B. J. Moyer, "High Energy Accelerators at the University of California Radiation Laboratory," *American Journal of Physics* **18**, 125 (1950).

17. G. F. Chew," The Inelastic Scattering of High Energy Neutrons by Deuterons and the Neutron-Neutron Interaction," *The Physical Review* **79**, 219 (1950).

18. G. F. Chew, M. Lax, H. Feshbach, and H. W. Lewis, "A Phenomenological Treatment of Photomeson Production from Deuterons," *The Physical Review* **82**, 324 (1951).

19. G. F. Chew and G. C. Wick, "A Quantitative Analysis of the Impulse Approximation," *The Physical Review* **83**, 239 (1951).

20. G. F. Chew, "High Energy Elastic Proton-Deuteron Scattering," *The Physical Review* **84**, 1057 (1951).

21. G. F. Chew, "A Theoretical Calculation of the Inelastic Scattering of 90-MeV Neutrons by Deuterons," *The Physical Review* **84**, 710 (1951).

22. G. F. Chew, M. L. Goldberger, J. L. Steinberger, and C. N. Yang, "Theoretical Analysis of the Process $\pi^+ + d \rightleftarrows p + p$," *The Physical Review* **84**, 581 (1951).

23. G. F. Chew and B. J. Moyer, "High Energy Nucleon-Nucleon Scattering Experiments at Berkeley," *American Journal of Physics* **19**, 203 (1951).

24. G. F. Chew and H. W. Lewis, "A Phenomenological Treatment of Photomeson Production from Deuterons," *The Physical Review* **84**, 779 (1951).

25. G. F. Chew and G. C. Wick, "The Impulse Approximation," *The Physical Review* **85**, 636 (1952).

26. G. F. Chew and M. L. Goldberger "The Scattering of Elementary Particles by Complex Nuclei — A Generalization of the Impulse Approximation," *The Physical Review* **87**, 778 (1952).

27. G. F. Chew, "Pion-Nucleon Scattering When the Coupling is Weak and Extended," *The Physical Review* **89**, 591 (1953).

28. G. F. Chew and J. S. Blair, "Subnuclear Particles," *Annual Review of Nuclear Science* **2**, 163 (1953).

29. G. F. Chew and J. S. Blair, "Fourth-Order Corrections to the Scattering of Pions by Nonrelativistic Nucleons," *The Physical Review* **90**, 1065 (1953).

30. G. F. Chew, "A New Theoretical Approach to the Pion-Nucleon Interaction," *The Physical Review* **89**, 904 (1953).

31. G. F. Chew, "One of Schwinger's Variational Principles for Scattering," *The Physical Review* **93**, 341 (1954).

32. G. F. Chew, "Renormalization of Meson Theory with a Fixed Extended Source," *The Physical Review* **94**, 1748 (1954).

33. G. F. Chew, "Method of Approximation for the Meson-Nucleon Problem when the Interaction is Fixed and Extended," *The Physical Review* **94**, 1755 (1954).

34. G. F. Chew, "Improved Calculation of the P-Wave Pion-Nucleon Scattering Phase Shifts in the Cut-Off Theory," *The Physical Review* **95**, 285 (1954).

35. G. F. Chew, "Comparison of the Cut-Off Meson Theory with Experiment" *The Physical Review* **95**, 1669 (1954).

36. W. P. Allis, K. A. Brueckner, G. F. Chew, H. Dreicer, M. L. Goldberger *et al.*, "Series of Lectures on Physics of Ionized Gases" March 1955–June 1956.

37. G. F. Chew, "Report on Theoretical Pion Physics at Illinois," *Il Nuovo Cimento,* Ser X, **4**, Suppl. **2**, 761 (1956).

38. G. F. Chew and F. E. Low, "Effective Range Approach to the Low-Energy P-Wave Pion-Nucleon Interaction," *The Physical Review* **101**, 1570 (1956).

39. G. F. Chew and F. E. Low, "Theory of Photomeson Production at Low Energies," *The Physical Review* **101**, 1579 (1956).

40. G. F. Chew, M. L. Goldberger and F. E. Low, "The Boltzmann

Equation and the One-Fluid Hydromagnetic Equations in the Absence of Particle Collisions," *Proceedings of the Royal Society* **A236,** 112 (1956).

41. G. F. Chew, M. L. Goldberger, F. E. Low and Y. Nambu, "Application of Dispersion Relations to Low-Energy Meson-Nucleon Scattering," *The Physical Review* **106,** 1337 (1957).

42. G. F. Chew, M. L. Goldberger, F. E. Low and Y. Nambu, "Relativistic Dispersion Relation Approach to Photomeson Production," *The Physical Review* **106,** 1345 (1957).

43. G. F. Chew, "Theory of Pion Scattering and Photoproduction," 1957 (Publication of Illinois University, Urbana and Institute for Advanced Study, Princeton, New Jersey).

44. G. F. Chew and H. P. Noyes, "Dispersion Relations for Scattering in the Presence of a Coulomb Field," *The Physical Review* **109,** 566 (1958).

45. G. F. Chew, "Forces Between Nucleons and Antinucleons," *Proceedings of the National Academy of Science,* U.S. **45,** 456 (1959).

46. J. S. Ball and G. F. Chew, "Nucleon-Antinucleon Interaction at Intermediate Energies," *The Physical Review* **109,** 1385 (1958).

47. G. F. Chew, R. Karplus, S. Gasiorowicz and F. Zachariasen, "Electromagnetic Structure of the Nucleon in Local Field Theory." *The Physical Review* **110,** 265 (1958).

48. G. F. Chew, "The Nucleon and its Interaction with Pions, Photons, and Nucleons and Antinucleons," in *Proceedings of the Eighth Annual International Conference on High Energy Physics, CERN,* 1958, p. 93.

49. G. F. Chew, "Pions and Antinucleons," in *Proceedings of the Second International Conference on the Peaceful Uses of Atomic Energy* **30,** 33 (1958).

50. G. F. Chew, "Proposal for Determining the Pion-Nucleon Coupling Constant from the Angular Distribution for Nucleon-Nucleon Scattering," *The Physical Review* **112,** 1380 (1958).

51. G. F. Chew and F. E. Low, "Unstable Particles as Targets in Scattering Experiments," *The Physical Review* **113,** 1640 (1959).

52. G. F. Chew "Theory of Strong Coupling of Ordinary Particles," in *Ninth International Annual Conference on High Energy Physics,* Kiev, 1959, p. 313.

53. G. F. Chew, "The Pion-Nucleon Interaction and Dispersion Relations," *Annual Review of Nuclear Science* **9**, 29 (1959).

54. G. F. Chew, "Dispersion-Relation Approach to the Nucleon-Nucleon Interaction," in *Proceedings of the 1959 London Conference on the Few-Nucleon Problem* (Permagon Press, New York, 1960), p. 153.

55. G. F. Chew, "Electromagnetic Structure of the Pion," in *Proceedings of the International Conference on High Energy Physics, Rochester,* 1960, p. 775.

56. G. F. Chew, "Three-Pion Resonance or Bound State," *Physical Review Letters* **4**, 142 (1960).

57. G. F. Chew and S. Mandelstam, "Theory of the Low Energy Pion-Pion Interaction, Part 1," *The Physical Review* **119**, 467 (1960).

58. G. F. Chew, S. Mandelstam and H. Pierre Noyes, "S-Wave Dominant Solution of the Pion-Pion Integral Equations," *The Physical Review* **119**, 478 (1960).

59. G. F. Chew, "The Pion-Pion Interaction." Presented at Tenth Int. Annual Conf. on High Energy Physics, Rochester, 1960, UCRL-9740.

60. G. F. Chew and S. C. Frautschi, "Unified Approach to High and Low-Energy Strong Interactions on the Basis of the Mandelstam Representation," *Physical Review Letters* **5**, 580 (1960).

61. G. F. Chew, "Double Dispersion Relations and Unitarity as the Basis for a Dynamical Theory of Strong Interactions," in *Relations de Dispersion et Particules Elementaires* [Proceedings of the 1960 Summer Session at Les Houches] (Hermann, Paris, 1961), p. 457.

62. G. F. Chew, *S-Matrix Theory of Strong Interactions,* W. A. Benjamin, New York, 1961.

63. G. F. Chew and S. Mandelstam, "Theory of the Low-Energy Pion-Pion Interaction II," *Il Nuovo Cimento,* Ser. X, **19**, 752 (1961).

64. A. Abashian, N. E. Booth, G. F. Chew and K. M. Crowe, "Double Meson Production in Proton-Deuteron Collisions," *Reviews of Modern Physics* **33**, 393 (1961).

65. G. F. Chew, "A Unified Dynamical Approach to High and Low Energy Strong Interactions," *Reviews of Modern Physics* **33**, 467 (1961).

66. G. F. Chew and S. C. Frautschi, "Dynamical Theory for Strong Interaction at Low Momentum Transfers but Arbitrary Energies," *The Physical Review* **123**, 1478 (1961).

67. G. F. Chew and S. C. Frautschi, "Potential Scattering as Opposed to Scattering Associated with Independent Particles in the S-Matrix Theory of Strong Interactions," *The Physical Review* **124**, 264 (1961).

68. G. F. Chew and S. C. Frautschi, "Principle of Equivalence for all Strongly Interacting Particles within the S-Matrix Framework," *Physical Review Letters* **7**, 394 (1961).

69. G. F. Chew and S. C. Frautschi, "Regge Trajectories and the Principle of Maximum Strength for Strong Interactions," *Physical Review Letters* **8**, 41 (1962).

70. G. F. Chew, S. C. Frautschi and S. Mandelstam, "Regge Poles in π-π Scattering," *The Physical Review* **126**, 1202 (1962).

71. G. F. Chew, "S-Matrix Theory of Strong Interactions Without Elementary Particles," *Reviews of Modern Physics* **34**, 394 (1962).

72. G. F. Chew, "The Reciprocal Bootstrap Relationship of the Nucleon and the (3,3) Resonance," *Physical Review Letters* **9**, 233 (1962).

73. G. F. Chew, "Strong-Interaction S-Matrix Theory Without Elementary Particles," in *Cargese Lectures in Theoretical Physics* (W. A. Benjamin, New York, 1963).

74. G. F. Chew, "The Self-Consistent S-Matrix with Regge Asymptotic Behavior," *The Physical Review* **129**, 2363 (1963).

75. G. F. Chew, "Artificial Singularity in the N/D Equations of the New Strip Approximation," *The Physical Review* **130**, 1264 (1963).

76. G. F. Chew, M. Gell-Mann and A. H. Rosenfeld, "Strongly Interacting Particles," *Scientific American* **210**, 74 (1964).

77. G. F. Chew, "Elementary Particles?" *Physics Today* **17**, 30 (1964) and *Proceedings of the National Academy of Sciences,* Vol. 51, No. 5, 965 (May 1964).

78. G. F. Chew, "What is the Nucleon?" in *Nucleon Structure,* edited by R. Hofstadter and L. Schiff (Stanford University Press, California, 1964).

79. G. F. Chew and C. E. Jones, "New Form of Strip Approximation," *The Physical Review* **135**, B208 (1964).

80. G. F. Chew, "The Dubious Role of the Space-Time Continuum in Microscopic Physics," *Science Progress* **L1**, 529 (1963).

81. G. F. Chew, "The Search for S-Matrix Axioms," Physics Publishing Company, Vol. 1 No. 2, 77 (1964).

82. G. F. Chew and M. Jacob, *Strong Interaction Physics,* W. A. Benjamin, New York, 1964.

83. G. F. Chew and V. Teplitz, "Dynamical Evidence that Regge Poles Control Small Momentum Transfer Scattering at High Energy," *The Physical Review* **136,** B1154 (1964).

84. G. F. Chew and V. Teplitz, "Total Cross Sections and Diffraction Scattering in the 10–100 GeV Range According to the Strip Approximation," in *Proceedings of the 12th International Conference on High Energy Physics, Dubna, 1964,* Vol. 1, p. 377.

85. G. F. Chew and V. Teplitz, "More Accurate Treatment of the Low Energy Potential in the Strip Approximation," *The Physical Review* **137,** B139 (1964).

86. G. F. Chew and V. Teplitz, "Approximation of Regge Potentials Through Form Factors," *Progress of Theoretical Physics,* Supplement, Extra Number, 118 (1965).

87. G. F. Chew, "Pomeranchuk Repulsion and Resonance Narrowing," *The Physical Review* **140,** B1427–1430 (1965).

88. G. F. Chew, "Decreasing $I = 0, J = 0$ $\pi\pi$ Phase Shift and Regge Ghosts," *Physical Review Letters* **16,** 60 (1966).

89. G. F. Chew, "Analyticity as a Fundamental Principle in Physics," *Il Nuovo Cimento* Supplement **4,** 369 (1966).

90. G. F. Chew, "The Analytic S-Matrix: A Theory for Strong Interactions," in *Grenoble University Summer School of Theoretical Physics, Les Houches, 1965, High Energy Physics* (Gordon and Breach, New York, 1965).

91. G. F. Chew, "Nuclear Democracy, Regge Poles and the Analytic S-Matrix," in *Tokyo Summer Institute of Theoretical Physics, 1965, High Energy Physics* edited by G. Takeda (W. A. Benjamin, New York, 1966).

92. G. F. Chew, "Bootstrapping with the Regge Boundary Condition," in *Tokyo Summer Institute of Theoretical Physics, 1965, High Energy Physics* edited by G. Takeda (W. A. Benjamin, New York, 1966).

93. G. F. Chew, "Aspects of the Resonance-Particle-Pole Relationship Which May Be Useful in the Planning and Analysis of Experiments," in *Old and New Problems on Elementary Particles,* in honor of Gilberto Bernardini's 60th birthday, edited by P. Papali (Academic Press, New York, 1968).

94. G. F. Chew, "Regge Pole Daughters and Reactions Involving Un-equal-Mass Particles," *Comments on Nuclear and Particle Physics,* Vol. **1,** 17, (1967).

95. G. F. Chew, *The Analytic S Matrix: A Basis for Nuclear Democracy,* W. A. Benjamin, New York, 1966.

96. G. F. Chew, "Crisis for the Elementary-Particle Concept" in *The Future of Science* (Zhanie Publishing House, Moscow, 1967).

97. N. Bali, G. F. Chew and Shu-Yuan Chu, "Mandelstam Iteration in a Realistic Bootstrap Model of the Strong Interaction S Matrix," *The Physical Review* **150,** 1352 (1966).

98. G. F. Chew, "Zeroes in the Regge Formula," *Comments on Nuclear and Particle Physics,* Vol. **1,** 58, (1967).

99. N. F. Bali, J. S. Ball, G. F. Chew and A. Pignotti, "Analytic S-Matrix Approach to Zero-Momentum-Transfer Symmetry," *The Physical Review* **161,** 1459 (1967).

100. N. Bali, G. F. Chew and A. Pignotti, "Kinematics of Production Processes and the Multi-Regge-Pole Hypothesis," *The Physical Review* **163,** 1572 (1967).

101. G. F. Chew, "The Pomeranchuk Trajectory: Actuality or Mirage?" *Comments on Nuclear and Particle Physics,* Vol. **1,** No. 6 (1967).

102. N. Bali, G. F. Chew and A. Pignotti, "Multiple-Production Theory Via Toller Variables" *Physical Review Letters* **19,** 614 (1967).

103. G. F. Chew, "S-Matrix Theory with Regge Poles," in *Fundamental Problems on Elementary Particle Physis* (Interscience Publishers, New York, 1968), p. 65.

104. G. F. Chew, "The Pion Mystery," *Comments on Nuclear and Particle Physics,* Vol. **1,** No. 10 (1967).

105. G. F. Chew, "Closure, Locality, and the Bootstrap," *Physical Review Letters* **19,** 1492 (1967).

106. G. F. Chew and A. Pignotti, "Dolen-Horn-Schmid Duality and the Deck Effect," *Physical Review Letters* **20,** 1078 (1968).

107. G. F. Chew, "Horn-Schmid Duality," *Comments on Nuclear and Particle Physics,* Vol. II, No. 3 (1968).

108. G. F. Chew and A. Pignotti, "Multiperipheral Bootstrap Model," *The Physical Review* **176,** 2112 (1968).

109. G. F. Chew, "Bootstrap, A Scientific Idea?" *Science* **161,** 762 (1968).

110. G. F. Chew, *"Nucleon* and *Particle* Physics: Two Different Subjects?,"* Comments on Nuclear and Particle Physics,* Vol. II, 107 (1968).

111. G. F. Chew, "Multiperipheralism and the Bootstrap," *Comments on Nuclear and Particle Physics,* Vol. II, No. 6 (1968).

112. G. F. Chew and C. DeTar, "Multiperipheral Dynamics at Zero Momentum Transfer," *The Physical Review* **180**, 1577 (1969).

113. G. F. Chew, M. L. Goldberger and F. E. Low, "An Integral Equation for Scattering Amplitudes," *Physical Review Letters* **22**, 208 (1969).

114. G. F. Chew, "Small Hadronic Parameters and a Principle of Complementarity for Bootstrap Models," *Physical Review Letters* **22**, 364 (1969).

115. G. F. Chew and W. R. Frazer, "Model of the Pomeranchuk Pole-Cut Relationship," *The Physical Review* **181**, 1914 (1969).

116. G. F. Chew and D. R. Snider, "Multiperipheral Model Suggestion of a Damped Oscillatory Component in High Energy Total Cross Sections," *Physics Letters* **31B**, 75 (1970).

117. G. F. Chew, T. Rogers and D. Snider, "Relation Between the Multi-Regge Model and the ABFST Multiperipheral Model," *The Physical Review* **D2**, 765 (1970).

118. H. Abarbanel, G. F. Chew, M. L. Goldberger and L. M. Saunders, "Magnitude of High Energy Meson-Meson Total Cross Sections," *Physical Review Letters* **25**, 1735 (1970).

119. G. F. Chew, "Hadron Bootstrap: Triumph or Frustration?" Physics Today **23**, 10 (1970).

120. G. F. Chew and D. R. Snider, "Multiperipheral Mechanism for a Schizophrenic Pomeranchon," *The Physical Review* **D1**, 3453 (1970).

121. G. F. Chew and D. R. Snider, "Partial Bootstrap of the Schizophrenic Pomeranchon," *The Physical Review* **D3**, 420 (1971).

122. G. F. Chew, "Generalization of Regge Asymptotic Behaviour." in *Properties of the Fundamental Interactions,* edited by A. Zichichi (Editrice Compositore, Bologna, Italy, 1973).

123. G. F. Chew, "Quark or Bootstrap: Triumph or Frustration for Hadron Physics?" in *Properties of the Fundamental Interactions,* edited by A. Zichichi (Editrice Compositori, Bologna, Italy, 1973).

124. G. F. Chew, "Platitudes on the State of Our Art," in *Properties of the Fundamental Interactions,* edited by A. Zichichi (Editrice Compositore, Bologna, Italy, 1973).

125. H. Abarbanel, G. F. Chew, M. L. Goldberger, and L. M. Saunders, "Small Dimensionless Parameter to Characterize Multiple-Pomeranchon Phenomena," *Physical Review Letters* **26**, 937 (1971).

126. G. F. Chew, "The Bootstrap Idea and the Foundations of Quantum Theory," in *Quantum Theory and Beyond,* edited by T. Bastin (Cambridge University Press, Cambridge, 1971).

127. G. F. Chew, "Hadron Bootstrap Hypothesis," *The Physical Review* **D4**, 2330 (1971).

128. H. D. I. Abarbanel, G. F. Chew, M. L. Goldberger, and L. M. Saunders, "Self-Consistent Pomeranchon Coupling Ratios in the Multiperipheral Model," *The Physical Review* **D4**, 2988 (1971).

129. H. D. I. Abarbanel, G. F. Chew, M. L. Goldberger and L. M. Saunders, "Diffractive Dissociation Within Multiperipheral Dynamics," *Annals of Physics* **73**, 156 (1972).

130. G. F. Chew and D. R. Snider, "Connection Between Nonlinearity of the Pomeranchuk Trajectory and an Intercept Below 1," *The Physical Review* **D6**, 2057 (1972).

131. G. F. Chew and S. D. Ellis, "Multiple-Counting in the Experimental Measurement of Diffractive Dissociation," *The Physical Review* **D6**, 3330 (1972).

132. G. F. Chew, "Arguments Supporting a Positive 2-Pomeron Discontinuity," *The Physical Review* **D7**, 934 (1973).

133. G. F. Chew, "An Estimate of the Magnitude of Triple Pomeron Coupling from the Observed Energy Dependence of Total and Elastic pp Cross Section," *The Physical Review* **D7**, 3525 (1973).

134. G. F. Chew, "Complex Regge Poles and the Sign of the Two-Pomeranchon Discontinuity," *Physics Letters* **44B**, 169 (1973).

135. G. F. Chew, "Weakly Recurrent Pomerons," AIP Conference Proceedings No. 15, Particle and Fields Subseries No. 7, High Energy Collisions (1973), p. 98.

136. G. F. Chew and J. Koplik, "Asymptotic Oscillation Hypothesis," *Physics Letters* **48B**, 221 (1974).

137. B. Bishari, G. F. Chew, and J. Koplik, "A Perturbative Approach

to the Pomeron," *Nuclear Physics* **B72,** 61 (1974).

138. G. F. Chew and J. Koplik, "Baryon-Antibaryon Threshold Resonances," *Nuclear Physics* **B79,** 365 (1974).

139. G. F. Chew, "Impasse for the Elementary-Particle Concept," in *The Great Ideas of Today* (Encyclopaedia Britannica, Inc., Chicago, 1974).

140. G. F. Chew and J. Koplik, "Peripheral Thresholds and Regge Asymptotic Expansions," *Nuclear Physics* **B81,** 93 (1974).

141. D. M. Chew and G. F. Chew, "Prediction of Double-Pomeron Cross Sections from Single-Diffraction Measurements," *Physics Letters* **53B,** 191 (1974).

142. G. F. Chew and C. Rosenzweig, "A Systematic lifting of Exchange-Degeneracy That Clarifies the Relationship Between Pomeron, Reggeons and SU_3-Symmetry Violation," *Physics Letters* **58B,** 93 (1975).

143. G. F. Chew and C. Rosenzweig, "Pomeron-Reggeon Relationship According to the Topological Expansion," *The Physical Review* **D12,** 3907 (1975).

144. G. F. Chew and C. Rosenzweig, "Asymptotic Planarity: An S-Matrix Basis for the Okubo-Zweig-Iizuka Rule," *Nuclear Physics* **B104,** 290 (1976).

145. G. F. Chew, C. Rosenzweig and P. R. Stevens, "The Pomeron-f Identity and Hadronic Total Cross Sections at Moderate Energy," *Nuclear Physics* **B110** 355 (1976).

146. G. F. Chew and C. Rosenzweig, "Asymptotic-Planarity Prediction of a Pomeron-Like Unnatural Parity Trajectory," *Physics Letters* **63B,** 429 (1976).

147. G. F. Chew and C. Rosenzweig, "A Statistical-Weight Interpretation for the $1/N^2$ Convergence Factors of the Topological Expansion," *Annals of Physics* **105,** 212 (1977).

148. G. F. Chew, "States of Baryonium Within the Hadron Family," in *Antinucleon-Nucleon Interactions* edited by G. Ekspong and S. Nilsson (Pergamon Press, Oxford and New York, 1977), p. 515.

149. G. F. Chew and C. Rosenzweig, "G Parity and the Breaking of Exchange Degeneracy," *The Physical Review* **D15,** 3433 (1977).

150. G. F. Chew and C. Rosenzweig, "Dual Topological Unitarization: An Ordered Approach to Hadron Theory," *Physics Reports* **41C,** 263 (1978).

151. G. F. Chew, J. Finkelstein, J. P. Sursock and G. Weissmann, "Ordered Hadron S-Matrix," *Nuclear Physics* **B136**, 493 (1978).

152. G. F. Chew, "Bootstrap Theory of Quarks", *Nuclear Physics* **B151**, 237 (1979).

153. G. F. Chew, "Topological Colour and Disc Mating as the Source of Zero Triality," *Physics Letters* **82B**, 439 (1979).

154. G. F. Chew, "Bootstrapping Quarks and Gluons," in *Proceedings of the XIVth Annual Rencontre de Moriond,* edited by J. Tran Thanh Van (Editions Frontières, Paris, 1979), v. 1, p. 21.

155. G. F. Chew, "Hadron Disc Spectrum of the Spherical S-Matrix", in *Proceedings of the VIIth International Winter Meeting on Fundamental Physics,* edited by M. Aguilar-Benitez and J. A. Rubio (Madrid, 1979), p. 117.

156. G. F. Chew, "Unusual Hadrons from Bootstrap Theory," in *Proceedings of the Orsay Workshop on Baryonium and Other Unusual Hadrons,* edited by R. Vinh-Mau (Paris, 1980).

157. G. F. Chew and V. Poénaru, "Topological Bootstrap Prediction of 3-Coloured 8-Flavored Quarks," *Physical Review Letters* **45**, 229 (1980).

158. G. F. Chew, J. Finkelstein, R. McMurray and V. Poénaru, "A Topological Theory of Electric Charge," *Physics Letters* **100B**, 53 (1981).

159. G. F. Chew and V. Poénaru, "Topological Bootstrap Theory of Hadrons," *Zeitschrift für Physik* **C11**, 59 (1981).

160. G. F. Chew, J. Finkelstein, R. McMurray and V. Poénaru, "Topological Theory of Electromagnetism," *The Physical Review* **D24**, 2287 (1981).

161. G. F. Chew, "Zero-Entropy Bootstrap and the Fine Structure Constant," *Physical Review Letters* **47**, 764 (1981).

162. G. F. Chew and J. Finkelstein, "Baryon Magnetic Moments from Topological Theory," *The Physical Review* **D24**, 3335 (1981).

163. G. F. Chew, J. Finkelstein and V. Poénaru, "Topological Theory of Electroweak Vector Bosons," *The Physical Review* **D24**, 2764 (1981).

164. G. F. Chew, J. Finkelstein and M. Levinson, "Topological Theory of Elementary Hadron Coupling Constants," *Physical Review Letters* **47**, 767 (1981).

165. G. F. Chew, "The Topological Bootstrap," in *Asymptotic Realms*

of Physics, edited by A. Guth, K. Huang and R. Jaffe (MIT Press, Cambridge, MA, 1983).

166. G. F. Chew, J. Finkelstein, "Topological Vector Gluons," *Zeitschrift für Physik* **C13,** 161 (1982).

167. G. F. Chew and J. Finkelstein and V. Poénaru, "A Single-Sheet Classical Surface for Electroweak Hadronic Currents," *Zeitschrift für Physik* **C14,** 363 (1982).

168. G. F. Chew and V. Poénaru, "Topological Representation of Leptons," *Zeitschrift für Physik* **C14,** 233 (1982).

169. G. F. Chew, J. Finkelstein, B. Nicolescu and V. Poénaru, "Topological Compositeness of Quarks, Leptons and Electroweak Bosons," *Zeitschrift für Physik* **C14,** 289 (1982).

170. G. F. Chew, "Electroweak Bootstrap," *The Physical Review* **D27,** 976 (1983).

171. G. F. Chew and M. Levinson, "Dual Feynman Rules — Topological Asymptotic Freedom," *Zeitschrift für Physik* **C20,** 19 (1983).

172. G. F. Chew, "Bootstrapping the Photon," *Foundations of Physics,* **13,** 217 (1983).

173. G. F. Chew and J. Finkelstein, "Topological Theory and the Standard Electroweak Model," *Physical Review Letters* **50,** 795 (1983).

174. G. F. Chew and V. Poénaru, "Parity Asymmetry from 'Diquarks'," *The Physical Review* **D30,** 1579 (1984).

175. G. F. Chew and J. Finkelstein, "Electrospin and Broken SU(2) Symmetry," *The Physical Review* **D28,** 407 (1983).

176. G. F. Chew, D. Issler and B. Nicolescu, "GeV Partons and TeV Hexons from a Topological Viewpoint" in *Proceedings of the 19th Rencontre de Moriond,* edited by Tran Thanh Van (Editions Frontières, Paris, 1984), p. 143.